Library
askalibrarian@bradfordcollege.ac.uk
capitadiscovery.co.uk/bradfordcollege

AF740618

BRADFORD COLLEGE LIBRARY
WITHDRAWN

BC 1203180 1

The Ethics of Technological Risk

RISK, SOCIETY AND POLICY SERIES
Edited by Ragnar E. Löfstedt

The Ethics of Technological Risk

Edited by
Lotte Asveld and Sabine Roeser

earthscan
publishing for a sustainable future

London • Sterling, VA

First published by Earthscan in the UK and USA in 2009

Copyright © Lotte Asveld and Sabine Roeser, 2009

All rights reserved

ISBN: 978-1-84407-638-3

Typeset by 4word Ltd, Bristol
Printed and bound in the UK by TJ International Ltd, Padstow
Cover design by Yvonne Booth

For a full list of publications please contact:

Earthscan
Dunstan House
14a St Cross St
London EC1N 8XA, UK
Tel: +44 (0)20 7841 1930
Fax: +44 (0)20 7242 1474
Email: earthinfo@earthscan.co.uk
Web: **www.earthscan.co.uk**

BRADFORD COLLEGE
GROVE LIBRARY
DATE 10/11 LOC. GR
ORDER NO. 11000271
CLASS NO. 174 ETH
BARCODE NO. 12031801

22883 Quicksilver Drive, Sterling, VA 20166-2012, USA

Earthscan publishes in association with the International Institute for Environment and Development

A catalogue record for this book is available from the British Library

Library of Congress Cataloging-in-Publication Data

The ethics of technological risk/edited by Lotte Asveld and Sabine Roeser.
p. cm.
Includes bibliographical references and index.
ISBN 978-1-84407-638-3 (hardback)
1. Technology–Risk assessment. 2. Ethics. I. Asveld, Lotte. II. Roeser, Sabine.
T174.5.E84 2008
174'.96–dc22

2008033036

The paper used for this book is FSC-certified. FSC (the Forest Stewardship Council) is an international network to promote responsible management of the world's forests.

FSC
Mixed Sources
Product group from well-managed forests and other controlled sources
Cert no. SGS-COC-2482
www.fsc.org
© 1996 Forest Stewardship Council

Contents

List of Figures and Tables

Figures

Table

List of Contributors

Lotte Asveld, Senior researcher at the Rathenau Institute, The Hague

Michael Baram, Professor of Law, Boston University School of Law, and Professor of Health Law, Bioethics and Human Rights, Boston University School of Public Health.

Yvo de Boer, Executive secretary of UNFCCC (United Nations Framework Convention on Climate Change), Bonn

Greg Bognar, Assistant professor/faculty fellow, Center for Bioethics, New York University

Mark Coeckelbergh, Assistant professor, Philosophy Department, Twente University, Enschede

Carl Cranor, Professor of philosophy, University of California Riverside

Marc D. Davidson, Research associate at the Philosophy Department of the University of Amsterdam

Nicolas Espinoza, PhD student at the Department of Languages and Culture, Luleå University of Technology

Arianna Ferrari, Research associate at the Institute of Philosophy, Darmstadt University of Technology

Melissa Finucane, East-West Center, Honolulu, Hawaii

Anke van Gorp, Researcher at TNO Quality of Life, Leiden

Armin Grunwald, Professor at the Institute for Technology Assessment and Systems Analysis (ITAS) at Karlsruhe Institute of Technology (KIT)

Sven Ove Hansson, Professor in philosophy and head of the Department of Philosophy and the History of Technology, Royal Institute of Technology, Stockholm

Gero Kellermann, Postdoctoral Research Associate, Center for Philosophy and Ethics of Science, University of Hannover

Donald G. MacGregor, MacGregor-Bates Consulting, Cottage Grove, Oregon

Douglas MacLean, Professor and director of the Parr Center for Ethics, University of North Carolina at Chapel Hill

Ellen Peters, Decision Research, Oregon

Sabine Roeser, Assistant professor at the Philosophy Department, Delft University of Technology

Paul Slovic, Decision Research, Oregon

Duff Waring, Associate professor of philosophy at York University, Toronto, Ontario

Henk Zandvoort, Associate professor at the Philosophy Department, Delft University of Technology

Foreword

Moral Considerations in Judging Climate Change Technologies

In 2007 the Intergovernmental Panel on Climate Change (IPCC) jolted the world with the release of its Fourth Assessment Report. It proved beyond doubt that climate change is happening and accelerating, and that much of it is caused by the continued and increasing emissions of greenhouse gases from human activities. It also showed that, if we fail to come to grips with it, the impacts of climate change will have devastating effects on economies, societies and eco-systems throughout the world, especially in developing countries.

But there was good news coming from the IPCC report as well. We *can* come to grips with climate change and this is possible at reasonable costs, but for this to happen we need to act now.

The crystal-clear signal from science called for a clear answer from politics. At the United Nations (UN) Climate Change Conference in Bali in December 2007, governments recognized the need to step up international efforts to combat climate change. A two-year negotiating process was kicked off. These negotiations are aimed at an agreement on stronger international climate change action to be concluded at the Copenhagen Climate Change Conference by the end of 2009.

Technology will be a key element of a Copenhagen deal. One of the main challenges of a Copenhagen deal is to put in place a clever set of financial and other incentives to scale up the development, deployment, diffusion and transfer of affordable climate friendly technologies, especially to developing countries. The world needs a green technological revolution that will shift the course of the world economy onto a low emissions path and will help us adapt to the unavoidable impacts of climate change that are already showing and will intensify over time, hitting the poorest members of the world community the hardest.

Many of the technologies to tackle climate change are already at our disposal. Others are still 'under construction' and need further development before they can make their way out of the research centres and into the real world. A number of them meet with a great deal of scepticism or criticism because of the risks they imply. Take nuclear energy for example, or Carbon Capture and Storage (CCS), the latter being identified by the IPCC as a potentially crucial technology to substantially reduce emissions from the use of fossil fuels on which the world will remain heavily dependent in the upcoming decades to meet its growing energy demand. Another example is the case of biofuels, which, especially over the last couple of months, have been heavily criticized due to their alleged effects on food prices.

These objections to technologies have to be considered carefully in order to assess their validity and to judge what is acceptable and what is not. Judging the acceptability of technological risks is not only a scientific but also a moral endeavour. This also holds for the assessment of climate-friendly technologies. It goes without saying that nuclear energy is only acceptable if it takes place under tight safety regulations and that scientific research will lead to the development of increasingly safer types of nuclear power stations. It also goes without saying there should be a sound and safe solution for nuclear waste. Biofuels should be produced in a socially responsible and environmentally friendly way, and it is necessary to speed up the development of second-generation biofuels, which can be made from waste instead of food crops. I also think that CCS needs more research and development (R&D) and pilot projects before it will be a proven technology.

As the IPCC report points out too, if left unchecked, climate change will have serious, destabilizing effects all around the globe, particularly in the poorest regions. Due to the melting of glaciers, the availability of fresh water in central, south, east and southeast Asia is projected to decrease, affecting more than a billion people by the middle of this century. By 2020, between 75 and 250 million people in Africa are projected to suffer from increased water stress. Many millions of people in the world's largest cities on coastlines are likely to be flooded every year due to sea-level rise by the 2080s.

Should these projected consequences be a legitimate moral consideration in judging the moral acceptability of technological risks? I very much hope that this volume will provide a better insight into this and other challenging ethical questions concerning technological risks. For me the answer is clear: yes, the impacts of climate change should play a role in assessing the acceptability of technological risks. I think it would even be immoral not to do so.

Yvo de Boer
Executive Secretary of the United Nations Framework
Convention on Climate Change
July 2008

Acknowledgements

The contributions to this volume have previously been presented at a conference on 'Ethical Aspects of Risk' which we have organized. The conference took place at the Philosophy Department of Delft University of Technology from 14–16 June 2006. The keynote speakers were Paul Slovic, Carl Cranor, Douglas MacLean and Ruth Chadwick. The contributions of Slovic, Cranor and MacLean are included in this volume. There were more than 80 participants from all over the world, and most of them presented a paper. A few months after the conference we received reworked papers from many participants, of which we selected the very best ones for this volume. We would like to thank Saskia Polder for her outstanding work as an editorial assistant during the preparation of this volume. Henneke Piekhaar did an excellent job in supporting us with the organization of the conference. The conference was generously sponsored by the Netherlands Organization for Scientific Research (NWO), the Royal Dutch Academy of the Sciences (KNAW), the Platform for Ethics and Technology of TU Delft and the Philosophy Department of TU Delft.

Lotte Asveld and Sabine Roeser
The Hague/Delft
May 2008

List of Acronyms and Abbreviations

A	standard therapy accepted by the medical community for treating the condition under study
AHRP	Alliance for Human Research Protection
ALARA	'as low as reasonably achievable'
B	non-validated therapy not accepted by the medical community for treating the condition under study
CBA	cost-benefit analysis
CCS	carbon capture and storage
CEST	Cognitive-experiential self-theory
DPT	Dual Process Theory
EMEA	European Medicines Agency
FDA	US Food and Drug Administration
GM	genetically modified
GNR	general notion of risk
GSM	Global System for Mobile communication, second generation mobile phone technology
HC	Health Council
ICNIRP	International Commission on Non-ionising Radiation Protection
IPCC	Intergovernmental Panel on Climate Change
IRB	Institutional Review Board(s)
IRGC	International Risk Governance Council
IXA	International Xenotransplantation Association
NBAC	National Bioethics Advisory Commission
OIRA	Office of Information and Regulatory Affairs
OSHA	Occupational Safety and Health Administration
PED	Pressure Equipment Directive
PERV	porcine endogenous retrovirus
STNR	standard technical notion of risk
TCE	trichloroethylene
TCP	Tri-Council Policy Statement
UHF EMR	Ultra High Frequency Electro Magnetic Radiation
UMTS	Universal Mobile Telecommunication System, third generation mobile phone technology
UNCED	United Nations Conference on Environment and Development
UNFCCC	United Nations Framework Convention on Climate Change
WCED	World Commission on Environment and Development
WRR	Netherlands Scientific Council for Government Policy
XTx	Xenotransplantation

Part I

Introduction

The ethics of technological risk is a new area of research, approaching the field of risk management from an ethical point of view. Risk management is a normative discipline that requires explicit ethical reflection. Sabine Roeser and Lotte Asveld provide for an introduction into the subject area and give a short overview of the contributions to this volume. Sven Ove Hansson develops an agenda for future research into the ethics of risk.

1 The Ethics of Technological Risk: Introduction and Overview

Sabine Roeser and Lotte Asveld

INTRODUCTION

Technology has advanced human well-being in a myriad of respects, for example in the areas of energy, communication and travel. Still, every technology has negative side-effects and may include risks from accidents and pollution. How to judge whether a risk is acceptable is a pressing ethical question that deserves thorough investigation.

There is a vast amount of sociological and psychological research on acceptable risks, but surprisingly, there is very little research from moral philosophy on risks. This is even more surprising given the fact that biomedical ethics has become a full-blown academic discipline. Moral philosophers, at least those in the analytic tradition, have largely avoided the discussion of technologies that belong to the domain of engineering. Continental philosophers have focused on technology, but mainly from a pessimistic perspective that sees technology foremost as a threat for a meaningful life. However, this is a very one-sided approach. It is true that technologies can change our lives for the worse; however, they can and do also change our lives for the better. It is too easy and too simplistic to reject technology as such. It is much more complicated, but much truer to the facts, to see technology as the bringer of a lot of good things but also a lot of problematic things. However, then it becomes far from obvious how we should judge whether we should accept a certain technology and its concomitant risks.

In risk management, the standard way to judge the acceptability of a specific technology is to calculate risk in terms of probabilities multiplied by unwanted outcomes and then apply cost-benefit (or risk-benefit) analysis. However, as well as the balance between the benefits and risks of a technology the following considerations seem to be important: the distribution of costs and benefits, whether a risk is voluntarily taken, whether there are available alternatives and whether a risk is catastrophic. This gives rise to the following questions. What are morally legitimate considerations in judging the acceptability of risks? Is cost-benefit analysis the best method to reach a decision or do we need additional considerations that cannot easily be incorporated into that framework? Is the precautionary principle a fruitful tool in dealing with risks? What role should the public play in judging the acceptability of risks? What role should emotions play in judging the acceptability of risks? Are they irrational and distorting or are they a necessary precondition for practically rational judgements?

This volume aims to spark research into ethical aspects of risk by bringing together moral philosophers, sociologists and psychologists who reflect on the questions above. It comprises discussions on biomedical risks, as well as on risks originating in other fields of technology such as electromagnetic radiation and energy systems.

Overview of the contributions

In the opening chapter for this volume, *Sven Ove Hansson* develops an agenda for the ethics of risk. He points out that risk and uncertainty have so far been blind spots in moral philosophy. Most moral philosophers presuppose a deterministic world in which outcomes of actions can be known for certain. Hence, the predominant ethical theories are not well suited for the real world, which is inherently risky and uncertain. Hansson also discusses the various meanings the notion 'risk' can have. Shifts in meaning can lead to conceptual confusions. The main part of Hansson's essay discusses four subareas of the ethics of risk. The first subarea shows the value dependence of risk assessments. The second subarea consists of ethical analysis as a supplement to standard risk analysis. The third subarea sees the ethical study of risk as a means to improve risk analysis. The fourth subarea sees the ethical study of risk as a means to improve moral philosophy. In short, Hansson argues that the ethics of risk should be a central part of risk analysis as much as of moral philosophy.

Furthermore, Hansson emphasizes ten points that should especially be taken into account in further studies into the ethics of risk: (1) pay attention to uncontroversial values; (2) pay attention to the influence of values on the burden of proof; (3) we need a systematic treatment of ways in which values enter risk assessments; (4) and (5) the notions and implications of voluntariness and consent require more clarification; (6) pay attention to the intertwinement of actions by harmed persons and others; (7) probabilistic risk analysis should pay more attention to individuals; (8) pay attention to incommensurable types of value; (9) develop a theory for a *defeasible* right against risk impositions; and (10) develop a theory of justice that takes risk into account. Some of these points are addressed in the other contributions to this volume.

The five papers in Part II discuss various principles and guidelines that should be taken into account in morally acceptable risk management.

Carl Cranor's contribution is a plea for a 'rich conception of risks'. Cranor argues that in theorizing about risks, researchers should recognize the wide variety of risks and their properties. There are limitations to the standard approach in risk management, which takes into account probabilities and magnitudes but overlooks other considerations that are morally important aspects of risk. There can also be limitations if researchers try to differentiate between risks where distinctions are not justified. In arguing for this thesis, Cranor makes several points. First, many people have life goals other than merely living as safely as possible. Secondly, in theorizing about risks, we should use a term that is neutral between risks that are imposed upon us and those that we have voluntarily taken, and he gives examples of cases that are ambiguous in that respect. Furthermore, we should distinguish between natural risks and humanly caused risks. He goes on to discuss the epistemic detection of risks, either through our senses or through technical tools, as well as the degree of control that we have over risks. Cranor also emphasizes the fact that people have different attitudes towards and value risks differently. In addition, benefits (or the lack thereof) associated with risks can make them more or less acceptable. Another important consideration is the extent to which risks are voluntarily incurred. Lastly, Cranor emphasizes that it is morally important how risks and benefits are distributed within a society; some risks raise explicit moral issues. According to Cranor, these considerations about risks should be taken into account in studying and theorizing about them.

In his contribution, *Henk Zandvoort* develops requirements for the social acceptability of risky technological activities. His argument is based on the assumption that all human activities should be in accordance with two ethical principles; that is, the principle of restricted liberty (the 'no harm principle') and the principle of reciprocity. Zandvoort argues that if applied to risk generating technological activities, these principles give rise to two requirements: the requirement of informed consent and the requirement of strict liability in the absence of informed consent. He relates these requirements to discussions of predominant views in economic theory and he points to the shortcomings of majority rule in political decision-making. For example, in the case of majority rule, there is the possibility that the rights of a minority, specifically the right to be safeguarded, are not respected. This is in conflict with the no harm principle and with the principle of informed consent. Such violations should be met with strict, that is full and unconditional, liability. Zandvoort then applies his requirements to the case of energy systems. In addition to the need for stricter liability legislation, he here also emphasizes the importance of transparent risk communication and risk information from the experts to the public, in order to allow for informed consent.

Duff Waring discusses different interpretations of 'clinical equipoise' in his contribution. Clinical equipoise is a principle in medical ethics that states that a novel, non-validated treatment may only be used for patients in a trial if therapeutic risks and benefits are approximately equal to those accepted by patients in clinical practice who consent to the standard treatment for the condition under study. If clinical equipoise pertains between the novel and standard treatments, then patients who become research subjects would not add to the therapeutic risk load they already carry by enrolling in a trial. Waring describes the types of trial clinical equipoise is meant to accommodate and then explores how the notion of 'approximate equal' can be applied to either sums or ratios of risks and benefits. He argues that 'approximate equality' is most plausibly construed as a prima facie requirement of acceptable therapeutic risk that can be overridden when it conflicts with a weightier, more favourable balance of benefits over risks. He concludes that the application of clinical equipoise will not always prevent research subjects from adding to their therapeutic risk load when they participate in a trial. He also discusses the tension between 'risk cautious' and 'risk friendly' value frameworks in the application of clinical equipoise. He relates this tension to the Institutional Review Board system and suggests that we ought to acquire greater empirical knowledge about which of these frameworks the application of clinical equipoise reflects.

Marc D. Davidson discusses our obligations to future generations and argues that giving shape to intergenerational justice revolves around dealing with risk and uncertainty. He discusses various perspectives on how a society is to deal with risk using Cultural Theory. The cultural ideal types distinguished in that theory offer a useful tool for understanding the different positions taken in the debates about managing risks. However, although people may differ in their attitudes towards risk, society has already institutionalized a certain general standard of conduct as being acceptable for handling risks to others. Davidson argues that intergenerational justice requires future generations to be treated according to these same standards. By means of examples, he shows that this general standard of conduct can indeed be meaningfully applied in the intergenerational context.

In her contribution, *Arianna Ferrari* discusses the use of genetically engineered livestock for biomedical research, such as xenotransplantation and gene-pharming. She argues that these developments give rise to ethical considerations that go further than those entailed in traditional risk assessment. The risks of these technologies are to a high degree unpredictable. In the case of xenotransplantation there is, for example, the risk of 'xenosis', that is, of cross-species diseases which might only manifest themselves in a far future. In the case of gene-pharming, there might be unforeseen toxological effects. Furthermore, these technologies give rise to increased concerns about animal welfare. Ferrari proposes to broaden all assessments of unpredictable risks in order to include morally relevant considerations such as consent and equity. In addition, she argues that in the case of these specific technologies three other considerations should be included: the interests of future generations, the possibility of alternative research strategies, and the implications for the suffering and death for genetically modified animals. Ferrari concludes that, based on these considerations and given the high risks involved, xenotransplantation and gene-pharming are not ethically acceptable.

Part III contains three papers that discuss methodological considerations in thinking about the ethics of risk.

Douglas MacLean discusses how risk analysts try to avoid making normative claims. They see themselves as neutral scientists who study the likelihood of risky events and the preferences of people. Risk analysts think that they should merely inform policy-makers without making ethical or normative claims, thereby supposedly respecting the freedom of individuals to make up their own mind about their preferences. According to MacLean, this is a mistaken view. Risk analysis is actually a branch of ethics, since it is inherently normative and concerns important ethical issues. MacLean argues that contrary to the standard view amongst economists and risk analysts, values and reasons for action cannot be reduced to preferences or willingness to pay. People can have irrational, self-destructive or immoral preferences, or preferences that are based on wrong information. Furthermore, we cannot determine what is good for society simply by aggregating preferences, since we also need to know how to value and balance the preferences of different individuals. Instead of just uncritically describing preferences of people, risk analysts should use their expertise by making explicit what are good reasons for or against options for action. They should not only advise policy-makers but also educate the public and influence individual preferences about risks.

Nicolas Espinoza unravels the different ways in which risks may be either evaluatively incommensurable or evaluatively incomparable. Both conditions may pose a serious risk to consistent weighing or prioritizing of societal risks. Risks are incommensurable if we fail to assign probabilities to potential negative consequences or if we fail to value the consequences of the risks. We are then unable to represent them on a cardinal scale. Cost-benefit analyses cannot be accurately performed on risks that are incommensurable because there is no common measure according to which a particular divide in the allocation of resources can be justified. Espinoza argues that incommensurable risks may still be comparable, in which case they can be ranked according to a common value. He shows that risks are only entirely incomparable if an additional condition pertains, namely if the evaluative relation that holds between the two risks is insensitive to small alterations in the probabilities or values associated with the risks.

Greg Bognar discusses how we should make welfare judgements about risks, and how far an ideal advisor model might be helpful in forming such judgements. Bognar understands an ideal advisor as somebody who is fully informed and ideally rational. An ideal advisor uses a 'fully developed theory of rational choice', plus a 'principle of reasonable levels of risk-taking' towards well-being, P. Bognar's argument is mainly targeted at possible candidates for this principle P. Principle P can either be: to be risk-neutral, to be risk-seeking, or to be risk-averse towards well-being. Bognar argues that for each of these principles we can give counter-examples. In contrast with an ideal advisor who makes decisions based on general principles, real people base their judgements also on contextual features. Not every risk is equally worth taking or avoiding. Furthermore, real people can decide to cooperate with others who are involved in a decision process. A purely principle-based approach for welfare judgements about risks fails to take such contextual features and substantive claims about risks into account.

Part IV contains four papers that argue for the view that there should be a more substantial role for the public in deciding about acceptable risks.

The contribution by *Paul Slovic, Melissa Finucane, Ellen Peters* and *Donald G. MacGregor* discusses empirical research about the role of affect and reason in judging risks. The authors base their views on ideas developed in cognitive psychology and neuroscience according to which human beings comprehend risks in two fundamentally different ways. This approach is also called Dual Process Theory. Our experiential system is intuitive, emotional and spontaneous; our analytic system is based on logic, rationality and is relatively slow. Slovic et al present studies that they have conducted which show that our feelings about a hazardous situation determine how we perceive its risks and benefits. Apparently, people base their risk judgements on feelings. This can lead to a clouded understanding of factual information about risks. For example, information about probabilities is prone to be misunderstood if we do not use our analytic system. On the other hand, risk judgements based on feelings can be useful in responding quickly to complex situations. In addition, feelings can convey meaning that purely rational information, based on numbers, fails to communicate.

Sabine Roeser argues for a different conception of the relationship between reason and emotion than is generally found in the literature about risk. Most authors who write about affective responses to risk see reason and emotion as categorically distinct faculties. In accordance with this distinction there is Dual Process Theory, which states that there are two fundamentally different systems by which we process information and form judgements. The first system is taken to be spontaneous, intuitive and emotional; the second system is supposed to be slow, reflective and rational. While the emotional system is seen to be prone to biases, the second, rational system is considered to be normatively superior. In her contribution, Roeser questions this dichotomy, specifically by focusing on moral emotions such as sympathy and empathy, but also on fear. She argues that these emotions cross the boundaries between the two systems. They have features that are central to both systems. Partly because of this, emotions can provide epistemic justification for moral judgements about risks. Rather than being biases that threaten objectivity and rationality in thinking about acceptable risks, emotions are crucial to come to a correct understanding of the moral acceptability of a hazard.

Mark Coeckelbergh discusses the role that images and imagination do and should play in judgements about technological risks. He analyses the current literature on risk perception and argues that the concepts used suggest that 'the public' has an inferior, misguided outlook on risks compared to that of experts, and that the views of the public should be corrected by those of experts. Examples of such tendentious concepts are 'stigma', 'image', 'risk perception' or 'risk as feeling' in the case of laypeople, versus 'risk as analysis' in the case of experts. According to Coeckelbergh, this merely enforces the polarization between laypeople and experts. Instead, he pleads that the views and imagination of the public should be taken seriously. According to Coeckelbergh, imagination should play a crucial role in the dialogue between experts and laypeople about acceptable risks. It enables both parties to understand different viewpoints and to critically assess their own views. Imagination should be understood as necessary to moral judgement and in that sense as an indispensable source of wisdom in decision-making about the moral acceptability of technological risks.

Lotte Asveld provides an analysis of a contemporary debate in the Netherlands on the acceptability of (alleged) risks associated with mobile phone technology. Trust is a main problem in this debate. Participation in decision-making about the acceptability of technological risks can serve as a means to increase trust and resolve the dispute. The dispute concerns the identification as well as the estimation and the acceptability of the alleged risks. The opponents of mobile phone technology, including both experts and laypeople, have articulated views on supposed fallacies in the risk-assessments that are central to current risk-policies.

Asveld argues that neither additional research nor precautionary measures will bring a resolution to the debate. The current system for participation will not move the debate further either. Asveld claims that for both ethical and instrumental reasons, the government should pursue a participatory method that focuses on the criteria for proof of risk, since the divergence in views on these criteria is the main reason for the lack of trust by the opponents in the authorities and the operators.

Part V comprises two papers that discuss how risk management could become more democratic.

Gero Kellermann discusses the role national ethics councils play in public debates on technological risks. The main task of national ethics councils is to evaluate scientific developments, in particular in the life sciences, on their moral dimensions. They usually consist of an interdisciplinary team of experts. Their recommendations often influence political decision-making. Kellermann asks whether these ethics councils can be said to possess ethical expertise that legitimizes their position in a democratic society. From a discussion on the possibility of the existence of ethical expertise in general, Kellermann concludes that ethics councils derive legitimacy from generating a specific kind of knowledge. Members of ethics councils are not necessarily better ethical experts than other individuals, but the process of producing ethical recommendations by ethics councils can be said to be robust enough to warrant their advisory status in democratic societies. This process includes discussions of an interdisciplinary nature, investment of allocated time and a systematic consideration of the relevant arguments. Ethics councils should not, however, exceed their advisory status and they should not have a binding impact on political decision-making, Kellermann argues, as this is irreconcilable with the values of a democratic, pluralistic society.

Anke van Gorp and *Armin Grunwald* take on the issue of the responsibilities of engineers in a deliberative democracy. They argue for a view on technology that recognizes the values implicit in the design of a technology, in which the role of engineers in designing that technology should not be overestimated. The work of engineers is constrained by what van Gorp and Grunwald term 'regulative frameworks'. These frameworks are supposed to provide the moral guidelines with regard to technological risks as required by society at large. However, at present many regulative frameworks do not adequately represent the perspectives of all actors that may be affected by a particular technology. Additionally, these frameworks do not always provide adequate guidance to engineers. Van Gorp and Grunwald make a distinction between normal and radical design. Especially in instances of radical design the regulative frameworks may fail to provide moral guidance to the engineer. Van Gorp and Grunwald illustrate this claim with four case studies. The authors argue that engineers have specific responsibilities to assure that the regulative frameworks are sufficiently adequate and that the different interests of relevant actors are incorporated.

The volume closes with a chapter by *Michael Baram* on risk governance. Baram discusses the way modern, developed countries manage risks. This involves many actors, including legislators, regulators, courts, industrial organizations, professional organizations, unions and interest groups. These actors give rise to regulation that developers of technologies have to adhere to. This can lead to complex and often impractical systems of rules. That is one of the reasons why recently there has been a shift towards self-regulation. However, self-regulation carries with it the danger that safety is only a minor concern in a competitive business environment. In addition, decision-making in such a context lacks transparency. Liability and control systems can prevent these pitfalls to a degree. In order to illustrate these issues, Baram discusses two cases of reforms towards self-regulation, i.e. concerning the offshore industry in Norway and in the United States, and concerning biotechnology and GM food in the European Union and in the United States. Baram concludes his essay with two messages: (1) most technocratic approaches to risk governance lack a sense of moral obligation; (2) it is not enough to comply with regulation, but organizations and individuals should also develop their own moral views and apply these to the 'eternal question' of 'how safe is safe enough'.

Outlook

The contributions to this volume vary between rather theoretical, conceptual papers and papers that engage directly with concrete technological case studies. What they all have in common, though, is their critique of conventional risk management. There seems to be a general consensus amongst scholars who study the ethics of technological risk that we need to come to a much more multidimensional approach of risk management than the conventional, technocratic approach which defines risk in terms of probabilities and outcomes and applies risk-benefit analysis. That we should come to a more multidimensional approach has been defended by social scientists for the last decades, but their research is mainly descriptive. Philosophical analysis adds to this research by providing for normative argumentations and conceptual analysis. The contributions in this volume provide such normative and conceptual arguments. The philosophical, normative perspective is an important addition to the sociological research about acceptable risk. So far, philosophers have been comparatively quiet in this debate, but this volume is evidence that this is changing. Given the significant impact that technologies and their concomitant risks and benefits have on the well-being of people, we hope that more philosophers get involved in discussions about the ethics of technological risk.

With this volume we aim to broaden the debate on the ethics of technological risk. Technology is pervasive; at its best, technology is a tool that we control in order to improve our lives. At its worst, technology is a process that unpredictably can turn against its initiators. It is up to us to choose which way we go with technology. However, we need to engage in ethical reflection about technology in order to direct it in the way that we human beings want it to go.

2 An Agenda for the Ethics of Risk

Sven Ove Hansson

Introduction

In the late 1960s, increasing public awareness of risks to human health and the environment from new technologies gave rise to a rapid growth in scientific and scholarly studies of risk (Otway, 1987). The area attracted specialists from many disciplines, including statistics, engineering, physics, biology, various medical disciplines, economics, geography, psychology, sociology and social anthropology. The new field was institutionalized as the discipline of 'risk analysis', with professional societies, research institutes and journals of its own. Moral philosophy has only had a small role in this development, but gradually an ethical discourse on risk has developed. Today, the ethics of risk is a small but growing subject that attracts increasing attention among philosophers and also among risk researchers in other disciplines.[1]

A blind spot in moral philosophy

It may be surprising that this is a new area for moral philosophy. Human life is a life in uncertainty; only very seldom do we know beforehand what the consequences of our actions will be. Of course, philosophers have been aware of this, and some have mentioned it. Leibniz complained in his *New Essays on Human Understanding* (1704) that moralists had an insufficient and too limited view of probability (Leibniz, [1704] 1962, p372 (IV:2, §14)). Risk-taking has an important role in Kant's essay 'On a supposed right to lie from philanthropy', in which he explains why telling a lie is always wrong, even it if is done for a good purpose (Kant, [1797] 1912). Suppose that an assassin asks you where his victim is. If you answer truthfully and the assassin finds and kills the victim, then according to Kant you have not really caused the death since you had no other choice than to speak truthfully. According to his view, the death was caused by 'chance'

(*Zufall*), that is, by contingent circumstances beyond your control. If you instead tell a lie in order to save the victim, then you cannot know for sure that your lie will have the intended effect. There is a possibility that it will in fact have the opposite effect. Perhaps it will induce the assassin to go to some other place, and the victim unexpectedly turns up in that place and is killed. In that case, says Kant, you have caused the death and are responsible for it. In a somewhat similar vein, Moore referred to the unpredictability of consequences as an argument why (act) utilitarianism could not be used in practical ethics; instead, commonsense ethical rules, such as the prohibition against lying, could be used (Moore, 1903, Chapter V, §§91–95).

However, Kant's and Moore's appeals to unexpected effects of actions are exceptions in the history of moral philosophy. Typically, moral philosophers from antiquity forwards have been predominantly concerned with problems that would fit into a deterministic world where the morally relevant properties of human actions are assumed to be not only determined but also knowable at the point in time of deliberation. We can see this deterministic bias not least in the choice of examples that are used in moral philosophy. It is a common feature of these examples that each option has well-defined consequences: you can be sure that if you shoot one prisoner, then the commander will spare the lives of all the others. You know for certain how many people will be killed if you pull or do not pull the lever of the runaway trolley, etc. This is of course unrealistic. In real moral quandaries we do not know for sure what the effects of our actions will be. The irrealism of moral philosophy in this respect can be contrasted with the frequent use of examples that are blatantly unrealistic in other respects. Moral philosophers do not hesitate to introduce examples that are far remote from the conditions under which we live our lives, such as examples involving teleportation or human reproduction with spores (Abbott, 1978; Rosebury, 1995, esp. pp499 and 505).

As a consequence of this blind spot in moral philosophy, common moral theories are incapable of dealing with decision-making under risk and uncertainty. If we turn for guidance to utilitarian, deontological rights-based or contract-based ethical theories, we will find recipes for how to act, but these recipes do not work unless we have prior knowledge of the consequences of our actions (Hansson, 2003a). Tools to deal with risk or uncertainty are lacking. (Such tools are available in decision theory, more about which below.) This is a major defect in current moral philosophy, and the ultimate task of the ethics of risk should be to mend this defect. Therefore, the ethics of risk should not be seen as one of many 'applied ethics' subdisciplines. It has a much more important role in moral philosophy than that. To the extent that we wish moral philosophy to deal successfully with the moral problems of human life as we know it, it is a central task for moral philosophers to develop tools and theories to deal with the issues of risk and uncertainties that have so long been neglected in the discipline.

THE NOTION OF RISK

The term 'risk' has several meanings and nuances (Hansson, 2007b). In everyday language, it has a non-quantitative ('qualitative') sense, and is used as an approximate synonym of 'danger'. When we speak for instance about the risk of future floodings due to global warming, we refer to certain undesirable events that may or may not occur. It is in practice impossible to determine the probability of these events. (Their occurrence depends not only on natural developments but also on human decisions on greenhouse gas emissions, dam reinforcements, etc.) We do not hesitate to use the word 'risk' when talking about such eventualities even though no probabilities are available.

In more technical language, 'risk' is used as a quantitative term, denoting a numerical value that indicates the size or seriousness of a danger. In everyday language a phrase such as 'the risk of a melt-down in the reactor' refers to the presence of a danger. In technical language, the same phrase refers to a numerical value that represents the size of that danger.

To make this even more complicated, there are two numerical measures that are called 'the risk'. First, 'risk' can denote the probability that a danger will materialize. Second, it can denote the expectation value of the severity of the outcome. An expectation value is a probability-weighted value. Hence, if 200 deep-sea divers perform an operation where the risk of death is 0.1 per cent for each individual, then the expected number of fatalities from this operation is $200 \times 0.1\% = 0.2$. We can then say that 'the risk' associated with this operation is 0.2 deaths. This usage of the term 'risk' was introduced into mainstream risk research through the influential Reactor Safety Study (WASH-1400, the Rasmussen report) from 1975 (Rechard, 1999, p776). Many attempts have been made to establish this usage as the only recognized meaning of the term. It is often called the 'objective risk'.

The use of one and the same term for these different meanings is bound to give rise to problems. It should be no surprise that attempts to reserve the well-established everyday word 'risk' for a technical concept have led to significant communicative failures. There is in fact often a pernicious drift in the sense of the word 'risk': a discussion or an analysis begins with a general phrase such as 'risks in the building industry' or 'risks in modern energy production'. This includes both dangers for which meaningful probabilities are available and dangers for which they are not. As the analysis goes more into technical detail, the term 'risk' is narrowed down to the expectation value definition. Before this change in meaning it was fairly uncontroversial that smaller risks should be preferred to larger ones. It is often taken for granted that this applies to the redefined notion of risk as well. In other words, it is assumed that a rational decision-maker is bound to judge risk issues in accordance with these expectation values ('risks'), so that an outcome with a smaller expectation value ('risk') is always preferred to one with a larger expectation value. This, of course, is not so. The risk that has the smallest expectation value may have other features that make it worse, all things considered. It may for instance be involuntary, or it may be a catastrophic risk with a very low probability that is considered to be of high concern in spite of having a low expectation value. This effect of the shift in meaning of 'risk' has often passed unnoticed.

Issues in the ethics of risk

The ethical problems of risk often concern factors that are not covered by probabilities or expectation values. Therefore, the ethics of risk takes 'risk' in the wide, everyday sense of the word as its subject-matter. The ethics of risk is not limited to any of the more technical senses in which the word 'risk' is used. To avoid misunderstandings about this, we can use the longer phrase 'ethics of risk and uncertainty'. 'Uncertainty' is the common decision-theoretical term for non-probabilizable lack of knowledge (Luce and Raiffa, 1957, p13).

Research into the ethics of risk can be divided into four (partly overlapping) subareas. First, there are investigations that aim at clarifying the value dependence of risk assessments. Second, ethical analysis can be undertaken as a supplement to standard risk analysis. This means that ethicists investigate issues related to justice, consent, voluntariness and other factors that are not covered in the usual (expected utility) framework of risk analysis. Third, ethical studies can have the aim of improving risk analysis, typically by providing means to include ethical issues in the main analysis, instead of relegating them to a supplementary analysis. Fourth, and finally, studies in the ethics of risk can have the aim of developing moral theory so that it can deal better with issues of risk.

In what follows, I will present ten important items on a research agenda for the ethics of risk (and uncertainty), organized according to this subdivision of the subject.

The value dependence of risk assessments

Before the development of risk analysis in the 1960s and 1970s, decisions on risk acceptance were largely delegated to scientists. Physicists and radiation biologists formed an international committee for radiation protection (the International Commission on Radiological Protection, ICRP) that issued exposure limits and other guidelines. Engineers in various organizations developed rules and regulations for building safety and other forms of technical safety. Toxicologists decided on exposure limits for chemicals.

In the 1970s, awareness grew that such standard-setting tasks go beyond the expertise of these various expert groups. It takes a radiation biologist to determine the risks of radiation at different exposure levels, but the decision as to what risks the regulation should allow is value based, and not an experts' issue. Similarly, structural engineers can determine how the risks that a building collapses depends on its construction, but the decision on what risks to accept in the construction of buildings is not a task for experts. Toxicologists are best qualified to determine the toxic risks from different exposures to toxicants, but in the decision as to what risks to accept they are no more qualified than the rest of us.

Considerations like this led to the development of a new view of the risk decision process that can be called the dichotomous model. Its most famous expression can be found in an influential 1983 report by the American National Academy of Sciences (NAS; National Research Council, 1983). In this report, and numerous others after it, the decision procedure has been divided into two distinct parts to be performed consecutively. The first of these, commonly called risk assessment, is a scientific undertaking. It consists of collecting and assessing the relevant information and, based on this, characterizing the nature and magnitude of the risk. The second procedure is called risk management. Contrary to risk assessment, it is not a scientific undertaking. Its starting-point is the outcome of risk assessment, which it combines with economic and technological information pertaining to various ways of reducing or eliminating the risk in question, and also with political and social information. Based on this, a decision is made on what measures – if any – should be taken to reduce the risk. An essential difference between risk assessment and risk management, according to this view, is that values only appear in risk management. The ideal is that risk assessment should be a value-free process.

In some areas of risk assessment, decision-making has been reorganized in accordance with the dichotomous model. This often means that work that was previously performed in a single committee has now been split into two. Hence, since 1978 occupational exposure limits in Sweden are developed in a two-committee system. One of these committees consists of scientists whose task is to determine the risks associated with different levels of exposure to a chemical substance in the workplace. The other committee combines this information with information about technical and economic feasibility, and decides on an exposure limit (Hansson, 1998, pp75–102). Similar two-committee systems can be found in many other countries, in particular in chemical risk assessment and management.

In spite of the seeming consensus about this division of the process, the old system with cohabitation of risk assessment and risk management still dominates in many areas. The ICRP still decides on international recommendations for radiation protection, and it does this in committees that are responsible for both the assessment and the management of risk. Similarly, in the building industry, risk assessment and standard-setting are still performed in the same committees (Mork and Hansson, 2007).

Exposure limits and other regulations are often presented as 'scientific' and 'value-free' in spite of containing obviously value-based judgements on what risks to accept (Hansson, 1998, pp35–73; MacLean, Chapter 8, this volume). However, it is important for the quality of risk decision processes that the hidden value assumptions in risk assessments are uncovered. This is a difficult task that often requires philosophical competence. It has indeed often been philosophers who discovered and reported the value-dependence of allegedly value-free risk assessments (Thomson, 1985; MacLean, 1986; Shrader-Frechette, 1991; Cranor, 1997). Such investigations have been the starting-point for most researchers who have worked in the area of risk and values, including myself. Often close cooperation between philosophers and natural or technological scientists has been the best way to ensure that hidden value assumptions in science-based assessments are discovered (Hansson and Rudén, 2006).

But although this is the most well-developed subarea in the ethics of risk, there is still much to be done. New risk assessments with hidden value assumptions are published all the time. Some types of risk assessments have not yet been subject to this type of analysis. (Building codes and other codes of structural engineering seem to be a case in point.) In addition, important methodological and theoretical issues remain to be investigated, among them the following three:

1 Since the focus has (understandably) been on the role of controversial values in risk assessments, very little attention has been paid to the role of *uncontroversial values*, i.e. values that are shared by virtually everyone or by everyone who takes part in a particular discourse. Medical science provides good examples of this. When discussing analgesics, we take for granted that it is better if patients have less rather than more pain. There is no need to interrupt a discussion on this topic in order to point out that a statement that one analgesic is better than another depends on this value assumption. However, in order to understand the role of values in risk assessments (or in science generally), it is necessary to have the full picture, which includes values generally considered to be uncontroversial.
2 Perhaps the most recalcitrant value assumptions in risk assessments are those that relate to the *balance between our strivings to avoid errors of type I and type II*. An error of type I (false positive) is a statement that a phenomenon or an effect exists when in fact it does not. An error of type II (false negative) consists of missing an existing phenomenon or effect. In scientific practice, errors of type I are the more serious ones, since they give rise to an unwarranted conclusion, whereas errors of type II merely keep an issue open that could have been closed. However, when the contested phenomenon is a potential risk, then a type II error may be more serious than a type I error from a social point of view. It may be worse to believe that a dangerous chemical is harmless than that a harmless chemical is dangerous (Hansson, 1995, 2008; Asveld, Chapter 14, this volume). Ideally, we should always separate the criteria for practical action from the criteria of sufficient scientific evidence. However, in practice this is often not done. It remains to investigate the actual influence of (controversial and uncontroversial) values on the burden of proof in different disciplines.
3 In addition to their effects on the burden of proof, values can enter risk assessments in several other ways. Appeals to naturalness or unnaturalness tend to introduce values into an assessment (Hansson, 2003b). The indetectability of an effect is often taken as an argument that it is small enough to be acceptable (Hansson, 1999). Decisions on whom to protect (e.g. the average individual, or the most sensitive individual) are often made without explicit clarification of the values involved, etc. We still lack *a systematic treatment of the different ways in which ethical values and other values enter risk assessments*.

Finally, it must be emphasized that the analysis of values in risk assessment is difficult precisely because risk assessments are complexly interwoven combinations of value statements and statements of fact. Risk has the double nature of being both fact laden and value laden. The statement that you risk losing your leg if you tread on a landmine has both a factual component (landmines tend to dismember people who tread on them) and a value component (it is undesirable that you lose your leg). There are two groups of discussants who deny this double nature of risk. Some claim that risk assessments are objective and value free, others that risk is a subjective phenomenon, unconcerned with matters of fact. Both these attempts to rid a complex concept of its complexity are misleading. The real challenge is to understand the complex combination of values and facts, and to understand the respective roles of these components in risk assessment and risk management.

ETHICS AS A SUPPLEMENT TO STANDARD RISK ANALYSIS

Our second approach to the ethics of risk is the use of ethical analysis as a supplement to standard risk assessment. As already indicated, standard risk assessment is based on the presumption that risks can be adequately assessed on the basis of numerical probabilities and utilities. Risk assessments that are based on this presumption can provide risk managers with important information. However, this framework also excludes information that can be highly decision relevant. Social risks give rise to problems of agency and interpersonal relationships that go beyond the probabilities and severities of outcomes. Issues such as consent, voluntariness, intentionality, justice and democractic participation need to be included in a discourse on risk (Cranor, Chapter 3, this volume; Roeser, Chapter 12, this volume). These are issues that are alien to probabilistic risk analysis but central in the ethics of risk.

There is a need for simple tools to deal with ethical aspects that are excluded from standard risk analysis. In joint work with Hélène Hermansson, we have proposed a framework for a systematic ethical analysis of risk to be used as a supplement to probabilistic risk assessment (Hermansson and Hansson, 2007). Its focus is on three (potentially overlapping) roles that people can have in social interactions on risks. We can distinguish between those agents who are potentially exposed to a risk, those who make decisions that affect the risk and those who gain from the risk being taken. An analysis of the relationships between these three groups can be used to identify major ethical aspects of a risk management problem. Some examples of the questions that are asked in an analysis according to this method include: are the risk-exposed the same (or partly the same) people as the beneficiaries? Are the risk-exposed dependent (economically or otherwise) on the decision-makers? Do the risk-exposed have access to all relevant information about the risk? Do the decision-makers benefit from other people's risk exposure?

Much would be gained if probabilistic risk assessments were routinely supplemented with an analysis along these lines. In addition, some of these ethical issues require a more thorough analysis that should include methodological development. Three such issues appear to be particularly important:

4 There seems to be widespread agreement that involuntary risks are, *ceteris paribus*, more problematic than voluntary ones. However, *the definition and implications of voluntariness* remain to be clarified. The distinction between voluntary and involuntary risk exposure seems to depend largely on social conventions that are taken for granted without much reflection. As one

example of this, the risks associated with smoking are regarded as voluntary, whereas risks associated with emissions from a nearby factory are usually regarded as involuntary. For many smokers, to quit smoking is much more difficult than to move to a safer neighbourhood. In this and other cases, our ascriptions of (in)voluntariness are strongly influenced by what we consider to be a morally reasonable demand on a person. There seems to be a circular relationship between moral assessments and appraisals of voluntariness; they influence each other in ways that remain to be clarified.

5 It is often taken for granted that if the persons at risk *consent* to the risk exposure, then it is morally acceptable. This is a problematic assumption since what we call consent to a risk is seldom consent to the risk per se. A person who consents to the risks of a surgical operation in fact consents to the combination of the risks and the advantages associated with that operation. She would not consent to the risks alone. Similarly, a person who chooses to bungee jump does not consent to the risk per se but to a package consisting of this risk and its associated advantages, primarily the thrill. If she had the choice of an otherwise exactly similar jump but with a safer cord, then she would presumably choose the safer alternative. In the same way, a worker who accepts a job with a high risk of serious injury actually consents to a package consisting of these risks and the benefits associated with the job, primarily the pay. He has not consented to the risk per se or to the construction of the packages that he can choose between. In view of this, the argument of consent is much weaker than what it may at first seem to be. It remains to clarify its relevance and to investigate what type of influence over the decision is required to make a risk imposition morally justified (Hansson, 2006a).

6 Harmful outcomes are often caused by complex *combinations of actions by the harmed person and by other persons*. The drug addict cannot use drugs unless someone provides her with them. Similarly, the smoker can smoke only if companies continue to sell products that kill half of their customers. In the latter case it is often taken for granted that if the smoker has a moral right to harm herself, then the tobacco company has a moral right to provide her with the means to do so. In contrast, the manufacturers and distributors of heroin are commonly held responsible for the effects that their products have on the health and well-being of those who choose to buy and use them. Cigarettes are legal and heroin illegal, but that does not settle the moral issue. The conventions surrounding such combinations of self-harming and other-harming actions are in need of careful investigation and moral reconsideration (Hansson, 2005).

ETHICAL STUDIES AS A MEANS TO IMPROVE RISK ANALYSIS

It is not a satisfactory procedure to perform a risk analysis that excludes major ethical issues, and then treat these issues separately in a supplementary analysis. It would be much better to include the ethical aspects into the main analysis. We should therefore investigate if it is possible to reform probabilistic risk analysis so that it includes at least some of the issues that are now relegated to a supplementary analysis. Two such possibilities seem particularly promising.

7 The first of these concerns the way in which values related to different persons are combined in a risk assessment. Standard risk analysis is similar to classical utilitarianism in its disregard for persons. Risks affecting different persons are added up, and the moral appraisal refers to this sum, said to represent the 'total' risk. In risk-benefit analysis, benefits are added in the same way, and finally the sum of benefits is compared to the sum of risks in order to determine whether the total effect is positive or negative.

For the sake of argument we can assume that risks and benefits accruing to different persons are fully comparable in the sense that they can be measured in the same units. It does not follow from this that they should be added up in a moral appraisal. The crucial issue here is not comparability but compensability; that is, whether an action that brings about the smaller harm (greater benefit) compensates for the non-realization of a greater harm (smaller benefit) accruing to another person. Such interpersonal compensability does not follow automatically from interpersonal comparability. We may agree that it is worse for you to lose your thumb than for me to lose my little finger without agreeing that you are allowed to sacrifice my little finger in order to save your own thumb (Hansson, 2004).

An obvious alternative to this utilitarian approach is to treat each individual as a separate moral unit. Then risks and benefits pertaining to one and the same person are combined into a single measure, whereas risks and benefits for different persons are kept apart. This is the type of risk-weighing that dominates in the individual-centred traditions of clinical medicine, including the ethics of clinical trials (Hansson, 2006b). In this tradition, the balance is struck separately for each individual.

There is no reason why probabilistic risk analysis should be so constructed that it can only be used in appraisals that allow for full interindividual compensability. Instead, the analysis should present information in a way that allows for moral appraisals that are based on different views in the compensability issue. This means that probabilistic risk analysis should be developed to include not only a total balance-sheet, but also a balance-sheet for each (representative) individual who is concerned by the risk.

8 The second proposal concerns a related issue, namely the way in which incommensurable types of value are dealt with. In risk-related decisions we often have to compare values that are difficult or impossible to compare to each other: losses in human life, disabilities and diseases, the loss of an animal species, etc. (Espinoza, Chapter 9, this volume). In standard risk analysis, this problem has surprisingly often been dealt with by disregarding all harmful outcomes other than losses in human life. In risk-benefit analysis (RBA), the comparability issue is dealt with by assigning an economic value to all potential losses and gains, including the loss of a human life and the extinction of an animal species. These are losses that do not have a market value, and it is important not to confuse them with prices in the ordinary sense of the word.

> Obviously, a risk-benefit analyst who assigns a monetary value to the loss of a human life does not thereby imply that someone can buy another person, or the right to kill her, at that price. The values of lives used in the analysis are for calculation purposes only. The same applies to the values entered for disease and environmental damage. These different losses are incommensurable not only in relation to money but also in relation to each other. There is no definite answer to the question of how many cases of juvenile diabetes correspond to one death, or what amount of human suffering or death corresponds to the extinction of an antelope species (Hansson, 2007a).

In this procedure, multidimensional decision problems are reduced to unidimensional ones. Proposals have been made to reject this reduction, and use multidimensional rather than unidimensional modes of presentation. In other words, different types of negative consequences should be reported separately for each of the alternatives (Fischhoff et al., 1984; Hansson, 1989). The use of such multidimensional presentations does not of course preclude the calculation of various simplified total sums. However, such aggregations should always be seen as tentative, and no aggregation method should be assigned the role of the uniquely correct way to combine different values.

Both these proposals for reforms of risk analysis point in the direction of multidimensionality. This will make the analysis somewhat more complex. However, it is difficult to see how this can be avoided. Both from an intellectual and a public relations point of view, the major problem of current probabilistic risk analysis is that its reduction of complex problems of risk to a single numerical value lacks credibility. In order to regain credibility, this reduction has to be revoked.

ETHICAL STUDIES OF RISK AS A MEANS TO IMPROVE MORAL PHILOSOPHY

As already mentioned, moral philosophy has paid very little attention to risk and uncertainty. It could be argued that this is no problem since there is another discipline, namely decision theory, that takes care of these issues. According to the conventional division of labour between these two disciplines, moral philosophy provides assessments of human behaviour in well-determined situations. Decision theory takes assessments of these cases for given, and derives from them assessments for rational behaviour in an uncertain and indeterministic world. Since decision theory operates exclusively with criteria of rationality, this derivation takes place without any additional input of values. However, this approach fails since it leaves out the ethical problems of risk-taking per se (Hansson, 2001). Such problems cannot be dealt with by a moral philosophy that has given up issues of risk to decision theory. It cannot either be dealt with in decision theory, since that discipline is devoted to instrumental rationality and lacks tools to analyse ethical problems. Admittedly, moral theory also lacks such tools, but it is in moral philosophy that they should be developed.

The following are two major challenges for the development of moral theories that are more adequate to deal with problems of risk.

9 Risk impositions in modern societies give rise to a *dilemma for person-regarding moral theories*. On one hand, if we take individual rights seriously, then each risk-exposed person should be treated as a sovereign individual with a right to fair treatment. It would seem to follow that each of us has a right not to be exposed to danger by others. On the other hand, modern society would be impossible if all risk impositions were prohibited. When I drive a car in the town where you live, then this increases (hopefully by a very small amount) your risk of being killed in a traffic accident or contracting a respiratory disease due to air pollution. If all persons who are exposed to small risks like these were given a veto, then it is difficult to see how modern society could be at all possible. Hence, we have good reasons both to prohibit and to allow risk impositions.

One plausible solution of this dilemma is to recognize a right against risk impositions, but make this right defeasible. In particular, it can be defeated in cases when each of us gains from reciprocal risk impositions. If others are allowed to drive a car, exposing me to certain risks, then in exchange I am allowed to drive a car and expose them to the corresponding risks. Such an arrangement (we may suppose) is to the benefit of all of us. As a first approximation, we consider the individual right against risk-impositions to be overridden in cases when a system of risk exposures is to the advantage of everyone (Hansson, 2003a). Much remains to be done in order to develop this into a workable moral principle and – in particular – to construct social processes for risk decision that conform with the principle.

10 We need to develop a *theory of justice* that takes the riskiness of human life into account. Currently, a dominant view of justice is that it consists of everyone having the same starting-line: 'Thus, if a number of people start out with equal shares of material resources, and fair opportunities (whatever exactly that may mean), other things being equal, there seems to be no basis for objecting to the justice of the outcomes of any voluntary exchange we might make' (Ripstein, 1999, p54).[2] According to a starting-line theory, justice is achieved if we all start out from equal starting-lines, in terms of educational opportunities and other resources in childhood and adolescence. However, the only credible reason why equal starting-lines should be sufficient seems to be the assumption that if we are provided with the same initial conditions, then any differences that follow will depend on our own actions and choices, and for these we can be held accountable. This assumption is incorrect. To be more precise, it might have been true in a deterministic world, but it is far from true in the world that we live in (Fleurbaey, 2001). Our living conditions are not determined exclusively by our starting-lines and our own actions. On the contrary, they are largely determined by events beyond our control that belong to the realm of risk and uncertainty. Since injustices arise throughout our lives due to events beyond our control, justice is not achievable by setting the initial conditions right and then leaving the system on its own. Instead, justice has to be a continuous counter-force to the various mechanisms that unceasingly give rise to injustices. A theory of justice along

these lines may have to be more complex than a starting-line theory. There seems to be no other way to go if we want to construct a plausible theory of justice that applies to human life as it actually is, not as it would have been in a hypothetical deterministic world.

References

Abbott, P. (1978) 'Philosophers and the abortion question', *Political Theory*, vol 6, pp313–335

Clausen Mork, J. and Hansson, S. O. (2007) 'Eurocodes and REACH – differences and similarities', *Risk Management*, vol 9, pp19–35

Cranor, C. F. (1997) 'The normative nature of risk assessment: features and possibilities', *Risk: Health, Safety & Environment*, vol 8, pp123–136

Dworkin, R. (1981) 'What is equality? Part 2: equality of resources', *Philosophy and Public Affairs*, vol 10, pp283–345

Fischhoff, B., Watson, S. R. and Hope, C. (1984) 'Defining risk', *Policy Sciences*, vol 17, pp123–139

Fleurbaey, M. (2001) 'Egalitarian opportunities', *Law and Philosophy*, vol 20, pp499–530

Hansson, S. O. (1989) 'Dimensions of risk', *Risk Analysis*, vol 9, pp107–112

Hansson, S. O. (1995) 'The detection level', *Regulatory Toxicology and Pharmacology*, vol 22, pp103–109

Hansson, S. O. (1998) *Setting the Limit. Occupational Health Standards and the Limits of Science*, Oxford University Press, Oxford

Hansson, S. O. (1999) 'The moral significance of indetectable effects', *Risk*, vol 10, pp101–108

Hansson, S. O. (2001) 'The modes of value', *Philosophical Studies*, vol 104, pp33–46

Hansson, S. O. (2003a) 'Ethical criteria of risk acceptance', *Erkenntnis*, vol 59, pp291–309

Hansson, S. O. (2003b) 'Are natural risks less dangerous than technological risks?', *Philosophia Naturalis*, vol 40, pp43–54

Hansson, S. O. (2004) 'Weighing risks and benefits', *Topoi*, vol 23, pp145–152

Hansson, S. O. (2005) 'Extended antipaternalism', *Journal of Medical Ethics*, vol 31, pp97–100

Hansson, S. O. (2006a) 'Informed consent out of context', *Journal of Business Ethics*, vol 63, pp149–154

Hansson, S. O. (2006b) 'Uncertainty and the ethics of clinical trials', *Theoretical Medicine and Bioethics*, vol 27, pp149–167

Hansson, S. O. (2007a) 'Philosophical problems in cost-benefit analysis', *Economics and Philosophy*, vol 23, pp163–183

Hansson, S. O. (2007b) 'Risk', *Stanford Encyclopedia of Philosophy*, http://plato.stanford.edu/entries/risk/

Hansson, S. O. (2008) 'Regulating BFRs – from science to policy', *Chemosphere*, vol 73, pp144–147

Hansson, S. O. and Rudén, C. (2006) 'Evaluating the risk decision process', *Toxicology*, vol 218, pp100–111

Hermansson, H. and Hansson, S. O. (2007) 'A three party model tool for ethical risk analysis', *Risk Management*, vol 9, no 3, pp129–144

Kant, I. ([1797] 1912) 'Über ein vermeintes Recht aus Menschenliebe zu lügen', in I. Kant (ed.) *Gesammelte Schriften* (Akademie-Ausgabe), Abt. 1, Bd 8., Königliche Preußische Akademie der Wissenschaften, Berlin

Leibniz, G. W. ([1704] 1962) *Sämtliche Schriften und Briefe*, Herausgegeben von der Deutschen Akademie der Wissenschaften zu Berlin, Sechste Reihe, Philosophische Schriften, vol 6, Akademie-Verlag, Berlin

Luce, R. D. and Raiffa, H. (1957) *Games and Decisions*, Wiley, New York

MacLean, D. (ed.) (1986) *Values at Risk*, Rowman & Littlefield, Totowa, NJ

Moore, G. E. (1903) *Principia Ethica*, Cambridge, Cambridge University Press

National Research Council (1983) *Risk Assessment in the Federal Government: Managing the Process*, National Academy Press, Washington, DC

Otway, H. (1987) 'Experts, risk communication, and democracy', *Risk Analysis*, vol 7, pp125–129

Rechard, R. P. (1999) 'Historical relationship between performance assessment for radioactive waste disposal and other types of risk assessment', *Risk Analysis*, vol 19, no 5, pp763–807

Ripstein, A. (1999) *Equality, Responsibility and the Law*, Cambridge, Cambridge University Press

Rosebury, B. (1995) 'Moral responsibility and "moral luck"', *Philosophical Review*, vol 104, pp499–524

Shrader-Frechette, K. (1991) *Risk and Rationality. Philosophical Foundations for Populist Reforms*, University of California Press, Berkeley

Thomson, P. B. (1985) 'Risking or being willing: Hamlet and the DC-10', *Journal of Value Inquiry*, vol 19, pp301–310

NOTES

1 See the philosophy of risk homepage (www.infra.kth.se/phil/riskpage/index.htm) and the philosophy of risk newsletter that can be ordered there.

2 See also Ronald Dworkin's (1981, pp308–312) discussion of the 'starting-gate theory of fairness'.

Part II

Principles and Guidelines

A fundamental challenge for including ethical considerations in risk management is to develop principles and guidelines that should be adhered to. Carl Cranor argues that the notion of 'risk' has to be broadened in order to do justice to the complex (ethical) issues involved. The other contributions to this part of the book discuss specific principles in more detail. Henk Zandvoort argues that agents who put others at risk without their consent should be subject to unconditional legal liability. Duff Waring points out ethical problems with the principle of clinical equipoise. Marc D. Davidson argues that risk assessment has to do justice to future generations. Arianna Ferrari discusses our moral obligations to animals in biomedical research.

3 A Plea for a Rich Conception of Risks

Carl Cranor

Introduction

Risks tend to loom large in contemporary industrialized societies (but are not restricted to them). In part this is because the industrial revolution and the later chemical revolution introduced risks that were previously unknown or much less extensive. In part we may now be more attentive to risks than we might have been before the environmental movements of the 1970s and 1980s. Moreover, risks catch our attention because the mere identification of something as a risk alerts us to potential adverse effects to ourselves, others or the environment.

Despite the attention they receive, there is less convergence on how we should respond to different risks. In particular some commentators, adopting a common theoretical apparatus, suggest that if one knows the probability and magnitude of the risks in question, this is the main or, in quite crude accounts, the only thing that one needs to know for social or legal regulation of risks. Others have noted this point, and regretted that commentators have such limited views of risks. For example, as Gillette and Krier put it:

> They may disagree about details, such as whether one looks at total expected deaths, deaths per person or per hour of exposure, or loss of life expectancy due to exposure, but generally speaking 'experts appear to see riskiness as synonymous with expected annual mortality and morbidity' … When experts write about relative risk, they implicitly or explicitly use body counts as the relevant measure. And, in a way seemingly consistent with the logic of their method, they insist that a death is a death is a death … (Gillette and Krier, 1990, p1072)

Gillette and Krier are correct to note this point; they, and I, believe that it is a mistake to approach risks in this manner. However, for the most part I will not address that issue in this chapter.

In considering the ethical, legal and social aspects of risks, we need to make some important conceptual distinctions between different kinds of risks and some of their properties. Elsewhere, I began this task and have even taken some modest steps towards proposing a normative justification of different kinds of risks (Cranor, 1995, 2007a). However, more remains to be done on these topics. In this chapter I do not directly address the normative issues. Instead, I want to step back and consider a variety of risks and their properties in order to have a rich conceptual field within which to consider risks and how they are to be addressed socially or by individuals.

Thus, the argument of this chapter is a plea to recognize the rich conceptual varieties of risks and their properties. I propose that these distinctions should be considered pertinent to assessing the acceptability from a personal point of view, or from a moral point of view or for considering them for various forms of legal regulation, but I do not explicitly argue for this. This chapter simply addresses several important conceptual distinctions about different properties of risks.

DISTINCTIONS

To begin, however, I adopt quite conventional conceptions of a risk. Thus, a risk is the chance, or the probability, of some loss or harm – the chance of mishap.[1] Another way of putting this point is to say that a risk is represented by the probability of a loss or harm times the severity of its outcome.

Risks should be distinguished from their *acceptability*, an assessment from some appropriate normative point of view, for example personal, moral or legal points of view (Cranor, 1995, 2007a). That is, all might agree that there is some small risk of being injured by an incoming meteor, perhaps a greater risk from crossing a busy train track, some degree of risk from drinking water contaminated with the degreaser trichloroethylene (TCE) (a carcinogen), and some risk from exposure to arsenic (another carcinogen) in drinking water. However, one can do little about incoming meteors, and there may be quite different views about the acceptability of exposure to TCE or arsenic in drinking water and the dangers of crossing a frequently used train track from various points of view.

THE PROBABILITIES AND MAGNITUDE OF RISKS

One important distinction we should want to know about risks are their comparative magnitudes of harms, as well as the probabilities of them materializing. These are part of the definition of particular risks. Having an accurate estimate of the severity of harms risked as well as the likelihood of a particular harm materializing are both important features we would like to know about risks. When one has such information, this informs one of one's chances of adverse effects, serious injury or, in the extreme, chances of death. Thus, for example, many commentators on risks go to great lengths to inform readers of the comparative statistics of dying from one risk versus another (see, for example, Morrall, 1986; Wilson and Crouch, 1987; Laudan, 1994).

This can be important information. Technical experts frequently point out that the lay public is often mistaken in their judgements about actual chances of risks materializing into adverse effects or about the comparative chances of being injured or killed as a result of one risk rather than another. Such information is significant because it provides individuals and social decision-makers with data (to the extent that it is data vs. merely guesses) that they can take into account in guiding social policies or choices in their individual lives.

This point should not be underestimated. In making choices about what risks to take as individuals or what risks to permit or to regulate as social decision-makers, *one* important element to consider is the probability and magnitude of the risk in question. Because we seek to avoid being harmed or killed, we should be concerned about how likely this is to occur as a result of different activities that pose risks to us. For example, I might be quite concerned about involuntary risks in my life, but come to realize that these are much lower than risks I might take in voluntary recreational activities (a view that technical writers often point out) (Wilson and Crouch, 1987). If I am mainly or only concerned about risk exposures that will shorten my life or inflict serious injuries on me, I should give great weight to such numbers. To oversimplify, if I sought to minimize my chances of adverse consequences of harm or death for myself, I should consult various sources that numerically compare the probabilities of serious injury and death and choose life paths that have a reasonable chance of keeping these to a minimum. Similarly, if in the area of governmental action, the body politic decides that all that matters socially is the frequency of adverse effects to citizens, then the numbers should receive great emphasis.

However, many of us have different life goals than merely living as safely as possible and would argue for social policies that are sufficiently nuanced to recognize this. If there are aspects of voluntary recreational activities that make my life worth living, for example being a mountaineer or an extreme skier, and I would cease to flourish, or in the extreme find it difficult to continue to live with any zest without engaging in these activities, then such statistics and courses of action might be much less important to me. We should not forget, as I present below, that not all risks we encounter give our lives zest, so we would want to take care not to conflate issues. One would want to make important conceptual distinctions for guiding social policies toward risks, although there tends to be a temptation for some theorists or officials to overestimate the importance such as the probability and magnitude of risks, judging them to be the only or the main determinants of the moral or legal acceptability of risks. Several writers have argued against this view, so I do not revisit it here (Slovic, 1987; Gillette and Krier, 1990; Cranor, 1995, 2007a).

NEUTRAL LANGUAGE FOR RISKS

As I have noted elsewhere (Cranor, 1995, 2007a, 2007b), when we are theorizing about risks, we need a term that is neutral between risks being *imposed* upon one and risks that one has *taken*. Some slightly awkward terms for this purpose include 'exposure to risks' or 'risk exposure'. Some writers tend to suggest that agents 'take' all kinds of risks, noting that 'Everyday we take risks and avoid others' (Wilson and Crouch, 1987). The subtitle of Larry Laudan's *The Book of*

Risks (1994) is *Fascinating Facts About The Chances We Take Every Day*. However, it seems to me that this way of putting it invites confusion, leading to both conceptual and normative obscurity. In fact not all risks are taken, but some are. Other risks clearly are imposed on one. More seriously, the conflation of risks *taken* with those *imposed* may not be an accidental slip of a keystroke. If one seeks to emphasize the similarity between risks obviously 'taken', such as recreational risks or some risks from driving a car, and risks more obviously imposed upon one, such as the risks from humanly caused air pollution or the risks from a hurricane, then one might use the language of one 'taking' these four different kind of risks. However, the choice of the term 'taken' will surely mislead the audience and it might even be a deliberate choice to make some normative point, for example to de-emphasize risk imposition in our lives and assimilate it to something like voluntarily undertaken risks. This tends coincidentally to suggest that imposed risks are not so serious after all.

Of course, there can be borderline cases between risks that are 'taken' and risks that are 'imposed' upon one. For example, we might 'take' risks in crossing a train track knowing that it is quite busy, but perhaps the route across the track might have been designed differently so that we are not forced to 'take' as much in the way of risks in getting to the other side (a walkway might have been built over the tracks, which would eliminate a good many risks). Is the fact that we have to cross the train track at ground level a risk that is 'imposed' upon us because a pedestrian way was not built over it or is it a risk we have 'taken' because in the present circumstances there is no other way to get to the other side of the track? In an important sense, both descriptions have some plausibility. Crossing the track necessitates risk exposure that might not have been necessary had the means of going over the tracks been designed differently. A more neutral term for risks would then force theorists to argue about which risks were taken, which were imposed and which were less determinate on this dimension. Also, a more neutral description might force an appropriate normative discussion about some appropriate design for approaching this particular problem.[2]

Sources of risks

We should distinguish between risks to humans that are mainly or predominantly humanly caused, those that are mainly or predominantly not humanly caused (one might think of these as naturally caused), and those that result from both natural and human sources. If a risk from any of these sources materializes, humans will suffer adverse consequences, such as diseases, injuries, disabilities or death. If it is possible to reduce the risks to humans from any of these sources, it will reduce human adverse effects and suffering to some extent.

There are risks from large natural phenomena, such as falling meteors, hurricanes, tsunamis, tornadoes, violent winds and floods. Microscopic entities such as bacteria, viruses, microbes, naturally occurring lead, arsenic and radon also can pose risks to humans and inflict harm. For such risky things we want to know how substantial the risks can be and to what extent individuals or the community as a whole can do about them. We might also want to know to what extent the community had some role in creating or exacerbating particular risks. Humans do not make any contributions to earthquakes. However, they could act or fail to act in ways that increase, amplify or reduce risks from earthquakes. They could build on soil that becomes liquefied in an earthquake. They could build over fault lines. Or, they could adopt some more protective guidelines. Because there are some naturally occurring risks over which we have little control, we may then inquire into the seriousness of any risks they pose, as well as what we can and should do in response to them. Of course, for earthquakes better building codes, as well as land use laws, can go some way towards reducing risks from earthquakes if they occur, so the results are not so severe. By contrast, there can be some naturally caused risks that are exacerbated or promoted by human activities. For example, humans may add to or exacerbate risks from microscopic risks if they do not dispose of wastes well or properly. Giardia, a natural flagellate protozoan that causes diarrhoea in humans, was increased in the natural world by humans polluting the natural environment, further spread by beavers and perhaps other animals, and now has returned to haunt humans when they drink water from natural sources that have been contaminated by giardia. Human failures likely exacerbated the damage done by Hurricane Katrina (Center for Progressive Reform, 2006).

For another example consider aflatoxin-contaminated peanut butter. Stored peanuts (as well as other nuts, oil seeds and grain) can become contaminated with a mould that produces aflatoxin, a substance that can cause liver cancer in humans (Kotsonis et al, 2001). However, the presence in peanuts of the mould that produces the aflatoxins is to some large extent a function of how the peanuts are grown and perhaps more importantly how they are stored. If humans store them poorly in humid or moist conditions, then the mould that produces the aflatoxins is more likely to grow and to infect the peanuts with the cancer-causing substance. Hence, if people are not careful in how they store peanuts, peanut butter may become infected with the cancer-causing aflatoxins. Are aflatoxins in peanut butter naturally caused or humanly caused? It is difficult to say clearly since these carcinogens are the joint result of both human and natural processes and activities. A careful assessor would consider a variety of examples. Aflatoxins also illustrate the taking-imposed-risk distinction. Do we *take* risks of cancer when we eat peanut butter (that has a very low probability of causing cancer, but we may not know it), or are they *imposed* on us by poor storage and processing conditions)?

Other risks can largely be the creation of individual or collective human activities, such as sulphur dioxide or nitrous oxide gases, the result of humanly created combustion, that can in turn harm humans. Radiation from a failing nuclear power plant is quite substantially a humanly caused risk. For risks such as these we could ask whether the community should allow such activities in its midst, how they should be conducted and what the conditions of carrying out the activities might be. Should the activities be done differently or permitted at all? The pertinence of the humanly caused versus naturally caused distinction is that for risks that are largely the result of human activities, at least collectively humans have considerable control over them and how they are done. For many naturally caused risks there may be much less collective control over the events that lead to risks. However, there will be a continuum from largely naturally caused risks, for example from tsunamis, over which humans have little or no control, to largely humanly caused risks, for example automobile accidents, over which individuals have much greater control individually or collectively, or both. Our normative responses typically are and should be quite different in the different cases for these reasons. Commentators that largely compare risks only on the dimensions of the magnitude of harm threatened and the probability of that harm materializing also significantly oversimplify their approach to risks; they in effect beg important questions about the activities (Morrall, 1986; Wilson and Crouch, 1987; Laudan, 1994).

EPISTEMIC DETECTION OF RISKS

Beyond the sources of risks, humans bring various abilities, skills and sensory apparatus that to some extent can assist them in dealing with risks. In turn, I submit, these features are pertinent characteristics that do and should affect our personal and community responses to risks. Some risks can be readily detected by our natural senses – for example, we can see oncoming cars, smell the presence of skunks (a minor risk), perhaps in some cases smell major poisons that are present at toxic doses, or hear an oncoming train. Sometimes one might taste a threat to one's health in a substance that one is about to imbibe (e.g. acids and strong bases are likely to taste bad or damage the mouth, providing a clue to the damage they can do elsewhere in the body). And of course, our sense of touch can inform us of various sharp or other dangerous objects. Some of these sensory inputs, for example sight and sound and combinations of these, are more useful than others. Some senses are much more limited in their ability to reveal risks, such as smell and taste. However, the possibility of sensory detection of risks importantly conditions some of our responses to both humanly and naturally caused risks.

Our senses can provide us with important warnings about the presence and sometimes the extent of risks. Various kinds of machinery, such as cars or saws, present fairly transparent risks. If we have substantial control over our activity with the aid of our senses we might be able to avoid or minimize the risks. For risks from largish macro-objects such as cars and other kinds of machinery, this natural ability can be especially helpful. When we are in the presence of other risks, less detectable by means of our senses, such as benzene near a rubber plant or in a workplace, or tasteless and odourless toxicants in our drinking water, we likely need greater protection and the approach to the risks should be substantially different (Cranor, 1995, 2007a, 2007b). This would apply to many toxicants that can harm us, but that are not detectable by means of the senses.

However, our senses can be extended by means of technical devices. To a large extent these assist experts, but have more limited use by ordinary citizens. For instance, humans have long used binoculars and microscopes to extend their eyesight and both can help in detecting some kinds of risks. Microscopes can help scientists identify or confirm microscopic threats, while binoculars can assist a wider range of people in detecting threats at some distance before they become proximate. Geiger counters are another technical aid that can reveal the presence of radiation, but most people are unlikely to have access to them or to use them.[3] Moreover, some of the US National Laboratories that conducted research for the Department of Defense in the past are developing detection devices for public spaces to provide early warnings of toxic substances placed in our midst by terrorists. While many of these technical extensions of our senses are impractical for the vast majority of citizens to use in any meaningful way to determine whether toxicants are in their midst, a few of them might hold promise, such as detection devices with warning horns when toxicants are present. However, even these will have limitations. Many will not have access to them as we all have to natural senses. Moreover, even if a horn warns us that we are in the presence of terrorist-placed toxicants, we are not likely to be aware of the exact nature and geographic extent of the risk. This is much different from when we detect heavy traffic or oncoming cars that can harm us; as for such risks, we have a much better sense of the risks, their dimensions and geographic extent.

Degrees of control over risks

Beyond our senses, humans have varying degrees of control over their own activity, over the extent to which they are exposed to risks, and whether or not risks to which they are subject materialize to harm them. Risks about which we know and can detect from exposures that we can control provide opportunities for avoiding them, if we choose to do so. Thus, we can avoid the risks of many recreational activities simply by not doing them, for example by not rock climbing, not scuba-diving or not bungee jumping. If we know that naturally caused risks from volcanoes, tsunamis or earthquakes occur in certain geographic regions and we have control over whether to live in such areas, we can avoid them simply by not putting ourselves in the way of risks. Still other activities may give us considerable control over their risks by how we conduct them, e.g. use of dangerous implements, such as table saws, chain saws, axes and the like. Such implements often make their threats quite manifest, so we are aware of risks they pose. Moreover, we can learn how to use them more rather than less carefully, and skilfully than in less risky ways.

However, there are risks over which we have little control, even if we know of them (and too often we do not have such knowledge). If our drinking water is contaminated by trichloroethylene and perchlorate as it is in many cities, but we are unaware of it, we are not likely to modify our ingestion of water that could pose risks to us. If we were aware of these toxicants, individually we could do some things to control our exposure to them and the community could do more. However, when our air is polluted with ozone or more serious toxicants, it will be much more difficult to control our exposures to them, without perhaps a substantial move out of the area, if this is possible and desirable from a personal point of view, given one's employment, spousal employment and so on. There can be some control in such circumstances, but it is limited and often constrained by competing concerns. Whether one should be forced to choose between exposure to risks and other vital interests is an important consideration that must be addressed in social policy decisions about such risks.

The degree of control we have over risks may play a role in policy arguments about who should have social control over the risks. If an individual has considerable control over risks and their materializing, to what extent should that person be protected or not from them as a result of legislation, regulation or, after the fact, legal compensation if risks materialize into harm? There are many different kinds of cases to consider here and no generalization will provide much guidance. It suffices for the purposes of this chapter to note that degrees of control may affect who has what degree of social responsibility over a risky thing or activity. For example, even though chain saws are dangerous objects and even though their risks are quite manifest to normal adults, nonetheless it is likely that existing doctrines of US product liability law require manufacturers to provide reasonable warnings about the hazards of using chain saws and even precautions about how to use them properly. In absence of such warnings, manufacturers might be open to suits for compensation if people are injured because of an absence of warnings. The extent to which protection from risks should be provided by users in such cases and the extent to which they should be provided by manufacturers may to some extent be the result of political and legal philosophic views. For another example consider the degree of control or not that humans have over the production aflatoxins in peanuts mentioned earlier (Kotsonis et al, 2001). To what extent should farmers and processors of peanuts have responsibility for the presence of aflatoxins in peanuts and their other commercial products, even though the moulds that produce them are 'natural'? This is a policy debate that should occur, but that cannot until we have a variety of distinctions at hand.

The point of this chapter is not to settle such issues, but to illustrate some of the richness of different risks to which we might be exposed so that there can be more clear-headed discussions about the normative issues. For risks over which individuals exercise little control and about which there is little awareness, there is likely to be a much greater need for protection by external agencies, but the exact form this should take is beyond this chapter. However, what seems clear is that the discussion is not much advanced by merely calling attention to a comparison between the probability and magnitude of risks posed by aflatoxins compared with some other risks, say those resulting from voluntary recreational activities or some other risks in our lives. It seems that the best way to have a fruitful discussion of social policy about a class of risks is to fully recognize their many features as well as likely human reactions to them.

ATTITUDES TOWARD RISKS

People are likely to have different approaches, attitudes or values toward the risks they encounter. Some risks to which one is *exposed*, or which one *takes*, are central to one's plan of life or are part of personal projects one has (Rawls, 1982). Some of these will be recreational, for example mountain climbing, scuba-diving or extreme white water rafting, while others may be part of one's employment, for example being an emergency medical technician, a lifeguard or a firefighter. Such risks are more central to the lives of those who take them than are other risks they might encounter. Part of this activity and its associated risks will be valued more highly and the risks either embraced or at least knowingly borne because of the high value given to the activity. When this is the case, those who are exposed to such risks are not likely to regard such risks as equivalent to other risks that may have equivalent numerical chances of materializing. Risks that are central to people's lives are *valued differently* than perhaps a more 'objective' account of risks would have it. And one would suppose that people *should* value differently risks that are not central to their lives, such as contaminants in drinking water or in the air. Moreover, there might be good moral reasons for treating these differently. Consequently, these differences, it seems to me, should be important considerations in forming social policies towards risk exposures. In addition, there will be degrees of centrality or importance of the risks from different activities to people's lives, ranging from risky recreational activity that adds zest to their lives to risks from bike riding to risks from working in a coal mine (Harris, 2006) to risks from pollutants in the air or drinking water.

Benefits associated with risks

In addition to the centrality (or not) of activities with risks to one's life, there may (or may not) be direct and substantial compensating benefits associated with the risks. For risks that are central to the activity which is centrally important to one's life (think of those engaged in mountaineering), there are obviously compensating benefits associated with the risks; they are what helps to make the activity attractive and one's life worth living. Even for risks that are not so central to one's life, there can be important compensating benefits. There are carcinogenic risks from chlorinated drinking water. However, chlorinating drinking water helps to protect those who drink it from quite serious illnesses or death in the short (or even the longer) run, even though over a much longer period of time consumers of water incur an increased risk of bladder cancer from trihalomethanes that are created by the interaction of chlorine with biological products in the water. These cancer risks, it is arguable, are personally worth it because of the compensating health benefits from chlorinating the water, at least until there is a less risky alternative for sanitizing the water. Consumers of water thus are exposed to low probability life-taking risks in order to obtain higher probability life-saving benefits. By contrast, consumers of water who are exposed to the degreaser trichloroethylene (TCE) in their drinking water because someone failed to dispose of it properly will probably have greater difficulty finding compensating benefits from drinking water with TCE in it.

Individuals may also be exposed to risks that have few obvious benefits or no very *direct* compensating benefits to themselves. Such circumstances pose substantial acceptability problems for the individuals affected; the value they place on those activities compared with other risky undertakings is likely to be quite different. It is barely conceivable that there could be substantial compensating benefits to individuals for being at low risk of injury or disease from nuclear power plants. That is, one might imagine that the general social benefits are sufficiently great when aggregated across many individuals that from some normative view (e.g. utilitarianism) the low level risks to those living around such plants and those exposed to risks from activities that dispose of the radioactive wastes are socially justified, even though it is difficult to argue to particular affected individuals that their individual risks are compensated for in the same way that chlorinating drinking water is. However, persuading random individuals that such risky activities are justified is likely a much more difficult task. A further point that these comparisons suggest is that when 'benefits' from risky activities or circumstances are sought there is a substantial difference between direct and substantial benefits to an individual and much more diffuse benefits across a society from which no particular individual benefits very substantially or directly. In the latter case, such risks are likely to be much more difficult to justify socially. Any risks from genetically modified plants may resemble this circumstance. Direct benefits to nearly all in a society are difficult to find, yet if there are risks (and I do not assert there are), they may fall equally on all those who are exposed to foods containing genetically modified plants.

Degree to which risks are voluntarily incurred

Individuals can voluntarily agree to risks. For some of these we might be inclined to attribute voluntary agreement to people, for example, when they engage in certain obvious risky recreational activities. They would not do them if they did not to some extent voluntarily commit to them. However, there are other circumstances in which people voluntarily agree to risks, but they have little or no control over most aspects of the risks other than agreeing to submit to them. For example, when patients give full voluntary consent to medical procedures or, more seriously, operations, the risks are judged to be acceptable, or at least the person is not in a position to complain about a characteristic risk of the procedure materializing, simply because he or she voluntarily consented to it, presumably in full knowledge of the benefits and risks of the operation. As we have learned from medical ethics, in order for risks to be voluntarily incurred one must have proper understanding and be aware of the risk, be competent to make decisions about them and then must have consented or agreed to them. Again there are degrees of voluntariness often associated with the knowledge condition on voluntary consent. Moreover, sometimes we should be quite sceptical that individuals have been aware of risks to which they are exposed, such as from cigarette smoking. For example, recent work by Paul Slovic shows that despite the public having some general knowledge about the health risks from smoking, and despite labels that warn that there are health risks from smoking, a much deeper appreciation and understanding of the nature of these risks is often lacking (Slovic, 2006). To the extent that this is correct, it suggests that decision-makers should exercise great care in attributing substantial knowledge to the public about risks to which they are subjected.[4]

Explicitly moral versus non-moral features of risky activities

Many of the above features of risk exposure are aspects of the risky circumstances that affect individual judgements about their acceptability, although as I have argued elsewhere many of these same characteristics can be utilized in constructing moral theories towards the acceptability of risks (Cranor, 2007a). However, some features of risk exposure explicitly require discussion of moral considerations. For example, when risk exposure is created by one agent and imposed on others, in economists' terms this is *an externality*. For philosophers this tends to raise issues about the justice of the risk distribution and certainly invites discussion about justice if the risks materialize into harm. Similarly, when risks clearly impact already burdened communities so that they are exposed to multiple sources of carcinogens or reproductive toxicants, for example, distributive issues are quite important. Concerns about already burdened subpopulations have rightly received increased theoretical and regulatory attention in recent years (Cranor, 1997, 2007c). Still other risks from toxicants, for example, will more seriously affect especially susceptible individuals and, to the extent that social policies should provide as close to equal protection for everyone in the moral community, such effects will pose particular distributive issues for regulatory policy (Cranor, 1997).

Conclusion

Why should theorists consider a rich conception of risks? First, a rich conception of risks is pertinent both to empirical studies of people's attitudes toward risks and to normative recommendations about how to address risks in our individual or collective lives. For empirical studies there are a wide and rich variety of risks with which we all have to cope as we make our way through the world and a lifetime. As the work of Slovic and others has shown, when members of the public consider the variety of risks, their attitudes towards them are quite different depending upon the risk in question (Slovic, 1987). In risk perception, researchers should begin with such broad data so their studies capture a wide variety of attitudes toward risks. Slovic and his collaborators have certainly done this.

When we consider normative approaches toward risks, again it seems that we should recognize the wide variety of risks to which we are exposed so myopia does not skew our recommended policies. A rich conception of the data suggests that we should not begin our theorizing by using narrow theoretical approaches, for example considering mainly or only the probability of outcome and severity of adverse effects from risks. Such an approach has attractions and it lends itself to a certain political view. It suggests a kind of technocratic state in which experts are responsible for making political determinations about what risks should be protected against, which not, and the degree of protection owed against different kinds of risks based largely on their chances of materializing. Moreover, the general public can and does sometimes make mistakes about the probability and severity of different kinds of risks. However, a technocratic approach could well disenfranchise the public and its much richer responses toward risks in their lives. It is also, I would argue, incompatible with quite different moral, social and political philosophic traditions that pay much greater attention to how social policies affect individuals or groups within a community (and for which the total utility in the community is of secondary importance) (Cranor, 2007a).

On a more theoretical note when we begin with a rich conception of risks and their probabilities, it not only forces us to keep many different kinds of examples in mind as we theorize, but also invites, or perhaps stronger, forces us to make arguments for our particular normative approach. If we argue for norms that recognize a wider range of approaches to the rich variety of risks, we should probably make arguments that they are indeed distinct enough in their properties and in how humans could and should cope with them to justify a nuanced range of normative responses. At the other end, if we argue for a simpler normative approach, the rich conception here more obviously forces us to *argue* for a normative approach that would lump many seemingly different kinds of risks together and treat them the same simply because they have more or less the same probability and magnitudes. Whichever way we go (or somewhere in between), we should recognize the variety of risks and their properties with which humans must cope and argue for our approach, not simply assume one theoretical apparatus or the other is automatically correct. This would be truer to the risky world in which we live, to our various abilities to cope with risks, to different kinds of values we put on them and to our responses to them as we wind our way through life.

References

Center for Progressive Reform (2006) 'An unnatural disaster: the aftermath of Hurricane Katrina', available at www.progressivereform.org/Unnatural_Disaster_512.pdf (accessed 10 July 2006)

Cranor, C. (1995) 'The use of comparative risk judgments in risk management', in A. M. Fan and L. W. Chang (eds), *Toxicology and Risk Assessment: Principles, Methods, and Applications*, Marcel Dekker, Inc.: New York

Cranor, C. (1997) 'Eggshell skulls and loss of hair from fright: some moral and legal principles that protect susceptible subpopulations', *Environmental Toxicology and Pharmacology*, vol 4, pp239–245

Cranor, C. F. (2007a) 'Toward a non-consequentialist approach to risks', in T. Lewens (ed.) *Risk and Philosophy*, Routledge, London

Cranor, C. F. (2007b) 'Learning from other technologies: acceptable risks and institutional safeguards', in M. A. Bedau and E. Parke (eds) *Social and Ethical Issues Concerning Protocells*, MIT Press, Cambridge, MA

Cranor, C. F. (2008) 'Risk assessment, susceptible subpopulations and environmental justice', in M. B. Gerrard and S. Foster (eds) *The Law of Environmental Justice*, 2nd edn, The American Bar Association, Chicago, Ill

Gillette, C. and Krier, J. (1990) 'Risk, courts and agencies', *University of Pennsylvania Law Review*, vol 38, pp1077–1109.

Harris, G. (2006) 'Endemic problem of safety in coal mining', *New York Times*, January 10

Kotsonis, F. N., Burdick, G. A. and Flamm, W. G. (2001) 'Food toxicology', in C. D. Claassen (ed.), *Casarett and Doull's Toxicology: The Basic Science of Poisons*, 6th edn, McGraw-Hill, New York

Laudan, L. (1994) *The Book of Risks: Fascinating Facts About the Chances We Take Every Day*, John Wiley and Sons, New York

Morrall, J. F. (1986) 'A review of the record', *Regulation*, November–December, 27

Rawls, J. (1982) 'Social unity and primary goods', in A. Sen and B. Williams (eds) *Utilitarianism and Beyond*, Cambridge University Press, Cambridge

Slovic, P. (1987) 'Perception of risks', *Science*, vol 236, pp280–285

Slovic, P. (2006) 'Written direct examination of Paul Slovic, Ph.D.', submitted by the United States Pursuant to Order 471, United States of America vs. Phillip Morris, Civil Action No. 99-CV-02496 (GK)

Sunstein, C. R. (2002) *Risk and Reason*, Cambridge University Press, New York

Wilson, R. and Crouch, E. A. (1987) 'Risk assessment and comparisons: an introduction', *Science*, vol 236, pp267–270

Notes

1 A typical risk assessment – where the outcomes of choices were known with high degrees of certainty and where probability distributions could be assigned with some confidence to such outcomes – should be distinguished from risk and uncertainty assessments – where the probabilities of loss or harm cannot be assigned with much confidence – and these should be distinguished further from assessments where there is great *ignorance* about the outcomes as well as their probability assessments. All of these might be called risks or risky situations calling for assessment for some purpose, but one would have much less confidence in risk and uncertainty assessments or assessments in considerable ignorance than in what might be considered a risk assessment properly considered.

2 Tim Lewens suggested a similar point for a related paper (Cranor, 2007a).

3 Mark Bedau suggested this point in connection with a related paper (Cranor, 2007b).

4 Even writers like Cass Sunstein, who may not otherwise be sympathetic to some or many aspects of the view presented here, recognizes that if some risks are especially 'hard or costly to avoid … [the] government should devote special attention to risks of this kind' (Sunstein, 2002, p77). This would likely apply to avoiding the risks of air pollution and the risks of water pollution, because both can be relatively costly to avoid. However, I would submit that when risks are difficult to avoid this affects the extent to which they are fully voluntarily incurred, despite the fact that people could have made different choices to have avoided them.

4 Requirements for the Social Acceptability of Risk-Generating Technological Activities

Henk Zandvoort

INTRODUCTION AND OVERVIEW

This chapter starts from the assumption that any human activity should satisfy two basic ethical principles in order to assert that the activity is ethically and socially acceptable. These ethical principles are the principle of restricted liberty, sometimes called the no harm principle, and the principle of reciprocity. As has been shown by Velsen (2000), the observance of these two principles is necessary and sufficient for peaceful coexistence. I will briefly elucidate why the principles are necessary for peaceful coexistence, but I will not repeat the exposition provided in Velsen (2000). The goal of the present chapter is rather to explore the implications of these two very general principles for risk-generating technological activities. I will focus on the production and consumption of energy as an example.

I assume that an activity can only be called socially acceptable in a non-arbitrary way if the necessary conditions for peaceful coexistence are respected by the activities. Hence, if the ethical principles of restricted liberty and reciprocity are necessary for peaceful coexistence, then an activity can only be called socially acceptable if the activity is in agreement with these two principles and their implications. I will state two requirements that follow from these ethical principles and that hence should be observed by a (technological) activity in order to qualify as socially acceptable: the requirement of informed consent and the requirement of strict liability in the absence of informed consent. I will explore the implications of these requirements for risk-generating technologies, with special reference to the production and consumption of energy, and I will explore how these implications can be satisfied.

In the second section, I will state and briefly elucidate the ethical principles of restricted liberty and reciprocity and their implications, the requirement of informed consent and the requirement of strict liability in the absence of informed consent. In this section I will also explain that the requirement of informed consent is implied by certain normative principles that underpin economic theory, and I will indicate that the requirement of strict liability in the absence of informed consent is at least consistent with these principles, even though several authors in economics appear to reject the requirement. In the third section, two general implications are described that can be drawn from the principles and requirements presented in the second section, in conjunction with the fact that actual collective (political) decision-making about technological activities proceeds under majority rule rather than unanimity rule. Finally, in the last section, I will present four implications for enhancing the social acceptability of energy systems and levels of energy supply/demand.

TWO ETHICAL PRINCIPLES AND TWO REQUIREMENTS FOR SOCIAL ACCEPTABILITY OF RISK-GENERATING TECHNOLOGICAL ACTIVITIES

Restricted liberty and informed consent

The ethical principle of restricted liberty, also called the no harm principle, states that everyone is free to do what he/she pleases as long as he/she does not harm others. The principle has a long history in both Western and non-Western thought. It was included as article 4 in the *Déclaration des droits de l'homme et du citoyen du 26 août 1789* of the French Revolution. The philosopher J. S. Mill defended the principle in his essay *On Liberty* (Mill, [1859] 1998). An equivalent of the restricted liberty principle is the right to be safeguarded (Velsen, 2000, p96): 'Everyone has the right to be safeguarded from the consequences of another person's actions.'

The restricted liberty principle or right to be safeguarded satisfies the principle of equal rights. Many people assume that this is a necessary requirement for any acceptable ethical principle. However, not every principle that respects the equal rights principle will qualify as a candidate for an ethical principle acceptable to all. Consider the alternative principle that everyone is free to do as he/she pleases, without the restriction that no one should be harmed. Under this principle, people could end up in a situation where mutual relations are only determined by physical force. For this reason, the principle would be an unlikely candidate for an ethical principle that could receive the acclaim of all people who through their actions mutually affect each other. Nevertheless, the principle does grant everyone the same right to act as he/she pleases. The example should serve to illuminate an asymmetry which exists between different possible conceptions of individual freedom to act: whereas peaceful coexistence among autonomous people endowed with equal rights can be expected if they observe the restricted liberty principle, the same cannot be expected from a liberty principle that does not in this way restrict people's actions towards others.

As harm has always subjective elements, there are only two ways in which it can be ascertained that other people will not be harmed by someone's activities. Either, there are no (actual or possible) consequences for those others. Or there are (actual or possible) consequences for others, but these others have given their informed consent to the activity under consideration. Hence, the right to be safeguarded implies the following requirement, to be called here the *requirement of informed consent*:

> For all (technological) activities, all those who may experience the negative effects including the risks of the activities must have given their informed consent to the activities and the conditions under which the activities are performed.

The requirement of informed consent should be imposed not merely upon actions that result in harm for others with certainty, but also upon actions that create *risks* for others.[1] Consent to activities that may affect others need not be given for each separate action, but could also be given by means of general rules specifying acceptable activities. In virtue of the restricted liberty principle, such rules should have the consent of all who may experience the consequences of the activities. Such general rules might be provided by laws, if these laws would have the consent of all those who are subjected to the possible consequences.

An objection that is often addressed against the restricted liberty principle and the requirement of informed consent is that it allows that activities, including beneficial or potentially beneficial activities, could be vetoed by a minority, even by a single person. In response it can be noticed that if (and only if) an activity is net socially beneficial, then a compensation scheme should be possible that makes all who are affected by the activity net beneficiaries, or at least do not make anyone worse off, in which case no one would have a reason to veto the activity. If for a contemplated activity no compensation scheme can be found that would make all involved better off or at least would make nobody worse off, then there is no ground for a claim that the activity is socially beneficial in an unambiguous, non-arbitrary way. And the only viable check that such a compensation scheme does exist is that it is accepted by all involved, that is, including all who are subjected to the harm or risk. It is true that, generally speaking, consensus decision-making is vulnerable to strategic behaviour (Mueller, 2003). The possibilities for strategic behaviour can be quenched, at least partially, by designing elaborate decision procedures based on unanimity rule (for examples, see Mueller, 2003, Chapter 8) and by agreeing and hence requiring that all participants to negotiation processes about compensation schemes will be consistent in their assessment and appraisal of negative effects including risks. In Zandvoort (2008a), I have elsewhere addressed the issue of the extent to which strategic behaviour can be constrained in discussions and negotiations about risk and risk compensation if parties agree to be consistent/coherent. Hence, a lot of work can and should be done to reduce the problems of strategic behaviour that as a matter of fact attach to consensus decision-making. The issue is of great relevance, as there are no other reasons besides informed consent and what can be derived from the reciprocity principle that would justify imposing harm or risks upon others. The matter is the more pressing because many actual technological activities are violating the right to be safeguarded on a large scale, and often the (actual or potential) harm done is irreversible (such as deaths or serious injuries or irreversible environmental harm), that is, can neither be repaired nor fully compensated.

Reciprocity and liability

The right to be safeguarded does not specify how a violation of that right may be reacted to. It is assumed here that a second principle is required that deals with violation of the right to be safeguarded. Such a principle is the reciprocity principle, which is here formulated as follows:

> He/she who violates a right of another one may be reacted to in a reciprocal way. That means that somebody who infringes a certain right of another, himself loses that same right insofar as that is necessary (and no more than that) in order to correct the original violation or to compensate for it and in order to, if necessary, prevent further infringement. (Velsen, 2000, § 7)

The reciprocity principle implies that anyone who does not respect another person's right to be safeguarded and who thereby inflicts harm upon another person may be forced to repair or compensate the harm. Hence the reciprocity principle implies the following *requirement of strict liability in the absence of informed consent*:

> Those who engage in activities without this consent can be held to full (unlimited, no caps) and unconditional (absolute) liability for the negative effects that their activities may cause to those who did not give their consent.

This requirement gives anyone who had not given his/her informed consent to a risk-creating activity the right to recover (in so far as is possible) from any harm ensuing from the activity that may fall upon him. It should be noticed that there is no obligation to execute this right. There may even be people (such as absolute pacifists) who do not ever want to invoke the reciprocity principle. However, it is also clear that many other people would not want to do without that principle, and hence the principle is needed in any set of behavioural rules if that set is to be acceptable for all. It should be noticed that someone who does not (intend to) invoke the reciprocity principle him/herself against others does not need to fear the adoption of that principle by others, as long as he/she respects the right to be safeguarded of those others.

The principle of restricted liberty requires that all activities that may cause harm for others should have the informed consent of all those who may be harmed. In some situations, activities that lack that consent may nevertheless be considered as unproblematic from the point of view of restricted liberty, namely when (1) the possible damage to non-consenters can be (physically) repaired, i.e. is reversible; and (2) actual repair by or on behalf of actors of any damage if it occurs is guaranteed. Many technological activities do not meet the first condition, however, as these activities may cause deaths and incurable injuries as well as irreversible environmental and ecological harm. If such activities are conducted without the consent of all who may experience these irreversible consequences, then the activities can be termed irresponsible in virtue of the ethical principles stated above. Alternatively, the responsibility of actors who engage in such activities can be called unbearable, in the sense that if harm materializes, the actors will be unable to repair or compensate for the harm for which they are responsible. It will be seen below that even for possible damage that can be repaired, current liability law often does not require (full) financial guaranties that damage, if it occurs, will in fact be repaired by on behalf of the actors.

Informed consent and economic theory

The requirement of informed consent is also implied by the basic principles and assumptions underlying economic theory. More precisely, the following holds. If the expectation is to be justified that technological activities that create external costs including risks lead to social progress in the sense of Pareto improvement, then the laws that regulate the activities should be adopted with unanimity among all who are subjected to the external costs. This will be briefly explained in the following.

Transitions that make at least some better off (in their own judgement) and no one worse off (in their own judgement) are called (subjective) Pareto improvements. It is uncontested that Pareto improvements represent social progress in an unequivocal and non-arbitrary way, hence can be considered good. Transitions that are *not* Pareto improvements cannot be called social progress in a similarly non-arbitrary and unequivocal way and hence cannot be considered good for that reason.

Under free market conditions, market parties will only enter into (market) transactions that make all parties to the transaction better off, in their own judgement. However, the conclusion that free markets lead to Pareto improvement does not follow if external costs are present. An external cost is here defined as a negative effect of one person's activity upon the utility or well-being of other persons that is not accepted by those other persons as an element of a voluntary (market) agreement, but instead is involuntarily imposed.[2] Involuntarily imposed risks from technological activities represent external costs. If the external costs of (market) activities are sufficiently large, then people will end up worse off rather than better off, in spite of the gains that they derive from the (market) activities that they are engaged in. In order to secure Pareto improvement, or in order at least to know that the external costs of an activity are acceptable, the consent is required of all non-contracting parties who may be negatively affected by that activity. If that consent is to be provided by general (legal) rules specifying which (market) activities are allowed and under which conditions, then these rules must have the consent of all those who may experience the consequences of the activities in order to justify the expectation that economic agents, by enhancing their personal welfare, at the same time contribute positively or at least not negatively to social welfare or social progress.[3]

It is sometimes objected to the Pareto-improvement criterion for social progress that the criterion protects the status quo, in the sense that it may block socially beneficial developments, namely if a consensus on a proposal cannot be obtained. As was said above, it is uncontested that Pareto improvements represent social progress in an unequivocal way, hence are good. Nevertheless, it is sometimes claimed that the requirement of Pareto improvement should not be rigorously imposed upon all proposed projects or activities. The reason given for this is that, by always requiring Pareto improvement (hence consent of all involved), socially beneficial developments might be blocked, namely when a consensus on a (socially beneficial) proposal cannot be obtained. This is a variation of the objection to the restricted liberty principle and the requirement of informed consent that was dealt with above. It can be responded to in a similar way: if a change represents social progress, then a compensation scheme is possible that can win the consent of all involved, and vice versa; only if the consent of all involved can be won (possibly after a compensation scheme has been established), then there is a non-subjective check that the change indeed represents social progress. It can be added to this, however, that the status quo may have resulted from infringements of someone's right to be safeguarded, and for that reason may be called unjust. Stealing is an obvious example of such an infringement; polluting the environment without the informed consent of all those who may experience negative effects from that is another example. In such cases, the reciprocity principle gives those who were harmed the right to corrective measures against the actors aimed at restoring the original situation before the infringement or, if that is impossible, compensation for the harm. In addition, it must be stressed that even in the absence of (charges of) historical infringements upon the right to be safeguarded, redistribution is always possible if it has the consent of those from whom it is being taken. It is interesting to note in this respect that all of the several possible justifications for redistribution through the tax system which are discussed in Mueller (2003, Chapter 3) are based on the consent of those who pay the tax that is being redistributed.

Analysis of legal liability in the law and economics tradition

According to the ethical principles and implications that have been stated above, the default rule for liability in the absence of prior agreement should be absolute and nonconditional. This conflicts with the approach towards liability law adopted in the law and economics tradition (for authors and sources see Zandvoort, 2004). As was explained in Zandvoort (2004), these scholars do not assume a default rule for liability. Instead, they purport to derive socially optimal liability rules from a criterion of social progress that they call the economic efficiency or wealth-maximizing criterion. More specifically, these authors deploy the so called Kaldor-Hicks criterion, in which a policy change is said to represent social progress if the winners from the change could compensate the losers, that is, if the winners gain more from the change than the losers lose. Actual compensation is not considered a requirement under the Kaldor-Hicks criterion. According to these authors, whether a liability rule should be strict or conditional to fault depends on the question which of both rules would optimize total wealth or income, disregarding the distribution. This approach was inspired by Coase's 'theorem' (1960) on external costs and (property) rights. I will discuss below Coase's theorem, and I will contrast the assumptions that lie behind it with the principles presented in the present chapter.

Coase (1960) (see also Mueller, 2003, Chapter 2) considered situations where the activities of persons or firms have external effects upon others. He argued that, if transaction and bargaining costs are absent or negligible, the affected parties will agree on an allocation of resources that is efficient (= socially optimal), and that is independent of how property rights are defined. Here, an allocation of resources is called socially optimal if the allocation maximizes the sum of individual incomes or wealth. In other words, Coase claimed that if transaction and bargaining costs can be neglected, a socially optimal outcome will arise out of spontaneous bargaining processes among parties who experience the external effects of each other's activities, irrespective of how property rights are defined. This is called 'Coase's theorem'. Coase argued for this theorem by means of providing specific examples. In one of his examples, Coase argued that for socially optimal outcomes (defined as the total sum of incomes or wealth) it is irrelevant whether a crop farmer has the right to be protected from his neighbour's cattle, or whether the cattle farmer has the 'right' to impose harm or risk upon the crop farmer, having no duty to repair or compensate harm done. In both cases, so Coase argued, the socially optimal outcome will result from a bargaining process between both farmers, as the sum of the individual wealths will in both cases be the same. However, the distribution of wealth over the individuals will be different in both cases. Thus, if the socially optimal outcome requires that a fence be built (because the costs of the harm done to the crops exceeds the costs of building a fence), then the cattle farmer will decide to erect one (and pay for it) if he is liable for harm done, whereas in the other case (no liability) the crop farmer will erect and pay for the fence. Hence, irrespective of the contents of the individual rights, the socially optimal outcome will result. Conversely, if the socially optimal outcome would arise without a fence (because the harm done to the crops is less than the costs of building a fence), then the fence will not be built. If the cattle farmer is liable, he will pay damages, which is cheaper for him than building the fence. If the cattle farmer is not liable, then the farmer will not be compensated, but he will not build the fence as that would cost him even more.

Examples like this are the basis for Coase's claim that in situations of externalities, bargaining processes among affected parties result in socially optimal outcomes irrespective of the contents of (property) rights (provided that transaction and bargaining costs are sufficiently small). This claim has been criticized in the economic literature. It has been remarked that if there is a right to inflict harm to others (hence no liability for harm done), then the fraction of cattle farmers to crop farmers will be higher than in the case where there is no right to inflict harm to others, hence when there is liability for harm done (see, for example, Kahn, 1998; Stringham and White, 2004). It has also been remarked by economists (quoted in Stringham and White, 2004) that the concept of economic value is indeterminate or undefined if there is no system of rights in place. Only when there is a fixed system of rights (and, it should be added, laws) do things get an economic value. Hence, economic calculations cannot be used to determine rights or laws in the way the law and economics scholars quoted above tried to do. Rather, economic calculations presuppose the existence of rights/laws. Hence, the question of which rights and laws should govern human interactions, if prior agreement on these rights and laws is lacking, should be determined in another way. It is here that the principles presented in the present chapter come in. Thus, considering once more the above example of the Coase theorem, the first system of rights/laws, granting the crop farmer the right to be safeguarded from the effects of his neighbour's cattle and requiring the cattle farmer to repair or compensate any harm actually done, can be expected to lead to peaceful coexistence, whereas the same cannot be expected from the second system of rights/laws, in which the crop farmer lacks the right to be safeguarded, and in which the cattle farmer lacks the duty to repair or compensate.[4]

From the above I conclude that the assumption of the law and economics scholars, that there are no default individual rights and liability principles that determine liability in the absence of prior agreement, is untenable. Opposite to this, I hope to have shown that the requirement of liability in the absence of informed consent, discussed in this chapter, is a necessary addition to the (ethical) principles that underpin economic theory and analysis.

THE IMPLICATIONS OF MAJORITY RULE IN POLITICAL DECISION-MAKING

Within democratic states, the actual political decision-making about (technological and other) activities proceeds under majority rule, often within the framework of a constitution which can only be changed with a larger majority. That implies that a technological activity that creates risks or other negative effects for others can in principle proceed in a state if a political majority in that state is in favour of it. Hence the procedures for political decision-making provide no basis for assuming that all who are subjected to the negative effects, including risks of contemporary technological activities, are consenting to the activities or the conditions under which the activities proceed, even in the case that relevant regulation has been enacted. In actual fact, it is almost certain that the latter is *not* the case.[5] Two very general implications of majority rule in political decision-making are as follows:

1. *The system of political decision-making cannot be relied upon for ethically and economically sound decisions about activities that generate risks or other external costs.*[6] This holds both for the collective (political) decisions themselves and for the private (market) decisions. As for the collective decisions, majority decision-making allows for violations of the ethical principle of restricted liberty and does not guarantee Pareto improvement.[7] In addition, market decisions constrained by a legal system subjected to majority rule cannot be relied upon for economically sound and ethically acceptable decisions about technological activities. Under such conditions it cannot be assumed that the external costs of these activities are adequately internalized into market decisions. It has already been noticed that the responsibility for an activity that creates a risk of irreversible harm and that is performed without the consent of those subjected to the risk is actually unbearable in the sense that if the harm materializes it cannot be repaired. Neither can the harm be fully compensated if the victims did not agree in advance, by having consented to the relevant laws, to the amount of compensation.
2. *The proper standard for liability in the legal systems is strict liability, i.e. liability that is unlimited (full) and unconditional.* The reason for this is that, because of political majority decision-making, it cannot be assumed that potential victims of a risk-creating activity are consenting to the laws that sanction that activity.

> On the contrary, active opposition to such laws is a normal phenomenon. It then follows from the requirement of strict liability that the standard for legal liability should be absolute (full, no caps) and unconditional. This gives all who are subjected to risks by others the right to full reparation of or compensation for any harm that may ensue from those risks. (As was remarked earlier, victims are free not to execute that right if they so desire.)[8] The current liability laws do not or only partially meet this standard of absolute and unconditional liability. Examples of non-absolute liability are the limited liability of corporations (see Zandvoort, 2000a) and various legal limits to liability which are unrelated to the potential damage. An example of conditional liability is the doctrine of 'no liability without fault' which has dominated much of liability law since the industrial revolution (see, for this issue, Zandvoort (2008b) and references therein, notably Horwitz (1977, 1992)).

The willingness to consent to risk-creating activities will increase as complete repair of or compensation for possible damage is better guaranteed. Also, to the extent that actual liability for risk-creating activities is less limited and less conditional, more external costs associated with the risks will be internalized. Hence, a development towards less limited and less conditional liability would diminish the negative aspects of majority decision-making summarized above, and therewith would diminish the ethical problems for those who work in risk-creating technological organisations.[9] Nevertheless, as was explained above, no liability law can completely compensate for the absence of consent when (part of) the potential harm is irreversible. Hence, the consent to activities that create risks of irreversible harm of all who are subjected to the risks remains necessary.

IMPLICATIONS FOR PROMOTING THE SOCIAL ACCEPTABILITY OF ENERGY SYSTEMS INCLUDING LEVELS OF ENERGY SUPPLY/DEMAND

I will now apply the insights that were obtained above to energy systems and levels of energy supply/demand. The aims are to formulate conditions for social acceptability of energy systems and levels of supply/demand, as well as to formulate possibilities for improving that social acceptability.

1. As political decisions about energy production and consumption are not taken on the basis of unanimity rule, the legal liability for the external costs including risks of energy should in principle be unlimited and unconditional.

In actual liability law, the ways in which liability has (or has not) been regulated varies enormously over different energy systems and their components through the chain of production, transportation, use, and handling of waste products. Nowhere have the requirements of unlimited and unconditional liability been fully met, but there are enormous differences across different energy systems or components thereof.

Thus, there is significant international legislation for the liability for harm from nuclear accidents (Radetzki and Radetzki, 1997; Pelzer, 2003; see also

Zandvoort, 2004). Likewise there are liability regulations for oil pollution due to tanker accidents, even though significant improvements are possible and desirable (Zandvoort, 2000b). In marked contrast with this, an international regime of liability for the adversarial effects of possible climatic change due to CO_2 production is completely lacking. This means that the recovery of people who will be harmed is not guaranteed. It also means that the costs of recovery from damage are excluded from the price of fossil energy. It is likely that the inclusion of such costs, even if only partially, into market prices by introducing market share liability[10] for climate effects and by requiring coverage of liability by financial security would lead to reduced energy consumption and/or increased use of renewable energy sources. As an example, consider the World Bank. It has been reported that this international agency has in the past invested 17 times more money in fossil energy projects than it has in renewable energy and energy efficiency projects (Vallette et al, 2004). If liability for CO_2 discharges were present, money would have been required to cover that liability, for instance through insurance, and this might have affected the investment decisions of the World Bank in favour of renewable energy.

2. People should be subjected to nuisance or risks from energy facilities only with their free and informed consent. To obtain that consent, compensation may be necessary.

I assume that individuals have the right to evaluate the hazards that they are subjected to in accordance with the 'axioms of rationality' of the theory of coherent decision-making under uncertainty.[11] A coherent ('rational') person, that is, a person who satisfies these 'axioms of rationality', may be willing to consent to the risk that a hazardous facility such as a nuclear power plant imposes upon him/her under one or both of the following conditions:

- Compensation is provided for being exposed to the risk ('ex ante compensation').
- Guarantees are provided that damage, if it occurs, will be repaired or compensated for in a specified way ('ex post compensation').

As part of the possible harm is irreversible, that is, cannot be repaired but at best be compensated, both conditions require prior agreement about the nature and amount of compensation. Hence, agreement about compensation must be an element of all negotiations aimed at the consent of those who are subjected to the risks of hazardous facilities.[12]

3. Risk communication and risk information are necessary conditions for social acceptability.

If people are not informed about a risk, then they cannot consent to it. Hence it is crucial that the public is adequately informed about the risks that technological facilities such as a nuclear power plant or a gas storage facility impose upon them. There is a potential conflict between openness about risk information on the one hand, and secrecy regarding risk-creating facilities motivated by security considerations on the other hand. Any decision to curtail openness of risk information because of secrecy considerations has potentially severe implications in view of the principles and requirements presented above. In order to justify a claim that a technological activity adds to social progress, the informed consent is required of all who are subjected to the risks created by that activity. That consent cannot be had if information is withheld; it is impossible to consent to a risk that one is not aware of. In addition, when lacking informed consent, the responsibility for any harm that may result from the activity rests entirely with those who actually decide about and operate the hazardous activity. It has already been explained that, for irreversible harm, this responsibility is always unbearable. It can be concluded that whenever it is decided that secrecy reasons prohibit the provision of relevant risk information to the public, it is doubtful that the technology can be run at all in a manner that respects ethical principles and assures social progress.[13]

4. The credibility and trustworthiness of risk assessment and risk management may be enhanced by imposing liability coupled to the requirement of (private) financial warranty such as insurance.

The risk assessment of hazardous technological activities is by no means a straightforward empirical activity. Possible accidents and the probabilities with which they may occur cannot simply be read from historical or statistical data. Instead, in any assessment of the risks of an existing or proposed technological activity, it is unavoidable to make assumptions that do not follow from either direct observation or logic. Hence, no one can be forced on the basis of empirical facts and logic alone to accept such assumptions, as they can be denied without denying any empirical fact or (deductive) logic. Any risk assessment must necessarily contain such assumptions. An outsider with no or incomplete access to a risk assessment and the assumptions that have been made is unable to evaluate the credibility of the assumptions and hence of the outcomes of the assessment.

Given the inability of lay members of the public to evaluate the credibility of the assumptions that have been made in a probabilistic risk assessment, it would be entirely legitimate if someone who is exposed to the risk would attach credibility or trust to a risk assessment only if an individual or a group of individuals (i.e. a market party) has agreed to insure the risk for a premium that is related to the expected costs of the risk.[14] It would be in agreement with the principles and requirements presented above if only those hazardous activities were allowed of which the risks are completely covered by private insurance or other financial warranty.[15] Under these conditions, private insurers could moreover act as effective and trustworthy risk assessors and safety inspectors. For if a private insurer assessed a risk too low, he would on average lose money. If he assessed the risk too high, he would lose market share to other insurers who could ask lower premiums and still earn money.

At present, there are virtually no hazardous technological activities of which the risks have been completely insured, or for which there are other guarantees that any damage resulting from the activity will be repaired or fully compensated. As was noted above, international regulations for liability for nuclear accidents are in place, but do not fully live up to the standards that have been formulated in this chapter. Notably, the international liability rules do not fully comply with the principle that the risks should be fully insured by private parties. Thus, the (privately) insured liability of operators is limited to legally fixed amounts that are below realistic levels of damage in case of accidents. The state in which the nuclear plant is located is liable for damage above the limited liability of the operator, again up to a limit. Limits to liability violate the principle, stated above, that only those hazardous activities are allowed of which the risks are completely covered by private insurance or other financial warranty.

Conclusions

Two requirements have been presented that should be satisfied in order to guarantee that risk-generating (technological) activities are socially acceptable in a non-arbitrary way. These are the requirement of informed consent and the requirement of liability in the absence of informed consent. The requirements are implied by very general ethical principles that are necessary for peaceful coexistence. It was explained that the requirement of informed consent is also implied by normative principles that underpin economic theory. It was also shown that the requirement of strict liability in the absence of informed consent is actually rejected in the analyses of scholars in the law and economics tradition, who therewith deny the ethical principles that are necessary conditions for peaceful coexistence.

An implication of the two requirements, in conjunction with the fact that actual collective (political) decision-making about technological activities proceeds under majority rule at best (as opposed to unanimity rule), is that the proper standard in the legal systems of liability for technological activities is strict liability, that is, liability that is unlimited (full) and unconditional.

The two requirements have been applied to the particular case of energy production and consumption, in order to formulate possibilities for improving the social acceptability of those activities. In addition to the conclusion that the legal liability for the external costs (including the risks) of energy should be unlimited and unconditional, the following conclusions were obtained. People should be subjected to nuisance or risks from energy facilities only with their free and informed consent; to obtain that consent, compensation may be necessary. If risk communication and risk information are lacking or inadequate, then the conditions for social acceptability cannot be satisfied. The credibility and trustworthiness of risk assessment and risk management may be enhanced by imposing liability and by requiring private financial warranty such as insurance.

References

Beaumol, W. J. and Oates, W. E. (1988) *The Theory of Environmental Policy,* 2nd edn, Cambridge University Press, Cambridge

Coase, R. H. (1960) 'The problem of social cost', *Journal of Law and Economics*, vol 3, pp1–44

French, S. (1986) *Decision Theory. An Introduction to the Mathematics of Rationality*, Ellis Horwood/Wiley, Chichester, New York

Horwitz, M. J. (1977) *The Transformation of American Law 1780–1860*, Cambridge (Mass.), Harvard University Press

Horwitz, M. J. (1992) *The Transformation of American Law, 1870–1960. The Crisis of Legal Orthodoxy*, Oxford University Press, New York and Oxford

Kahn, J. R. (1998) *The Economic Approach to Environmental and Natural Resources*, 2nd edn, The Dryden Press, Fort Worth, etc.

Kunreuther, H. and Rajeev Gowda, M. V. (eds) (1990) *Integrating Insurance and Risk Management for Hazardous Wastes*, Kluwer Academic Publishers, Boston, etc.

Mill, J. S. [1859] (1998) *On Liberty*, Oxford University Press, Oxford

Montague, P. (1996) 'Dealing with uncertainty', *Rachel's Environmental & Health Weekly*, No. 510, 4 September 1996. Environmental Research Foundation, Annapolis, In. Online at: http://www.Rachel.org/en/node/3931

Mueller, D. C. (2003) *Public Choice* III, Cambridge University Press, Cambridge

Pelzer, N. (2003) 'Modernizing the international regime governing nuclear third party liability', *Oil, Gas and Energy Law Intelligence*, vol 1, no 5

Radetzki, M. and Radetzki, M. (1997) 'Liability of nuclear and other industrial corporations for large scale accident damage', *Journal of Energy & Natural Resources Law*, vol 15, no 4, pp366–386

Stringham, E. and White, M. D. (2004) 'Economic analysis of tort law: Austrian and Kantian perspectives', in M. Oppenheimer and N. Mercuro (eds) *Law and Economics: Alternative Economic Approaches to Legal and Regulatory Issues*, M.E. Sharpe, New York

Vallette, J., Wysham, D. and Martinez, N. (2004) *A Wrong Turn from Rio. The World Bank's Road to Climate Catastrophe*, IPS (Institute for Policy Studies). Available at www.seen.org

Velsen, J. F. C. van (2000) 'Relativity, universality and peaceful coexistence', *Archiv für Rechts- und Sozialphilosophie*, vol 86, no 1, pp88–108

Zandvoort, H. (2000) 'Controlling technology through law: the role of legal liability', in D. Brandt and J. Cernetic (eds) *Preprints of 7th IFAC Symposium on Automated Systems Based on Human Skill*, Joint Design of Technology and Organisation, 15–17 June, Aachen Germany, VDI/VDE-GMA Düsseldorf

Zandvoort, H. (2000b) 'Self determination, strict liability, and ethical problems in engineering', in P. A. Kroes and A. W. M. Meijers (eds) *The Empirical Turn in the Philosophy of Technology*, Elsevier, Amsterdam, pp219–243

Zandvoort, H. (2004) 'Liability and controlling technological risks. Ethical and decision theoretical foundations', in C. Spitzer, U. Schmocker and V. N. Dang (eds) *Proceedings of the International Conference on Probabilistic Safety Assessment and Management PSAM 7 – ESREL '04*, Springer, Berlin, pp2815–2820

Zandvoort, H. (2005) 'Good engineers need good laws', *European Journal of Engineering Education*, vol 30, no 1, pp21–36

Zandvoort, H. (2008a) 'Risk zoning and risk decision-making', *International Journal of Risk Assessment and Management*, vol 8, no 1/2, pp3–18

Zandvoort, H. (2008b) 'What scientists and engineers should know about the history of legal liability and why they should know it', Proceedings of the International Conference on Engineering Education 2008. 27-31 July, Pecs, Budapest, INEER. Available at: http://icee2008hungary.net/download/fullp/full_papers/full_paper167.pdf

NOTES

1 The word risk will be used to denote the exposure to a potential loss created by a hazard. A hazard is a situation or an activity that, if encountered, could produce undesired

consequences to humans or what they value. A (quantitative) risk assessment is a quantitative estimate of a risk in terms of possible consequences and probabilities with which the consequences occur. As will be elaborated in note 11 below, someone who is exposed to a hazard and who satisfies the axioms of the theory of decision-making under uncertainty can evaluate the risk ensuing from this as an expected cost, which is equivalent to a cost.

2 For expositions and discussions of the concept of external costs in economic theory, see Beaumol and Oates (1988) and Kahn (1998).

3 The above analysis can also be stated in terms of Prisoner's Dilemmas and solutions of Prisoner's Dilemmas through contractual agreements between those involved in the dilemmas. See Mueller (2003).

4 In spite of this seemingly obvious observation, Coase's claim, that (if bargaining costs are absent) for socially optimal results not the contents of 'property' rights is important but only whether rights are well defined, has been widely repeated. Coase's theorem has been uncritically embraced not merely in part of the scientific literature but also in government documents, witness the following quotation: 'An externality occurs when one party's actions impose uncompensated benefits or costs on another party. Environmental problems are a classic case of externality. For example, the smoke from a factory may adversely affect the health of local residents while soiling the property in nearby neighborhoods. If bargaining were costless and all property rights were well defined, people would eliminate externalities through bargaining without the need for government regulation. [Reference to Coase (1960).] From this perspective, externalities arise from high transaction costs and/or poorly defined property rights that prevent people from reaching efficient outcomes through market transactions.' (Quoted from: USA Office of Management and Budget, Circular A-4, Regulatory analysis, 17 September 2003, available at www.whitehouse.gov/omb/circulars/a004/a-4.html#3#3)

5 Decision-making between states does proceed according to consensus rule, at least in principle. However, given majority decision-making at a national level, consensus among governments, for instance about laws governing technological activities, does not at all guarantee consensus among the citizens of the states involved.

6 The problems of majority rule as compared to unanimity rule have been intensively studied in the field of public choice. For an overview of results, see Mueller (2003).

7 Majority decision-making does not even guarantee Kaldor-Hicks improvement, as the following example may show. Consider a proposal for building an incinerator. Suppose that the benefits (after subtracting the costs of building and operating the facility) for 10,000 people are 2 euros per year, and that the costs for 100 people living nearby amount to 500 euros per year, due to nuisance and health risks. Under majority rule, the proposal can be adopted as 99% of the voters are in favour. However, the project is not net euro beneficial, in the sense that there is no compensation scheme possible that would result into a Pareto improvement.

8 The statements in the text are particularly relevant for the case of 'bystanders', i.e. persons who in no way participate in an activity, at least not on a voluntary basis, and who hence have not given their informed consent to the activity. It could be argued that someone who buys and uses a product, after having been adequately informed about its potential risks, does not fall under this category of bystanders, as the act of buying and using a product could qualify as informed consent to the risks attached to the product's use. In that case, the producer would not be liable for harm that the product might cause to that user, according to the principles explored in this chapter.

9 For more on the relation between legal liability and ethical problems of professionals working in technology, see Zandvoort (2005).

10 For the concept of market share liability in environmental law, see Zandvoort (2000b).

11 The theory of coherent decision-making under uncertainty, also called utility theory, is the best available account of what it means to take coherent ('rational') decisions under uncertainty. See French (1986) for an account of this theory. It would be incoherent, and inconsistent with the basic principles underlying economic theory, if individuals were denied the right to evaluate the circumstances in which they find themselves in agreement with the axioms of utility theory ('axioms of rationality'). Anyone who satisfies these axioms and who is facing a risk, which is a cost expected not for sure but with a probability, is capable of identifying a cost (a negative utility) for sure, such that he/she is indifferent between the cost for sure and the cost expected with a probability. Any hazard can be evaluated by someone who is subjected to the hazard as creating a risk for him/her, and he/she may always analyse the risk in terms of negative consequences that will materialize not with certainty but with some probability. Hence if individuals have the right to evaluate risks in agreement with the axioms of utility theory, then it must be assumed that any hazardous human activity is equivalent to a real cost for anyone who is exposed to the hazard. This is true, even though that cost may and will be evaluated differently by different individuals, because of differences in risk estimates, i.e. different estimates of the possible effects and of the probabilities with which the effects will occur; and differences in circumstances and values of different individuals, including differences in attitudes towards risks. In addition, because of uncertainties in the risk estimates, that cost will be vague to a varying degree.

12 I have addressed elsewhere (Zandvoort, 2008a) the question of how a requirement to the effect that negotiating parties should be consistent in their evaluations of and decisions about risks would constrain the legitimate demands/desires of the parties to such a negotiation.

13 In Zandvoort (2008a), I address the additional requirement that the public should be properly educated in order to be capable of taking coherent decisions about risks.

14 Something similar is expressed in the following statements made in the context of the management of hazardous wastes: 'We all have a stake in insurability, not only because of the financial security that it provides, but also because of the psychological security it provides to the public. There is force to the assertion that if insurance isn't able [to] deal with the risk, then the lay member of the public is not going to be able to do so either' (F. Henry Habicht II in Kunreuther and Gowda, 1990, p337).

15 The idea to allow a hazardous activity only when its external risk has been completely insured is also the basic idea of the so-called '4P' principle ('the precautionary polluter pays principle'). See Montague (1996) and references therein.

5 Clinical Equipoise and the Assessment of Acceptable Therapeutic Risk

Duff Waring

Introduction

Clinical equipoise is an ethical standard for the inception of random-controlled trials and a normative vehicle for the calibration of acceptable therapeutic risks to human research subjects. It requires a null hypothesis or a state of honest, professional disagreement among members of the expert clinical community as to the relative merits of the treatments being compared in the trial. If those treatments are in clinical equipoise, then trial subjects are not randomized to a treatment that is known to be inferior. It was first introduced by the late philosopher Benjamin Freedman in a seminal article published in the *New England Journal of Medicine* in 1987 (Freedman, 1987) and has since become an influential, some would say foundational, standard in North American biomedical research ethics. It is endorsed in Canada's Tri-Council Policy Statement (2005) as pivotal to the assessment of benefits and harms and the use of placebos in clinical trials. It is also an important concept in the recommendations of the US National Bioethics Advisory Commission (NBAC) for reforming the federal regulations that prescribe standards for the Institutional Review Board (IRB) analysis of benefits and harms in research (NBAC, 2000; Miller and Weijer, 2003, p93).

This chapter will examine how IRB members can apply the ethical standard of clinical equipoise to determine acceptable therapeutic risk.[1] I will use the terms 'nonvalidated' and 'novel' treatment interchangeably and will focus primarily on drug treatments. A is the standard drug treatment and B is the novel or nonvalidated one. A nonvalidated treatment has some evidentiary and theoretical basis for use in clinical practice but is otherwise unproven and experimental. Questions about its efficacy have not been resolved by Phase III clinical trials. Examples of nonvalidated treatments would be 'new chemical compounds or biological agents, new combinations of treatments or adjuvant treatments' (Freedman et al, 1992, p655). A validated treatment has been accepted by the expert clinical community for treating patients in clinical practice. Questions about its efficacy are supposedly resolved by sufficient research and testing. A validated treatment can become a standard treatment if it is the treatment usually recommended for patients with a given condition.

If an IRB confirms that standard treatment A and novel treatment B are in clinical equipoise, then the risks and benefits to research subjects of taking B in a trial are required to be approximately equal to those accepted by patients outside the trial who take A for the condition under study. The therapeutic risks of B are thus acceptable. We then distinguish the therapeutic interventions A and B from the trial procedures that are administered solely to answer the research question and to generate data. These research procedures will pose any remaining risks to subjects in the trial. If we distinguish these risks from the therapeutic risks that are accommodated by clinical equipoise, then 'demarcated research risks' are supposedly the only additional risks of trial participation. These are salient ideas in the clinical equipoise literature. I want to question them by examining two types of trial that clinical equipoise is meant to accommodate.

There can be trials in which A and B are in clinical equipoise even though B poses 'considerably more [therapeutic] risk to subjects' than A. For clinical equipoise to be confirmed in such a trial, B must also offer 'the prospect of considerably greater benefit' (Weijer, 2000, p354; cf Weijer, 1999, p2). I call these markedly greater risk-benefit trials. I will posit two types of such trial. In the first type, B is also available outside the trial to patients in clinical practice and in the second type, B is only available to research subjects in the trial that tests it. If clinical equipoise is meant to accommodate both types of markedly greater risk-benefit trial, then I argue that it will include some studies that expose research subjects to greater therapeutic risk than they would face as patients taking A in clinical practice. These would be trials of the second type. Consequently, 'demarcated research risks' will not always be the only additional risks of trial participation.

I will explore some related ideas in developing this argument. The clinical equipoise literature does not elaborate on what approximate equality means and how it is to be applied in determining acceptable therapeutic risk. How might the approximate equality requirement enable both types of markedly greater risk-benefit trial to fall within the purview of clinical equipoise? I will use the standard definition of approximate equality that is used in physics, engineering and occasionally mathematics. The clinical equipoise literature indicates two ways of applying this definition. An approximate equality of risks and benefits between A and B could mean that the aggregate risk and benefit sums of A and the aggregate risk and benefit sums of B are close enough to make the difference inconsequential in practical terms.[2] Alternatively, we might use the standard definition to mean that the risk-benefit ratios of A and B are so close as to make any difference inconsequential.

I aver that if the standard definition of approximate equality is applied as an absolute requirement admitting of no exceptions, then clinical equipoise will exclude some markedly greater risk-benefit trials. This would have the counterintuitive result of limiting research on novel treatments that pose considerably greater potential benefits than their standard practice comparators. I think approximate equality is more plausibly construed as a prima facie requirement of acceptable therapeutic risk, i.e. the standard definition is applied first but it can be overridden when it conflicts with a weightier, more favourable balance of benefits over risks. Whether applied to risk-benefit sums or to ratios that reflect different sums of risks and benefits, a prima facie requirement of approximate equality will include both types of markedly greater risk-benefit trials in the purview of clinical equipoise.

As a standard applied by IRBs, clinical equipoise can accommodate both 'risk-friendly' and 'risk-cautious' perspectives in the evaluation of therapeutic risk. Given the documented concerns about research-friendly conflicts of interests between sponsoring companies and IRB members (Campbell et al, 2006), we may want to pay closer attention to how IRBs are applying the 'inherently imprecise and multifaceted' concept of clinical equipoise (Miller and Weijer, 2003, p100). Given a basic commitment to protecting human research subjects, a predominantly risk-cautious perspective might be most apposite for IRB members.

I will develop these arguments further in this chapter. I begin by elaborating on the constituent ideas of clinical equipoise and component analysis. I then cover applying the standard definition of approximate equality to a comparison of the aggregate risk sums of A and B. I expound my analysis of the first and second type of markedly greater risk-benefit trial and draw three conclusions that pertain to the second type. First, research subjects randomized to B will add significantly to the therapeutic risk load they carry as patients taking A for the condition under study. Second, these greater therapeutic risks add to the risk load of trial participation. Third, demarcated research risks are not the only additional risks of trial participation. I then claim that proponents of clinical equipoise do not mean to determine acceptable therapeutic risk by always requiring the aggregate risk sum of A and the aggregate risk sum of B to be approximately equal. This would make approximate equality an absolute requirement admitting of no exceptions. To do so would unduly narrow the purview of clinical equipoise by excluding the second type of markedly greater risk-benefit trial. If clinical equipoise is to cover this type of trial as well, then I think approximate equality is more plausibly construed as a prima facie threshold requirement of acceptable therapeutic risk.

I next look at applying approximate equality to a comparison of the risk-benefit ratios of A and B. I argue that approximate equality cannot be applied to risk-benefit ratios as an absolute requirement admitting of no exceptions. To do so will exclude some trials in which B indicates markedly greater potential benefits over A from the purview of clinical equipoise. Here again, I think we can avoid this difficulty if approximate equality is a prima facie requirement.

Finally, I attempt to clarify the values of those members of the expert clinical community who endorse B as the initial basis on which IRB members determine ranges of acceptable therapeutic risk. I distinguish between risk-friendly and risk-cautious perspectives in research review. I argue that a risk-cautious approach is the most suitable expression of a basic commitment to the protection of human subjects.

Component Analysis, Clinical Equipoise and the Approximate Equality Requirement

As applied by IRBs, clinical equipoise is part of a systematic approach to the ethical analysis of risks and potential benefits of biomedical research known as 'component analysis'. Component analysis distinguishes between therapeutic and nontherapeutic risks to human subjects. It recognizes that clinical research protocols are often mixed studies of new treatments that combine therapeutic and research procedures. Under component analysis, these different procedures require separate ethical standards for the evaluation of their attendant risks to human subjects (Freedman and Weijer, 1992, p656; Weijer, 1999, p2; Miller and Weijer, 2000, p7; Weijer, 2000, p351; Weijer and Miller, 2004, pp570–571).

Consider a trial testing a new, nonvalidated treatment B against an accepted, standard treatment A that is currently used in clinical practice for the condition under study. As such, A falls within acknowledged criteria of competent care. By definition, B 'has not been accepted as within the range of standard treatments by the medical community' (Freedman et al, 1992, p655). The two treatments in this trial are administered with therapeutic warrant, that is 'on the basis of evidence sufficient to justify the belief that they may benefit research subjects' (Weijer and Miller, 2004, p570). These procedures will present treatment-related or therapeutic risks to subjects. The trial will involve other procedures that are administered without therapeutic warrant; for example, venipunctures for pharmacokinetic drug levels, additional imaging procedures or blood tests not used in clinical practice. These procedures do not offer the prospect of direct benefit to research subjects. They are administered solely to answer the research question and to generate data. These procedures can present nontherapeutic or research-related risks to subjects (Freedman et al, 1992, pp655–657; Weijer, 1999, p2; Miller and Weijer, 2000, p7; Weijer, 2000, pp354–355; Weijer and Miller, 2004, pp570–571).

The first step in the component analysis of a mixed study is to demarcate the therapeutic and nontherapeutic procedures. There are two stages of risk analysis that correspond to these two types of procedures and the two types of risk they present. In the first stage, the therapeutic risks and benefits of A and B are assessed by the IRB and must be found to satisfy the ethical standard of clinical equipoise. In the second stage, the research risks of the nontherapeutic procedures are assessed by the IRB according to two ethical standards. First, the IRB must conclude that the research risks are minimized consistent with sound scientific design. This is known as the minimal risk standard. Second, the IRB must conclude that the research risks 'are reasonable in relation to the knowledge that may be gained from the study' (Freedman et al, 1992, p656; Weijer, 1999, p2; Miller and Weijer, 2000, p7; Weijer, 2000, p355; Weijer and Miller, 2004, pp570–571). Input from community representatives as well as scientific experts is required for this conclusion (Weijer, 2000, p355). I will focus exclusively on the first stage of analysis that accommodates therapeutic risks under clinical equipoise. Issues pertaining to the minimization of research risk will not be addressed.

Clinical equipoise was offered by Freedman as a 'research friendly' (Weijer and Miller, 2004, p571) resolution to the moral tension between the physician's therapeutic commitment to the care of her patients and her scientific commitment to a research protocol (Miller and Weijer, 2003, p98). The therapeutic commitment prioritizes fidelity to the welfare of the patient. The scientific commitment prioritizes fidelity to the methodology of the trial and the generation of reliable research data. Randomization seems antithetical to a patient-centred treatment plan. Attentive and responsible physicians do not usually resort to chance when deciding which treatment is best for their patients. Under what conditions might a physician-investigator randomize patients in a trial while maintaining her therapeutic commitment? To answer this moral question, Freedman argued that the 'basic reason' for conducting a trial is 'current or imminent conflict in the clinical community over what treatment is preferred for patients in a defined population' (ibid, p98). As a rule, there must be an honest null hypothesis at the start of a trial. Is it a priori quite likely that either arm of the trial may be found inferior, superior or equivalent to the alternative arm(s)? 'If not, the trial is unethical, for at least some subjects will be denied access to the best known form of medical treatment because of their trial participation' (Freedman and Weijer, 1992, p6; see also Freedman et al, 1996, p253).

Clinical equipoise is confirmed when an IRB determines that a state of honest, professional disagreement exists, or may soon exist, among members of the relevant expert community as to the publicly available evidence on the relative merits of A and B. The IRB can obtain this evidence from the study justification in the protocol and the relevant medical literature. Where necessary, it can also be obtained from consultation with one or more clinical experts not affiliated with the study or its sponsors. The trial must have the potential to eliminate this disagreement upon its completion (Miller and Weijer, 2003, pp99, 101, 106). The IRB does not survey practitioners to make this determination. Clinical equipoise can be confirmed if the IRB concludes that the evidence supporting the two treatments 'is sufficient that, were it widely known, expert clinicians would disagree as to the preferred treatment' (Miller and Weijer, 2003, p102; Weijer and Miller, 2004, p571). If the community of expert clinicians is in a state of clinical equipoise, then 'good medicine' finds the choice between A and B 'indifferent' (Freedman, 1987, p144).

A 'significant' or 'respectable' minority of expert clinicians who favour B is sufficient to establish this disagreement (Freedman et al, 1992, p654; Miller and Weijer, 2003, p101). There are no set quantitative criteria for determining this minority. This idea of a standard of care endorsed by an expert minority of physicians is derived from the 'respectable minority' principle in Canadian and US health law, which functions as a defence to allegations of medical malpractice. A defendant physician whose treatment preference, or approach to administering it, is endorsed by a respectable minority of physicians is not in breach of the relevant standard of care (Picard and Robertson, 1996, pp278–280; Furrow et al, 2000, pp259–309). The court does not survey medical practitioners to make this determination; 'rather, it considers expert testimony and relevant literature in making its [qualitative] judgement'. Like a court, an IRB 'can gather evidence from the literature and expert clinicians' in determining whether a significant minority endorses the novel treatment (Miller and Weijer, 2003, p105). As a strictly legal determination, this minority can be quite small (Freedman and Weijer, 1992, p96).

Clinical equipoise requires that physicians who prefer one drug treatment respect the fact that 'their less favored [drug] treatment is preferred by colleagues whom they consider to be responsible and competent' (Freedman, 1987, p144). There are numerous ways in which a state of clinical equipoise can arise. Evidence might emerge from early animal studies or basic knowledge of how the drug functions that B offers advantages over A. Or the clinical community might be split, with some physicians preferring A and others preferring B. This split should be so well documented in the literature that a trial is called for to settle the issue of which is the better treatment (Weijer, 2000, p354).

Freedman argued that the development of medical knowledge is an inherently social process that places a moral locus on the community of expert physicians as opposed to the individual practitioner. The physician's therapeutic commitment to the patient requires the provision of competent care, that is the provision of treatment that falls within the standard norms of care. These 'derive not from the individual clinician's preferences, but from practices accepted by the physician's peers in the community of expert practitioners. Again, a treatment is consistent with the standard of care if it is endorsed by at least a respectable minority of expert clinicians' (Miller and Weijer, 2003, p101). Thus physician-investigators with an informed preference for A may justifiably request patients to consent to random assignment of A and B 'insofar as colleagues they recognize as "responsible and competent" prefer the other treatment' (Freedman, 1987, p144; Miller and Weijer, 2003, p99). Research subjects should understand that the fact that they are being seen by a physician with a treatment preference for A, rather than an equally competent physician who prefers B, is likely a matter of chance (Freedman, 1987, p144).

Confirmation of clinical equipoise relies on a comparison of the risks and potential benefits of B with the standard treatments for the condition under study that are accepted by the medical community. Researchers must have some pretrial evidence to suggest that B will be an improvement over A (Miller and Weijer, 2003, p98). But in order to confirm clinical equipoise, the IRB must determine that there is enough pre-trial evidence to warrant the assumption that there is a 'risk-benefit equivalency' between A and B. This evidence can also be acquired from the study justification, a review of the relevant medical literature, animal or other uncontrolled studies, or from consultations with independent clinical experts. The following factors can contribute to this determination: the efficacy of the treatments, reversible and irreversible side effects, ease of administration, patient compliance and possibly costs. Some risks will be shared between the two treatments but variations may exist (Freedman and Weijer, 1992, p6).

Clinical equipoise does not require numeric equality of the potential risks and benefits of the study treatments. It requires a 'rough' equivalence (Freedman et al, 1992, pp656, 658; Weijer, 1999, p2; cf Miller and Weijer, 2003, p107) or 'approximate equality' (Weijer, 2000, p354) of each treatment's therapeutic index that can be summed up as a 'compendious measure' of risks and benefits. The unproven treatment to be tested in the trial will usually pose greater uncertainty about risks and benefits than the standard treatments used currently in clinical practice (Weijer, 1999, p2; Weijer, 2000, p354).

For 'a nonvalidated intervention to be in equipoise with a standard treatment arm, its associated expectation of risk and benefit must be roughly equivalent to those of treatments commonly used in clinical practice (or placebo if no treatment is commonly accepted)' (Freedman et al, 1992, p656). When applied properly, clinical equipoise ensures that 'the *sum of risks and potential benefits* [italics mine] of therapeutic procedures in a clinical trial are roughly similar to that which a patient would receive in clinical practice' (Weijer and Miller, 2004, p572). Proponents of clinical equipoise have also argued that the 'treatment *risk-benefit ratios*' [italics mine] of A and B must be assessed and found to satisfy the requirement of clinical equipoise (Freedman et al, 1992, p656). I note this distinction because equal ratios can reflect different sums of risks and benefits. But there can be other trials in which A and B are in clinical equipoise, even though B poses 'considerably more [therapeutic] risk to subjects as long as it also offers the prospect of considerably greater benefit' (Weijer, 2000, p354; cf Weijer, 1999, p2). These are what I term markedly greater risk-benefit trials.

By the standard of clinical equipoise then, the physician may randomize when the therapeutic procedures of the trial are consistent with competent medical care (Weijer and Miller, 2004, p571). If each of the trial arms are consistent with a standard of care, then 'offering a patient enrollment in an RCT is consistent with the physician's duty of care to the patient'. As such, clinical equipoise 'acknowledges that the ethics of clinical practice and the ethics of clinical research are inextricably intertwined' (Miller and Weijer, 2003, pp93–94, 101). Clinical equipoisc is the 'keystone' of the IRB's ethical analysis of risk in research. It directs the attention of IRBs to assessing the available evidence of the 'comparative efficacy of treatment alternatives' for the population under study. Clinical equipoise should thus 'be understood as a condition governing the approval of research by IRBs, and thereby as a controlling condition in the state's oversight of research involving human participants' (Miller and Weijer, 2003, p113).[3]

The application of clinical equipoise 'presupposes agreement or justification about who should be in the community of expert clinicians deciding which treatments are equally good and whether their views adequately represent the views of the potential patients' (Kopelman, 1995, p2337). These presuppositions are contentious. Some critics disvalue the views of 'any but the most acclaimed clinical investigators' while others 'contend that many perspectives, including those of investigators, clinicians, and patient advocates, represent patients' sometimes differing values' (ibid, p2337).

Under component analysis, high risk therapeutic procedures can fall within the purview of a minimal risk research protocol. Patients who incur high therapeutic risks from A in clinical practice can become research subjects and incur high therapeutic risks from B in a trial that compares them. As long as the high risks of B are within the range of therapeutic risks that are acceptable in clinical practice, they are acceptable in research. Kopelman has raised the following concern:

> This view is untenable. It permits high-risk research to be called 'minimal risk' for some people. Moreover, it raises justice issues since it has different standards for different people leaving some to bear more of the research risks of harm than others in order to gain information that benefits all of us. (Kopelman, 2004, p367)

Put simply, 'If some people have high-risk interventions routinely then, on this view, comparable high-risk research for most people would be minimal *for them*' (Kopelman, 2004, pp366–367). One might argue that component analysis somehow justifies an assessment that the therapeutic risks are lower in the research context than they are outside of it. Research subjects who are randomized to the standard treatment arm will only be incurring minimal risk from what would otherwise be a high risk intervention in clinical practice. One might interpret this as meaning that subjects can reduce their high level of therapeutic risk from taking A in clinical practice merely by enrolling in a trial that uses A as a standard control arm.

That would be a misinterpretation. There is no inconsistency in maintaining that high risk procedures that are available to patients in clinical practice can be within a range of acceptable therapeutic risk in a minimal risk research protocol. That research could not proceed if it were unacceptable to test novel treatments that pose roughly the same measure of high therapeutic risk as their standard practice comparators. Clinical equipoise does not change the magnitude of therapeutic risk in a trial. The magnitude of a therapeutic lumbar puncture's harm and the probability of its occurrence remain the same in both clinical practice and research. If there is an approximate equality of therapeutic risks, then the additional risks to research subjects would supposedly come from the non-therapeutic procedures necessary to conduct the trial and generate data. There is nothing unjust about different ranges of acceptable therapeutic risk for different persons as long as those ranges reflect the morally relevant differences between them, that is, some patients consent to high risk treatments and some do not.

Proponents of component analysis have responded to Kopelman by noting that she overlooks the accommodation of acceptable therapeutic risk by clinical equipoise (Miller and Weijer, 2000, p7). We just have to be clear about the risks we aim to minimize in clinical research on therapeutic interventions. We aim to minimize the nontherapeutic risks from the demarcated research procedures that are used only to answer the research question. If the treatment-related risks of B are approximately equal to those of A, then research subjects would not add significantly to the therapeutic risk load they already carry as patients who take A outside the trial. If the demarcated risks from the nontherapeutic trial procedures are minimized, then trial participation will present minimal research risk. These protocols are usually eligible for expedited review (Kopelman, 2004, pp351, 356–357; US Department of Health and Human Services, National Institutes of Health, and Office for Human Research Protections, 2001, in Emanuel et al, 2003, p44; Tri Council Policy Statment, 2005, p1.8).

This response to Kopelman turns on the idea that she would have much less to worry about if she just focused on demarcated research risks as the additional risks of trial participation. But one might respond that it is not sufficiently clear how clinical equipoise uses the notion of approximate equality to calibrate an acceptable balance of therapeutic risks if it accommodates studies in which B is both unavailable outside the trial and thought to pose considerably greater therapeutic risks and benefits than A. I will argue in the next section that the second type of markedly greater risk-benefit study presents additional therapeutic risks of trial participation to subjects who are randomized to B. While these risks might be acceptable to the expert clinicians who favour B, they would only be born by research subjects who enroll in the trial those clinicians propose. One might argue that the additional therapeutic risks in the second type of markedly greater risk-benefit trial pose more than minimal risk to subjects randomized to B. Consequently, such trials should not be eligible for expedited review.

In summary, an IRB's determination of clinical equipoise confirms the following requirements: (1) that there is an evidence-based disagreement in the expert clinical community about the relative merits of A and B; and (2) that there is between A and B an approximate equality or rough equivalence of therapeutic risks and benefits (requirements 1 and 2).[4] Again, I take an approximate equality of risks between A and B to mean that the risks are close enough in probability and magnitude to make the difference inconsequential in practical terms. Component analysis holds that the standard of minimal risk applies only to research risks. We do not aim to minimize therapeutic risks. Apparently, we do not have to since a determination of clinical equipoise confirms requirement 2. Demarcated research risks are supposedly the only additional risks of trial participation.

The approximate equality requirement is meant to limit additional therapeutic risk to an acceptable range. If there is no appreciable addition to the subjects' therapeutic risk load, then it is easy to see how demarcated research risks would be the only additional risks of trial participation. Clinical equipoise can certainly accommodate trials in which the risks of A and B are so close as to make the difference inconsequential. Will the risks of B always be so limited if clinical equipoise is met? I aver not. How then might we understand the approximate equality requirement in the application of clinical equipoise? I will argue in the next two sections that we should understand approximate equality as a prima facie requirement that can be applied to the risk sums of A and B or to their respective risk-benefit ratios.

Approximate equality of aggregate risk sums

A sum is the total amount resulting from the addition of two or more numbers or amounts. It is the whole amount, quantity or number. Assume that an IRB is reviewing a protocol for testing B against A and that its members have a reliable methodology for summing risks in terms of their magnitudes and probabilities of occurrence.[5] We could then compare the benefit sum of A to its risk sum, for example A presents 30 units of benefit as compared to 10 units of risk. We could do the same with B, for example B presents 170 units of benefit as compared to 60 units of risk. We could then compare the respective benefit and risk sums of A to those of B to determine whether they are approximately equal, that is whether 'the sum of risks and potential benefits of therapeutic procedures in a clinical trial are roughly similar to that which a patient would receive in clinical practice' (Weijer and Miller, 2004, p572). I do not think that proponents of clinical equipoise mean to determine acceptable therapeutic risk by always requiring the aggregate risk and benefit sums of A and B to be approximately equal. This would make approximate equality an absolute requirement admitting of no exceptions. To do so would unduly narrow the purview of clinical equipoise by excluding some of the trials that clinical equipoise is meant to accommodate.

My reasons for thinking this derive from a consideration of the two types of markedly greater risk-benefit trial that I assume to fall within the purview of clinical equipoise. In the first type, B is available outside the trial as a treatment to patients in clinical practice. In the second type, B is not available as a treatment to patients in clinical practice, that is, it is only available to research subjects in the trial that tests it. I argue that the first type of markedly greater risk-benefit trial allows for an application of approximate equality as an absolute requirement admitting of no exceptions where the second type does not. If clinical equipoise is to cover both types of trial in a determination of acceptable therapeutic risk, then I think its proponents are referring instead to a prima facie requirement of approximate equality.

Consider the first type of markedly greater risk-benefit trial. Some nonvalidated treatments that are tested in trials are also available to patients in clinical practice, for example innovative departures from standard practice in surgical or medical treatments or the administration of drugs (Levine, 1986, pp3–4). Here is an example from the clinical equipoise literature: the accepted approach to surgical interventions for hypotensive patients with penetrating torso injuries (e.g. gunshot wounds) involves fluid resuscitation before the patient reaches the operating room. An expert minority of clinicians endorses 'withholding fluid resuscitation in penetrating trauma until the patient reaches the operating room'. An IRB reviews the protocol. It concludes: (1) that the study justification presents 'a sound theoretical basis for thinking that delayed fluid resuscitation is advantageous' that is supported with data from animal models; (2) that the relevant literature includes one previous trial that generated some evidence of a survival advantage to delayed resuscitation; and (3) that consultations with one or more expert clinicians not affiliated with the study or its sponsor confirms that 'the clinical community is divided as to the preferred approach to fluid resuscitation'. An IRB could conclude on the basis of these three considerations that a trial 'is both morally permissible and necessary' as a step towards eliminating disagreement in the clinical community (Miller and Weijer, 2003, pp105–107).

Even though the controversial approach to delayed fluid resuscitation has not yet been accepted as a standard treatment by the medical community, it falls within a minority standard of care as any such treatment must. It is also a treatment that some patients actually receive in clinical practice. Hence clinical equipoise might be said to render the sum of risks and benefits of the trial's therapeutic procedures approximately equal to the sum of risks and benefits which a patient could receive from the therapeutic procedures available in clinical practice (cf Weijer and Miller, 2004, p572). We might say 'approximately' equal because adherence to the research protocol may preclude giving the 'individualized attention to the specific and evolving needs' of particular patients that is expected in clinical practice (Emanuel et al, 2003, p193). The other possibility is that subjects in this trial receive greater clinical attention than they would as patients in clinical practice.[6] Note that this does not require the risks of A and B to be close in magnitude or probability. It just requires that A and B are available in clinical practice.

Now consider the second type of markedly greater risk-benefit trial. Suppose we have a new drug for treating schizophrenia that is chemically unrelated to any other currently available antipsychotic.[7] By definition, B 'has not been accepted as within the range of standard treatments by the medical community' (Freedman et al, 1992, p655). It is at the Phase III trial stage and thus not yet approved by regulatory authorities. B is only available to patients who become research subjects in a trial that tests it. These trials are not uncommon. For instance, B could be an investigational drug not approved by regulatory authorities for legal marketing and sale and not available to patients through compassionate access programmes. There is no indication in the literature that this second type of trial is excluded from the purview of clinical equipoise. The expert minority proponents of B suspect that it poses a considerably greater risk than A but even greater potential benefits. The majority of clinical experts claim that A is less risky and at least as beneficial as B. Clinical experts propose a trial to determine the preferred treatment.[8]

I argue that this type of markedly greater risk-benefit trial does not allow for an application of approximate equality to the respective risk and benefit sums of A and B. As to benefits, we would rule out research on nonvalidated treatments that indicate considerably greater benefits than their standard comparators. As to the risks, it is not as if a standard of care that accommodates both A and B somehow negates the considerable differences between these respective risk sums. By the standard definition, approximate equality would not prohibit *all* additional risks from the new treatment. We would prohibit much research if novel treatments had to present only as much or less risk than the standard ones. The measure of equality is supposed to be close but not exact and the measure of equivalence can be uneven. Hence the qualifiers 'approximate' and 'rough'. To be meaningful, these adjectives still have to add some limits to the nouns they qualify. The approximate equality requirement would be vacuous if it were completely open ended. I think approximate equality can be plausibly construed as meaning that the risk sum of B can be slightly greater than the risk sum of A. But there is a wide discrepancy between sums of risk that are close and sums of risk that differ considerably. If we use the standard definition as an absolute requirement admitting of no exceptions, then the considerably greater aggregate risks of B will exceed a plausible range of approximate equality, or closeness, to those of A.

At least three conclusions follow from a consideration of this second type of markedly greater risk-benefit trial. First, research subjects randomized to B will add significantly to the therapeutic risk load they carry as patients taking A for the condition under study. A sets the limit of therapeutic risk they incur outside the trial. B raises that limit inside the trial. Second, these greater therapeutic risks add to the risk load of trial participation. Patients will not incur those greater therapeutic risks unless they enroll in the trial that tests B. Third, demarcated research risks are not the only additional risks of trial participation.

When comparing risk and benefit sums, the approximate equality requirement can be applied to the first type of markedly greater risk-benefit trial but not to the second. I do not think that proponents of clinical equipoise mean to exclude the second type of markedly greater risk-benefit trial from the purview of clinical equipoise. Consequently, I do not think they mean to always require the respective risk sums of A and B to be approximately equal by the standard definition. In terms of pharmaceutical research, applying the standard definition of approximate equality as an absolute requirement would largely limit the purview of clinical equipoise to 'me-too' drugs, that is, imitative compounds that are very close in structure to the drugs already available to patients. Me-too drugs are understood to present no significant clinical advantage over the drugs they mimic.

If clinical equipoise is to cover the second type of markedly greater risk-benefit trial as well, then approximate equality is more plausibly construed as a prima facie threshold requirement of acceptable therapeutic risk; that is, the standard definition is applied first but it can be overridden when it conflicts with a weightier, more favourable balance of benefits over risks. At the very least, the risks and benefits of A and B should be so close as to make the difference inconsequential. This would be a minimal threshold of acceptable therapeutic risk. We presume A and B to meet this requirement unless it conflicts in a particular trial with a more favourable balance of potential benefits over risks. As a prima facie requirement, approximate equality is conditional on not being outweighed by better balances of benefits over risks. A prima facie requirement of approximate equality would not exclude the second type of markedly greater risk-benefit trial from the purview of clinical equipoise. But note as well that it would not prevent research subjects randomized to B in these trials from being exposed to greater therapeutic risks than they would face as patients taking A for the condition under study. Nor would its application ensure that demarcated research risks are the only additional risks of participation in this type of trial.

Approximate Equality of Risk-Benefit Ratios

We have seen that the 'compendious measure' of approximate equality has also been construed as a ratio, that is, a quantity that denotes the proportional amount or magnitude of one quantity relative to another. Any fraction, quotient, proportion or percentage is a ratio. A ratio is usually expressed as the quotient of one quantity divided by the other. It is thus a comparison of two numbers or quantities by division. More generally, a risk-benefit ratio weighs, balances or trades off benefits against risks. Suppose we claim that A and B present roughly equivalent ratios of benefits to risks. We might also claim that the therapeutic risks of A and B fall within an acceptable comparative range. I aver that approximate equality cannot be applied to risk-benefit ratios as an absolute requirement without excluding some trials indicating markedly greater potential benefit from the purview of clinical equipoise.

Ratios can compare the relative magnitudes of two sums measured in similar units. Assuming a reliable methodology that can be expressed in quantitative terms, we might claim that A presents 30 units of benefit to every 10 units of risk where B presents 150 units of benefit to every 50 units of risk. Since ratios reduce like standard fractions, this would make the ratios of benefits to risks approximately equal to three to one. The point to remember is that equal risk-benefit ratios can reflect different sums of risks and benefits. Call this the ratio interpretation of approximate equality. Depending on the probability of occurrence and the magnitude of the risk involved, a study presenting these ratios could be seen as a markedly greater risk-benefit trial. Forty additional units of possible harm from B could be seen as posing considerably greater therapeutic risk than the ten units of A. It would seem that clinical equipoise could accommodate both types of markedly greater risk-benefit trial on the ratio interpretation. It would make no difference to the approximate equality of the ratios whether B is, or is not, available to patients outside the trial that tests it.

Even so, an approximate equality of risk-benefit ratios in this type of trial entails three familiar conclusions: When B is not available to patients outside the trial that tests it, subjects randomized to B would still incur considerably greater therapeutic risks than they would as patients taking A in clinical practice for the condition under study. While ratios representing units or levels of risk can reduce like fractions, the actual risks do not reduce, that is, B still presents 40 more units of risk than A when the ratios are exactly equal. These additional therapeutic risks from B add to the risk load of trial participation because subjects would not incur them outside the trial taking A for the condition under study. Demarcated research risks are thus not the only additional risks of trial participation.

But not all therapeutic interventions will have approximately equal risk-benefit quotients when the potential benefit is divided by, balanced with or weighed in terms of, the degree of anticipated risk. There would obviously be trials to which we would not want to apply an absolute requirement that the risk-benefit ratios of the treatments being compared be approximately equal, for example one in which B's ratio of benefits to risks is 13 to 1 and A's ratio is 3 to 1. Consequently, we do not want to make approximate equality a requirement admitting of no exceptions. Here again, we can avoid this difficulty if the standard definition of approximate equality is a prima facie requirement that can be overridden when it conflicts with a weightier, more favourable balance of benefits over risks. Since we aim to develop superior new treatments, its application by IRB members is not intended to exclude trials indicating that a nonvalidated treatment poses greater potential benefit with little or no additional risk over its standard comparator.

Once again, we can question whether we are assuming too much in speaking of a reliable methodology for determining a risk-benefit ratio that can be expressed in quantitative terms. While the term 'risk-benefit ratio' is prominent in evidence-based medical literature, Ernst and Resch found that, circa 1996, none of the 420 studies which they found to use the term (1986 to June 1994) actually provided a definition: 'Everyone seemed to take a definition for granted.' Nor could they find formulae or instructions for arriving at a ratio 'even though all one seems to need is the benefit, which is divided by the risk' (Ernst and Resch, 1996, p1203). Thus we might take the sum, level or degree of benefit, express it as a number and divide it by another number describing the sum, level or degree of risk. According to Ernst and Resch, this notion is not only 'simplistic' but presents a host of conceptual and methodological difficulties for risk assessment. Benefits might be quantified from the results of clinical trials but:

> risk matters at a more qualitative level: a few severe cases of adverse reactions can already be enough, a formal quantitative statistical significance is not necessarily required. Hence RBR [Risk Benefit Ratio] would, in most cases, reflect a mathematical impossibility: a fraction of a qualitative over a quantitative variable. (Ernst and Resch, 1996, p1203)

They claim that the RBR equation 'explodes with complexity' if we start comparing the RBR of one therapy to that of another (Ernst and Resch, 1996, p1204).

It seems that a risk-benefit ratio is at least as much of a qualitative as it is a quantitative determination. According to the US Belmont Report, to speak of risks and benefits of biomedical research as being 'balanced' and presenting 'a favorable ratio' is to speak metaphorically. Precise judgements will be difficult and exceptional. Only rarely will 'quantitative techniques be available for the scrutiny of research protocols' (National Commission for the Protection of Human Subjects of Biomedical and Behavioral Research, 1979, p37). Even so, the notion of a nonarbitrary, systematic analysis of risks and benefits should be emulated. Physician-investigators and IRBs should distinguish 'the nature, probability, and magnitude of risk...with as much clarity as possible'. They should also have an 'explicit' method of ascertaining risks (National Commission for the Protection of Human Subjects of Biomedical and Behavioral Research, 1979, p37).

More recently, Schosser claims that the German approach to evaluating the therapeutic risks of drugs 'requires balancing the sum of risks versus the sum of benefits in a given indication' (Schosser, 2002, p204; see also *German Drug Law*, 1998). This balancing involves consideration of four basic parameters: the incidence of desired versus adverse effects and the severity of the condition under study versus the severity of adverse reactions. Statistical incidence aside, the words 'desired,' 'adverse' and 'severity' are qualitative terms. Schlosser writes:

> It is clear that the general formula (incidence of damage versus magnitude of damage) is not applicable to risk/benefit evaluation of drugs in a straightforward manner. Instead, medical judgement and consensus are necessary. (Schosser, 2002, p204)

Indeed, the evaluation of acceptable therapeutic risk might be as inherently imprecise and as multifaceted as the concept of clinical equipoise. It is certainly not a task for which the algorithm rules supreme. I want now to explore some qualitative dimensions of risk assessment by discussing the normative role of value judgements.

Value Frameworks and Acceptable Therapeutic Risk

Given the second type of markedly greater risk-benefit trial, on what basis could we assume that additional therapeutic risk is acceptable as long as there are greater countervailing benefits? Input from the patient population with the condition under study is not required before an IRB can confirm that A and B are in clinical equipoise and the pre-trial evidence supporting B has to be interpreted. At this stage of evaluation, determinations of acceptable therapeutic risk have as their basis the values of those members of the expert clinical community who endorse B and the IRB members who agree with them. The therapeutic risks of B are justified as if B were available in clinical practice: 'In other words, there is no limit to the risk that may be posed by such [therapeutic] procedures as long as they are reasonable in relation to potential benefits' (Weijer, 2000, p350). A and B are thus favourably 'comparable' (Weijer, 2000, p358) because they both fall within legal criteria for a standard of care.

This stage is unavoidably normative. Since it 'involves appeal to a norm or standard of acceptability, it is not value-free' (Brunk et al, 1991, p4). A determination that A and B are in clinical equipoise reflects a two-stage process. The first stage involves risk assessment, or the estimation that measures the magnitude of a potential harm and the probability of its occurrence. Quantitative methodologies can be used here (cf Brunk et al, 1991, note 6, p4). Kristin Schrader-Frechette's argument that the quantitative risk assessment of hazardous substances is laden with value judgements in the face of uncertainty can be applied to risk assessments of novel pharmaceutical treatments. 'Assessors must make value judgements about which data to collect; how to simplify myriad facts into a workable model; how to extrapolate because of unknowns', and how to choose the statistical tests, sample sizes and any other criteria that will be used (Schrader-Frechette, 1991, p57).

The second stage involves risk evaluation, or a normative determination of the risk's acceptability. With respect to clinical trials, it can involve setting standards to provide for the safety of research subjects and the level of care and observation they will receive during the course of the study. Do we factor in the risk of physician-investigator error? If so, then by how much? Should the IRB assessors expect that the physician-investigators will always take every effective precaution to manage the risks to subjects of adverse drug reactions? What constitutes a serious adverse reaction (cf Brunk et al, 1991, pp4, 28–29; Waring and Lemmens, 2005, pp159–161, 162–163)? By what standards do we measure the magnitude of a harm in terms of different qualities and degrees (e.g. pain, disability)? These are not questions of pure fact. They oscillate between facts and values (Kasperson, 1992, p163). Nor is the process by which they are answered exclusively descriptive. It is also prescriptive because the risk assessor's value framework will contribute to the framing of the risk assessment (Waring and Lemmens, 2005, p163). Values can thus inform both the risk assessment and the risk evaluation stages in the application of clinical equipoise.

We can appreciate the role of values here by thinking of risk as a Janus-faced term. The analysis of Brunk, Haworth and Lee is instructive. One face of risk is that of the gambler, the other is that of the worrier. Consequently, when faced with the question 'Is the risk acceptable?', the persons who must answer it have to decide whether they ought to approach the proposed trial as persons who are risk-friendly or as persons who are risk-cautious (cf Brunk et al, 1991, p141). A risk-friendly perspective can reflect a value framework that prescribes the importance of certain biomedical technologies or the type of benefits that should be realized in the healthcare system. These values can influence risk evaluations.

They may lead researchers and IRB members to conclude that it is reasonable to assume considerable risks in an attempt to realize greater benefits that might be lost if the study did not proceed (cf Brunk et al, 1991, p141). This perspective has the potential to be too research-friendly.

Thus the values of the IRB members and those members of the expert clinical community who endorse B can lead them to conclude that a markedly greater risk-benefit trial is a good gamble. The prospect of benefits to be gained can be a decisive reason for accepting the risks (Brunk et al, 1991, pp141, 144). These values are not unique to clinicians and IRB members. Given a risk-friendly perspective, some prospective research subjects might choose to run greater risks in what they consider to be a sensible trade-off for even greater potential benefits.

Persons who take a risk-cautious perspective can see the matter differently. A risk-cautious perspective can reflect a value framework that prescribes being on the *qui vive*, or being guarded or prudent about adding to one's risk load. Risk caution does not reflect a commitment 'to assume considerable risks in order to realize benefits that would otherwise be lost' (Brunk et al, 1991, p141). Put another way, risk caution does not reflect a bias in favour of conducting research that characterizes 'the greater risk as the loss of opportunity to realize potential benefit if the study does not proceed' (Waring and Lemmens, 2005, p165).

Risk-cautious persons would not regard a preponderance of potential benefits as rendering otiose the questions 'Are the benefits worth the risks?' and 'Are the risks acceptable despite the greater benefits?' It would be mistaken to assume that the only rational decision a prospective research subject can make is to increase one's risk load in the pursuit of greater benefit. A determination that the risk-benefit ratios are equal does not mean that the respective sums of the risks are equal. Differences in the respective sums of risks might be very significant in practical terms, especially if you are a research subject who might bear them. Given a risk-cautious value framework, greater therapeutic risks might be rejected by prospective research subjects because the additional risks exceed their 'tolerance limit' even when offset by potential benefit (cf Brunk et al, 1991, p145). There would be nothing irrational about that decision. A preponderance of benefits may not be enough by itself to justify additional risk even if the ratios are approximately equal.

The fact that a minority of physicians in the expert clinical community find the therapeutic risks of B initially acceptable says nothing about whether patients would concur with that determination. Nor should it, since clinical equipoise is an ethical basis on which physicians can offer patients the option of trial participation without breaching standards of care. This is not an unreasonable basis on which to determine a conception of acceptable therapeutic risk that prospective research subjects can accept or reject. In the case of the second type of markedly greater risk-benefit trial, giving subjects the option of voting with their feet would require informing them that if they are randomized to B they will be adding to their therapeutic risk load regardless of greater potential benefit. This means informing them that demarcated research risks will not be the only additional risks of trial participation.

A RISK-CAUTIOUS PERSPECTIVE FOR IRB MEMBERS

Clinical equipoise relies on the notion that the good conscience and competent judgement of IRB members, many of whom are physician-researchers, is the best assurance that reasonable qualitative evaluations of acceptable risk will be made. Historically, the good conscience of the physician-investigator who conducts the research has not afforded adequate protection to the welfare of research subjects. With the pervasive and growing influence of corporate funding, we cannot assume that IRB members are immune to the biases of private-interest science. Private-interest science asks how knowledge can generate a profitable product or defend a corporate client regardless of whether it has social benefits and regardless of whether the product is distributed fairly. It turns the risks of publicly funded research into private wealth (Krimsky, 2002, p180). One recent study has shown that some IRB members are involved in financial conflicts of interest with the corporate sponsors of the proposed research (Campbell et al, 2006). As such, they can have a 'sensitivity to benefits achievable' only if the research proceeds. This could establish 'a mind-set biased in favour of such deployment' (Brunk et al, 1991, p143). In the risk environment of increasingly commercialized, private interest science, researchers' and IRB members' interests can also reflect a shift in values towards profit and economic growth (cf Brunk et al, 1991, p133).

Wynne made a point in the early 1990s about risk assessment in the field of toxic wastes that can be applied to the oversight of biomedical research and the protection of human subjects. People's concerns are increasingly institutional, hence the concern that some decision-makers might be unduly influenced by the financial interests of the biotech and pharmaceutical industries and be overly committed to the 'endless future expansion' of their products. A risk-cautious approach might best reflect an independent and primary commitment to protecting human subjects. Research subject advocacy groups that take a cautious approach to risk are concerned that the controlling authorities (e.g. IRBs) are not independent of the research promoters (cf Wynne, 1992, p290; see also Waring and Lemmens, 2005). Consider the *Alliance for Human Research Protection*, a US network of lay and professional persons with a mandate to advance ethical research practice, to protect the rights of subjects and to minimize the risks of trial participation (see AHRP http://www.ahrp.org/cms/content/view/18/87, date accessed 16 September 2008). Members argue that the 'explosion' of biomedical research over the past decade has not been accompanied by an effective oversight and enforcement system to protect research subjects. Conflict of interest in commercially funded research and the incomplete disclosure of risks are two systemic issues this group addresses (Waring and Lemmens, 2005, p179).

It does not take much for IRBs to establish that a disagreement exists, or may soon exist, among members of the expert community as to the evidence on the relative merits of A and B. Consequently, the amenability of clinical equipoise to the research enterprise might be seen as favouring the approval of protocols. But we should not assume that all IRB members would object to being risk-cautious. A risk-cautious value-framework would favour a review of risk assessments by those with no financial or competing interest in the research. It would appreciate the potential importance of biomedical research without assuming that proposed studies are prima facie benign and worth running considerable risks in order to realize benefits that might otherwise be lost. It would raise questions that reflect a predominant concern for the risks to research subjects and the independence of science (Waring and Lemmens, 2005, p177).

Clinical equipoise can accommodate both 'risk-friendly' and 'risk-cautious' perspectives. While I am not convinced that we can say at this point whether the application of clinical equipoise has been too risk- and research-friendly, I do think we should raise the question. As noted above, there are concerns about research-friendly conflicts of interest between sponsoring companies and IRB members. Financial relationships between IRB members and industry have been documented and members have sometimes reviewed protocols sponsored by companies with which they had a financial relationship (Campbell et al, 2006; see also Waring and Lemmens, 2005, pp169–174). These conflicts arguably compromise the honest professional disagreement about the relative merits of A and B that clinical equipoise requires. Although clinical equipoise is no substitute for the rigorous enforcement of a conflict of interest policy, we may want to pay closer attention to how IRBs are using this inherently imprecise concept. After 20 years of focus on how clinical equipoise should be defined, we have little empirical knowledge of how it is actually translated into the practice of research ethics review. Systemic studies on its application could give us a better sense of how risk-friendly or risk-cautious that translation has been.

Conclusions

The application of clinical equipoise will not always limit the therapeutic risks of nonvalidated treatments to being close to their standard practice comparators. Clinical equipoise is supposed to accommodate the second type of markedly greater risk-benefit trial. In those trials, subjects randomized to B will add significantly to the therapeutic risk load they carry as patients taking A for the condition under study. Those greater therapeutic risks add to the risk load of trial participation. Consequently, demarcated research risks are not always the only additional risks of trial participation. These trials should not be eligible for expedited review by IRBs.

If the standard definition of approximate equality is applied as an absolute requirement that admits of no exceptions, then it will exclude the second type of markedly greater risk-benefit trial from the purview of clinical equipoise when applied to the respective risk sums of A and B. When applied as an absolute requirement to the respective risk-benefit ratios of A and B, it will exclude some trials that pose greater potential benefits from B over A. If approximate equality is applied as a prima facie requirement of acceptable therapeutic risk, then it will include both types of markedly greater risk-benefit trial under clinical equipoise.

The values of the physician-investigators who propose a clinical trial and the IRB members who review it will be a significant influence on the determination of acceptable therapeutic risk. Their values can reflect risk-friendly or risk-cautious perspectives. The latter perspective might best reflect a primary commitment to protecting the welfare of human research subjects.[9]

REFERENCES

Brunk, C., Haworth, L. and Lee, B. (1991) *Value Assumptions in Risk Assessment: A Case Study of the Alachlor Controversy*, Wilfred Laurier University Press, Waterloo Ontario

Campbell, E. G., Weissman, J. S., Vogeli, C. and Clarridge, B. R. (2006) 'Financial relationships between institutional review board members and industry', *New England Journal of Medicine*, vol 355, pp2321–2329

Emanuel, E., Crouch, R., Arras, J., Moreno, J. and Grady, C. (2003) 'Informed consent in research', in E. Emanuel, R. Crouch, J. Arras, J. Moreno and C. Grady (eds) *Ethical and Regulatory Aspects of Clinical Research: Readings and Commentary*, Johns Hopkins University Press, Baltimore and London, pp189–195

Ernst, E. and Resch, K. L. (1996) 'Risk-benefit ratio or risk-benefit nonsense?', *Journal of Clinical Epidemiology*, vol 49, pp1203–1204

Foster, K. R., Vecchia, P. and Repacholi, M. H. (2000) 'Science and the precautionary principle', *Science*, vol 288, p979

Freedman, B. (1987) 'Equipoise and the ethics of clinical research', *New England Journal of Medicine*, vol 317, pp141–145

Freedman, B. and Weijer, C. (1992) 'Demarcating research and treatment interventions: a case illustration', *IRB*: *A Review of Human Subjects Research*, vol 14, pp5–8

Freedman, B., Fuks, A. and Weijer, C. (1992) 'Demarcating research and treatment: a systematic approach for the analysis of the ethics of clinical research', *Clinical Research*, vol 40, pp653–660

Freedman, B., Cranley Glass, K. and Weijer, C. (1996) 'Placebo orthodoxy in clinical research II: ethical, legal, and regulatory myths', *Journal of Law, Medicine and Ethics*, vol 24, pp252–259

Freudenburg, W. R. (1992) 'Heuristics, biases, and the not-so-general publics: expertise and error in the assessment of risks', in S. Krimsky and D. Golding (eds) *Social Theories of Risk*, Praeger, Westport, CT, pp229–250

Fried, C. (1974) *Medical Experimentation: Personal Integrity and Social Policy*, North Holland Publishing, Amsterdam

Furrow, B., Greaney, T., Johnson, S., Jost, T. and Schwartz, R. (2000) *Health Law*, 3rd edn, West Group Publishing, St. Paul, MN

German Drug Law: In the version of the law reform of the drug law of 24 August 1976 (Federal Law Gazette 1, pp2445, 2448); last amended by article 1 of the eighth law amending the law of 7 September 1998 (Federal Law Gazette 1, p2649) = Arzneimittelgesetz. With the Ordinance of the transition of EC law: of 18 December 1990 (Federal Law Gazette 1, p2915). Aulendorf, Editio-Canter-Verlag, 1999

Kasperson, R. E. (1992) 'The social amplification of risk', in S. Krimsky and D. Golding (eds) *Social Theories of Risk*, Praeger, Westport CT, pp153–178

Kopelman, L. (1995) 'Research methodology II. Clinical trials', in S. Post (ed.) *Encyclopedia of Bioethics*, 3rd edn, Thomson-Gale, New York, pp2334–2342

Kopelman, L. (2004) 'Minimal risk as an international ethical standard', *Journal of Medicine and Philosophy*, vol 29, pp351–378

Krimsky, S. (2003) *Science in the Private Interest: Has the Lure of Profits Corrupted Biomedical Research?*, Rowman and Littlefield, Lanham, MD

Levine, R. (1986) *Ethics and Regulation of Clinical Research*, 2nd edn, Urban and Schwartzberg, Baltimore

Lilford, R. (2003) 'Ethics of clinical trials from a Bayesian and decision analytic perspective: whose equipoise is it anyway?', *British Medical Journal*, vol 326, pp980–981

Medical Research Council of Canada, Natural Sciences and Engineering Council of Canada & Social Sciences and Humanities Research Council (2005) *Tri-Council Policy*

Statement: Ethical Conduct for Research Involving Humans, Public Works and Government Services of Canada, Ottawa

Miller, P. and Weijer, C. (2000) 'Moral solutions in assessing research risk', *IRB: A Review of Human Subjects Research,* vol 22, pp6–10

Miller, P. and Weijer, C. (2003) 'Rehabilitating equipoise', *Kennedy Institute of Ethics Journal,* vol 13, pp93–118

National Bioethics Advisory Commission (NBAC) (2001) *Ethical and Policy Issues in Research Involving Human Participants,* NBAC, Bethesda Maryland

National Commission for the Protection of Human Subjects of Biomedical and Behavioral Research (1979) 'The Belmont Report: Ethical Principles and Guidelines for the Protection of Human Subjects of Research', in E. Emanuel, R. Crouch, J. Arras, J. Moreno and C. Grady (eds) *Ethical and Regulatory Aspects of Clinical Research: Readings and Commentary*, Johns Hopkins University Press, Baltimore and London, pp33–38

Picard, E. and Robertson, G. B. (1996) *Legal Liability of Doctors and Hospitals in Canada,* 3rd edn, Carswell, Toronto

Schosser, R. (2002) 'Risk/benefit evaluations of drugs: the role of the pharmaceutical industry in Germany', *European Surgical Research*, vol 34, pp203–207

Schrader-Frechette, K. (1991) *Risk and Rationality: Philosophical Foundations for Populist Reforms*, University of California Press, Berkeley

US Department of Health and Human Services, National Institutes of Health, and Office for Human Research Protections (2001) 'The Common Rule, Title 45 (Public Welfare), Code of Federal Regulations, Part 46 (Protection of Human Subjects), Subpart A', in E. Emanuel, R. Crouch, J. Arras, J. Moreno and C. Grady (eds) (2003) *Ethical and Regulatory Aspects of Clinical Research: Readings and Commentary*, Johns Hopkins University Press, Baltimore and London, pp39–48

Waring, D. and Lemmens, T. (2005) 'Integrating values in risk analysis of biomedical research: the case for regulatory and law reform', in Law Commission of Canada (ed.) *Law and Risk*, University of British Columbia Press, Vancouver and Toronto, pp156–199

Weijer, C. (1999) 'Thinking clearly about research risk: implications of the work of Benjamin Freedman', *IRB: A Review of Human Subjects Research,* vol 21, pp1–5

Weijer, C. (2000) 'The ethical analysis of risk', *Journal of Law, Medicine & Ethics,* vol 28, pp344–361

Weijer, C. and Miller, P. (2004) 'When are research risks reasonable in relation to anticipated benefits?', *Nature Medicine,* vol 10, pp570–573

Wynne, B. (1992) 'Risk and social learning: Reification to engagement', in S. Krimsky and D. Golding (eds) *Social Theories of Risk*, Praeger Publishers, Westport CT, pp275–300

NOTES

1 I define risk as the possibility that a harm will befall a patient or research subject. It involves estimations of both the probability of that occurrence and the magnitude of the harm.

2 See http://whatis.techtarget.com/definition/ø,,sid9_gci822424.øø.html. Date accessed 16 September 2008.

3 Clinical equipoise does not 'explain fully the fiduciary duties of individual physicians to particular patients' once they have been 'identified … asked for participation, and enrolled in a trial'. These duties relate to Charles Fried's concept of equipoise (Fried,

1974). His concept stipulates that '*a physician* [my italics] may offer trial enrollment to her patient' only when she is 'genuinely uncertain as to the preferred treatment' (Miller and Weijer, 2003, pp93, 113–114). If the individual physician is not uncertain, i.e. if she is convinced that B is inferior given the therapeutic needs of her patients, then she may refuse to ask them to participate in a trial even though an IRB has verified clinical equipoise and approved the study. Miller and Weijer lucidly parse the relationship between clinical equipoise and the fiduciary duties that individual physicians have to patients in their innovative paper 'Rehabilitating Equipoise'.

4 Perhaps the null hypothesis is relevant to approximate equality. IRB members will confirm clinical equipoise once they are satisfied that a sufficient number of medical experts accept, or would accept, the scientific convention of assuming A and B to be therapeutically equivalent unless a trial affords us enough evidence that one is superior. It is one thing to assume equivalence as a standard procedure when we test for statistical significance. It would be quite another to use this methodological assumption alone to claim that the therapeutic indices of A and B are approximately equal. The investigator is supposed to assume the null hypothesis even if the pre-trial evidence indicates greater risks and potential benefits of B over A. Any determinations of approximate equality are based on this pre-trial evidence. When that evidence indicates that the risks and potential benefits of B are considerably greater than A, then formulating the null hypothesis is just good research procedure. It is not a substitute for a risk assessment. We can say that there is genuine uncertainty about which is the best treatment and that A and B are both suitable for carefully selected research subjects. But in the markedly greater risk-benefit cases, we could not use the scientific rationale for starting a trial to say that a subject 'might participate at no personal cost' (cf Lilford, 2003, p980). It would be research-friendly indeed to claim that the conventions of good scientific procedure are all we need to assess the acceptability of additional therapeutic risk.

5 Some would argue that this is assuming too much since studies have shown that 'the parties to a risk debate can assess the same data with widely divergent results' (Waring and Lemmens, 2005, pp160–161). This is a problem that allegedly affects risk assessment in general. It would not be unique to biomedical research and the application of clinical equipoise. This problem is thought to be especially relevant to the risk assessment of environmental pollutants (Foster et al, 2000, p979; see also Freudenburg, 1992, p236). It might be less relevant to biomedical research if extensive toxicological and epidemiological data on health risks are available to IRB members. For a more detailed analysis of how this problem might apply to biomedical research, see Waring and Lemmens (2005, pp161–163).

6 I owe this point to Dr Joel Lexchin.

7 Numerous examples of such novel antipsychotics come to mind. Risperidone was chemically unrelated to any other available antipsychotic when the US Food and Drug Administration (FDA) approved it for use in 1993. See http://www.tutorgig.com/ed/Risperidone (date accessed 16 September 2008). Aripiprazole is also chemically different from other atypical antipsychotics and is believed to have unique pharmacological actions that distinguish it from other antipsychotics like clozapine and risperidone. It received FDA approval in 2002. See www.bipolarchild.com/Newsletters/0302.html (date accessed 16 September 2008). Another novel antipsychotic is bifiprunox mesilate which is currently under development as a treatment for schizophrenia and possibly for bipolar disorder. Regulatory submission for FDA approval was made in August 2007. The FDA expressed concerns about the efficacy and safety of bifiprunox and rejected the submission. See http://www.drugdevelopment-technology.com/projects/bifeprunox/ (date accessed 16 September 2008).

8 Clozapine comes closest to the hypothetical greater risk-benefit case that I want to consider. It was a novel antipsychotic circa 1989 when the FDA approved its exclusive use for treatment-resistant schizophrenia. It was thought to pose greater potential benefits in that it was indicated for the treatment of severely ill schizophrenic patients who failed to respond adequately to other drugs. Like other antipsychotics, it posed risks of serious side effects like tardive dyskinesia and neuroleptic malignant syndrome. But unlike other antipsychotics, it also posed a risk of agranulocytosis, a potentially life-threatening reaction where the body's bone marrow does not produce enough white blood cells. See http://www.fda.gov./cder/drug/infopage/antipsychotics/default.htm (date accessed 16 September 2008).

9 Thanks to Sabine Roeser and Lotte Asveld, Joel Lexchin in the Faculty of Health at York University and Adam Rawlings, PhD candidate in the Philosophy Department at York University for their helpful comments on earlier drafts. Special thanks to Dorrit Kane for the use of her study in San Miguel de Allende.

6 Acceptable Risk to Future Generations

Marc D. Davidson

Introduction

In 1994, the Scientific Council for Government Policy, one of the Dutch government's key advisory councils, dropped a bomb on the public debate on sustainable development in the Netherlands. Until then, the notion of 'environmental utilization space' (Siebert, 1982) had been pivotal in the customary elaboration of sustainable development policy. This notion implicitly assumed that it is scientifically feasible to determine the limits to the burden that may be imposed upon the environment. In other words, scientists were deemed able to determine the carrying capacity of the earth and a 'safe zone' for human activities, giving policy-makers an unequivocal and objective precept by which to steer their environmental policy. In its report *Sustained Risks: a Lasting Phenomenon* (WRR, 1994), the Scientific Council argued, however, that sustainable development hinges on dealing with uncertain risks and therefore requires inherently value-driven and hence political choices that cannot be made by scientists. At the core of the Council's argument was the Cultural Theory of risk (see, for example, Douglas and Wildavsky, 1982; Schwartz and Thompson, 1990), which holds that, faced with incomplete and often contradictory information, people perceive the world through a cultural filter that influences the way issues are defined and preferences as to how they should be handled. Since, in this view, no one 'risk filter' is superior to others, completely opposing perspectives on courses of action may be equally worthy of the predicate 'sustainable'. In order to elaborate the concept of sustainability as a genuinely operative policy concept, the Scientific Council therefore recommended that normative choices in relation to identified risks and uncertainties be rendered explicit. In more recent reports, the Scientific Council has reiterated its views and recommendations (WRR, 1999, 2002, 2006).

The publication of *Sustained Risk* did not lead to a public debate about these normative choices, however. Instead, the result has been that much weaker interpretations of sustainable development have come to dominate the Dutch public debate and Dutch policy-making more than before. This move towards less stringent long-term environmental policy is hardly a surprise, though. After all, sustainable development may well require present generations to give up long-cherished patterns of consumption and production, while the benefits are reaped first and foremost by future generations. Due to the inertia of the climate system, for example, fossil fuel consumption has to be reduced today to prevent impacts of climate change decades to centuries from now. If a stringent environmental policy could not be argued on the basis of objective, scientific facts, why not then opt for a less stringent and consequently less costly policy? The Scientific Council's full argument in fact allows such reasoning. The Council's argument has been unnecessarily relativistic, however. Although the idea of an objective 'environmental utilization space' to be determined by scientists has justifiably been criticized, the relativism regarding the concept of sustainable development on the basis of Cultural Theory has gone too far – not because of flaws in Cultural Theory as such (see, for example, Boholm, 1996; Sjöberg, 1997), but because, so I believe, concepts such as sustainable development and intergenerational justice are not shaped in a moral vacuum. The Scientific Council has observed, correctly, that dealing with uncertain risk requires value-laden choices. However, society has already adopted certain general standards of conduct, as expressed in tort law, for instance, as to how present generations should handle *contemporary* uncertain risks. The aim of intergenerational justice, which is encompassed in the notion of sustainable development, would require future generations to be treated as moral equals. This means that any interpretation of how to handle uncertain risks to future generations is bound by the general standards of conduct as to how present generations handle contemporary uncertain risks. In other words, attitudes towards the handling of risk to others ('risk filters') cannot be chosen simply to suit one's own interests. The purpose of the present chapter is to support this claim.

Of course, this chapter will draw heavily on a heroic assumption: the idea that the handling of risk to future generations is a matter of justice in the first place. This idea is by no means uncontroversial. In moral philosophy a heated debate about intergenerational justice has been going on for at least three decades now and it has certainly not yet been brought to a conclusion (for an overview of this debate see, for example, de-Shalit, 1995; Visser't Hooft, 1999). Some moral philosophers have argued, for example, that there is no meaningful sense in which present generations can be held to harm future generations (see, for example, Parfit, 1984) or that people cannot have rights if they cannot claim them (see, for example, De George, 1979). I wish neither to defend such positions nor refute them. While ethicists continue to debate our moral relation to posterity, society has already declared itself in favour of taking the interests of future generations into account. For example, the international community has expressed its willingness to take intergenerational justice seriously by accepting the goal of sustainable development as a cornerstone of governmental policy (WCED, 1987; UNCED, 1992; UNESCO, 1997). It is therefore an issue of both theoretical and political importance how sustainable development and the concept of acceptable risk to future generations are to be interpreted *if* future generations were to be included under the umbrella of justice.

This chapter is organized as follows. Section two aims to show that giving shape to intergenerational justice revolves around dealing with risk and uncertainty. In section three, I discuss various perspectives on how a society is to deal with risks to others. In section four, it is argued that intergenerational justice requires handling risks to future generations according to the general standard of conduct that present generations apply when it comes to handling risks to other contemporaries. Section five seeks to make plausible that this general standard of conduct can indeed be meaningfully applied in the intergenerational context. The chapter closes, in section six, with some conclusions.

INTERGENERATIONAL JUSTICE, RISK AND UNCERTAINTY

As mentioned in the introduction, I endorse the point of view expressed by the Dutch Scientific Council for Government Policy that there are no such things as a clear-cut environmental utilization space, carrying capacity of the planetary ecosystem or no-effect levels of pollution which can be determined by natural scientists alone. When considering intergenerational justice, environmentalists and moral philosophers have nevertheless generally assumed such objective limits, often giving the impression that the answer to the question of how to treat future generations is relatively straightforward once it has been decided that we do have moral obligations to future generations or that future generations hold rights against us. Intergenerational justice would then simply mean staying within the carrying capacity of the earth, for to exceed that capacity would harm future generations, while remaining within it would not. It would then simply be up to natural scientists to determine the carrying capacity of the planetary ecosystem for the emission of gases contributing to global warming, acidification and nitrification of the soil, for fisheries, etc.

However, the notion of a clear-cut carrying capacity to be determined by natural scientists alone is an illusion. In the first place, for most human interventions in the planetary ecosystem there is no clear-cut boundary between the level of present-generation activities that harms future generations and the level that does not. For example, the risks to future generations posed by global warming are a continuous – though not necessarily smooth or monotonic – function of the level of greenhouse gas emissions by present generations. Since zero emissions can never be achieved, neither can zero risks. However stringent environmental policy may be, risks will always remain.[1]

Second, the further ecological risks are reduced, the greater the social costs of risk reduction and mitigation will become. These costs are borne not only by present generations: through their introduction into the economy, they also imply a risk for future generations. After all, our obligations to future generations include the obligation to leave behind not only a healthy environment but also a healthy economy and society, these also being prerequisites for a good life. Economic cost-benefit analysis, however rudimentary, is therefore a useful tool for establishing the point at which risk reduction efforts should be halted. The overall risks implied by additional policy measures must be weighed up against those of a policy in which no further measures are implemented (Wiener, 1995).

Third, science can map future risks to a limited extent only. Much will always remain uncertain, and consequently no quantitative probabilities can be assigned to conceivable future states. In some cases scientists may arrive at (widely) different conclusions or, faced with inadequate information, make no judgement at all. The available information is often no more than qualitative. Risk management, and the required rudimentary weighing of cost and benefits described earlier, therefore depends on the translation of such qualitative information into quantitative estimates on the basis of subjective estimates of ecological and economic resilience, future technological developments and the preferences of future generations.

In short, once we have opted to include future generations under the umbrella of justice, many ethical questions still remain. What decision rules are we to adopt for situations of long-term risk? How are we to treat uncertainty regarding future developments, concerning technological progress, for example? How much may we anticipate? Et cetera.

Conflicting moral positions on risk management

The idea that giving shape to intergenerational justice requires dealing with *risk* has led many to relativism: the idea that any interpretation of intergenerational justice can be argued for. After all, so it has been argued, people differ widely in their attitudes towards the handling of risk. In particular, proponents of Cultural Theory claim that attitudes towards risk management are, in the end, culturally determined (see, for example, Holling, 1979, 1986; Douglas and Wildavsky, 1982; Schwarz and Thompson, 1990; Thompson et al, 1990; Adams, 1995). Faced with incomplete and often contradictory information, people are deemed to perceive the world through a cultural 'filter', which influences the way issues are defined and preferences as to how they should be handled. Since attitudes towards risk management are thus culturally determined, a diversity of interpretations of intergenerational justice will always remain, a diversity which cannot converge through scientific discussion.

Although I shall challenge this relativism in the context of intergenerational justice, as Cultural Theory is gaining ground in the debate on how to manage long-term risks, I will first give a brief description of the four human ideotypes distinguished in that theory (see also Mamadouh, 1999). Along the way I will discuss the various perspectives on the handling of risk that have been adopted in ethical debates, as these dovetail nicely with Cultural Theory. It is noteworthy that while there is an extensive literature dealing with the question of how to take decisions in situations of risk to oneself, that is, how to make *rational* choices in the context of uncertainty (see, for example, Von Neumann and Morgenstern, 1944; Resnik, 1987), in comparison the literature on the moral issue of acting in the face of (uncertain) risks to *others* is remarkably limited.

The first ideal type distinguished in Cultural Theory is the *individualist*, who tends to prefer a laissez-faire lifestyle, favouring few controls beyond those required to establish and maintain property rights and control criminal behaviour. The autonomy of the individual is the highest political and social good.

Fairness consists of equality of opportunity. Blame is put on personal failure (or lack of competition). Corresponding to this viewpoint is the myth[2] of nature as benign and robust; it can suffer experimentation, trial and error. There are high expectations that human creativity and future technological developments will solve any problems encountered along the way (see, for an exponent of this view, Simon, 1996). Strongly related to the individualist viewpoint is the moral position of libertarianism. Libertarians advocate the maximum freedom of individual action compatible with equal freedom for all. Applied to risks, this point of departure leads to two completely opposing views – a 'moral split', as it were: on the one hand, that no risk at all may be imposed on others without their consent, since this would violate the individual entitlement to property and the right to bodily integrity (see Nozick, 1974; Magnus, 1983); on the other hand, that the burden of proof is always on those who wish to curtail liberty, to interfere. In environmental affairs this so-called 'presumption principle for liberty' means that the burden lies with those who claim that some course of action is causing environmental damage: 'more research is needed before curtailment of our action is justified' (O'Neill, 1993).

The second ideal type is the *egalitarian*, who fights against the exploitation of some groups by others and favours the levelling of the social pyramid. Fairness is equated with equality of result. Blame is put on the 'system'. Corresponding to this viewpoint is the myth of nature as ephemeral or fragile. Confidence in technology as a means of solving (future) problems is low. Related to risk management from the egalitarian viewpoint is the political liberalism of John Rawls. In Rawls' theory, decision-making under conditions of uncertainty plays a key role. To design a just society, Rawls advocates application of a so-called maximin principle: 'The maximin rule tells us to rank alternatives by their worst possible outcomes: we are to adopt the alternative the worst outcome of which is superior to the worst outcomes of the others' (Rawls, 1972, p153; see also Rawls, 1974; Shrader-Frechette, 1991). Rawls' maximin principle follows primarily from the egalitarian myth of society. Another political principle in the egalitarian view is the 'precautionary principle', following primarily from the myth of nature as ephemeral or fragile. Although many definitions of the precautionary principle exist, it boils down roughly to the principle *in dubio pro natura.* [In case of doubt regarding the possibility of damage to the environment, any decision must favour the protection of the environment.]

The third ideal type is the *hierarchist.* Corresponding to this viewpoint is the myth of nature as perverse/tolerant: although there is a safe zone, things will go wrong if one goes too far. This myth therefore justifies the power given to experts, the people able to evaluate the safety zone. Hierarchists consider the whole more important than the parts, the collective more important than the individual. Fairness consists of equality before the law. Blame is put on deviants who do not endorse the established procedures. The moral theory that might be related to the hierarchist point of view is utilitarianism. Utilitarians advocate a Bayesian strategy, involving optimization of expected aggregate social utility on the basis of subjective probabilities (Harsanyi, 1975, 1977, 1978). In the hierarchist point of view, these subjective probabilities should be based on expert judgement.

The last ideal type is the *fatalist*. Fatalists are generally apathetic about how society is structured, believing it to be inevitable that powerful groups will exploit weaker groups. Fairness is not to be found on this earth. Blame is put on fate (bad luck). Corresponding to this viewpoint is the myth of nature as capricious. It is a lottery, one does not know what to expect, one cannot learn from experience.

Of course, these ideal types are caricatures and the particular choices made in Cultural Theory have been challenged. Perhaps attitudes towards risk can be classified according to other ideotypes as well. It is not my aim here to champion Cultural Theory, like Wildavsky and Dake (1990, p42), for whom Cultural Theory is able to 'predict and explain what kind of people will perceive which potential hazards to be how dangerous'. Nevertheless, the ideal types distinguished in Cultural Theory offer a useful tool for understanding the various positions taken in the scientific and social debate about managing risks. For example, they help explain the differences in the probabilities assigned (subjectively) by different experts to future states of affairs (Thompson, 2000; see, for example, the results of a survey conducted by Nordhaus (1994) among experts about their estimates of the effects of global warming).

One conclusion that may be drawn from (theories like) Cultural Theory is that the question of how society ought to deal with risks to others can only be answered in public debate – a debate in which people will necessarily discuss their perception of risks and risk management from different points of view and different conceptual and ethical frameworks. Scientific information may play an important role, but final decisions cannot be made on scientific grounds alone. The situation is similar to the way in which other moral issues such as fair distribution of income are discussed, where no one can 'prove' objectively that the opinion of the other party is unjust. One can examine the pros and cons of the various views, discuss them publicly on the basis of as much (scientific and other) information as possible, and finally decide democratically. The general standard of conduct to emerge as being acceptable for handling risks to others may consequently differ from society to society and from time to time (see Lowi, 1990; Bernstein, 1996).

TREATING FUTURE GENERATIONS AS EQUALS

In the previous section it was argued that the question of how society ought to deal with risks to others can only be answered in the political arena. This conclusion is frequently extended to the case of long-term risks, and the question of how to approach risks to future generations is likewise seen as mainly a political issue. Since 1994 this has been the position of the Dutch Scientific Council for Government Policy, for example (see also Azar and Rodhe, 1997). This conclusion I believe to be wrong, however. The question of what justice implies for a specific group cannot be treated in the same way as the question of what justice implies in general.

What, then, does sustainable development and intergenerational justice imply? Definitions abound, ranging from giving equal weight to present and future utility when maximizing utility (Sidgwick, 1874), to leaving the earth in the same state we encountered it (Routley and Routley, 1978). However diverse the various interpretations of intergenerational justice (see, for example, de-Shalit, 1995), one idea lies at their heart: that future generations should be included in our moral community. To be included in a moral community means to be treated as equals, to be entitled to equal consideration and respect in the organization of society (Dworkin, 1977, 1983, 2000). It is important to note that to treat people as equals is not the same as treating them equally. For example, to treat future generations as equals in a utilitarian calculus means that future utility matters as much as present utility. It does not mean that no correction may be made for a lower marginal value of utility if one has reason to assume that future generations will be wealthier (for the debate about discounting, see Portney and Weyant, 1999).

It may be illuminating to link intergenerational justice to the concept of emancipation. In the past, women and coloured people were not recognized as part of the (white, male) European moral community. Today the right of women to be treated as equals is recognized and slavery has been abolished. All races and sexes are entitled to equal consideration and respect. Intergenerational justice might thus be seen as the next step in an ongoing process of emancipation. What makes the link between intergenerational justice and emancipation illuminating is that emancipation as such does not say anything about *how* people should be treated: it says merely that they should be treated as equals. The important conclusion is that a debate about justice towards a specific group cannot just start from scratch. Once there is a prevailing moral view or general standard of conduct in a society, one cannot abstract away from that view. Treating people as equals means treating them as equals according to the existing general standard of conduct. In the historical case of women's emancipation, the question of how civil rights should in general be shaped was irrelevant. Emancipation implied that women should be treated as equals and obtain the same rights as men, *whatever these rights entailed*. The same consideration holds for the interpretation of intergenerational justice. Intergenerational justice implies that present generations should treat future generations with equal concern and respect, whether that concern and respect be individualistic, egalitarian or hierarchical in nature.[3] In this sense, any plausible theory of intergenerational justice finds itself on the 'egalitarian plateau' (Kymlicka, 1990). This latter term 'egalitarian' should not be confused with the egalitarian myth of society and nature in Cultural Theory. Here, 'egalitarian' denotes a more abstract and fundamental idea of equality in political theory, namely that a government should treat all of its citizens with equal consideration, that each citizen is entitled to equal concern and respect (Dworkin, 1977, 1983, 2000; Kymlicka, 1990). In this sense, every 'valid' cultural filter – individualistic, egalitarian or hierarchic fatalistic – is egalitarian.

The link between this interpretation of intergenerational justice and Cultural Theory is readily made. The general standard of conduct acceptable in a given society is a cultural construct, which may differ from society to society. It is a reflection of the (prevailing) cultural filters in that society. This also means that the substantive content of 'intergenerational justice' may differ from society to society, from culture to culture, and from time to time. In a risk-seeking society, intergenerational justice entails something different than in a risk-averse society. The fact that standards and circumstances may change with time does not complicate equal treatment of future generations. Even though we do not know what moral standards future generations will hold, we can and indeed should still apply present-day social standards to the handling of risks to future generations. The emancipation of women was in no way rendered impossible through ignorance of the rights men would have in the future.

At first sight, this interpretation of intergenerational justice may seem relativistic, for the concept of intergenerational justice may differ from time to time and from society to society. However, this interpretation strongly confines the way in which intergenerational justice can be shaped at any *specific* time in a *specific* society. Given the – culturally determined – general standard of conduct acceptable in a society, intergenerational justice means that the present generations may not apply different standards to future generations, or, in terms of Cultural Theory, put on a different pair of cultural glasses to view long-term risks, when this is favourable for present vested interests.

JUSTICE BETWEEN CONTEMPORARIES

Is it practically feasible in the first place to judge policies towards long-term risks with reference to justice between contemporaries, as currently institutionalized in everyday practice? When it comes to the acceptability of imposing risks on our contemporaries, this general standard of conduct is sufficiently substantial and concrete to be accessible to law (tort law, for example). Of course, there is a theoretical debate between economists and moral philosophers as to how positive law is to be interpreted (see, for example, Coase, 1960; Posner, 1972; Coleman, 1992). This is not to say, however, that there are no limits to that interpretation. Otherwise, positive law could not differ from country to country. The fact that it does could even lead to the conclusion that intergenerational justice, with respect to the handling of long-term risks, will necessarily differ from country to country. Likewise, the rights of women may differ from country to country, while at the same time women and men are treated as equals in each. It may be objected, though, that risks to future generations differ from present risks to such an extent that justice between contemporaries cannot be applied to future generations – because of the incomparable spatial and temporal scale of risks to future generations, for example, or the enormous costs and interests associated with risk reduction, or the major scientific uncertainties surrounding the risks in question (Beck, 1986; Funtowicz and Ravetz, 1991). Furthermore, society is not always consistent in the way it deals with the risks of today. Nonetheless, society does seem to have a general standard of accepted conduct vis-à-vis risks to others that is independent of the kind of risk involved. I am thinking here not of yardsticks like maximum acceptable lifetime risk (one in a million, say), but of written and unwritten general standards of conduct regarding a variety of concrete issues. Let me provide some examples to indicate how general standards of conduct may conflict with approaches currently adopted towards long-term risks.

Anticipating technological development

A typical distinguishing feature of the various attitudes towards risk ('cultural risk filters') is people's attitudes towards technological progress (Schwarz and Thompson, 1990). Whereas the individualist, as distinguished in Cultural Theory, is highly optimistic about the capacity of technological development and innovation to solve future environmental problems, egalitarians are much more pessimistic and cautious. The individualistic point of view, frequently employed in cost-benefit analyses, results in very low estimates of the future costs of damage and mitigation, obtained by extrapolating past technological developments to the future. It is then argued that scarcely any environmental policy is required to mitigate long-term risks, or that mitigation should be deferred to the future (for an example from the climate debate, see Wigley et al, 1996). However, although one could not argue for one objectively 'right' approach to technological progress, it is a matter of fact that in today's society there are strong de facto limits to the degree of anticipation of future technological or scientific developments that is considered appropriate in the case of risk to others. One could hardly imagine someone responsible for infecting another person with HIV or Creutzfeldt-Jacob disease defending themselves by saying: 'The risks were known to me, but the disease only manifests itself several decades after infection. History shows that medical science has found a cure for almost every disease in such a time span.' It is unthinkable that such a defence would convince a judge, even if it were accompanied by a sound cost-benefit analysis. In our culture, then, in the case of risks to others, one's decisions must be based at least on currently available technology or seriously account for the risk that the expected technological developments will not materialize.

Likewise, when we consider the treasurers of public or private organizations such as schools, the general standard of conduct is that he or she should play safe with respect to the investment of saved capital. It is not deemed acceptable for capital to be invested in high-risk activities with potentially high returns, such as the information technology sector. In this context a maximin strategy (investment in low-risk government bonds) is deemed appropriate, rather than a Bayesian strategy of maximizing expected utility (investment in high-risk funds). The general standard of conduct here appears to be that outcomes with a low probability but major negative consequences are to be avoided.

Burden of proof

At the core of Cultural Theory is the idea that people differ in their perception of risk and preferences as to how they should be handled. Long-term environmental problems like climate change provide pivotal examples of situations in which views differ about what is the case and what should be done. Given controversial information, to make a decision we must first weigh up the judgements of the various 'experts' on the basis of their credibility as well as our own attitude towards risk. If we are generally 'rather safe than sorry', we will attach greater importance to information that is unpleasant rather than reassuring. If we are risk seeking, on the other hand, we will attach rather less weight to unpleasant information. Nevertheless, the standards of conduct currently in force in a given society can and do provide considerable leverage for restricting the wide range of potential policy options. What intergenerational justice requires is *consistency* between the attitudes adopted towards the management of intergenerational risk and those reflected and expressed in the handling of contemporary risk.

For example, most commercial products, such as medicinal drugs, must be thoroughly tested before they can be marketed. Although testing products once they are out on the market may be more cost effective from society's point of view, such an approach is deemed unacceptable. In many societies a precautionary approach is adopted: a producer of potential risk needs stronger arguments or evidence to show that the risks are acceptable than those required by the party facing the risks to show that the risks are unacceptable. In the debate on long-term risks, however, the situation often appears to be reversed. While there is an insatiable demand for stronger evidence and indication of the risks of, say, climate change, indications vis-à-vis the (short-term) economic costs of risk prevention are generally readily accepted. What if the economic models used by governments to predict, say, economic growth and future employment were to be scrutinized with the thoroughness with which climate models are examined by the International Panel for Climate Change and further questioned in public debate? Again we see a discrepancy between the standard of conduct applied to future environmental risk and that generally adopted in other areas.

Take, as a second example, the discrepancy between the attitudes of US congressmen towards scientific information about climate change and their attitudes towards the perceived threat of Saddam Hussein possessing weapons of mass destruction. For example, the same senators who insisted upon 'sound science', consensus among scientists and complete scientific certainty before devoting funds to climate mitigation found sufficient justification in inconclusive information from the US intelligence services, contradicting the conclusions of the chief UN weapons inspector, to start a war against Iraq (see, for example, Senator Inhofe: CNN Late Edition, 25 August 2002). In short, although there is no uniquely 'right' approach to risk assessment, consistency is a prime consideration in any intellectual debate.

As a third example, consider the lawsuits in the United States against the tobacco industry. Even today's state-of-the-art knowledge about the health risks of smoking offers no absolute proof that smoking indeed causes cancer. There are still scientists who question their colleagues' results, and someone with an extremely individualistic cultural filter might therefore still remain optimistic. However, although the relationship between smoking and cancer is still the subject of research, US courts recently ruled that the *indications* of health risks reported in scientific journals in the 1970s should already have been sufficient for the tobacco industry to change its ways (Engle vs. Reynolds Tobacco Co, 2000). It seems reasonable to assume that an 'intergenerational court' would consider the first or second assessment report by the Intergovernmental Panel on Climate Change (IPCC, 1990, 1996) as providing at least as much of an indication of risk to future generations as the reports in the 1970s of the health risks of smoking. Nonetheless, there are still governments today requiring greater proof of climate change before changing their ways.[4]

Discounting the future

A common practice in cost-benefit analysis of long-term risk mitigation is to assign consumption losses in the distant future far less weight than those occurring in the present. Economists commonly proffer two arguments for such discounting of future losses. First, people living in the distant future are expected to be much wealthier than we are in the present, and consequently a dollar of damage will harm them less. To paraphrase Alfred Marshall (1890): 'a pound's worth of satisfaction to present generations is a much greater thing than a pound's worth of harm to the much wealthier future generations'. Second, citizens are deemed simply to care less about causing harm to future people than about losing consumption in the event of them having to incur expenditures on harm prevention, and governments should respect this attitude. Here too, however, it can be shown that this attitude towards long-term risks conflicts with the general standards of conduct; that is, national and international legal regimes, laying down standards of behaviour when acts involve risk of harm to other *contemporaries* (Davidson, 2006). Under these national and international laws, neither differences in wealth nor 'empathic remoteness' qualify as an extenuating circumstance when considering the reasonableness of creating risk of harm to another. For example, international law forbids the owner of a chemical plant to offer less risk protection to people simply because they are living across the border. Neither does international law allow developing countries to offer citizens in developed countries less protection against transboundary air pollution on the basis of differences in per-capita income between the countries.

CONCLUSIONS

People may differ widely in their views on how society should deal with risks imposed on others, that is, what is to be deemed an acceptable risk. After all, faced with incomplete and often contradictory information, people perceive the world through fundamentally different 'risk filters', influencing the way issues are defined and preferences as to how they should be handled. Therefore, scientific or objective arguments alone cannot settle disputes about the acceptability of the risks we impose on our fellow human beings. If people disagree with the institutionalized standard of conduct with respect to the handling of risk, the political arena is the obvious place to express one's ideas. At the same time, though, as I have endeavoured to show in this chapter, the debate on what to consider acceptable risk to future generations cannot just start from scratch. This is not an open question to be answered by one and all, each from their own personal perspective. For example, once we include immigrants in our society, we cannot debate whether the social security they are entitled to should be based upon individualistic or egalitarian principles. Such a debate can only relate to the whole of society, that is, both immigrants *and* the already existing population. Likewise, once we include future generations in our moral community, we cannot debate what standard of conduct to apply to the handling of specifically long-term risks. Intergenerational justice demands first and foremost that future generations be treated in line with justice between contemporaries, as institutionalized in actual practice. Since positive law exists, such as tort law, which indeed regulates how risk to others ought to be treated, the moral choices underlying positive law should guide us in the handling of long-term risks as well.

It has not been my intention here to provide a thorough survey of the general standards of conduct in force in various societies for handling risks to others. How the hierarchical, individualistic and egalitarian viewpoints in Cultural Theory terminology, for example, have amalgamated in the general standard of conduct of a given society is a question mainly for lawyers and is beyond the scope of the present chapter. Indeed, the main aim of this chapter is to indicate the importance of such research for the project of intergenerational justice. There is already ample indication, however, that such research would indeed yield meaningful results and that the point of departure of treating future generations as equals would function as an effective sieve for much of what is today deemed to be acceptable risk to future generations. Long-term policy could then be evaluated, first, with respect to whether an appropriate analytical framework has been used in decision-making. Society, after all, proves far more risk averse and clings far more to the right not to be harmed than long-term policy generally assumes. Second, it could be assessed whether the reasoning employed is biased in favour of present generations, for example through neglect and overexposure of different kinds of information. This might possibly require the creation of a special court dedicated to judging the acceptability of the risks we impose on future generations.

REFERENCES

Adams, J. (1995) *Risk*, University College London, London

Azar, C. and Rodhe, H. (1997) 'Targets for stabilization of atmospheric CO_2', *Science*, vol 276, no 5320, pp1818-1819

Beck, U. (1986) *Risikogesellschaft. Auf dem Weg in eine andere Moderne*, Suhrkamp, Frankfurt am Main

Bernstein, P. L. (1996) *Against the Gods: The Remarkable Story of Risk*, John Wiley and Sons Inc, New York

Boholm, A. (1996) 'A critique of cultural theory', *Ethos*, vol 61, pp64–84

Coase, R. H. (1960) 'The problem of social cost', *Journal of Law and Economics*, vol 3, no 1, pp1–44

Coleman, J. L. (1992) *Risks and Wrongs*, Cambridge University Press, Cambridge

Davidson, M. D. (2006) 'A social discount rate for climate damage to future generations based on regulatory law', *Climatic Change*, vol 76, no 1–2, pp55–72

de-Shalit, A. (1995) *Why Posterity Matters: Environmental Policies and Future Generations*, Routledge, London

De George, R. (1979) 'The environment, rights and future generations', in K. Goodpaster and K. Sayre (eds) *Ethics and Problems of the 21st Century*, University of Notre Dame Press, Notre Dame, Ind., pp93–105

Douglas, M. and Wildavsky, A. (1982) *Risk and Culture: An Essay on The Selection of Technological and Environmental Dangers*, University of California Press, Berkeley

Dworkin, R. (1977) 'Taking rights seriously', in R. Dworkin (ed.) *Taking Rights Seriously*, Harvard University Press, Cambridge, pp184–205

Dworkin, R. (1983) 'In defense of equality', *Social Philosophy and Policy*, vol 1, no 1, pp24–40
Dworkin, R. (2000) *Sovereign Virtue: The Theory and Practice of Equality*, Harvard University Press, Cambridge
Engle vs. R. J. Reynolds Tobacco Co. (2000) *Final Judgment and Amended Omnibus Order*, No. 94-08273 (Fla. 11th Cir. Ct. Nov. 6, 2000)
Funtowicz, S. O. and Ravetz, J. R. (1991) 'A new scientific methodology for global environmental issues', in R. Costanza (ed.) *The Ecological Economics*, Columbia University Press, New York, pp137–152
Harsanyi, J. C. (1975) 'Can the maximin principle serve as a basis for morality? A critique of John Rawls's theory', *American Political Science Review*, vol 69, no 2, pp594–606
Harsanyi, J. C. (1977) 'Morality and the theory of rational behaviour', *Social Research*, vol 44, no 4, pp621–627
Harsanyi, J. C. (1978) 'Bayesian decision theory and utilitarian ethics', *American Economic Review*, vol 68, no 2, pp223–228
Holling, C. S. (1979) 'Myths of ecological stability', in G. Smart and W. Stanburry (eds) *Studies in Crisis Management*, Butterworth, Montreal
Holling, C. S. (1986) 'The resilience of terrestrial ecosystems: local surprise and global change', in W. C. Clark and R. E. Munn (eds) *Sustainable Development of the Biosphere*, Cambridge University Press, Cambridge, pp292–317
IPCC (1990) *First Assessment Report: 1990*, Cambridge University Press, Cambridge
IPCC (1996) *Second Assessment Report: Climate Change 1995*, Cambridge University Press, Cambridge
Kymlicka, W. (1990) *Contemporary Political Philosophy: An Introduction*, Oxford University Press, Oxford
Lowi, T. J. (1990) 'Risks and rights in the history of American governments', *Daedalus*, vol 119, no 4, pp17–40
Magnus, E. von (1983) 'Rights and risks', *Journal of Business Ethics*, vol 2, pp23–26
Mamadouh, V. (1999) 'Grid-group cultural theory: an introduction', *GeoJournal*, vol 47, no 3, pp395–409
Marshall, A. (1890) *Principles of Economics*, Macmillan and Co., Ltd., London
Neumann, J. von and Morgenstern, O. (1944) *Theory of Games and Economic Behavior*, Princeton University Press, Princeton NJ
Nordhaus, W. D. (1994) 'Expert opinion on climatic change', *American Scientist*, vol 82, no 1, pp45–52
Nozick, R. (1974) *Anarchy, State, and Utopia*, Basic Books, New York
O'Neill, J. (1993) *Ecology, Policy and Politics*, Routledge, London
Parfit, D. (1984) *Reasons and Persons*, Clarendon Press, Oxford
Portney, P. R. and Weyant, J. P. (eds) (1999) *Discounting and Intergenerational Equity*, Johns Hopkins University Press, Baltimore
Posner, R. A. (1972) *Economic Analysis of Law*, Little Brown, Boston
Rawls, J. (1972) *A Theory of Justice*, Oxford University Press, Oxford
Rawls, J. (1974) 'Some reasons for the maximin criterion', *American Economic Review*, vol 64, no 2, pp141–146
Resnik, M. D. (1987) *Choices: An Introduction in Decision Theory*, University of Minnesota Press, Minneapolis
Routley, R. and Routley, V. (1978) 'Nuclear energy and obligations to the future', *Inquiry*, vol 21, pp133–179
Schwarz, M. and Thompson, M. (1990) *Divided We Stand: Redefining Politics, Technology and Social Choice*, Harvester Wheatsheaf, Hemel Hempstead
Shrader-Frechette, K. (1991) *Risk and Rationality*, University of California Press, Berkeley

Sidgwick, H. (1874) *The Methods of Ethics*, Macmillan, London
Siebert, H. (1982) 'Nature as a life support system: renewable resources and environmental disruption', *Journal of Economics*, vol 42, no 2, pp133–142
Simon, J. (1996) *The Ultimate Resource 2*, Princeton University Press, Princeton
Sjöberg, L. (1997) 'Explaining risk perception: an empirical evaluation of cultural theory', *Risk Decision and Policy*, vol 2, no 2, pp113–130
Thompson, M. (2000) 'Understanding environmental values: a cultural theory approach', *Environmental Values Seminar*, 2 October 2000, Carnegie Council on Ethics and International Affairs, New York
Thompson, M., Ellis, R. and Wildavsky, A. (1990) *Cultural Theory*, Westview Press, Boulder, Colorado
Tol, R. S. J. (2007) 'Europe's long-term climate target: A critical evaluation', *Energy Policy*, vol 35, no 1, pp424–434
UNCED (1992) *Rio Declaration on Environment and Development*, The United Nations Conference on Environment and Development, Rio de Janeiro
UNESCO (1997) *Declaration on the Responsibilities of the Present Generations Towards Future Generations* (Resolution 44: Article 1 and 5.2), Adopted on 12 November 1997 by the General Conference of UNESCO at its 29th session
Visser't Hooft, H. P. (1999) *Justice to Future Generations and the Environment*, Kluwer Academic Publishers, Dordrecht
WCED (World Commission on Environment and Development) (1987) *Our Common Future: The Bruntland Report*, Oxford University Press, New York
Wiener, J. B. (1995) 'Protecting the global environment', in J. D. Graham and J. B. Wiener (eds) *Risk vs. Risk: Tradeoffs in Protecting Health and the Environment*, Harvard University Press, Harvard, pp193–225
Wigley, T. M. L., Richels, R. and Edmonds, J. A. (1996) 'Economic and environmental choices in the stabilization of atmospheric CO_2 concentrations', *Nature*, vol 379, no 6562, pp240–243
Wildavsky, A. and Dake, K. (1990) 'Theories of risk perception: Who fears what and why?', *Daedalus*, vol 119, pp41–60
Woolf, Lord H. K. (1992) 'Are the judiciary environmentally myopic?', *Journal of Environmental Law*, vol 4, no 1, pp1–14
Woolf, Lord H. K. (2001) 'Environmental risk: the responsibilities of the law and science', *Environmental Law and Management*, vol 13, no 3, pp131
WRR (Netherlands Scientific Council for Government Policy) (1994) *Sustained Risks: A Lasting Phenomenon*, nr 44, Sdu Uitgeverij, The Hague
WRR (Netherlands Scientific Council for Government Policy) (1999) *Generationally Aware Policy* (in Dutch: *Generatiebewust beleid*), nr 55, Sdu Uitgeverij, The Hague
WRR (Netherlands Scientific Council for Government Policy) (2002) *Duurzame ontwikkeling. Bestuurlijke voorwaarden voor een mobiliserend beleid*, Rapporten aan de regering, nr 62, Sdu Uitgeverij, The Hague
WRR (Netherlands Scientific Council for Government Policy) (2006) *Climate Strategy Between Ambition and Realism* (in Dutch: *Klimaatstrategie – tussen ambitie en realisme*), nr 74, Sdu Uitgeverij, The Hague

Notes

1 In their quest for an objective boundary between dangerous and safe interference with the climate system, governments have eagerly accepted as a long-term target for climate policy that the global mean temperature should not rise more than 2°C above

that of the pre-industrial era. As has been argued by Tol (2006), this target seems unfounded.

2 Please note that in Cultural Theory the term myth does not denote a false belief but a generalized idea or perception of reality, which by definition lies beyond the possibility of scientific falsification.

3 The position of the 'fatalist' has deliberately been omitted here. Since the fatalist does not believe fairness to be found on this earth, the fatalist has no particular view on what it would mean to treat people as equals.

4 Interesting to note in this respect is the plea of Lord Woolf, the Lord Chief Justice of England and Wales, for an environmental court, which he believes should have 'general responsibility for overseeing and enforcing the safeguards provided for the protection of the environment which is so important to us all' (Woolf, 1992, 2001).

7 The Ethical Assessment of Unpredictable Risks in the Use of Genetically Engineered Livestock for Biomedical Research

Arianna Ferrari

INTRODUCTION

The possibility of modifying the genome of animals offered by genetic engineering has opened new fields in biomedical research, which are now mainly in the stage of experimental research: gene-pharming and xenotransplantation. In the scientific discussion, the use of transgenic livestock in these fields entered the debate as a case of regulation of risks in biomedicine; that is, as a problem of assessing the dangerous potentials of medicines for gene-pharming (through appropriate toxicological tests) and of assessing the risks of rejection in xenotransplantation. Besides these great promises, the use of transgenic livestock is also connected with the possibility of great threats to the safety of people receiving the xenotransplants or consuming the drugs derived by transgenic livestock due to the presence of so-called endogenous retroviruses (cross-species viruses). Moreover, genetic modification has the potential to cause suffering and distress to the animals especially created and involved in these practices. It is unclear in how far this is justified in our society, which recognizes in some way the moral relevance of animals. In most debates, gene-pharming and xenotransplantation are discussed as cases of assessing unpredictable risks and of balancing benefits for human kind and costs for the animals. However, special reflections on the normative implications of these unpredictable risks both for human beings and for animals are missing.

The purpose of this chapter is first to clarify the ethical dimension of the unpredictable risks connected with the use of transgenic livestock in the biomedical fields of xenotransplantation and gene-pharming and then to offer criteria for the ethical assessment of this use. Particularly relevant here is the risk of 'xenosis', that is, of cross-species diseases: in the case of xenotransplantation, it is particularly relevant because they might also only manifest themselves in the far future. In the case of gene-pharming, there also might be unforeseen toxological effects.

GENETICALLY ENGINEERED LIVESTOCK IN BIOMEDICINE

The term genetically modified animal (GM animal)[1] refers to an animal in which there has been a deliberate incorporation of external DNA into the genome through human intervention, in contrast to a spontaneous mutation. Through addition, selection or substitution of the genetic make-up of the animal, it is possible to change the characteristics of its phenotype. In biomedicine, besides the traditional use of animals in experimental research (in the basic research and as disease and toxicity models), the creation of transgenic animals, in particular of livestock, has led to new possible experimental fields: xenotransplantation and gene-pharming.

In xenotransplantation live cells, tissue and organs from GM animals are used for transplantation into humans or for clinical ex-vivo perfusion[2] (US Department of Health and Human Services, 1999). In gene-pharming,[3] animals are genetically modified so that their bodily products (such as milk, blood or eggs) contain human proteins having medicinal value. These proteins are then collected and purified and can be used as drugs (examples are antithrombin, a human anticoagulant, and alpha-1-antitrypsin for emphysema and cystic fibrosis).

Both xenotransplantation and gene-pharming have been accompanied by great expectations. Because of the shortage of organs in our society, the vast number of people who die while on the waiting list and the increasing number of neurodegenerative diseases, xenotransplantation is seen as having the potential to bridge the shortfall in human materials for transplantation. Moreover, the production of medically useful human proteins in the bodily fluids (especially milk) of transgenic livestock seems to provide an efficient and convenient method for generating large quantities of biologically active proteins, thereby reducing the cost of pharmaceutical manufacturing.

However, it was soon realized that xenotransplantation and gene-pharming also pose serious risks which seem difficult to assess, as they are not predictable in the near term nor in the long run: these risks are connected with endogenous retroviruses, also called cross-species viruses.

Retroviruses are RNA viruses containing a reverse transcriptase enzyme that allows the genetic information of the viruses, upon replication, to become part of the genetic information of the host cell. Retroviruses produced by GM animals (endogenously) could be pathogenic for the human body, but they are not dangerous for the animals themselves (Coffin et al, 1997). Through either the transplantation of organs, tissues or cells from GM animals to humans and through the consumption of bodily products from these animals, the retroviruses could be carried in the host recipient or in the consumer and then be activated, giving rise to infection. The worst case scenario would be the pandemic spreading of this virus through the entire human population. Although this scenario has never been documented and there are no data available regarding it, regulatory authorities must take the presence of unpredictable risks in xenotransplantation and gene-pharming into account. In the current debate, outbreaks of bird flu[4] and the ongoing discussion about HIV,[5] which are examples of pathogenic retroviruses derived from animals, well document the massive social impact as well as the relevance of the discussion about these kinds of viruses for the health of the population.

THE ETHICAL DIMENSION OF UNPREDICTABLE RISKS IN XENOTRANSPLANTATION

The debate on cross-species viruses in xenotransplantation began later compared to the discussion of other risks posed by immunological and physiological barriers,[6] and it was not until the middle of the 1990s that a special concept, 'xenozoonosis' or 'xenosis', was formulated for describing cross-species diseases (Fishman, 1997). However, since the announcement that the porcine endogenous retrovirus (PERV) could infect human cells in vitro (Weiss, 1998), the focus of the debate on xenotransplantation has progressively shifted from the initial concerns about the problem of compatibility between animal and human materials to the need to assess and deal with risks of xenosis.

The problem of transmission of xenosis has catalysed the debate precisely because of the special ethical challenges posed.[7] This is a difficult situation for biomedical research: on the one hand we want to save more lives and reduce the clinical shortage of suitable organs, tissues and cell donors. On the other hand we are dealing with a risky practice connected with the possible spread of animal-derived pathogens to the patient and then to the entire population, which obviously would be contrary to the goals of medicine.

Many different PERVs have been isolated, and three infectious classes have been identified (PERV-A, PERV-B and PERV-C, Wood et al, 2004). Furthermore, it has been demonstrated that they are integrated into the genome of all pig strains and that normal pig cells produce viral particles, so that these viruses seem to be less susceptible to exclusion by careful breeding.

However, until now all retrospective studies on patients who received porcine xenografts (i.e. tissues, organs or cells from GM animals) have shown no evidence of PERV transmission. As a consequence, in the debate the role and the assessment of risks connected with PERVs among scientific experts is very controversial. Some authors tend to underline the lack of transmission in human recipients (Patience et al, 1998); others show a more cautious attitude and ask for more basic research and more refined animal studies (Magre et al, 2003). Further difficulties result from the fact that not every retrovirus can be analysed with current testing methods, thus there is a general need to develop new research instruments. It remains unclear whether and how consistently these methods can be developed.

Moreover, due to the peculiar strategy of xenotransplantation, the unpredictable risks of xenosis due to retroviruses are connected with the predictable risks of rejection[8] and this complicates the risk assessment: After a transplant of xenograft, the human recipient will require immune suppression to prevent graft rejection. The combination of immune suppression, use of organs (or tissues or cells) in the presence of molecular differences of tissue cells and the absence of pre-existing immunity to animal organisms makes the organ recipient more susceptible to xenosis. This strategy is a sort of double-edged sword: on the one hand the immune system is treated in order to accept the animal material and hence to minimize the risk of rejection; on the other side, the protection of the patient from the xenosis risk is fundamental, while exactly these risks are augmented by the fact that the treated immune system is impaired.

The seriousness of the unpredictable risks in xenotransplantation is documented by the fact that despite recent progress, pre-clinical experiments so far do not yet justify human clinical trials, even if there are careful ongoing trials of the transplantation of animal cells and tissues into humans. Moreover, a recent paper of the World Health Organization explicitly stressed the dangers posed by clinical studies performed in some countries – such as Russia and China – which lack rigorous regulations with particular regard to risk assessment: it was said that these experiments raise 'unacceptable infectious public health risks and should be stopped' (WHO, 2005, p1).

Last but not least, xenotransplantation involves the use and the killing of animals, and this needs to be ethically scrutinized and justified. In our society, animal experimentation is a very complex matter that raises particular ethical concerns. Animal experiments are even required by authorities and prescribed by the law (such as, for example, in toxicological assessment of chemical substances and of pharmaceuticals), but they are perceived as an ethically controversial field and they are usually designed so as to balance the costs for the animals and the benefits expected for human beings. The case of xenotransplantation requires a further ethical analysis. Since xenotransplantation involves a *new* use of animals as sources for organs, tissues and cells, which was not possible before, and since animals here are specially created (through genetic engineering) and bred for this purpose, the question of animal experimentation in the case of xenotransplantation has to be discussed again. Furthermore, the presence of unpredictable risks connected to the use of xenotransplants represents a new factor both for the assessment of the risks connected to this practice and for the balancing of costs and benefits by evaluating the acceptability of the use of animals.

THE ETHICAL DIMENSION OF UNPREDICTABLE RISKS IN GENE-PHARMING

At the beginning of the 1990s the possibility of creating transgenic animals as bioproducers of therapeutical proteins for human beings was seen as a largely promising, low-cost and highly effective field (Janne et al, 1992). After the first big success of the production of human haemoglobin in the blood of transgenic pigs and the successful realization of the technique of animal cloning using transfected somatic cells as nuclear donor, hopes of reaching similar positive results also in other animals and in other body parts (especially the mammary glands) arose (Houdebine, 2000). However, over the last decade various technical problems and serious risks connected with the developed drugs have emerged.

Notwithstanding decades of experimentation,[9] until now only one drug has entered the market: the ATryn®, a recombinant form of human antithrombin derived from the milk of genetically modified goats, produced by the American biotech company GTC Biotherapeutics and distributed in Europe by LEO Pharma (LEO Pharma, 2006). After an initial refusal by the European Medicines Agency (EMEA) in February 2006, in September of the same year the final authorization from this agency was given. In the United States,

ATryn® is currently still under review by the Food and Drug Administration, which however assigned in September 2008 the priority Review to GTC Biotherapeutics.[10]

The initial refusal by EMEA in the case of ATryn® was due to difficulties in the assessment of antibody stimulation and to the realization of clinical trials, since the number of the patients in these trials was judged as too low (Heuser, 2006; Peplow, 2006).[11]

After that refusal, the producing company had asked for a re-examination of the data, and EMEA convened a panel of European experts on blood and blood clotting, which concluded that all the data from all the patients could be used, since all faced the risk of blood clotting (EMEA, 2006a). The panel of experts in June 2006 finally agreed that the benefits connected with ATryn® outweigh the risks, and so recommended the authorization for the market only for the cure of the rare disease of inherited reduction of the protein antithrombin (the hereditary AT deficiency) when the patients undergo surgery[12] and under 'exceptional circumstances'. These circumstances imply that GTC has to carefully monitor clinical uses for antibody reactions and that EMEA will review any new information available and make an update if necessary (EMEA, 2006b, 2006c, 2006d; Schmidt, 2006). These special circumstances are motivated by the fact that, since the hereditary AT deficiency is very rare, it has not been possible to obtain complete information about the substance (EMEA, 2006c).

Interesting is the fact that recently EMEA refused the approval for another drug from GM animal, Rhucin, with a similar motivation as the initial refusal of ATryn®, because the results were done on a low number of patients and the risks were judged as not outweighing the benefits (see EMEA, 2008). In particular, EMEA has expressed concern over the lack of data concerning the dose of Rhucin, the possible allergic reactions in patients as well as the possible presence of impurities in this drug, 'which could come from the rabbit milk from which the active substance is extracted and could affect the medicine's safety' (EMEA, 2008, p2). Rhucin entails a recombinant human C1 inhibitor produced in the milk of GM rabbits and it aims at helping the treatment of acute attacks of a rare disease, the hereditary angioedema (HAE),[13] in patients who have low levels of the protein 'C1 inhibitor' due to a congenital (inborn) deficiency.[14]

There are three areas of concern regarding proteins derived from GM animals: toxicology issues pertaining to the differences in pharmacodynamic properties of the proteins obtained from animals, 'intrinsic toxicity' (i.e. toxicological effects due to the molecule itself) and adverse issues pertaining to the cellular systems or processes that lead to the production or secretion of the macromolecule (Thomas and Fuchs, 2002). The last area is the one connected with the greatest and most difficult to assess risks, and the highest risks; that is, risks of microbiological contamination that could have the consequence of causing allergic reactions, risks of infection, risks of immunogenic responses and risks of autoimmune reactions through consumption of these drugs. Among the biological contaminants which could pose risks of infections, prions[15] are seen as the most dangerous (EMEA, 2004). In particular, it is not clear if blood and blood products can transmit prions to humans, because viruses in blood and cell products are more complex and labile, that is, difficult to remove. In any case, it has been demonstrated that blood could potentially transmit prion infections in experimental animals (Lubon, 1998; Hunter et al, 2002). Furthermore, autoimmune reactions also pose some concerns, that reactions that could arise if the transgenic proteins broke tolerance to their endogenous, self-protein counterparts (Celis and Silvester, 2004).

With respect to xenotransplantation, there is a quite different discussion in the case of gene-pharming about the risks of cross-species diseases: here it is surprising how few systematic studies and analyses of the implications of risks for the individual consumer and for the society there are. The main reason for that lies in the general claim that the safety of the product can be assured through toxicology (National Research Council, 2002; Clark and Whitelaw, 2003). Moreover, the opinion is common that risks of cross-species diseases can be controlled and efficiently managed through the careful selection and breeding of transgenic animals together with a progressive refinement of the methods of genetic engineering for the expression of proteins in the bodily products of the animals (especially in the mammary glands).

In the literature on risk assessment by gene-pharming, there is particular emphasis on the risk of escape of GM animals, in particular connected to the fact that genetically modified material can be released into the environment and to other organisms, for example through the mating of the GM animals with conventional ones, or through contact with other animals (National Research Council, 2002). This focus seems to be a reflection of some concerns expressed in the debate on GM crops. Experts tend to assure the public and politicians that these risks are minimized because the animals are carefully monitored and kept under specific conditions, such as isolation and pathogen-free conditions. In any case, there is confidence in the possibility of controlling the risks posed to the environment, for two main reasons: first of all, the human proteins secreted in the mammary gland proteins are expressed primarily in the milk of the animal and are not present in significant amounts in meat, urine or other secretions, so that they cannot be easily transferred to the environment; second, since the animals created for biomedical purposes are very expensive there is no interest in setting them free, so there is no need to worry (National Research Council, 2002).

This confidence seems to be also indirectly supported by the public: although in agricultural and food production the rejection of genetic engineering among the public is prevalent mostly because of perception of risks together with the absence of recognition of direct benefits for the consumer, there is no equally strong opposition to the therapeutical applications of genetic engineering in general, in particular to drugs derived from GM animals. However, when people are directly asked about the possibility of alternative research on transgenic plants for example, they are more likely to support the alternatives (Einsiedel, 2005). Furthermore, among the public, concerns about the use of GM animals are more significant when there are uncertainties over long-term impacts on human health and environment. As I already noted, there is very little literature about risks from these drugs, so it seems legitimate to ask if the opinion on the use of GM animals would be affected (and in which sense) by more information about risks of cross-species diseases.

However, it seems to be difficult to exclude the possibility of developing these diseases via toxicological tests. In an interview, Amy Rosenberg, supervisory medical officer with the US Food and Drug Administration's (FDA) Center for Drug Evaluation and Research, has declared: 'And each product poses its own unique risk – for instance, recombinant versions of endogenous proteins might pose immunogenicity risks that you might not encounter if the protein doesn't have a human counterpart' (Schmidt, 2006, p877). Furthermore, Louis Marie Houdebine, pioneer researcher in the field of gene-pharming,[16] regards the shift of opinion of EMEA regarding the approval of Atryn® as an effort in supporting the experimental field of gene-pharming. Houdebine has indeed declared: 'It's possible that given Atryn®'s low risk and infrequent use, EMEA chose to give an agreement that could have a significant impact on the development of processes to prepare recombinant pharmaceutical proteins. [...] They want good proteins and they *hope* the method will work' (Schmidt, 2006, p877 – emphasis is mine). Houdebine's declaration – although not officially commented on by EMEA officials – is interesting because it explains indirectly that other factors play a role in regulative risk assessment: sometimes it is not only a matter of 'objective' assessment of risks (especially when some risks are unpredictable!), but decisions are often taken considering the special context. EMEA's approval sounds as the very first and important step for legitimating and supporting the use of recombinant proteins produced in transgenic animals.

The discussion on risks in gene-pharming therefore presents interesting elements of risk perception and conceptualization: in this context there seems to be a general trend towards transforming the unpredictable risks into predictable ones, in order to facilitate the risk assessment; this is much more evident here than in the case of xenotransplantation. For good or ill, as I already wrote, up to now only one drug has officially entered the market.

Similarly to the case of xenotransplantation, gene-pharming also involves a *new* use of animals that are specially created and bred. Moreover, in some cases the production of therapeutical proteins in bodily fluids of animals represent a reintroduction of the use of animals for the obtainment of proteins which were previously produced in plants or microorganisms. In these cases the use of animals is motivated only by the need for more efficient and cheap ways to produce these proteins, that is, for economic purposes. Anyway, the presence of unpredictable risks, as in the case of xenotransplantation, introduces a new variable that reframes both the risk assessment in the context of biomedical applications and the balancing of costs for animals and benefits for human beings in the evaluation of the acceptability of animal experimentation.

Difficulties of Risk Assessment and the Ethical Dimension of Unpredictable Risks

In the classical formula for risk assessment, risk is calculated as the product of the magnitude of possible harm (including kind, degree, duration and timing) and the probability of its occurrence. Accordingly, the risk is viewed as completely identifiable and determined. The presence of unpredictable risks complicates the scenario of risk assessment and also lets the normative dimension of risk emerge with particular force.

Decision-theory distinguishes between decision-making under risk, in which each action is connected with a set of possible outcomes, and decision-making under uncertainty, in which probabilities are either not known or known with little precision. In this theory many different criteria have been proposed to cope with decisions under uncertainty in mathematical form (Hansson, 2005), but these calculations present some limitations, particularly when they deal with socially sensitive problems, so that alternative solutions, especially in the sociological debate, have been proposed. Bonß (1995) speaks for example of 'second-order dangers'[17] derived from many present practices, characteristics of our 'risk-society' (*Risikogesellschaft*). Many current techniques lack the conditions for fulfilling the factual/descriptive component of risk assessment (which are predictability, imputability and the possibility to quantify these), such that other considerations such as the political, ethical and economical consequences of the introduction of these technologies should be included in the assessment.

The discussion of ethical implications of xenotransplantation and gene-pharming is characterized by these situations of uncertainty, indicated by the fact that we are dealing with topics in the particularly sensitive and important field of biomedical research, whose goals can be identified as maintaining and protecting people's health and ameliorating illness. Furthermore, both these practices involve the generation and the use of animals, which in our society are ethically relevant practices and which therefore have to be ethically scrutinized. However, in this debate – particularly in the one about xenotransplantation, given that the one about the risks in gene-pharming is not as popular – the prevalent view is that the most appropriate ethical model for dealing with these risks is cost-benefit analysis. In other words, common is the idea that in order to solve the ethical dilemma posed by these technologies, we have to weight the costs and the benefits. An example of this procedure is represented by the position paper of the Ethics Committee of the International Xenotransplantation Association (Sykes et al, 2004), which argues for moving carefully towards clinical trials under highly controlled conditions, once the other ethical principles discussed in the papers are met. The ethical principles are: questions of informed consent, of safety precautions with respect to the countries where such standards are not satisfied, and of the ethical concerns about the use of animals in research. The paper presents a clear tendency to analyse and judge the different issues connected with the main topic of xenotransplantation separately, and the question of risks is regarded as the most important. The strategy is based on the reduction of ethical analysis to a matter of risk-benefit calculus: as soon as the other topics are discussed and an 'ethical solution' is proposed for them, the core problem remains that of risk. And the problem of risk ought to be assessed so far as possible in an objective manner, that is, through scientific methods: Despite the above limitations, existing guidelines and the lack of evidence of PERV transmission so far, and evidence that some pigs may be incapable of producing PERV particles that can infect human cells, are encouraging. These developments lead the IXA[18] Ethics Committee to conclude that, when such monitoring practices are followed, it is appropriate to move forward with XTx[19] trials that also satisfy the other ethical principles discussed in this paper (Sykes et al, 2004, p1103).

But what does this mean exactly from the ethical point of view of balancing the risks and the benefits when the risks are unpredictable, that is, not foreseeable in quantitative terms? It seems to me that if we stop at the consideration of risks in the view of the risk-benefit calculus we meet two options: either we find ourselves in an impasse because we simply don't know how to decide, or we try in some way to transform the unknown risks to make them some way calculable. The strategy of transforming uncertainties into calculable risks is identified as one of the possible answers to the 'second-order dangers' by Bonß (1995). He argues that sometimes uncertainties are transformed by the application of the standard method of risk assessment (calculation) in the so-called 'rest-risks', which are perceived as positive elements, because they are in some way intrinsically connected with the technological development and which show at the same time how society is plastic, flexible and capable of adapting itself to new conditions (Bonß, 1995). This strategy is however very problematic because it jumps over the very problem of these practices.

The problem arises from the fact that the nature of the decision and the factors that determine it also both need to be discussed. In order to judge biomedical procedures connected with unpredictable risks, I think that the risks should be seen in a broader context; that is, they should be attached to other considerations, such as the implications of the use of these procedures for the subjects involved: the individuals, the society and the animals. These elements should in any case not be treated separately but should be directly integrated in the ethical assessment of risks, because the risks themselves are embedded in a normative framework. Biomedical research and its applications are social practices that involve sensitive spheres of our lives, such as health and safety, and the use of animals, which have to be ethically justified. Moreover, the regulation of these practices results from political decisions, such as for example whether a research field should be financed or not. The challenge for the ethical analysis consists exactly of scrutinizing this framework and in making the normative premises of the decision explicit. For this purpose, I think it is necessary to analyse the deep implications of the presence of unknown risks for the different subjects involved.

IMPLICATIONS FOR HUMAN BEINGS

In gene-pharming and xenotransplantation the presence of unpredictable risks poses some challenges to different human subjects: to the patient or the consumer of drugs from GM animals, to his/her close contacts (family and friends), to the medical staff or research staff, and to society in general.

For the individual patient, in particular one who is critically ill, it is indisputable that the benefits expected from xenotransplantation – assuming that rejection can be controlled – outweigh any risk of infection. In this sense, the application of the risks-benefit model for the individual patient offers simple but trivial answers. However, other areas of conflict emerge for the individual: because of the xenosis risk it is necessary that the patient be monitored in clinical trials (as I already wrote, until now xenotransplantation is only possible in clinical trials and not as a standard procedure). This monitoring is lifelong and may include avoidance of blood donation as well as sexual contacts, and also following patterns of behaviour with close contacts that will minimize infectious risks. Moreover, the patient is also expected to agree to postoperative measures such as autopsy and, in the case of clinical trials, people are expected to give up the traditional right to withdraw from a trial – which is a fundamental right protected in the Declaration of Helsinki – until the risk of late-developing viruses is reasonably known not to exist. Consumers of protein-based-drugs from GM animals are also expected to be monitored and their reactions observed in the long term. However, as I already wrote, there is not sufficient literature about these topics, since the debate is characterized by the opinion that the risks of drugs are normally assessed and then ensured during the clinical phase, that is, before the drugs enter the market. In this case there are no sufficient data because the first drug has just now begun to be commercialized.

This extraordinary monitoring of the patient does conflict with the respect for his or her autonomy. Moreover, the fact that the patient is going to be required to comply with these measures in some way alters the character of voluntary consent, and renders it more binding (Daar, 1997). Monitoring and safety measures also affect the family and friends of the patient or consumer and the medical or research staff, who are also exposed to the risks. The necessity of notification of close contacts to the medical staff for the patient or consumer and then the necessity for the staff to notify authorities conflicts with the principle of confidentiality, which is another fundamental right to which human research subjects are entitled. These elements alter the traditional character of 'informed consent' so much that the Swiss Academy of medical sciences among others proposed rather to speak of 'informed contract' (SAMW, 1999). The idea is that the physician and the medical staff provide the patient with the organ (or tissue or cells) from a GM animal and they undertake the necessary monitoring measures to protect his/her health and safety, and that the patient agrees to face the monitoring measures all his/her life to guarantee the protection of public health.

Moreover, xenosis risks can also occur later, in subsequent generations, and current testing methods do not seem to be adequate for clearly excluding the substances which will pose potential risks in the future. As a consequence, in the risk assessment it is necessary also to take into account the possible health threat to future generations.

All the implications of risks previously observed for xenotransplantation are potentially valid also for the case of gene-pharming. However, there is no specific literature about the possibility of monitoring the consumer of drugs derived from GM animals because, as I already wrote, when a drug enters the market it is expected to be safe; this safety is also assured through the usual monitoring of pharmacovigilance authorities. Since so far only one drug has entered the market, in order to make provisions we need to wait to see what happens with this drug in the future. In the approval process of ATryn® two elements are very interesting: the fact that it has been approved under a very limited and specific use and under the condition of a careful monitoring and of the possible reevaluation due to the presence of new data. First, as I already noticed, EMEA has chosen the way of approving the drug from transgenic goat under special monitoring because the data are very scarce. The decision was, consequently, also a matter of choice of research politics. Second, ATryn® serves as an anticoagulant for patients suffering from a very rare disease who undergo surgery; that is, who are in a *risky* situation because they need the surgery but they also need to compensate their coagulation problem. In this sense, for the individual patients the use of Atryn® could in some cases be a matter of life and death – a similar situation as the case of xenotransplantation – so that at the individual level it is not really a matter of balancing costs and benefits. The risk assessment assumes, as a consequence, a social connotation, in the sense that society should deliberate about the impact of the introduction of biomedical procedures which present unpredictable risks.

At the societal level, especially for the case of xenotransplantation, there are some concerns about the newly created scenario with regard to the question of allocation of resources. Xenotransplants are not expected to reach the same degree of safety and success as allotransplants, and thus the introduction of xenotransplantation in medical practice could generate inequalities between patients who immediately receive human organs or cells and others who receive animal ones. Some argue for conceptualizing xenotransplantation, instead of a routine procedure, as a 'bridge-therapy' in patients who are nearing death while waiting for a graft, but this also poses some difficulties, because the performance of two major surgical procedures instead of one (allotransplant following xenotransplant) is expected to diminish survival following the allograft, since the body's recipient may be sensitized against a future allograft (Steele and Auchincloss, 1995). Moreover, it remains open whether this solution effectively addresses the fundamental issue of the shortage of human donor organs. Similarly, in gene-pharming the question of the opportunity of producing therapeutical proteins in GM animals remains also open, due to the fact that rapid developments have taken place, for example in the creation of therapeutical proteins in transgenic plants, bacteria, yeast or animal cells (Twyman et al, 2005). One of the strongest arguments against the use of GM animals as bioreactors relies indeed on the assumption that the largest part of the drugs currently under clinical trials are in some ways already present on the market and that biotech companies are only trying to find more lucrative ways to produce them.

IMPLICATIONS FOR ANIMALS

Beyond the many implications for human beings, unpredictable risks of xenotransplantation and gene-pharming pose important animal ethical concerns. A great number of animals are involved in the production of GM animals,[20] both at the stage of creation (as animals are involved in obtaining zygotes, which is a necessary step in the creation) and at the stage of breeding the genetic modification into the desired genetic background (since not all of the modified animals will express the transgene in the manner requested in the experiment; Ferrari, 2006, 2008).[21] The animals that are not useful for the experiment are normally killed.

Procedures for genetic modification of farm animals have a very low efficiency: for example, with the pronuclear microinjection (the usual method applied to farm animals) the average successful rate of the injected eggs which develop to GM animals is below 1 per cent (0.2 per cent for pigs and 0.7 per cent for sheep, goats and calves; Van Reenen et al, 2001). An essential and complementary technique for the creation of GM livestock in gene-pharming is the technique of cloning via somatic cell nuclear transfer, because it permits targeted genetic changes in farm species.[22] In addition, this technique presents a very low efficiency (between 1 and 10 per cent; National Academy of Science, 2002; Nationaler Ethikrat, 2004; Clausen, 2006).

Although the genetic modification of an animal does not necessarily mean that it will havc welfare problems, in most cases, a number of factors connected with this modification increase the risks of the animal suffering and of manifesting negative effects at the phenotypic level, more than in conventional breeding. The cloning techniques via somatic cell nuclear transfer are also often connected with welfare problems such as embryonic and foetal losses, various birth abnormalities (especially oversize problems) and a greater propensity in the later stages of life for respiratory problems and immunodeficiencies compared with conventional animals (Wells, 2005).

First of all, the methods used in the genetic modification of farm animals allow only a random integration of the inserted gene-construct in the genome.[23] The mechanism of integration is not known; hence the consequences of the modification to the phenotype cannot be predicted with accuracy. It has been observed that genetic modification can have a significant impact on an animal's biological functioning and fitness because it is often connected with a decrease in the survival rate of the pups, reductions in fertility and a higher occurrence of pathologies (such as lameness and mastitis, especially in cows; FAWC, 1998). Moreover, animal welfare can be affected, even if the phenotypic effects are subtle, because damaging mutations may not surface for many generations, so that generally the unpredictability of the techniques means that it is extremely difficult, or impossible, to reliably anticipate negative effects on the phenotype of the animal and to be able to ameliorate them (Buehr et al, 2003).

The unpredictability of the phenotype also implies that each animal can present unique characteristics that complicate the application of welfare measures in breeding and use (Ferrari, 2006). Furthermore, due to the safety requirements connected with the use of genetically modified materials, GM livestock have to be constantly monitored, and kept under pathogen free conditions and in isolation. These conditions are not suitable to the specific needs of the animals: for example, pigs are social animals that like to wallow in the mud.

Another important issue is the use of non-human primates as recipients of organs, tissues and cells from GM pigs in the experimental research on xenotransplantation. In their reports, both the Nuffield Council of Bioethics (1996) and the Advisory Group on the Ethics of Xenotransplantation (1997) proposed to exclude primates from this research, partly on the basis of pragmatic reasons (because the phylogenetical closeness of them to human beings increases the risk of infection), partly for ethical reasons (because of their great capability of suffering and their cognitive and emotional capabilities). Precisely because of these reasons, the use of them as recipients in experimental research is very controversial in the current debate.

Ethical assessment of the risks: a proposal

It seems that a consideration of the implications posed by these biomedical practices to the different subjects involved, such as individuals, society and animals, is fundamental when we are dealing with practices connected with unpredictable risks. Hansson (2003) recently proposed an interesting scheme for the evaluation of actions with certain outcomes. Hansson is unsatisfied with the traditional view of solving the so-called problem of 'appraising mixtures' for human actions with undetermined properties, that is, in assessing the value of these actions. According to Hansson, this view is dominated by the idea that actions with indeterminate outcomes can be evaluated by combining the moral appraisal of actions with determinate outcomes with their probabilities. The problem recognized by Hansson is that in real life, in addition to probabilities and utilities, there are always other factors that can influence a moral appraisal of a situation with risk; some of these are consent, intentions, agency, duties, rights and the question of equity for the distribution of resources.

These elements are very important because they permit a personalization of the risk-benefit calculus by taking in account how the individual considers the benefits and the risks as well as how the individual interests correlate or conflict with those of the public. As a consequence, Hansson proposes to reformulate the problem of appraising mixtures, focusing on the search for the conditions under which 'the right not to be exposed to risks has been overridden, but not necessarily cancelled' (Hansson, 2003, p303). The non-cancellation of the risk (since its outcome is uncertain) permits us to save some residual obligations, such as to inform and to reduce the risk whenever possible, which for Hansson play an important role in the risk assessment.

Applying this to the particular case of the creation and use of transgenic livestock for biomedical purposes, we have to reflect upon the following: in order to assess the ethical acceptability of xenotransplantation and gene-pharming we must not only consider the probability of a particular scenario (such as the spreading of a pandemic as the worst case) and the utility of the outcome for the patient or the consumer, but we should also consider the impact on the rights of the individuals involved in the distribution of the resources for society, and the impact on the animals. It is important to consider how the extraordinary monitoring of the patient is consistent and compatible with the respect for his/her autonomy and with the principle of non maleficence and beneficence,[24] and what the possible conflicts are between the individual interests and duties of society to protect itself, along with duties towards future generations.

The case for biomedical research is a very sensitive topic because, as I already wrote, it deals with the protection of health and amelioration of illness, and because in this case it is based upon the use of animals. Consequently, for the ethical assessment of unpredictable risks in these practices, we must also consider three other factors in addition to the ones mentioned by Hansson, which seem to me specifically connected with this particular case.

First of all, I think that the consideration of the possible conflict of interests among generations should constitute a factor to be taken into account in the ethical assessment of these practices. The presence of unpredictable risks in these fields is connected with the possibility of the so-called 'decoupling phenomena' by the assignment of responsibility (*Entkopplungsphänomene*, Bonß, 1995), which consists of a sort of separation between the responsible actors and the subjects who will suffer the consequences of the decisions. The presence of unpredictable risks in xenotransplantation and gene-pharming renders the assessment of the responsibility for the identification of the responsible subjects problematic (Hüsing et al, 2001, pp221–222). Since it is indirectly suggested that the monitoring system can guarantee the safety of the patient and the society, who will be identified as responsible in case of the widespread of a pandemy? Furthermore, a decoupling phenomenon in assigning responsibility can also occur because the possibility of the pandemy might only occur in later generations. Who will be responsible for a pandemy in the future?

The possibility of decoupling phenomena renders the social dimension of unpredictable risks connected to the practices discussed very evident. It would not only be a matter for the individual patient who took drugs or underwent xenotransplantation, but also for society and future generations. Society should be responsible for the future consequences of technologies that it has allowed. As a consequence, I propose that in the ethical assessment of these practices, society should not only take into account its responsibility for its current members, but also its responsibility for future generations.

Second, I propose taking into account the possibility of alternative research strategies. Choices in biomedical research are a matter of political decision-making because research money and means are limited – they are not available for every experimental sector – so that the financial support for one field means at the same time lack of support for one other. Choices of research policy are embedded in a normative framework. There are criteria for defining an acceptable research, both in the case of research on human subjects and on animals. What should be deliberated about is whether the creation of further risks for public health, and for patients as drug-consumers or as recipients of non-human materials, justifies the allocation of research funding in these procedures and not in others. Moreover, the ethical acceptability of pursuing a research strategy also depends on the advantages of the strategy in contrast to others, especially if they appear less problematic. Specifically in the case of xenotransplantation, it ought to be considered that quality of life appears to be severely reduced by the required lifelong monitoring of the patients and their close contacts. Moreover, alternative strategies are also connected to the possibility of other methods, which do not involve the use of animals. It could be argued, for example, that the general presupposition of a long-term trend of increasing numbers of patients requiring transplants, on which the idea of xenotransplantation is based, is not exactly realistic in these terms because improved diagnostic and surgical procedures, for example, may eliminate the need for many organ transplants. As a consequence, the consideration of alternatives seems to me to be urgent both in xenotransplantation and in gene-pharming: in xenotransplantation because of the unclear implications of this practice for the question of allocation of resources and the implications in terms of suffering and killing for the animals, and in gene-pharming because of the possibility of creating drugs in different ways which do not involve the creation of GM animals, such as, for example, in GM plants and bacteria. The example of ATryn® is a very interesting lesson: due to the difficulties in the purification of the proteins and the associated risks, ATryn® has been approved only as a substitute for more traditional anticoagulants in cases where patients with hereditary deficiency undergo surgery and hence undertake the risk of a haemorrhage, that is, in very specific contexts.[25] It is now definitely too early to judge if the approval of ATryn® is only the first and small step for a broader acceptance of many other substances obtained from GM livestock or not, but it remains clear that notwithstanding decades of experimentation until now the production of therapeutical proteins in these animals is a very expensive, inefficient and risky way of producing only a very limited number of substances. As a matter of fact only one has been approved and will be on the market.

Third, I propose direct consideration of the implications in terms of suffering and death for the GM animals deliberately created and used. Since these practices are connected with serious risks for individual and public health, animal ethical concerns about the use of animals and the creation of suffering carry an even stronger authority. The genetic engineering of animals poses higher risks for the individual animal to suffer and to have unexpected negative alterations of its phenotype, which are not foreseeable and therefore not controllable. Moreover, the special breeding conditions and the use of animals are not suitable to their specific needs and cause them suffering in many cases.

The complexity of the challenges posed by the unpredictable risks in the biomedical uses of transgenic livestock obliges us to think in a broader and more complex way than the one offered by the risk-benefit calculus. It is not sufficient to draft the expected benefits and the supposed risks, but it is necessary to scrutinize the interactions of these risks with other important factors such as claims of intergenerational justice, protection of animal welfare, respect for the autonomy of people and the possibility of alternative research strategies. In the debate, it is necessary to rethink the risks and, as a consequence, also the benefits, connecting the different implications of an introduction of these practices with the goals which are to be pursued and in order to be able to judge whether the unpredictable risks are really ethically acceptable.

To conclude, I think that the burden of proof should be on those who defend these practices because they have to show that we are dealing with a reasonably safe and above all ethically acceptable practice. Since it seems to me that the posed risks are very great, the implications for all the subjects involved are very serious, as well as the benefits are disputable and ambiguous, I judge these practices as not ethically acceptable. Furthermore, they implement further and new uses of animals, thus they stay in contrast with ethical commitments to reduce and replace animal experimentation.

References

Advisory Group on the Ethics of Xenotransplantation (1997) *Animal Tissue into Humans*, London, TSO

Beauchamp, T. L. and Childress, J. F. (1994) *Principles of Biomedical Ethics*, 4th edn, Oxford University Press, Oxford

Beauchamp, T. L. and Childress, J. F. (2001) *Principles of Biomedical Ethics*, 5th edn (1st edn 1979) Oxford University Press, New York

Bonß, W. (1995) Vom Risiko. Unsicherheit und Ungewissheit in der Moderne, Hamburger Edition, Hamburg

Buehr, M. et al (2003) 'Genetically modified laboratory animals – What welfare problems do they face?', *Journal of Applied Animal Welfare Science*, vol 6, no 4, pp319–338

Celis, P. and Silvester, G. (2004) 'European regulatory guidance on virus safety of recombinant proteins, monoclonal antibodies and plasma derived medicinal products', *Developments in Biologicals*, vol 118, p310

Clark, J. and Whitelaw, B. (2003) 'A future for transgenic livestock', *Nature Reviews Genetics*, vol 4, pp825–833

Clausen, J. (2006) *Biotechnische Innovationen verantworten: Das Beispiel Klonen*, Wissenschaftliche Buchgesellschaft, Darmstadt

Coffin, J. M., Hughes, S. H. and Varmus, H. E. (1997) *Retroviruses*, Cold Spring Harbor Laboratory Press, Cold Spring, Harbor

Cozzi, E., Bosio, E., Seveso, M., Vadori, M. and Ancona, E. (2006) 'Xenotransplantation – current status and future perspectives', *British Medical Bulletin*, vol 75–76, no 1, pp99–114

Daar, A. S. (1997) 'Ethics of xenotransplantation: animal issues, consent, and likely transformation of transplant ethics', *World Journal of Surgery*, vol 21, pp975–982

Dyck, M. K., Lacroix, D., Pothier, F. and Sirard, M.-A. (2003) 'Making recombinant proteins in animals – different systems, different applications', *Trends in Biotechnology*, vol 21, no 9, pp394–399

Einsiedel, E. F. (2005) 'Public perceptions of transgenic animals', *Revue Scientifique et Technique*, vol 24, no 1, pp149–157

EMEA (2004) 'Note for guidance on minimising risk of transmitting animal spongiform encelopathy agents via human and veterinary medicinal products', *Official Journal of the European Union*, 28 January, www.emea.europa.eu/pdfs/human/bwp/TSE%20 NFG%20410-rev2.pdf

EMEA (2006a) *Press Release, 2 June 2006*, Doc. Ref EMEA 203163/2006, European Medicines Agency adopts first positive opinion for a medicinal product derived from transgenic biotechnology, www.emea.europa.eu/pdfs/general/direct/pr/20316306en.pdf

EMEA (2006b) *Questions and Answers on Re-Examination Opinion for ATRYN*, EMEA Doc. Ref. 191862/2006, www.emea.europa.eu/pdfs/general/direct/pr/19186206en.pdf

EMEA (2006c) *European Public Assessment Report (EPAR) ATRYN. EPAR summary for the public* EMEA/H/C/679, www.emea.europa.eu/Humansdocs/Humans/EPAR/ atryn/atryn.htm

EMEA (2006d) *European Public Assessment Report (EPAR) ATRYN. Scientific Discussion*, www.emea.europa.eu/Humansdocs/Humans/EPAR/atryn/atryn.htm

EMEA (2008) *Questions and Answers on Recommendation for the Refusal of the Marketing Authorisation for Rhucin*, http://www.emea.europa.eu/pdfs/human/opinion/Q&A_ Rhucin_14310508en.pdf

Farm Animal Welfare Council (FAWC) (1998) *Report on Implications of Cloning for the Welfare of Farmed Livestock*, www.fawc.org.uk/reports/clone/clonetoc.htm

Ferrari, A. (2006) 'Genetically modified laboratory animals in the name of the 3Rs?', *ALTEX*, vol 23, no 4, pp294–307

Ferrari, A. (2008) *Genmaus & Co. Gentechnisch veränderte Tiere in der Biomedizin*, Harald Fischer Verlag, Erlangen

Fishman, J. (1997) 'Xenosis and xenotransplatation: addressing the infectious risks posed by an emerging technology', *Kidney International*, vol 51, pp41–45

Hansson, S. (2003) 'Ethical criteria of risks acceptance', *Erkenntniss*, vol 59, no 3, pp291–309

Hansson, S. (2005) *Decision Theory. A Brief Introduction*, www.infra.kth.se/~soh/decision-theory.pdf

Houdebine, L. M. (2000) 'Transgenic animal bioreactors', *Transgenic Research*, vol 9, no 4, pp301–304

Hunter, N. et al (2002) 'Transmission of prion diseases by blood transfusion', *Journal of General Virology*, vol 83, pp2897–2905

Hüsing, B., Engels, E., Gaisser, S. and Zimmer, R. (2001) *Zelluläre Xenotransplantation*, Studie des Zentrums für Technikfolgen-Abschätzung beim Schweizerischen Wissenschafts- und Technologierat, TA 39/2001

Janne, J., Hyttinen, J. M., Peura, T., Tolvanen, M., Slhonen, L. and Halmekto, M. (1992) 'Transgenic animals as bioproducers of therapeutic proteins', *Annals of Medicine*, vol 24, no 4, pp273–280

LEO Pharma (2006) 'Europäische Kommission erteilt Zulassung für ATryn®', www.leo-pharma.de/C1256B06003CCFBF/, last consultation 1 December 2006

Lubon, H. (1998) 'Transgenic animal bioreactors in biotechnology and production of blood proteins', *Biotechology Annual Review*, vol 4, pp1–54

Magre, S., Takeuchi, Y. and Bartosch, B. (2003) 'Xenotransplantation and pig endogenous retroviruses', *Reviews in Medical Virology*, vol 13, no 5, pp311–329

Mepham, T. B. et al (1998) 'The use of transgenic animals in the European Union – the report and the recommendations', *Alternatives to Laboratory Animals*, vol 26, no 1, pp21–43

National Academy of Science (2002) *Scientific and Medical Aspects of Human Reproductive Cloning*, The National Academy of Science, Washington

National Research Council (2002) *Animal Biotechnology: Science-Based Concerns*, The National Academies Press, Washington, www.nap.edu

Nationaler Ethikrat (2004) *Klonen zu Fortpflanzungszwecken und Klonen zu biomedizinischen Forschungszwecken*, Stellungsnahme, Druckhaus Berlin-Mitte, Berlin

Nuffield Council on Bioethics (1996). *Animal-to-Human Transplants: The Ethics of Xenotransplantation*, Nuffield Council on Bioethics, London

Patience, C. et al (1998) 'No evidence of pig DNA or retroviral infection in patients with short-term extracorporeal connection to pig kidneys', *Lancet*, vol 352, p699

Peplow, M. (2006) 'Drug from GM animal gets thumbs down', http://www.nature.com/news/2006/060224/full/news060220-17.html

Salomon, B. et al (2001) 'Erfassung und Bewertung des Leidens sowie der Belastung transgener Tiere im Tierversuch im Vergleich zu konventionellen Tierversuchen', in Auftrag von Bundesministerium für Bildung, Wissenschaft und Kultur, Wien

SAMW (1999) *Medizin-ethische Grundsätze zur Xenotransplantation*, Basel, Schweizerische Akademie der medizinischen Wissenschaften

Schmidt, C. (2006) 'Belated approval of first recombinant protein from animal', *Nature Biotechnology*, vol 24, p877

Steele, D. J. and Auchincloss, H. (1995) 'The application of xenotransplantation in humans – reasons to delay', *Institute for Laboratory Animal Resources Journal*, vol 37, no 1, pp13–15

Sykes, M., d'Apice, A. and Sandrin, M. (2004) 'Position Paper of the Ethics Committee of the International Xenotransplantation Association', *Transplantation*, vol 78, no 8

Thomas, J. A. and Fuchs, R. L. (2002) *Biotechnology and Safety Assessment*, Elsevier Science, San Diego

Twyman, R. M., Schillberg, S. and Fischer, R. (2005) 'Transgenic plants in the biopharmaceutical market', *Expert Opinions on Emerging Drugs*, vol 10, no 1, pp185–218

US Department of Health and Human Services (1999) *Guidance for Industry. Public Health Issues Posed by the Use of Nonhuman Primate Xenografts in Humans.* www.fda.gov/CBER/gdlns/xenoprim.htm#iii

Van Reenen, C. G., Meuwissen, T. H., Hopster, H., Oldenbroek, K., Kruip, T. H. and Blokhuis, H. J. (2001) 'Transgenesis may affect farm animal welfare: A case for systematic risk assessment', *Journal of Animal Science*, vol 79, pp1763–1779

Weiss, R. A. (1998) 'Retrovirus zoonoses', *Nature Medicine*, vol 4, no 4, pp391–392

Wells, D. J., Playle, L. C., Enser, W. E. et al. (2006) 'Assessing the welfare of genetically altered mice', *Laboratory Animals*, 40, pp111–114. Report at www.nc3rs.org.uk/GAmice or www.lal.org.uk/gaa.

Wood, J. C. et al (2004) 'Identification of exogenous forms of human-tropic porcine endogenous retrovirus in miniature swine', *Journal of Virology*, vol 78, no 5, pp2494–2501

World Health Organization (WHO) (2001) 'Communicable disease surveillance and response', Guidance on Xenogeneic Infection/Disease Surveillance and Response: A Strategy for International Cooperation and Coordination. WHO/CDS/CSR/EPH/2001.2, whqlibdoc.who.int/hq/2001/WHO_CDS_CSR_EPH_2001.2.pdf

World Health Organization (WHO) (2005) *Animal To Human Transplantation – Future Potential, Present Risk*, WHO Media Centre, www.who.int/mediacentre/news/notes/2005/np08/en/index.html

NOTES

1 The term transgenic animal refers to an animal which has been genetically modified by stable incorporation, using genetic engineering techniques, that is, in which the inserted gene construct can be transmitted to the next generation (Mepham et al, 1998). Genetically modified animals which do not have a stable integration cannot be properly defined as 'transgenic'. However, in many cases the word 'transgenic' is simply used as synonym for 'genetically modified'.

2 Ex-vivo perfusion means those procedures in which human body fluids, cells, tissues or organs are removed from the body, come into contact with live animal cells, tissues or organs, and are then placed back into a human patient. This precise definition is particularly relevant for the case of human embryonic stem cells which have come into contact with animal material.

3 The term 'pharming' comes from a combination of the words 'farming' and 'pharmaceuticals'.

4 Bird or avian flu refers to influenza A viruses found in birds, which can however be pathogenic for human beings. Since 1997 more than 200 confirmed cases of human infection with avian influenza viruses have been documented and the topic is currently monitored by the WHO. Most cases of infection are thought to have resulted from direct contact with infected poultry or contaminated surfaces. The differences between the various strains of viruses and their different impact on public health risks still remain unknown.

5 Human immuno-deficiency virus, also known as HIV, is a lentivirus – which is part of the family of retroviruses – described as the cause of acquired immunodeficiency

syndrome (AIDS). There are two species of HIV infected humans (HIV-1 and HIV-2) and there are different theories to explain the transfer of this virus to humans. In any case, the WHO estimates that AIDS has killed more than 25 million people since it was first recognized in 1981, making it one of the most destructive pandemics in recorded history. See UNAIDS, *2006 Report on the Global Aids Epidemic* http://data.unaids.org/pub/GlobalReport/2006/2006_GR-ExecutiveSummary_en.pdf.

6 Even the process of allotransplantation (i.e. the human-to-human transplantation) is associated with safety risks, xenotransplantation presents a more complex scenario than allotransplantation, due to the antigenic disparities present on tissue derived from different species. Moreover, there are also relevant differences between the immunological barriers by the xenotransplantation of solid organs and of cells (cf Cozzi et al, 2006).

7 Retroviruses are not the only viral agents which raise concerns in xenotransplantation: there are also viruses whose zoonotic potential is already known (such as rabies) and viral agents which are normally not considered zoonotic, but which are so closely related to their human counterparts that they are normally connected with a high risk potential (e.g. herpes-viruses) (Coffin et al, 1997).

8 Rejection primarily involves how the immune system uses several lines of defence against infection from foreign organisms such as parasites and bacteria, and specifically when the system attacks transplants. Various methods of modifying xenotransplantation procedures have been created to solve this problem. These procedures go mainly in two directions. One method is to attempt to alter the recipient's immune system to increase the transplant tolerance. Another is to use genetic engineering to change the organs, cells and tissues of the donating animal, especially by deleting certain animal genes to be replaced by human genes. In the debate it has been consistently assumed that the transplant rejection risk can be adequately managed (Eurosurveillance, 2005).

9 A bunch of biotech companies is exploring the field of gene-pharming: Origen Therapeutics, located in Burlingame, California, is developing a transgenic production line that employs chickens for the production of human anticancer proteins and other antibodies in their eggs (see www.origentherapeutics.com). In 2007 they received a grant of $2 million from the National Institute of Standards and Technology (NIST), a division of the US Department of Commerce, to develop a new method for discovering and producing human polyclonal antibodies in eggs from genetically modified chickens. In Athens, USA, AviGenics is using a transgenic-chicken system to make a protein compound that stimulates the bone marrow to make more white blood cells, in order to help cancer patients bounce back after chemotherapy (on the internet this company is available under Synageva; see http://www.synageva.com/).

10 Products that, if approved, are expected to provide a significant improvement in the safety or effectiveness of the treatment, diagnosis or prevention of a serious or life-threatening disease are granted the Priority Review by the Food and Drug Administration. See http://www.gtc-bio.com/pressreleases/pr090408.html.

11 The company GTC tested from the beginning the drug on 19 patients with antithrombin deficiency, a hereditary lack of anticoagulant protein in their blood: five surgical patients, nine pregnant women and five indicated as 'compassionate use cases' (Schmidt, 2006). Since changes have occurred in the middle of the study regarding how the drug was administered to nine of the patients, the European authorities considered only the remaining five surgical patients, also refusing to take into account data from the nine pregnant women. EMEA judged that the data from five patients was too few to determine whether the drug worked safely (the minimum requested for this kind of review is 12 cases). GTC explained the low number of patients by the fact that the drug was thought to cure a very rare disease, i.e. the hereditary AT deficiency,

which affects just one in 3000–5000 people. That is typical for biotechnology companies, which are specialized in the selling of high-priced drugs that treat very few patients.

12 This disease causes swelling of the blood vessels.

13 Rhucin has been produced by the Dutch biotechnology firm Pharming (PHAR.AS). See also http://www.reuters.com/article/rbssHealthcareNews/idUSWEB946220080320.

14 Atryn® is given only under medical prescription and to patients suffering from hereditary AT deficiency who undergo surgery. Atryn® is given to prevent problems due to the formation of clots in the vessels and is normally given in combination with another anti-clotting medicine (heparin). See EMEA (2006c).

15 'Prion' is the short form for proteinaceous infectious particle that indicates an abnormally structured form of a host protein, which is able to convert normal molecules of the protein into the abnormal structure.

16 Houdebine is director of the animal gene study laboratory at the French Institute for Agronomy Research and he is also co-founder of BioProteins Therapeutics.

17 Bonß (1995) uses the term 'dangers' instead of risks because he wants to stress the new character of the challenges of many current practices. These dangers are not quantifiable and not assignable to precise subjects, so that they differ from the classical notion of risk. However, in the current debate they are also called 'second-order risks'.

18 IXA is the International Xenotransplantation Association.

19 XTx is xenotransplantation.

20 The animals needed to create the 'right' transgenic one and which are not directly used in the experiment are called 'waste-animals' (Salomon et al, 2001).

21 Furthermore, many animals are also used in order to maintain a GM line. The breeding of a line of animals is an essential step in animal experimentation, because in order to assess the scientific validity of experiments they should be repeatable (cf Ferrari, 2006, pp295–296).

22 The technique of cloning via somatic cell nuclear transfer permits targeted genetic changes in virtually all species: these targeted changes are only possible via the usual genetic engineering only through the method of gene targeting using embryonic stem cells, which is only possible in the mouse.

23 The only genetic engineering method which allows a precise integration of the gene construct in the animal's genome is the site-specific recombination (gene targeting technique), which uses embryonic stem cells. This method is so far only possible in mice.

24 The four principles of respect for autonomy, non maleficence, beneficence and justice were described by Beauchamp and Childress in 2001 as solution 'tools' for conflicts in the biomedical practice. They were argued to be mid-level principles mediating between high-level moral theory and low-level common morality, and they immediately became very popular in writings about medical ethics. The principle of beneficence relies upon the moral idea of doing good and avoiding evil, which has obviously a longer tradition than just the one in the biomedical context. The principle of non maleficence espouses the belief in not inflicting harm on an individual (cf Beauchamp and Childress, 1994).

25 As a matter of fact, GTC is now working with another company (LEO Pharma A/S) to develop ATryn® as an anti-coagulant specific for sepsis patients who have acquired an antithrombin deficiency.

Part III

Methodological Considerations

Integrating ethical considerations into risk management gives rise to methodological problems. Risk analysis becomes more complex. But the supposed simplicity and objectivity of conventional risk analysis is illusionary. The methodology is inherently limited and biased. Douglas MacLean argues that ethical considerations are inherent to risk analysis, but they cannot be reduced to preferences or willingness to pay. Nicolas Espinoza discusses problems for cost-benefit analysis that arise from the fact that risks can be evaluatively incommensurable or incomparable. Greg Bognar shows the limits of an ideal advisor-approach to welfare judgements about risks, as it insufficiently takes into account contextual features and the fact that people can cooperate.

8 Ethics, Reasons and Risk Analysis

Douglas MacLean

> Economists are right to be diffident about their own ethical opinions if they are not founded on good arguments and well worked-out theory. In that case, their opinions will not prosper in the market place of ideas. Perhaps this is indeed the reason why so many economists are reticent. The solution is for them to get themselves good arguments, and work out the theory. It is not to hide behind the preferences of other people, when those preferences may not be well founded, and when the people themselves may be looking for better foundations. (Broome, 2005, p88)[1]

INTRODUCTION

The role of reasons in risk analysis is a subject that has not only received insufficient attention, it is regarded with antipathy and suspicion among risk and policy analysts. This may seem a surprising fact, because the fundamental aim of risk analysis (and policy analysis more generally) is to assist rational agents in making choices that will realize their values to the fullest extent. We live in a world of uncertainty, and we face situations that require trade-offs among our most desired ends. Risk analysis tries to identify and measure the severity of the risks we face and to compare them to the costs and benefits of eliminating, reducing, increasing or ignoring them. All of this is aimed at helping us figure out what we ought to do. How could this not be seen as, for the most part, a normative activity? But if it is normative, then it must be governed by reasons, for how else are we to determine what ought to be, or what we ought to do, except by appealing to reasons? Yet risk analysis avoids getting involved in reasons. This fact needs to be explained.

AVOIDING NORMATIVITY

Inquiries into what ought to be or what we ought to do or believe are normative: that's what 'normative' means. But most risk analysts, in my experience, are reluctant to acknowledge that their work is part of a normative enterprise. Rather, they see themselves as engaged in a two-step scientific process. The first step involves identifying and measuring risks, such as risks to human life and health. This is basically an empirical matter. The second step is to identify and measure individual preferences for risk reduction and to determine the public's aggregate willingness to pay to reduce risks. This is also basically an empirical matter, however preferences are understood. Risk analysis thus helps to evaluate the severity of different risks, not just in physical terms but also as they matter to people, and the results of the analysis provide useful advice to policy-makers. Risk analysis so conceived will include a good bit of evaluation, but this is not necessarily normative. It is meant only to give decision-makers useful information, not to tell individuals what they ought to think or policy-makers what they ought to do.

No risk analyst would deny that ethical issues matter to how people think about risk and how policy-makers make decisions. But in its aspiration to be as scientific and ethically neutral as possible, risk analysis typically tries to sequester the ethical dimensions of risk into two arenas that it need not enter. Individuals should be left free to work out the ethical claims on their thinking about risk as they develop their own preferences for trading off the cost of risk reduction against other costs. Risk analysis is concerned only with measuring and aggregating these preferences. As for the ethical issues that arise at the social level – matters of justice, giving priority to certain risks or certain groups of people, weighing present gains against future risk, or taking into account the special reasons we may have for protecting specific areas or eliminating a particular kind of risk – these should be left to the political process.

If this is a correct, rough portrait of the self-conception of the risk analyst's conception of his subject, then we can begin to comprehend his suspicion of appeals to consider the reasons people may have for their preferences or the reasons for making different decisions about trading off risks, costs and benefits. Reasons for having some preference or making some decision take us into the realm of the normative, and this can only invite controversy about the proper role of risk analysis or about who has the right to challenge the sovereignty of individuals to embrace their own values and form their own preferences. The risk analyst believes he has good reasons for avoiding these controversies: they threaten to compromise his neutrality and the scientific aspirations of his profession. They may also compromise his influence as a trusted and indispensable advisor to those who are entrusted with the power to make policy decisions and want advice that they believe reflects the public will in a non-partisan way.

RISK EVALUATION, POLICY ANALYSIS AND ECONOMICS

This claim about compromising influence requires some further explanation. The explanation I offer here is also drawn from personal experience and reflection.

The foundations of risk analysis are partly in engineering and the natural sciences, where risks are identified and quantified, and partly in economics, where the methods for assessing the costs of reducing risk and measuring preferences for trading off risks and costs have been developed.

The part of risk analysis that is concerned with identifying and measuring risk – risk estimation, as it is sometimes called – includes elements of toxicology and epidemiology; it includes fault tree analyses, computer simulations and stress tests of natural systems and engineered structures; and it includes much more. It is a remarkable human achievement that we are able to understand and forecast risks as well as we do, an achievement made possible in part by one of the great intellectual advances in human history, the discovery of the laws of probability and statistics. We can predict with great accuracy many things that will happen to aggregate populations even when we cannot know what will happen to any individual within the population. The application of statistics and probability theory in risk analysis has improved our lives immeasurably.

To be sure, some interesting ethical issues are involved in this part of risk analysis. Even here we cannot avoid normative questions, such as what we ought to identify or count as a risk. That we consider smoking to cause a health risk but not the human susceptibility to lung cancer, or that we consider the genes that cause Down's syndrome to be a risk factor but not the genes that are responsible for ageing, involve normative judgements that can raise ethical issues. But I will not discuss these ethical issues here. I will not address the part of risk analysis that is involved primarily with prediction and estimation.

It is the part of risk analysis that is related to economics – the part that is sometimes called risk evaluation – that takes what we know about the risks we face and tries to help decision-makers figure out what, if anything, to do about them. Here the prevailing method is either to look for evidence in which people reveal their preferences for risk reduction – that is, how they trade off risk reduction against other costs and benefits – or to create settings in which people can express preferences about risk reduction that may not be revealed in ordinary (economic) behaviour. The methods for getting people to express these preferences are generally known as contingent valuation methods. There is an extensive literature on methods for revealing risk preferences, contingent valuation methods for expressing risk preferences and the relative strengths and weaknesses of each approach (Stern and Finebergs, 1996).

Almost entirely lacking in this literature is any normative discussion of the *role* of individual preferences in evaluating risks and the benefits of reducing them. This role is often taken for granted in the research literature, and in many places it is acquiring the force of law about how societies should approach these issues.

For example, in the curricula for training policy analysts, the field in which risk analysis is supposed to be located, it is generally assumed (though seldom argued) that the goal of public policies and other government actions is primarily to promote the welfare of those affected by them. It is also generally assumed (but again seldom argued) that welfare is promoted by satisfying the preferences of individuals. Thus in one of the most widely used and highly respected policy analysis textbooks in the United States, the authors state that 'individual welfare is all that matters in policy choices'. Without further explanation, they also claim that preference satisfaction is the criterion by which we are to judge a person's well-being: 'In the United States, we usually take the position that it is the individual's own preferences that count, that he is the best judge of his own welfare' (Stokey and Zeckhauser, 1978, p262).

The story of how this way of thinking comes to be legally binding in the United States is clearly seen through a series of Presidential Executive Orders and ensuing Executive Office directives that were issued to interpret and implement legislation passed primarily to regulate various risks to human life and health and to the environment. These Executive Orders, going back to the 1970s, impose increasingly explicit requirements on administrative agencies to justify proposed major regulations with a cost-benefit analysis that attempts to show that the benefits of the regulation are greater than the costs imposed in meeting it. The benefits could include things that range from reducing a health risk, to saving a species, improving workplace conditions, protecting an area of natural beauty, or almost anything else. How are these benefits to be measured and compared to the costs of producing them? The answer is by measuring the public's preferences for these benefits as expressed by the aggregate of individual willingness to pay to satisfy them. This is the proposed neutral method that will avoid fundamental normative issues.

In 1999, President Clinton signed Executive Order 12866, which required that proposed regulations be submitted for approval to the Office of Management and Budget, along with a justifying cost-benefit analysis of the proposal.[2] To help regulatory agencies meet this requirement, the Office of Information and Regulatory Affairs (OIRA – part of the Office of Management and Budget) issued in 2003 guidelines that are known as 'Circular A-4: Regulatory Analysis'.[3] These guidelines give government sanction to the preference satisfaction criterion of benefit as measured by willingness-to-pay. Circular A-4 states that to the fullest extent possible, the benefits and costs that result from a proposed regulation should be expressed in monetary units, because these measures give a clear indication of the most efficient alternatives for decision-makers. It also includes detailed discussion of techniques for measuring willingness-to-pay for goods that are not normally traded in established markets. To be fair, Circular A-4 recognizes that it will not make sense to value every kind of benefit from risk reduction (and other proposed regulatory benefit) in monetary terms, so it instructs agencies at least to try to quantify the benefits that cannot be monetized.

I served on a committee convened in 2004 to try to consider and assess the value of some particularly difficult kinds of environmental benefits.[4] The Director of OIRA wrote a letter to our committee to explain the process set out in Circular A-4, and he went on in that letter to acknowledge that:

> Circular A-4 recognizes that it is often not possible to quantify all of the effects of a regulation. In such cases, the Circular requires and encourages the analyst to identify the non-quantitative factors of sufficient importance to justify consideration in developing a regulatory decision.[5]

The letter suggests that the Director is bending over backwards to avoid admitting that someone might want to appeal to a reason for acting – something that cannot easily be quantified – to reduce a risk or protect something valuable in the environment. But when he allows an analyst to 'identify the non-quantitative factors of sufficient importance', isn't he opening the door to reasons? The Director pretty clearly felt that this clause in Circular A-4 can only invite trouble, for, as his letter quickly went on to explain, 'we believe that ... efforts to better quantify ... effects are more likely than valuation efforts to prove productive in providing useful information for regulatory analysis'. And why is that? Because in the view of people who adopt this way of thinking, reasons do not fit within the neutral confines of science, including the decision sciences. As the Director explains near the close of his letter to our committee, Circular A-4 is explicit that 'valuation' processes 'would ideally use "willingness-to-pay" measures to reflect ... valuation ... rather than the subjective values of the regulatory analyst'.

RISK ANALYSIS AS A BRANCH OF ETHICS

I have been trying to describe a way of thinking that I am convinced is pervasive and is an essentially accurate picture of risk analysis. It is, I admit, a sketch drawn largely from anecdote and personal reflection. I assume nevertheless that the picture will strike many readers familiar with risk analysis as pretty much on the mark. Now I want to criticize this conception of the risk analyst's role in the policy-making process as fundamentally misconceived. Risk analysis does not simply raise unavoidable normative and ethical questions; it should be seen as a part of ethics. If risk analysis is supposed to help us figure out what to do, then it cannot avoid tracking in reasons; more specifically, it cannot avoid reasons by hiding behind individual preferences and measurements of willingness-to-pay to avoid or reduce risk. Risk analysts see themselves as scientists who study the pulse of the public, record its preferences and use what they know to advise policy-makers. They shy away from using their very real expertise to advise the public and help people figure out what they should think and want about some very complicated matters that are of the greatest importance.

In order to make clearer this criticism of risk analysis, we should look more closely at reasons and values, and how they are related. Reasons are an essential part of moral philosophy. This is because the philosophical study of ethics is normative, and reasons are an essential part of the normative. Historians, anthropologists and psychologists might study the actual ethical beliefs of individuals and the ethical codes that societies have accepted. These are empirical matters, which require observation and an understanding of causes, but which do not rely essentially on an appeal to reasons. Philosophical meta-ethics is the study of the meaning of ethical concepts and their logical relationships. This kind of conceptual analysis may also be able to avoid appeals to reasons. But normative ethics, which is still a main part of moral philosophy, cannot avoid them. Normative ethics aims to discover which ethical claims are best justified or true, and there is nowhere else to turn but to reasons for accepting or rejecting them.

I take this to be a relatively uncontroversial philosophical claim. Consider, for example, how Thomas Nagel begins the general article on ethics in the current edition of the *Encyclopedia of Philosophy*:

> Morality of some kind seems to be a universal human phenomenon; it is a subpart of the broader domain of the normative, which seems also to be characteristically human. Normative questions and judgements are about what we ought to do or want or believe or think (rather than just about what we actually do), and about the reasons for and against doing or believing one thing rather than another. Only rational beings, and probably only beings with language, are capable of normative thinking. (Nagel, 2006, p380)

Of course not all normative questions and judgements are part of ethics. Epistemology is a normative subject about what we ought to believe, especially in empirical matters, and it is not part of ethics. Rules of etiquette are about what we ought to do, but etiquette may also not be part of ethics. Actually, the relation between etiquette and ethics is complicated and a matter of some debate, but it is not important for our purposes to get it straight here.

Ethics is also about what we value, but not all matters of value are matters of ethics, either. Aesthetics is about what we value in the realm of beauty, and although objects of beauty may make ethical claims on us, aesthetics is not a part of ethics. Still, ethics includes a large part of the normative domain, including many kinds of questions and judgements about what we ought to do and how we ought to think or feel about our lives and our actions, especially where other people are involved. Most of the normative issues in these areas are part of ethics.

The aim of risk analysis, as I have claimed, is to help us figure out what we ought to do in response to different risks to life and health that we face. Some of these risks are caused naturally, but many are themselves the result of human activities and technology. The goal of risk analysis is to help us understand the nature and magnitude of these risks and make reasonable decisions about reducing, controlling or living with them. This means that risk analysis is also a normative subject. It also involves questions and judgements about what we ought to do or believe. If risk analysis to this extent has the purpose of helping decision-makers figure out what to do, then it is indistinguishable in its aims from ethics. It is the normative study of what we ought to do or believe or think, applied to a certain domain of activities. Risk analysis is therefore a part of ethics.

I am not claiming that risk analysis raises some important ethical issues. Nobody denies that. I am claiming that this whole part of risk analysis should be seen as a branch of ethics, that is, as part of the subject of moral philosophy. People involved in it therefore need to understand ethics. It is not enough for risk analysts to be ethically sensitive individuals or to recognize that ethical questions are important in public policy decisions involving risk. They need to have as much sophistication about moral philosophy as they often have about economics or decision analysis. But this kind of sophistication is sadly lacking among risk analysts, and this fact is most apparent when we examine the role of reasons in normative questions and judgements.

The role of reasons

Risk analysis assumes that the goal of figuring out which risks to control, to what degree and at what cost, is to promote human well-being. This is its fundamental normative commitment. If other values are to be taken into account in making public risk policies, it should be done through the political process. These other values are not part of risk analysis. In order to avoid any further controversies that might arise if we were to allow experts to determine what best promotes well-being, however, risk analysis needs a second assumption, which is that well-being is a function of satisfying people's actual preferences. Thus, risk analysis is the process of describing to people what risks they face and getting them to express their preferences for reducing these risks and trading off risk reduction against other costs and benefits. Risk analysis does this by measuring an individual's willingness-to-pay to reduce risk.

These assumptions can be combined into a more workable normative judgement: risk management decisions ought to be based on citizen preferences for reducing risk as measured by their willingness-to-pay. This judgement is compatible with a conception of value that claims that the value of anything is simply a measure of what a person is willing to give up or exchange for that thing. And this, in turn, is a familiar conception of value in economics.

If risk analysis is a branch of ethics, as I have argued, then we should examine these fundamental normative claims from a philosophical perspective. Two problems stand out, both of which are familiar to those who work in moral theory (see, for example, Sagoff, 2004, chapters 2–3). First, to assume that well-being consists simply of the satisfaction of preferences simply avoids a question that philosophers have debated for centuries: whether well-being consists of pleasure, living virtuously, achieving some human ideal or some other trait (Broome, 2005). Some of our preferences, moreover, are surely based on desires that it may not be in our interest to satisfy. The reasons for this may vary from poor information to weakness of will. In any event, whether or not the satisfaction of a preference will contribute to a person's well-being is something that can be determined only by knowing more about the meaning of well-being and the nature of the particular preference. It begs the question simply to assume that we can cash out well-being in terms of preference satisfaction. Reasons have a role to play here: they can explain the connection between preference satisfaction and well-being.

The second problem is with understanding the meaning of the value of something as a measure of what a person is willing to give up or exchange for that thing. Whether or not this is an accurate way to understand the meaning of economic value, it is not a plausible way to understand other kinds of value, such as religious or aesthetic value, the value of respect or the value of commitments we make to other people and some objects. Things and people have different kinds of value for us, and the specific natures of these values prescribe appropriate ways of acting and responding to them, as (for example) ways of honouring or respecting what should be honoured or respected. None of this has any necessary connection to what we are willing to pay for things. Reasons have a role to play here, too: they help us understand the nature of particular values and how they differ from one another. The proper expression of some things we value may well be a measure of what we are willing to give up or sacrifice for those things, while the proper expression of some other values may be revealed in different kinds of behaviour altogether.

Reasons and values

Without getting too deeply into issues of moral theory, we can make somewhat more explicit here the connection between reasons and values. We might begin with a general characterization of value:

> *Value*: To value something is to believe that there exist reasons for holding certain positive attitudes and acting in ways that are appropriate in regard to that thing.[6]

Different kinds of values can be distinguished by the different kinds of attitudes and actions that are appropriate to what we value. This characterization also allows us to distinguish values from *mere* preferences (or desires) because mere preferences, whether fleeting or persistent, will not have the backing of reasons. Whether a mere preference is destructive or harmless, it will be something different from a value; and if a preference can be backed by a reason, then it is a value after all.[7]

A reason on this account is nothing mysterious. It is merely a fact – any fact – that we take to support or rationalize the kinds of positive attitudes and actions that we associate with valuing. For example, suppose I perform some action, and you ask me to explain why I did it. I might reply that I did it for the following reasons, and then I list them. I would thus be referring to the reasons I hold or accept. They may refer to the objects of beliefs or attitudes to which I appeal in order to explain or justify my action. I take it that we all understand what it means to give reasons in this sense. But there is also another perfectly ordinary sense of having reasons. Suppose you want to go to a concert that has just been announced, which is scheduled to take place next month, and suppose I know this about you. Imagine further that many people want to go to this concert, and the tickets will sell out very quickly. Given these assumptions, you have a reason to call early to buy tickets. You have this reason whether or not you (or anyone else) are aware of it. If you want to go to the concert, then you have a reason to do what is necessary to make it possible for you to go. In this perfectly ordinary sense, a reason is mind-independent.

Reasons are not empirical entities. They do not exist in our heads, and nor can they be reduced to behaviour, as we suppose is the case with preferences. They cannot simply be measured or recorded in any empirical manner. That is the nature of the normative; it is accessed not via our senses but through our rational capacities.

Reasons are thus not strictly subjective. To cite a fact as a reason for acting or holding a certain positive attitude is to commit oneself to claiming that others should similarly be moved by the acknowledgement of that fact or, at the very least, that others should recognize the appropriateness of your response. In this way reasons are public, even when they are personal reasons. Personal reasons must be recognizable by others, even if they need not be shared. Most ethical reasons make stronger claims on others, and in some cases we believe that a reason should move all rational people in similar ways, regardless of their other differences. My reason for doing something special for my daughter on her birthday is a reason anyone can appreciate; but my reasons for not torturing innocent children for fun are reasons that should motivate every rational person to respond in similar ways.

Preferences and Individual Well-Being

I have been arguing that risk analysis is a part of ethics, and I have described what it means to say that ethics is a normative activity and how the normative is connected to reasons. It follows that risk analysis cannot avoid tracking in reasons. It needs to make its basic assumptions explicit and to give a good philosophical account of them. But risk analysis avoids doing this by holding onto the myth that it is essentially a science and can be practised in an ethically neutral way. It appeals to preferences as a way of avoiding ethics. As part of this process, risk analysis assumes that people have their own views about what is good for them; these views are reflected in the preferences that they have; and these preferences exist, waiting to be uncovered and measured.

Psychologists have challenged this assumption of risk analysis on empirical grounds. There are good reasons to doubt that preferences for trading off risk against other costs and benefits exist in individuals, waiting to be measured. Many studies and considerable psychological evidence suggest that individual preferences are often constructed in the elicitation process and do not exist independently of that process. But I will leave this important issue aside (see Lichtenstein and Slovic, 2006).

I want to look more closely at the strategies that risk analysts borrow from economics to avoid ethics. In order to figure out what we ought to do about any particular risk, economists and risk analysts must assume that we can know two things. First, we need to know what is good for people individually. Then, having worked that out, we need to know how to put together the good of different individuals to arrive at an overall assessment of the social good. Even this basic way of conceiving the issue makes two philosophically controversial assumptions: that reference to an overall or social good makes sense; and that overall good is a function of what is good for individuals. But I will also set aside these issues here and grant the assumptions.

Let us begin therefore with the idea of what is good for individuals. This certainly has the appearance of an ethical issue. To avoid getting involved in ethics, as I have said, risk analysts insist that people should be left to work out for themselves what is good for them. Their risk preferences will reflect their conclusions.

If we think of what is good for people as their well-being, then it takes some theory to connect preferences to well-being. There are two general ways to try to make this connection. One way is to assume that a person's well-being or good simply consists of the satisfaction of her preferences. This is to accept a preference-satisfaction theory of good. The other way is to avoid commitments to a theory of the good but to insist that whatever constitutes the good for a person, individuals are the best judges of their own well-being. We should for that reason defer to individual preferences. We might call this the epistemic strategy: whatever we mean by good or well-being, people know better than others what is good for them.

As it turns out, the preference satisfaction theory of good is not very plausible. I have already mentioned one reason for rejecting it, which is that our preferences are sometimes based on false beliefs or are in other ways irrational or crazy. If a person has self-destructive impulses, these will be reflected in her preferences. Now, there may be reasons having to do with autonomy or reasons based on claims of individual rights or freedom to defer to a person's irrational or self-destructive preferences, but these reasons will certainly not be based on any conceptions of a person's good or well-being. We need not assume that an individual's preferences commonly or even very often diverge from his well-being. The very possibility of such a divergence is enough to refute the preference satisfaction theory of good. What a person prefers is conceptually distinct from what is good for a person.

John Broome gives another argument for rejecting the preference satisfaction theory (Broome, 2005). Sometimes, and perhaps often, a person's preferences derive from her beliefs about what is better for her or what is in her interest. The preference satisfaction theory says that a preference for A over B makes A better for you than B. That's what it means to say that A is better for you than B according to the theory. But if a person's preference is based on her belief about what makes her better off or what is in her interest, then her preference guarantees the truth of her belief. Her belief would ensure its own truth. As Broome recognizes, some beliefs do ensure their own truth, such as the belief that you exist or the belief that you have a belief, but beliefs about what is good or beliefs about the nature of well-being are not plausibly beliefs of this sort.

The other way of connecting preference satisfaction to a person's good – the epistemic strategy – also fails as a universal strategy. No doubt it is often true that a person is the best judge of what is best for him, but it is equally obvious that this is sometimes false. People can fail to prefer what is best for them because they are poorly informed, because they exhibit weakness of will, and for other reasons. Most significantly, a person's preferences can fail to track what is good for him in situations that are complex or that require sophisticated computations to figure out what is good. Whether it is good to avoid certain risks, and at what cost, can depend on computations that are complex in two sorts of ways. First, the nature of the risk itself may be complicated. There may be complications about intensity or duration of exposure to risk, complications having to do with latency between exposure and the onset of disease or illness, and so on. And the reasonableness of avoiding or reducing a risk will also have to take into account some complicated computations about one's own future. How long do you expect to survive? How well do you believe your life will go? What responsibilities do you expect to have to other people? Should you discount the future or be neutral with respect to time? And so on. These beliefs have to be factored into rational preference for reducing or avoiding some risk and reflected in your current willingness to pay to do so.

I think it is reasonable to assume that even when we have preferences for reducing some risks or accepting others, most of us are not basing these preferences on these kinds of computations. Even if all the relevant information is available to us, the computations may be too difficult for most people to carry out. If this is right, then our preferences are not always accurate representations of what is good for us or what best promotes our interests. Even when we are not irrational in any familiar sense, we are often not fully or even sufficiently rational to justify our assuming that people are invariably the best judges of their own well-being.

Well-being is a complicated matter, and in other areas we commonly cope with these complications by seeking the advice of experts. Thus a prudent person who wants to promote her own well-being might seek advice about how to invest her savings from a financial expert; or a person who wants to stay healthy might seek advice from a physician or healthcare professional. We seek advice in these areas either because we believe that these experts are better judges of what is best for us than we are, or because we believe that they can help us with the complicated reasoning required to figure out what is best for us.

Risk analysts, however, resist advising people about how to form preferences that will best promote their well-being. This resistance is motivated by the desire to remain ethically neutral, but this stance itself can be ethically criticized. The fact that people are often the best judges of what is best for them is not an excuse for risk analysts never to try to help them do better and to form better preferences. The risk analyst avoids giving advice to individuals whose preferences he is trying to measure. He sees his responsibility as neutrally measuring these preferences and using these results to advise policy-makers. But risk analysis is a profession that embodies expertise that could help individuals to form risk preferences that will better promote their own well-being. It is bad faith to avoid getting involved in giving this kind of advice under the guise of ethical neutrality. But to be willing to advise individuals about the preferences they should be adopting would require a commitment to seeing the connection between an individual's risk preferences and her well-being as an ethically significant connection to establish.

Finally, if our ethical beliefs have any practical impact, then we must be able sometimes to form preferences on the basis of ethical reasons. Ethical reasons are often not self-interested; they make no reference to a person's own well-being. If we look only at an individual's preferences for trading off risk against other costs and benefits and assume that satisfying these preferences adds to a person's good or well-being, then we will face deep problems if a person's preferences are based on disinterested ethical beliefs. Broome gives a perfectly normal but compelling illustration of a preference of this sort. He writes:

> I was faced with a [non-self-interested ethical] question … when Greenpeace asked me to contribute to saving the Atlantic from oil exploration. When I decided my willingness to contribute, I thought a bit about the true value of the clean Atlantic, and also about what I ought to contribute given my financial and other circumstances. Greenpeace helped me with the first consideration by telling me about the purity of the area and the whales that live there. It never tried to persuade me that the existence of the unpolluted Atlantic is good for *me*, and it never occurred to me to think in those terms when I determined my willingness to contribute. Indeed, it simply is not good for me, so far as I can tell, and even if it is, my willingness to contribute has nothing to do with the benefit to me. (Broome, 2005, p86)

It would be absurd to make inferences about a person's well-being from this kind of preference, and it is no less absurd to try to invent some preference for an existence or non-use value to try to account for such an ordinary bit of ethical reasoning. It is also absurd to deny the importance of such preferences in understanding what matters to individuals in many kinds of risk decisions. We cannot avoid assessing a person's reasons in determining how to take into account preferences of this sort.

Preference aggregation and social good

I will conclude with some brief remarks about how we are supposed to bring our assumptions about the good of different individuals together to determine the social good. In the first place, it takes some ethical reasoning even to justify that the social good is an aggregation of individual well-being. Suppose we face an issue about how much we should be willing as a society to pay to reduce different health risks. Should we give equal priority to reducing risks to all people regardless of their age, or should we give greater priority to reducing risks to children than we do to reducing similar risks to older people? How are considerations of justice relevant to determining which social policies we should support? We can't hope to answer questions like these (or many others that may involve direct appeals to social values) by aggregating individual preferences. These may be the kinds of values that risk analysts insist should be left to the political process, but then it is unclear what information an aggregation of individual willingness-to-pay is supposed to be providing.

The risk analyst has another argument for taking into account the aggregation of individual preferences, as measured by willingness-to-pay in deciding risk policies or regulations. This is an appeal to democracy or citizens' sovereignty. Risk analysis is seen in this light as a midwife that helps to uncover and hand to the policy-maker the will of the people.

But this way of thinking again misconceives the role of risk analysis as one of adviser to policy-makers instead of adviser to a broader public. This argument, as Broome explains, mistakes the nature of democracy with the role of experts like risk analysts in the democratic processes (Broome, 2005, p87). It is a basic principle of democracy that our public policies should reflect the will of the people. But it is an equally basic responsibility of democratic systems to be concerned with how the will of the public and the preferences of individuals are formed. It is this responsibility that explains the need for establishing deliberative processes as an essential part of democratic decision-making. Consider, for example, the processes that we use to elect our representatives and government officials. We don't do this simply by measuring the preferences of citizens. Elections are preceded by campaigns, which are supposed to inform the electorate and help people to establish their preferences in responsible ways. These processes are highly imperfect, to be sure, but nobody would favour doing away with campaigns altogether and simply surveying public attitudes or determining how much people would be willing to pay to see their preferred candidate in office. The process by which preferences are supposed to be formed is an essential part of any adequate conception of democracy.

Risk analysts insist that they do not make decisions. They act simply as advisers to policy-makers. But the more important role of risk analysis is as part of the preference formation process. This involves educating the public, but also helping to structure discussion and debate over important risk issues. The important role that risk analysis should play in a democratic society is to help influence individual preferences about risk. This involves giving up the myth of risk analysis as an ethically neutral science. It requires a willingness to get one's hands dirty. Risk analysts should not take individual preferences as given; nor should they hide behind them.

References

Broome, J. (2005) 'Why economics needs ethical theory', *Pelican Record*, vol 42, pp80–88

Lichtenstein, S. and Slovic, P. (eds) (2006) *The Construction of Preferences*, Cambridge University Press, Cambridge

Nagel, T. (2006) 'Ethics', *Encyclopedia of Philosophy*, vol 3, 2nd edn, Macmillan Reference, Detroit

Sagoff, M. (2004) *Price, Principle, and the Environment*, Cambridge University Press, Cambridge

Scanlon, T. M. (1998) *What We Owe to Each Other*, Harvard University Press, Cambridge MA

Stern, P. and Finebergs, H. (eds) (1996) *Understanding Risk: Informing Decisions in a Democratic Society*, National Academy Press, Washington, DC

Stokey, E. and Zeckhauser, R. (1978) *A Primer for Policy Analysis*, Norton, New York

Notes

1. This paper is a transcript of a talk given to the British Association for the Advancement of Science, 2000. A transcript of this talk is also available at: http://users.ox.ac.uk/~sfop0060/pdf/Why%20economics%20needs%20ethical%20theory.pdf. My debt to Broome in my paper is very large. His paper deserves to be widely known.
2. 'Executive Order 12866 – Regulatory Planning and Review', 4 October 1993, at www.whitehouse.gov/omb/inforeg/eo12866.pdf.
3. Circular A-4 can be found at www.whitehouse.gov/omb/circulars/a004/a-4.html.
4. US EPA Science Advisory Board Committee on Valuing Ecological Systems and Services. Description and materials available at www.epa.gov/sab/panels/vpesspanel.html.
5. Letter from John Graham, Administrator, Office of Information and Regulatory Affairs, to Dr Angela Nugent, Designated Federal Officer, US Environmental Protection Agency, Science Advisory Board, 20 October 2003. This letter was circulated and discussed by the CVPESS. See note 4 above.
6. This general characterization of value is discussed and defended at length by Scanlon (1998, chapter 2).
7. Although this characterization of the connection of values to reasons seems to me generally correct, it needs further refinement. Thomas Hill has pointed out to me that we sometimes come to cherish objects for no reason at all. (Think, for example, of some not significant object that a person places on her desk and which, over time and for no reason she is aware of, she develops a fondness for that object such that she now makes an effort to protect it and would resist attempts to move it.) Examples like this raise questions for the connection between reasons and values that I am claiming to exist, but I cannot pursue these questions or their significance here.

9 Incommensurability: The Failure to Compare Risks

Nicolas Espinoza

Introduction

A risk is something bad that may or may not happen. Since we do not want bad things to happen we take preventative measures, that is, we try to reduce risk. Of course, with limited resources we must choose wisely which risks to reduce and how much we should spend doing so. Some risks we even choose to accept because the cost of taking the risk is outweighed by its associated benefits. This is the kind of reasoning that motivates, for example, mountain climbing, skydiving and also driving to work. In order to determine whether a risk is of the unbeneficial kind we wish to reduce, or of the beneficial kind we wish to take, it is necessary that we can compare risks to each other and also compare risks to their associated benefits. The problem is, however, that comparisons do not always come easy. In some situations we may be unable to compare risks because they are *incommensurable*.

The aim of this contribution is to examine incommensurability and incomparability in their connection to the comparison of risks. The main question is: is it ever the case that risks cannot, or perhaps ought not, be compared, rendering it impossible to rank them along a single scale, whether this scale be ordinal or cardinal? Of course, if we have in mind the standard technical notion of risk (let us call it STNR), that is, probability multiplied with negative consequence, it is easy to imagine cases where we would have to answer the above question in the affirmative. Take, for example, the comparison between the risk of one person dying in a traffic accident with a probability of 0.1 and the risk of an indigenous bird species becoming extinct with a probability of 0.03.[1] In this case it would be meaningless to say that one risk is *greater* than the other since the potential consequences of those risks are not of the same *kind* and cannot be expressed in terms of each other – they are in a sense incommensurable.[2] Since many risk comparisons are between risks that have consequences of different kinds, it is a great disadvantage of STNR that it allows only *in-kind* comparisons. The present discussions of incommensurability will take this disadvantage into account by presupposing a more general notion of risk (let us call it GNR). According to GNR, a risk is the *disutility* of some event multiplied by the probability of that event occurring, which is to say that a risk is the expected disutility of some event.[3] By incorporating the *value* of the negative consequence, this notion of risk is not as vulnerable to trivial incommensurabilities, due to differing kinds of consequences, as that of STNR. We shall see, however, that there may still be cases of incommensurability of an *evaluative* sort even under this interpretation of risk.[4]

I shall say that two risks are *evaluatively incommensurable* if and only if there is no cardinal scale with respect to which the severity of both risks can be compared. In addition, two risks are *evaluatively incomparable* if and only if it is not the case that they can be ordinally ranked, which is to say that it is not the case that one risk is better, worse or equally as good as the other. Note that incommensurability thus defined does not necessarily imply incomparability; the failure to compare two risks cardinally, for instance the failure to say that risk A is, say, *three times more* severe than B, does not automatically imply that we cannot say that risk A is *more* severe than risk B. It may be helpful to view the distinction between incommensurability and incomparability, namely that between ordinal and cardinal measurement, as analogous to the distinction between quantitative and qualitative comparison.

My argument will proceed in two steps. First, I will motivate why risk comparison failures pose a problem for risk evaluation. Second, I will distinguish several types of incommensurability among risks and show when these respective incommensurabilities occur. Furthermore, I will distinguish incommensurable risks from incomparable risks. First, however, in order to give some substance to the argument, it will be helpful to consider a few examples.

EXAMPLES OF INCOMMENSURABILITY

According to Swedish law, cars must be equipped with high traction winter tyres, either studded or non-studded, during the mid-winter season. Although studded tyres are generally more expensive, a majority of car owners prefer them over the non-studded alternative because of the common perception that studded tyres are safer (Wester-Herber, 2006).[5] However, one of the effects of using studded tyres is that they tear up microscopic particles which are hazardous to inhale. It may thus be argued that any potential safety benefits gained from using studded tyres should be weighed against the health hazards that are due to inhaling suspended particulate matter from stud-induced roadway wear. The trade-off we face, should we consider a restriction on the use of studded tyres, is that between the probable declines in health-related fatalities caused by exposure to hazardous road wear and the probable rise in traffic incident fatalities due to the use of less safe tyres.

However, even if experts could accurately assess the number of lives that would be saved due to the respective risk preventative measures of using either studded or non-studded tyres, the above risk comparison would still be notoriously difficult from an evaluative point of view. Simply using the numerical death toll as the basis for evaluation is unsatisfactory because even if the number of lives lost is indeed a weighty factor, there are other aspects that must be taken into account. For example, is there a reasonable alternative to studded tyres, and if so, do people really perceive them to be so? Are the people who benefit from the safety benefits of studded tyres the same people who run the risk of inhaling hazardous particles? Do people value the safety of driving higher than the safety of dying from pollution-related illnesses? Can we trust the road services agency if they recommend a less safe tyre? And so on.

Indeed, a common view nowadays is that an ethically acceptable risk evaluation should take these kinds of considerations into account; something which is usually not done in traditional comparative risk assessments (Hornstein, 1992; Jenni, 1997; Hansson, 2003). However, it appears that the more considerations we take into account, the harder it is to consistently and non-arbitrarily aggregate them into a unified measure suitable for comparative evaluations. Suppose, for example, we believe that an ethically informed risk decision, concerning the restricted use of studded tyres, must take the following aspects into account: (1) the expected number of lives that will be lost (in traffic) due to using alternative tyres; (2) the expected number of lives that will be saved (in healthcare) due to using alternative tyres; (3) the level of public acceptance for the use of alternative tyres; and (4) the cost of subsidizing a nationwide transition from studded to non-studded tyres. Then, in order to determine a single measure for this multidimensional evaluation, several trade-off relations must be determined: what is the monetary value of a life? How much public acceptance loss are we willing to accept per saved life? How many lives in traffic should we trade for lives in healthcare? These questions are of course difficult, and perhaps impossible, to answer. In situations like these, when trade-offs between the different considerations that determine the severity of a risk are impossible, we say that risks are incommensurable.[6]

One way to circumvent this problem would be to artificially construct a common measure along which all these ethically relevant criteria could be evaluated. An influential effort to this effect is cost-benefit analysis (CBA). In the broadest sense, CBA can be seen as a systematic approach to implementing the common sense principle that advantages should be weighed against disadvantages. In a recent article, Hansson writes:

> In a typical CBA, two or more options in a public decision are compared to each other by careful calculation of their respective consequences. These consequences can be different in nature, e.g. economic costs, risk of disease and death, environmental damage etc. In the final analysis, all such consequences are assigned a monetary value, and the option with the highest value of benefits minus costs is recommended or chosen. (Hansson, 2007)

However, while experts and decision-makers tend to argue that the assignments of monetary prices are necessary for making comparisons between different alternatives – so that the most cost-efficient alternative can be chosen – laypersons often feel that it is unethical to assign monetary prices to risks imposed upon humans or the environment (Margolis, 1996). In fact, some people think that some of their values are protected from trade-offs with other values (Tetlock et al, 1996; Baron and Spranca, 1997). So-called sacred or protected values can be defined as 'any value that a moral community implicitly or explicitly treats as possessing infinite or transcendental significance that precludes comparisons, trade-offs, or indeed any other mingling with bounded or secular values' (Tetlock et al, 2000). Indeed, a growing body of empirical evidence suggests that not only do people express moral outrage when asked to perform trade-offs between a protected value and money, but they fail to be consistent in doing so (Tetlock, 2003). As a result, several researchers have noted that protected values cause problems for quantitative elicitation of values, as is done in cost-benefit analysis or decision analysis (Baron, 1997; Bazerman et al, 1999). For instance, people who hold a protected value for forests might say that it is just as bad to destroy a large forest as a small one.

So it seems that it is not only the multidimensional aspect of risks that gives rise to evaluative incommensurability, since it may also be the case that one single value associated with one risk (or simply a single-valued risk) is incommensurable to another single value of another risk. This is further illustrated in the following example. Jet fuel is today transported by tank trucks to Arlanda Airport (Stockholm) from the harbour just outside Stockholm. On their way to the airport the trucks must pass through a densely populated area in the city centre. A risk analysis has shown that the probability of an accident in which a large number of lives in the city centre are lost, due to an exploding tank truck, is about 1 in 10,000 per year. Another safer alternative is to use an existing railway. If that alternative is chosen the cost will be considerably higher, but the risk that many lives are lost in a catastrophe is avoided. There is, however, a risk that a nearby groundwater reservoir will be polluted if two trains collide. The probability for this event is about 2x10E-6 per year according to the best estimates available.

Now, one might ask whether the choice between the two alternatives described above can really be made by first assigning monetary values to the different kinds of accidents, and then calculating the expected monetary loss from each alternative, and finally comparing the expected monetary losses to the economic gains of implementing the two alternatives. One could claim that the risk that many people die is incommensurable to the risk that a groundwater reservoir is polluted. For even if the separate probabilities that two different risks materialize are commensurable, there is no guarantee that the negative values associated with these risks are, since the values may be fundamentally different.[7]

Risk comparisons in risk evaluation

It seems obvious that incommensurability or incomparability may, if either materializes, pose a serious threat to consistent weighing or prioritizing of societal risks. For if risks are incommensurable, and thereby resistant to accurate comparisons in terms of severity, we will not be able to perform accurate and cost-effective trade-offs between risks and their associated benefits. Risk regulators may well be able to determine that one risk is *more* severe than another, and thus demands *more* risk preventative resources (assuming of course that the more severe risk is more expensive to reduce), but they cannot justify a *particular* divide in the allocation of resources to these risks based on their relative severity. Whatever reasons they may have for such a divide will ultimately be arbitrary because of incommensurability. The reassurance we may find in the fact that incommensurability does not *always* preclude the possibility of rational *prioritization* among risks – since exact (cardinal) comparisons are not always necessary – would be effectively eradicated by the added presence of incomparability. For according to most scholars of philosophy and economics, rational choice requires that our choice options must, indeed, be comparable.

What I shall call the *standard view* of risk evaluation is essentially comprised of two parts, one consequentialist part and one maximizing part. According to the consequentialist part, risks are evaluated with respect to their outcomes, which in turn can be divided into costs and benefits. Depending on whether a collectivistic or an individualistic view is adopted, costs are weighed against benefits so that a positive beneficial balance is achieved for the entire population or for every individual (Hansson, 2004c).[8] According to the maximizing part, risks are ranked and should then be dealt with in order of the magnitude of their cost/benefit ratio. In other words, risk regulators should maximize risk reduction effectiveness, that is, they should try to achieve the greatest amount of risk reduction for the least amount of money.[9]

There are two different kinds of situation where risks are evaluated: either a single risk is evaluated in terms of acceptability or unacceptability, or several risks are weighed against each other, in order to determine which is the most acceptable. In both cases comparisons are crucial to the evaluation of risk. It may seem odd to say that a comparison is necessary even in the single risk case, but comparative evaluation is necessary for at least two reasons. First, in order to determine the acceptability of a risk, the risk must be compared to its associated benefits. A risk is taken/accepted, or imposed upon others, only if the risk bears with it some benefit to those submitted to the risk or to those imposing the risk onto others: 'It seems undeniable that risks have to be weighed against benefits' (Hansson, 2004c, p145). Second, even in the single risk case, the evaluation of a risk entails comparing two separate risks: the risk we initially face, that is, the status quo, and the risk we face after a risk-preventative measure. To evaluate the cost-effectiveness of a particular risk-reductive intervention, we must compare the existing risk to the reduced risk that is expected to result from the intervention. We would in such a case have to ask: has the risk become less severe (answering this question involves a risk comparison), and if so, was it worth the cost? The risk is unacceptable only if the outcome of regulating it is better than not doing so, and acceptable when regulating it would be too costly (or even impossible). For an example of the latter: meteor risks are acceptable because the costs of preventing them would be ridiculously high.

A comparative evaluation of two separate risks R_1 and R_2 is meant to establish which risk is the worst or most severe (least acceptable). If, for instance, R_1 and R_2 are the consequences of two different courses of action (one of which must be taken for the fulfilment of some societal goal), we will, of course, want to choose the course of action which leads to the lesser of these two evils (though this does not necessarily imply choosing the monetarily most cost-effective alternative). Of course, for the comparison to be possible, we must be able to determine, from an assessment point of view, how risky R_1 and R_2 are. Moreover, in some cases we would like to know *to what extent* one risk is riskier than the other, since even though R_1 may be a *greater* risk than R_2 (from an assessment point of view), R_1 may be worth taking (from an evaluative point of view) if its associated benefits are more valuable than the benefits associated with R_2.[10]

If we are on the other hand confronted with a single risk R, we categorize this risk as either more or less acceptable than W, the worst risk we have previously found acceptable (within a relevant context).[11] If R is less acceptable than W, then R is unacceptable. If R is more acceptable than W, then R, like W, is also acceptable. This rationale lies at the heart of the fallacious claim that people are irrational if they choose to drive a car but are opposed to living in the vicinity of a nuclear power plant: given that the risk of a meltdown is not higher than the risk of dying in a car accident, people should be more opposed to driving than to nuclear power, which in fact most people are not.[12] Granted that comparisons of this type are crucial to the evaluation of risk, we should be careful in situations when comparisons are inappropriate or unethical for some reason. As for the risks of traffic death and nuclear meltdown, one may claim that this comparison is inappropriate for several different reasons:

1 Driving is voluntary while, presumably, living close to a power plant is not.
2 The very nature of the probability estimate for the single occurrence of a core meltdown is essentially different from the probability estimate of having a car accident.[13]
3 The societal benefits resultant from the power plant may not befall those in its immediate vicinity while driving is supposedly always beneficial to the driver.
4 When driving we are to a great extent in control of what happens while the potential accidents at a power plant are out of our control.
5 The horrific and dreadful consequences of radioactive fallout are not comparable to the consequences of an ordinary car accident.

This list of reasons why a risk comparison may be inappropriate can be made much longer if we take into account all the various risk factors that people generally find relevant when evaluating risks.[14] Despite these problems, traditional risk-benefit analysis presupposes that there exists a common measure, for example societal willingness to pay, which can be used to compare different risks. Incommensurability among risks seriously threatens this presupposition.

INCOMMENSURABLE RISKS

Incommensurability among risks may arise in several different ways. First, as was mentioned at the outset, two risks that do not have the same kind of consequences will not be commensurable under STNR.[15] Incommensurability of this kind does not, however, necessarily imply that the risks are evaluatively incommensurable, so we shall not discuss the matter further. Second, and more importantly, it may be that one of the risks of a comparison is undefined because the probability has not been precisely estimated (or is completely lacking). In this case the resulting evaluative incommensurability is due to one of the risks in the comparison not in fact being a risk, in which case the relevant comparison predicate, '*more severe risk than*', '*less severe risk than*' or '*equally as severe risk as*' simply does not apply. Comparing such undefined risks would be analogous to posing the nonsensical question: which is the highest mountain, Mount Everest or Lake Placid?[16] Third, failures may occur despite the risks under comparison being well defined, that is, when the probabilities are known. Incommensurability in these cases is due rather to the fact that the *negative values* associated with the risks are incommensurable. More precisely, assessing the value of a risk in a particular situation primarily involves: (1) assigning a numeral v_e to the disvalue of the potential unwanted event *e;* and (2) determining the probability p of e. The severity (i.e. the value) of risk R is then given by $R = v_e \times p(e)$. So failures of commensurability occur when either, or both, of (1) and (2) cannot be fulfilled. In such cases the risk (which then does not really qualify as a risk in a stricter sense) cannot be accurately compared to any other risk, since it, itself, cannot be expressed accurately. It would not make sense to say, for instance, that risk R_1, with an undefined probability and/or an undefined utility is, say, 0.7 times worse than risk R_2.

We start off with the failure to assign a numeral to the disvalue of an unwanted event. What is needed here is mathematical structure that can truthfully represent the relational structure between the values of different events (Luce and Suppes, 1965; Krantz et al, 1971). In other words, we must be able to assign a number that tracks the value of the event – the higher the value of the event, the higher the number, and, if one event is better than another, the number representing the magnitude of value of that event must also be higher. This can be expressed as $v(e_1) > v(e_2)$ *if and only if* $e_1 B e_2$, where > is the usual *larger than* relation and B is the relation *better than*. If the numbers assigned do not satisfy these conditions then the numbers will fail to represent the internal structure amongst entities that they were meant to measure – a very severe risk could end up being conceived of as less severe than another risk that is not severe at all.[17]

The most common way of measuring the disvalue of some event, which satisfies the tracking conditions above, is by examining the preferences of those who evaluate it.[18] According to standard expected utility theory, most famously axiomatized by von Neumann and Morgenstern, a utility function, which is a description of how strongly an agent desires something, can be derived given that certain technical conditions are satisfied (von Neumann and Morgenstern, 1947). One of the conditions is the so-called completeness axiom, which requires that a system of individual preferences is complete; that is, for any two mutually exclusive choice options u and v, exactly one of the following relations holds: $u > v$, $u < v$, or $u \sim v$.[19] Hence, in order to assign a numeric utility to, for instance, a household accident, like slipping in the shower, we must be able to rank the disvalues of every relevant household accident.

However, there are those who claim that we sometimes fail to compare some alternatives in terms of the relations *better than*, *worse than* or *equally as good as*, and can thus not be said to have complete preferences.[20] So-called *incomparable preferences* are presumably very common. Consider for instance this household example: which accident is worse, burning your hand on the stove or banging your thumb with the hammer? It is plausible that under some circumstances, given some particular temperature of the stove and particular size of the hammer, you find neither accident to be worse than the other. One might then assume that the two accidents are equally as bad. However, this may be unjustified. For we can imagine a third accident, another one in which you burn your hand on the stove, but where the temperature is now just slightly higher, which therefore is worse than the first burning accident but still not worse than the hammer accident. If this is the case, neither of the two burning accidents is better or worse than the hammer accident. This means that the original two accidents were incomparable.[21] Arguably, if it is easy to imagine household cases where we fail to have a complete preference ordering then it should also be a very common phenomenon in more serious cases. Thus, in many cases concerning the potential occurrence of a highly disvalued event, we are unable to accurately assess the level of risk, since we are unable to assign numeric utilities to the events.

Probability is the second component of the conception of risk. Hence, if the probability is unknown the risk is undefined. The main characteristic of probabilistic assertions is that they are testament of a lack of knowledge. In general this lack of knowledge is due to either one of two reasons:

1 There is a fact of the matter concerning whether or not the event will occur, but we do not have sufficient knowledge of the causally relevant parameters that may bring about the event, or, even with such knowledge, the chain of events that leads up to the event is too complex for us to determine with certainty.
2 There is no fact of the matter concerning whether or not the event will occur because the world is fundamentally indeterminate (in which case of course it is not a question of a lack of knowledge in a stricter sense since there is no fact of the matter to lack knowledge of); hence, even if we had complete knowledge of all the parameters, and had infinite computational powers, we could still, at best, only make a probabilistic assertion. This distinction is essentially one between aleatory and epistemic uncertainty (Clausen-Mork, 2006).

Furthermore, we can distinguish essentially two interpretations of probability, *objectivist* and *subjectivist* probability.[22] According to the objectivist interpretation of probability, which is often interpreted as the *frequency* view of probability – 'the probability of an attribute A in a finite reference class B is the relative frequency of actual occurrences of A within B' (Hajek, 2003) – there are probabilities 'out there' that we may or may not know. This is captured by the distinction that is usually made between *risk* and *uncertainty*. The word 'risk' in *this* context should not be confused with the ordinary notion of risk discussed in this chapter. It is a technical term used in decision analysis to separate the cases when we know what the probabilities are (cases of decision under risk), from the cases when we do not (decisions under uncertainty). From an objectivist viewpoint it is very seldom that we do know what the precise probabilities are – most decisions are made under uncertainty.[23] Hence, from the objectivist viewpoint of probability there will be many situations in which risks will be undefined due to unknown probabilities.

The subjectivist view of probability, on the other hand, rejects the idea that there are probabilities 'out there'. According to subjectivists, probability is rather a mode of judgement 'in your mind'. According to this interpretation, there are no 'true' probabilities that people fail to have knowledge of. Probabilities are instead assigned to events for indicating that there is a certain amount of genuine indeterminacy involved. Consequently, the expression 'there is a 70 per cent chance that event e will happen' does not mean that the event will occur seven times out of ten. It rather means that the person who expresses it has a degree of belief, that e will happen, corresponding to the number 0.7. In the Bayesian approach to subjective probability, dating back to the works of Ramsey (1931), De Finetti (1931) and Savage (1954), this entails that the agent will be willing to accept a seven to ten bet that e will occur. For example, suppose John wishes to measure the subjective probability that he assigns to the event e occurring. If John judges $7 to be the highest price he is prepared to pay for a bet in which he wins $10 if the proposition x = 'the event e occurred' turns out to be true, but wins nothing otherwise, then his subjective probability for x is approximately 7/10.

By accepting this view, one would expect that one could always assign a probability to the occurrence of any event, no matter how unfamiliar one is with the event. However, there are cases when probabilities cannot be assigned even under the subjectivist view. The reason for this is intimately connected to the failure of assigning utilities described in the former section. For reasons we shall not go into here, determining probabilities requires (according to Savage) complete preferences over lotteries (various betting situations). But again incomparability or incomplete preferences would stop subjective probabilities in their tracks. Hence, even under the subjectivist interpretation of probability we see that risks may be undefined and give rise to failures of commensurability.

Incomparable risks

We have seen that risks may be evaluatively incommensurable for different reasons. If we fail to assign probabilities to potential negative consequences or fail to value the consequences of the risks, we are not able to represent them on a single cardinal scale. This does not, however, mean that the risks are not evaluatively *comparable.*

An example that illustrates this distinction is the process of comparing mineral rocks with respect to hardness. Minerals can be compared with respect to hardness by scratching them against each other. If one leaves a scratch on the other then it is harder. However, there is no way of saying that one mineral is, say, twice as hard or, for instance, 3.5 times as hard as another. In that respect we could say that any two minerals are incommensurable with respect to hardness, but nevertheless comparable, since they, after all, can be scratched against one another.

Now recall the example in the introduction where we compared a potential traffic fatality (A) with the potential extinction of a bird species (B). The corresponding values may in this case very well be incommensurable and so also the risks. But what if we knew that the probability for A was 0.1 and the probability for B was 0.00000001? Then it would be absolutely evident that the former risk was *worse* than the latter, even though we could not say how much worse. In this section I shall discuss the cases when risks are incommensurable *and* it is not evident that one is better or worse than the other.

In order to say something about the cases in which we fail to compare the value of two objects, we must first have some idea of what it means to successfully compare two objects. In the most general sense, comparing two objects involves seeing how they are different and how they are alike. In this sense it is obvious that any two objects are comparable, because we can always think of *some* ways in which they differ and some ways in which they are alike. For instance, a trip to the zoo is comparable to a trip to the dentist – they differ in that a trip to the zoo is pleasant while a trip to the dentist is not, whereas they are alike in that they both, say, require taking the bus. For another example, the risk of dying from mountain climbing is comparable to that of dying from cancer – they differ, amongst other things, in that the former risk is voluntary while the latter risk is involuntary (lung cancer set aside), whereas they are alike in that they may both result in death.

However, this way of viewing comparison is innocuous because it has little to do with comparisons, as they are usually understood (at least comparisons that are of any practical value). When we make comparisons we are usually interested in particular aspects; we wish to determine which of the compared outcomes have or do not have a particular property, or which outcome has more or less of some property. For instance, when we compare two risks, we are interested in which of the risks is the most costly to society, the most unequally distributed or, more generally, the most severe. In all such cases the comparison regards a particular 'measure'. Our interest lies in determining which outcome exhibits the most (or least) of each measure. We thus say that two outcomes are evaluatively comparable if they have in common that they realize some value *with respect to* which we can say that one is better, worse or equally as good as the other.

The 'with respect to' qualification denotes the value-measure that functions as a standard or reference for assessing the value of an object; which is what Chang (1997) and others call the *covering value*. Chang introduces the notion of a covering value because she believes that it does not make sense to talk about 'better than' *simpliciter*; something can only be better than something else *in a certain way*, that is, with respect to some specific value. This is parallel to the point made by Judith Thompson that it is only meaningful to speak of 'goodness' as 'goodness-in-a-way' (Thompson, 1997). Practically speaking, the covering value is applied to narrow down the countless different ways in which two items may be compared, moving from a very wide comparison to a narrower one by restricting the comparison to a particular set of aspects.

Employing this view, a comparison can be seen as a three-place value relation; A is better than B with respect to V, where V can be any value. Under different covering values the result of the comparison may vary; A may be better than B with respect to V_1, but A may be worse than B with respect to V_2, but also A may be equal to B with respect to V_3. Incomparability arises when we are not willing to admit that any of the relations better than, worse than or equally as good as hold in a comparison of A and B, with respect to the relevant value V. Accordingly, Chang defines incomparability as: 'Two items are incomparable with respect to a covering value if, for every positive value relation relativized to that covering value, it is not true that it holds between them' (Chang, 1997, p6).[24]

As far as evaluative comparisons are concerned, it is often assumed that the logical space of positive value relations that may be obtained between any two outcomes is exhausted by the trichotomy of relations *better than*, *worse than* and *equal to*. So, when we claim that a positive value relation of the trichotomy is true, say 'it is true that x is better than y', we are also implicitly saying that 'it is false that x is worse than y' and that 'it is false that x is equal to x'. But if we merely say that 'it is not true that x is better than y' it is still possible that x is worse than y or that x and y are equally good.

I have not yet offered a reason to believe that objects are ever incomparable, nor will I try to do so. But what I will offer is a simple test with which one can determine *if* objects are incomparable. Roughly the test works as follows: suppose that you value two objects x and y in such a way that you find x to be better than y and y to be better than x. According to the trichotomy thesis it then follows that you find x and y to be equally good. However, if a small bonus is added to x, and it turns out that you still do not find this slightly improved x^+ better than y, it cannot have been the case that you found x and y to be equally good. If you *had* thought them to be equally good then the small bonus would have tipped the scale in favour of the improved object. If x and y pass this test it proves that you find them incomparable. How is this applicable to the comparisons of risks?

Consider for instance the previous example involving transportation of jet fuel. Let x be the outcome that five people die due to the explosion of a tank truck in the centre of Stockholm. Let y be the outcome that a particular water reservoir is destroyed. Arguably it is neither the case that x is better than y nor that y is better than x with respect to severity (if you find this implausible simply adjust the size of the reservoir or the number of people so that it becomes true). Are these outcomes then equally as bad? No, for if we slightly improve one of the outcomes, for instance if we change x to four rather than five fatalities, x will still not be better than y. Hence, x and y are not equally as bad. Had they been equally as bad then any slight improvement on x would have made it the better outcome. Another way of doing this would be to adjust the probabilities of one of the risks so that it becomes more or less likely. If it is still not possible to determine which of the risks are more severe, then they were incomparable to begin with.

Conclusion

In this chapter it has been argued that two risks A and B are incommensurable if and only if the severity of risk A cannot be represented on the same cardinal scale as the severity of risk B. If risks are incommensurable in this way, and thereby resistant to accurate comparisons in terms of severity, we cannot perform accurate and cost effective trade-offs between risks and their associated benefits. According to the developed account, incommensurability among risks is due to when at least one of the two risks is undefined. However, the fact that risks are incommensurable does not automatically imply that they cannot be compared or ranked. Incomparability among risks, when risks cannot even be ranked, arises in situations in which the following two conditions are satisfied: (1) the risks are incommensurable; and (2) the evaluative relation that holds between the two risks (*more severe than*, *less severe than* or *equally as severe as*) is insensitive to small alterations in the probabilities (or values) associated with the risks. This latter point can be demonstrated via a risk-modified version of the so-called small-improvement argument.

References

Adler, M. (1998) 'Incommensurability and cost-benefit analysis', *University of Pennsylvania Law Review*, vol 146, pp1371–1418

Aumann, R. (1962) 'Utility theory without the completeness axiom', *Econometrica*, vol 30, pp445–462

Baron, J. (1997) 'Biases in the quantitative measurement of values for public decisions', *Psychological Bulletin*, vol 122, pp72–88

Baron, J. and Ritov, I. (1994) 'Reference points and omission bias', *Organizational Behavior and Human Decision Processes*, vol 59, pp475–498

Baron, J. and Spranca, M. (1997) 'Protected values', *Organizational Behavior and Human Decision Processes*, vol 70, no 1, pp1–16

Bazerman, M. H., Moore, D. A. and Gillespie, J. J. (1999) 'The human mind as a barrier to wiser environmental agreements', *American Behavioral Scientist*, vol 42, pp1277–1300

Beck, U. (1992) *Risk Society: Towards a New Modernity*, translated by Mark Ritter, Sage, London

Bewley, T. (1986) 'Knightian uncertainty theory: Part I', *Cowles Foundation Discussion Paper* No. 807, Cowles Foundation, Yale University

Chang, R. (1997) 'Introduction', in R. Chang (ed.) *Incommensurability, Incomparability, and Practical Reason*, Harvard University Press, Cambridge MA

Chang, R. (2002) 'The possibility of parity', *Ethics*, vol 112, pp659–688

Covello, T. (1991) 'Risk comparisons and risk communication: issues and problems in comparing health and environmental risks', in R. Kasperson and P. J. M. Stallen (eds) *Communicating Risks to the Public*, vol 79, Kluwer

Danan, E. (2003) 'Revealed cognitive preference theory', mimeo, http://www.u-cergy.fr/edanan/research/revealed_cognitive.pdf

De Finetti, B. (1931) 'Probabilismo: saggio critico sulla teoria della probabilità e sul valore della Scienza', Napoli

Eliaz, K. and Ok, E. A. (2006) 'Indifference or indecisiveness? Choice theoretic foundations of incomplete preferences', *Games and Economic Behavior*, vol 56, no 1, pp61–86

Elvik, R. (1999) 'Assessing the validity of evaluation research by means of meta-analysis, Institute of Transport Economics', mimeo, Norwegian Centre for Transport Research

Espinoza, N. (2006) 'The small improvement argument', mimeo, Luleå University of Technology

Espinoza, N. and Peterson, M. (2006) 'Human choice behaviour: A probabilistic analysis of incomplete preferences', mimeo, Luleå University of Technology

Gillies, D. (2000) *Philosophical Theories of Probability*, Routledge, London
Hajek, A. (2003) 'Interpretations of probability', *Stanford Encyclopedia of Philosophy* http://plato.stanford.edu/entries/probability-interpret/
Hansson, S. O. (2003) 'Ethical criteria of risk acceptance', *Erkenntnis*, vol 59, no 3, pp291–309
Hansson, S. O. (2004a) 'Fallacies of risk', *Journal of Risk Research*, vol 7, no 3, pp353–360
Hansson, S. O. (2004b) 'Philosophical perspectives on risk', *Techné*, vol 8, no 1
Hansson, S. O. (2004c) 'Weighing Risks and Benefits', *Topoi*, vol 23, no 22, pp145–152
Hermansson, H. (2005) 'Consistent risk management: three models outlined', *Journal of Risk Research*, vol 8, pp557–568
Hornstein, D. T. (1992) 'Reclaiming environmental law: a normative critique of comparative risk assessment', *Columbia Law Review*, vol 92, no 3, pp562–633
Jenni, K. (1997) 'Attributes for risk evaluation', PhD dissertation, Carnegie Mellon University, Pittsburgh
Krantz, D. H., Luce, R. D., Suppes, P. and Tversky, A. (1971) *Foundations of Measurement*, vol 1, Academic Press, New York
Luce, R. D. and Suppes, P. (1965) 'Preferences, utility, and subjective probability', in R. D. Luce, R. R. Bush and E. Galanter (eds) *Handbook of Mathematical Psychology*, vol III, Wiley, New York
Mandler, M. (2005) 'Incomplete preferences and rational intransitivity of choice', *Games and Economic Behaviour*, vol 50, pp255–277
Margolis, H. (1996) *Dealing With Risk: Why the Public and the Experts Disagree on Environmental Issues*, University of Chicago Press, Chicago
Mellor, D. H. (2005) *Probability: A Philosophical Introduction*, Routledge, London
Peterson, M. (2006) 'Indeterminate preferences', *Philosophical Studies*, vol 130, no 2, pp297–320
Ramsey, F. (1931) 'Truth and probability', in R. Braithwaite (ed.) *The Foundations of Mathematics and other Logical Essays*, Humanities Press, London
Savage, L. J. (1954) *The Foundation of Statistics*, John Wiley and Sons, New York
Sen, A. (2004) 'Incompleteness and reasoned choice', *Synthese*, vol 140, pp43–59
Sinott-Armstrong, W. (1988) *Moral Dilemmas*, Blackwell, Oxford
Tetlock, P. E. (2003) 'Thinking the unthinkable: sacred values and taboo cognitions', *Trends in Cognitive Sciences*, vol 7, no 7, pp320–324
Tetlock, P. E., Peterson, R. S. and Lerner, R. S. (1996) 'Revising the value pluralism model: Incorporating social content and context postulates', in C. Seligman, J. M. Olson and M. P. Zanna (eds) *The Psychology of Values: The Ontario Symposium Volume 8*, Routledge
Tetlock, P. E., Kristel, O., Elson, B., Green, M. and Lerner, J. (2000) 'The psychology of the unthinkable: taboo trade-offs, forbidden base rates, and heretical counterfactuals', *Journal of Personality and Social Psychology*, vol 78, pp853–870
Thompson, J. J. (1997) 'The right and the good', *The Journal of Philosophy*, vol 94, no 6, pp273–298
von Neumann, J. and Morgenstern, O. (1947) *Theory of Games and Economic Behaviour*, Princeton University Press, Princeton NJ
Wester-Herber, M. (2006) 'En enkätundersökning om stockholmares attityder till dubbdäck: frågor om partiklar, hälsa och säkerhet', *Naturvårdsverket rapport*, nr. 5613

NOTES

1 Imagine, for instance, that we wish to build a stretch of highway for safety reasons, but that this would then potentially destroy the breeding grounds (trees) for some rare species of birds.

2 While there is nothing wrong with saying that the 0.2 probability of X is a *greater* risk than the 0.1 probability of X under STNR (where the two Xs represent the same kind of consequence), it is difficult to see how it could be meaningful to say that some probability of X is a greater or smaller risk than some probability of Y (where X and Y are different kinds of consequences). It seems that the only circumstance under which such a comparison would be meaningful is one in which there was some presupposed comparison-value with respect to which either risk would be found to be *better or worse*. Hence, either all risks that are not of the same kind are incommensurable under STNR, or comparisons among them are value-laden under STNR.

3 Note that not all scholarly risk theorists endorse this notion of risk. Ulrich Beck, for example, wishes to equate risk with risk perception (1992, p55). For a listing of various common usages of the word risk, see Hansson (2004b).

4 This entails that the values of negative consequences can be incommensurable. It should be noted that under GNR the values of two incommensurable *consequences* may be commensurable or at least comparable (one fatality is worse in terms of value than one sick person for example). On the other hand, the commensurability of consequences is not a guarantee for the commensurability of the values of those consequences – ten fatalities is ten times one fatality, but we might not be able to express the negative value of one fatality as an exact fraction of ten fatalities (I thank the anonymous referee for pointing this out to me). Furthermore, we should note that even though the negative values of the potential consequences of two risks are incommensurable it does not mean that the *risks* cannot be compared. This will be discussed in detail below.

5 However, studies have recently shown that studded tyres actually only confer a slight safety benefit during wintertime (Elvik, 1999).

6 One may question, of course, if a single measure really is necessary. It is quite conceivable to employ a multidimensional risk evaluation, one in which each attribute is considered separately: '[E]ach risk and benefit is measured in the unit deemed to be most suitable for that attribute. Perhaps money is the right unit to use for measuring the construction costs of a new road, whereas the number of lives saved is the right unit to use for measuring increased traffic safety. The total value of each act is thereafter determined by aggregating the attributes, eg money and lives, into an overall ranking of the act' (Peterson, 2006, p5). However, multi-attribute risk analysis of this kind is fundamentally problematic. For how can the decision-maker determine the relative importance of each attribute? In order to do so one would have to determine trade-off relations between the different attributes, whereby we would end up with a single measure after all.

7 Whether or not the value of human life *actually is* fundamentally different from the value of a ground water reservoir is a substantial value-theoretical question. From a *value-monistic* point of view all values are ultimately reducible to one single *supervalue*, but according to *value-pluralists* there are potentially infinitely many different values. I shall not have anything to say about this discussion here. It should be noted though that values need not be different in a value-pluralistic sense in order to be incommensurable. Some values may even be incomparable despite being of the same kind (Chang, 1997).

8 One of the main assumptions of the standard view (the collectivistic version) is that harms inflicted on one individual may be compensated by benefits to another individual.

This compensability assumption is often criticized for not taking into account the *rights* of individuals exposed to risks. The absolutist alternative, to take into account every individual's rights, is also problematic. Besides being unpractical, perhaps even impossible, to implement, it is doubtful if even a single individual can always be given compensation that is *commensurate* to the harm to which she may potentially be exposed.

9 The standard view can be contrasted against other methods of evaluation according to which risks are taken or imposed upon others only if they are acceptable with respect to some, perhaps, non-maximizing standard (cf Hermansson, 2005).

10 For example, say that course of action A leads to a certain risk R_1 that a person dies and that course of action B leads to a slightly higher risk R_2 that a person dies. If the benefits associated with taking each of these courses of action were valued the same then we should of course go with A. However, it may be the case that B results in significantly more valuable benefits. We must then weigh the difference in value against the difference in risk; if the benefits outweigh the risks then we should perhaps go with B after all.

11 *W* may be some acceptable risk standard.

12 According to Hansson (2004a), risk comparisons of this kind are fallacious because '[c]omparisons between risks can only be directly decision-guiding if they refer to objects that are alternatives in one and the same decision' (p353).

13 The probability of a car accident is derived from accident statistics while there is no corresponding statistics for nuclear power plants.

14 See Vincent Covello's (1991) list of 19 factors that could account for expert/lay conflicts of risk intuition.

15 It may, of course, be difficult to determine whether or not two consequences are of the same kind; it may be a matter of degree or there may be borderline cases. For instance, is the consequence that a young child dies in a car accident the same kind of consequence as that of a very old person dying in a car accident? Arguably, there are evaluative reasons to view them as different kinds of consequences since we tend to value a young person's life higher than an old person's life. But then, again, evaluative considerations should not be taken into account when comparing risks under STNR. However, it is difficult if not impossible to draw a line that distinguishes young from old. This difficulty is not due to evaluative reasons but rather to semantic ones. Accordingly, it would then, perhaps, be meaningful to talk of both partial and complete cases of formal incommensurability.

16 Chang (1997) calls items that do not fall within the domain of application of the comparison predicate *non-comparable*.

17 This is analogous to what Adler (1998) calls a conventional ordering failure in cost benefit analysis.

18 This could be anyone: the risk-taker, the decision-maker, or the risk-beneficiary. In the following we can assume, however, that we wish to measure the preferences of an objective, maximally rational decision-maker behind a 'veil of ignorance'. How such a decision-maker comes to have her preferences and how she *ought* to evaluate different risk situations is a different matter. There are those who suggest that risks should be evaluated with monetary cost-benefit analyses involving contingent valuation methods. Of course, incommensurability is also a problem for cost-benefit analysis, but these issues are left for another time.

19 The symbols $>$ and $\sim$ stand for the relations *preferred to* and *indifference* respectively. For axiomatizations of utility theory without the completeness axiom, see for instance Aumann (1962) and Bewley (1986).

20 There is a growing literature in both economics and philosophy dealing with incomplete preferences. See, for instance, Sen (2000), Danan (2003), Eliaz and Ok (2005), Mandler (2005), Espinoza and Peterson (2006) and Peterson (2006).

21 This is an instance of the so called *small improvement argument*, originally proposed by Sinott-Armstrong (1988) and further developed by Chang (2002). A detailed critique can be found in Espinoza (2006). More about the small improvement argument will be discussed below.

22 There are many interpretations of probability that satisfy the classic probability axioms proposed by Kolmogorov. For introductions to these various interpretations of probability, see Gillies (2000) and Mellor (2005).

23 In many cases only probability *intervals* can be ascertained.

24 A positive value relation is a relation that affirms something about how items relate, whereas negative value relations merely say how items do not relate. Take for instance the proposition 'x is better than y' as an example of the former, and 'x is not better than y' as an example of the latter. Suppose that no matter what and how many different kinds of value relations there are, only one can be true at a time, that is, they are mutually exclusive. Now, if we can relate two items positively as in the first case, then we have automatically excluded all other possible relations. But, if we merely state a negative relation, as in the second case, we have only excluded one of the potentially infinite set of relations that may be obtained between two items. Needless to say, we should be able to say something affirmative about a relation if what we say is to be of any use at all.

10 Welfare Judgements and Risk

Greg Bognar

Welfare judgements

When we try to decide what to do, or we evaluate actions and policies, we are often concerned with welfare effects: how good an action or policy is for those who are affected. In such cases we attempt to make *welfare judgements.*

There are different kinds of welfare judgements. In many cases, we are interested in comparative judgements: how well off certain people are or will be compared to some other situation or compared to some other people. Such judgements are often elliptical – cast in non-comparative language. Other times we may be interested simply in whether something is good or bad for some person without comparing it to something else or someone else's lot. Welfare judgements may also concern the past or the present – when for instance we evaluate how well a person's life is going, or has been going, for that person – but they often concern the future: in such cases, we ask how well off people may be, given that this or that action or policy is chosen. These are prospective welfare judgements.

In recent years, philosophers have expended considerable effort clarifying and proposing theories of welfare.[1] In contrast, they have devoted much less attention to the problem of welfare judgements. One might think that given a theory of welfare, it is a straightforward task to evaluate actions, policies, institutions and the like. Thus, we do not need a separate model of welfare judgements – having the best theory of welfare at hand, we can make all the welfare judgements we want to make. But even though theories of welfare and models of welfare judgements are not unrelated, they are different. A theory of welfare is a view of that in virtue of which certain things are good (or bad) for people; it gives an account of what we mean when we say that a person is well off or her life is going well for her. It provides the basis on which we can evaluate welfare. A model of welfare judgements, on the other hand, tells us how we can make these evaluations: it answers questions about the scope and limits of the judgements we can make on the basis of our account of well-being.

Another way in which theories of welfare and models of welfare judgements differ is this: a theory of welfare is usually understood as an account of what is *intrinsically* good for a person; it is not concerned with what is good only as the means (for achieving what is intrinsically good) for a person. But when our objective is to promote welfare, we often have to deliberate about means as well as ends. Even though such deliberation makes essential reference to what is intrinsically good for the people we are concerned with, we need to take into account how different means might contribute to what is intrinsically good for them. In other words, we need to deliberate about what is merely instrumentally good.

As an example, suppose you accept a simple hedonist account on which a person's well-being consists of that person's having some conscious mental state. Then facts about that mental state are the truth-makers of claims about welfare: you are well off just in case you have this mental state. But your theory of welfare is not going to be sufficient to evaluate all welfare claims. How can we tell what your level of well-being is? How can we tell how that level compares to your level of well-being at other times or to the level of well-being of other people? Can we compare not only levels, but also units of welfare, such that we can determine how much better off you are than another person (or how much better off you are at one time than at another time)? In order to determine how to answer such questions, and whether they can be answered on your theory at all, we need a model of welfare judgements.[2]

As a matter of fact, there is one model of welfare judgements which is often implicit in discussions of well-being as well as in our ordinary, everyday practice of making welfare judgements. On this model, very roughly, welfare judgements are made and justified by appealing to what people in more privileged epistemic and cognitive circumstances would want, desire, prefer, seek or choose for themselves. That is, welfare judgements involve idealization. This model is most naturally connected to informed desire or full-information accounts of well-being.[3] It is not incompatible, however, with any theory of well-being which allows that the desires or preferences formed in these circumstances can serve as *indicators* of a person's well-being, hence welfare judgements can be made in terms of them – even if there may be other, perhaps often more adequate, methods for making those judgements, or the judgements made on this model track the truth of welfare claims less than perfectly reliably.[4]

I shall call this sort of model of welfare judgements the *ideal advisor model.* One of the considerations in its favour is that it seems to give a reasonably adequate picture of how people ordinarily make welfare judgements. When giving advice to someone, we often appeal to what that person would want if she was in a better position to decide what to do; normally, we give more weight to the advice of those who are better informed, more experienced, or make a sound case for their opinion; and we might prefer not to make decisions when we are tired, depressed, inattentive or lack information.

A further consideration in favour of the ideal advisor model is that it is relatively uncontroversial insofar as it does not stipulate that there are pursuits or goods in terms of which welfare judgements should be made. By starting from people's actual desires and preferences and determining how these would change in more ideal conditions, the model does not include *substantive judgements* – judgements about the content of desires and preferences. All we need to rely on in order to evaluate people's well-being are rationality and facts.

Nevertheless, I will argue that neither of these considerations hold for some kinds of welfare judgements. The ideal advisor model fails to capture an important component of what we do when we make such judgements. It also fails as their philosophical model, since these judgements are inevitably substantive. The root of these problems is that the assessment of risks plays a central role in these kinds of welfare judgements.

The welfare judgements I have in mind are *comparative* and *prospective*. Such judgements are perhaps the most important kind there is: people make them all the time when they want to decide what may be best for them or for others. Politicians and other public officials make them when they formulate policies. Economists and other social scientists make them when they evaluate those policies.

I begin by characterizing the version of the ideal advisor model which seems to be the most plausible. If this version is not the best formulation, it can at least serve as a starting point for my arguments. The last section explains why I do not think the model can be reformulated to meet my objections, and it concludes by discussing the general implications of my argument.

The ideal advisor model

On the ideal advisor model, judgements about a person's well-being are made in terms of the preferences that person would have were she in ideal conditions for forming her preferences.[5] There are, of course, other possible models which make use of the same idea, depending on how the ideal conditions for forming preferences are specified. For instance, one version may hold that a person is in ideal conditions for forming preferences if and only if she is in Buddhist meditation. What sets the ideal advisor model apart is that its ideal conditions are *epistemic* and *cognitive*: on the one hand, the person in ideal conditions for forming preferences is informed about her circumstances, range of options and the possible consequences of her choices; on the other hand, when she forms her preferences, she does not make any mistakes of representation of fact or errors of reasoning, and she is free of distorting psychological influences such as depression, anxiety, stress and the like. In short, the person in ideal conditions is informed and rational in some appropriate sense.

The ideal advisor model involves specifying counterfactuals about preferences. It takes the person's actual preferences and determines how they would change if the person was given information about her situation, provided that she does not make any mistake of reasoning and avoids other sorts of cognitive error. It is usually assumed – and I will also assume this – that the counterfactuals about the person's preference changes can be evaluated on some best theory for the evaluation of counterfactuals, whatever that theory is.

To save words, I will say that the preferences of a person in ideal conditions for forming preferences are the preferences of the 'ideal advisor' of that person.

Of course, distinguishing between the preferences of the 'actual person' and the preferences of her ideal advisor is no more than a useful metaphor that makes the exposition easier. Both are the preferences of the same person: the former are her actual preferences, the latter are the preferences she would form were she informed and rational in the appropriate sense.[6]

What is the appropriate sense? Since the epistemic and cognitive conditions of ideal preferences can be interpreted in different ways, the ideal advisor model has further sub-versions. On the interpretation I will be working with, the person in ideal conditions for forming preferences is *fully informed* and *ideally rational*. Let us consider these conditions in turn.

'Being fully informed' is usually understood to require that *all relevant* information is available to ideal advisors. Any piece of information is relevant which could make a difference to the preferences of the person, and all such information should be made available, since the recommendations based on the preferences of the person's ideal advisor would have less normative force if she was to work with limited information only.

Being fully informed, however, cannot mean that ideal advisors are omniscient. They cannot have certitude of what *will* happen given their actual person's choice; they only know what *is likely to* happen, given that choice. This restriction is necessary because if the model assumed that ideal advisors are omniscient, then it would involve counterfactuals which *in principle* cannot be evaluated. In that case, the ideal advisor model would be useless for making prospective welfare judgements (even though it may continue to be useful for making welfare judgements which concern the present or the past). Of course, it is true that we hardly ever have all the information to determine what we would prefer if we were fully informed and ideally rational, even if no prospective judgements are involved. But the idea is that as long as the relevant information is in principle available, we can make rough-and-ready judgements and use the model as a heuristic device. If, however, the model was such that in many cases we could not even in principle evaluate the counterfactuals about preference changes, there would seem to be a fatal flaw in it. Since many of our welfare judgements are indeed prospective, the restriction is inevitable.[7]

Therefore, an ideal advisor knows what options are open to her actual counterpart, the relevant features of the choice situation and the objective probabilities with which the possible outcomes might obtain – and, since she is ideally rational, she forms and handles subjective probabilities appropriately when objective probabilities of some options cannot be obtained.

Consider now the cognitive condition. The ideal advisor model treats ideal advisors as ideally rational; but it is controversial what rationality is and what it is to be ideally rational. For ideal advisors, rationality may consist of forming rational preferences, and representing and processing information appropriately. Or it may also consist of some further cognitive capacities. I propose therefore to make the following distinction. The cognitive capacities of ideal advisors include that:

(a) they form their preferences according to the canons of a fully developed theory of rational choice;

(b) in addition, they have further cognitive capacities.

By a 'fully developed theory of rational choice', I mean a formal theory that tells rational agents how to order their preferences under conditions of certainty, uncertainty and risk. This theory also involves rules for assigning to and updating the probabilities of uncertain options. I will call this complete theory of rational choice *R* for short. Needless to say, we do not now have such a fully developed theory, but rather we have a number of competing theories. Nevertheless, an intuitive idea of what such a theory would look like in broad outline is this: *R* tells a rational agent how to form her preferences with a view to maximize their satisfaction in decision problems, including problems in which her choice may be influenced by states of nature or the consequences of the choices of other agents, and it tells her only this much. In contrast, by 'further cognitive capacities' I mean cognitive capacities that are not part of that theory, even though they are necessary for an agent to have in order to be able to employ that theory. These further cognitive capacities are needed by the agent to be able to understand her situation – to describe and represent the options and possible strategies, the influences of the choices of other agents and so on. As it were, (a) enables a rational agent to make a choice, while (b) enables an agent to understand what is involved in making that choice.

Therefore, we can think of the difference between (a) and (b) this way. The former says that ideal advisors follow the norms of rationality, hence their preferences must be formally representable on theory *R*. The latter describes what capacities an agent must have to count as rational – what it takes to be able to follow the norms of rationality and to have preferences representable by *R*.

Of course, we do not make welfare judgements in exactly these terms. But this model is intended to capture the central features of what we do when we advise ourselves or others: we appeal to having the relevant information (insofar as we can have it), processing that information correctly and weighing the options on the basis of that information. Also, more needs to be done to work out the details of the model: we would have to specify more precisely what relevant information is, say more about the theory of rational choice used in the model, and spell out the details of component (b) in the cognitive condition.

In what follows, however, I am going to bracket (b).[8] In order to make my argument against the ideal advisor model of welfare judgements, all I need to suppose is that ideal advisors are ideally rational in the sense given by (a) – that is, they follow the norms, and their preferences satisfy the axioms, of *R*.

A COUNTERARGUMENT

Consider the following example. I am faced with the choice of what career to pursue in my life. For simplicity, I assume that only my success in my chosen career determines how well my life goes. Now suppose that due to my circumstances, inclinations and talents, the two relevant options open to me are becoming a philosopher and becoming a concert pianist. In order to decide which of these would be better for me, I turn to my ideal advisor. My ideal advisor knows the following. I have talent for both pursuing an academic career in philosophy and a career in the performing arts as a pianist. But he also knows that my talent for philosophy is somewhat modest: I can become a reasonably successful, average philosopher, and therefore have a reasonably good life. If, on the other hand, I pursue a career in music, I have the ability to become an exceptionally good pianist and have an immensely rewarding life.

There is, however, a problem. If I do decide to pursue the career in music, there is a high likelihood that I will develop rheumatoid arthritis in my fingers in a few years – which will destroy my career completely, and I will end up with a miserable life. My ideal advisor knows that the probability that I do develop this condition after a few years is in fact 0.9 – since he fulfils the epistemic condition, that is, he has full information of the possible consequences of my choice and the relevant probabilities. As I suppose now, he also uses a fully developed theory of rational choice, *R*, to form his preferences over what I should prefer and choose. In other words, he knows that the decision problem I face is the one depicted in Figure 10.1.

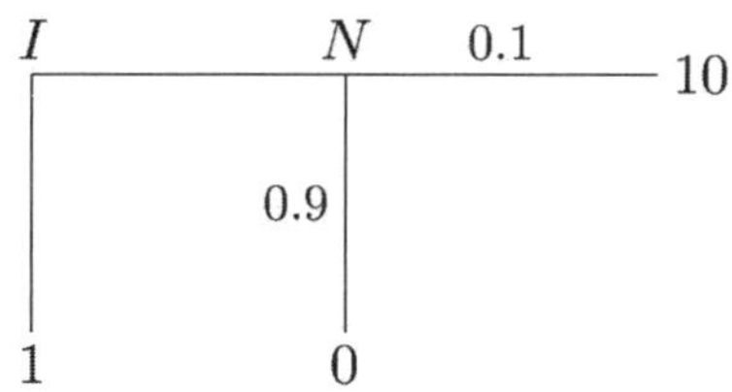

Figure 10.1 *Career choice*

The numbers 0, 1 and 10 represent my well-being: how well my life may go for me overall if I choose to become a philosopher or a concert pianist.[9] Node *I* shows my move, and node *N* shows Nature's 'move'. If I move 'down', that is, become a philosopher, my life will be alright, although not great. If, on the other hand, I move 'across', it is Nature's move – 'she' will either move down, with the consequence that I develop rheumatoid arthritis, or she will move across, in which case I do not develop the condition. There is a 0.9 probability that Nature moves down, and a 0.1 probability that she moves across. If she moves down, my career is ruined and my life will be miserable. Should she, however, move across, my life will be extraordinarily good. Note that the *expectations* of the two prospects are equal. If I move down, I realize a life with 1 'unit' of well-being. If I move across, my expectation of well-being is $0.9 \times 0 + 0.1 \times 10 = 1$ as well.

The preference my ideal advisor forms over these prospects determines which one is likely to be better for me – whether it is the sure prospect I can choose by moving down (that is, by becoming a philosopher), or the lottery prospect I can choose by moving across (that is, by trying to become a concert pianist). So what will his recommendation be?

Now, we know that my ideal advisor forms his preference based on the norms and axioms of *R*. But in order to form his preference over the prospects I am now facing, he has to use some norm or principle of *R* that tells him how to form his preferences when I have to choose between a sure and a lottery prospect with the same expected values. Thus, he needs a norm or principle that tells him what risk-attitude he should have towards these prospects – more generally, he needs what could be called a *principle of reasonable levels of risk-taking* towards well-being, which I will abbreviate as P.[10]

Let me ask the following question: will principle P be a part of a fully developed theory of rational choice *R*, and what are the consequences of its inclusion or omission for the ideal advisor model?

First, suppose that P is *not* part of *R*. In this case, my ideal advisor will not be able to form a preference in cases like my career choice. Since no principle determines which prospect he should prefer, he cannot give recommendations to the actual person. He cannot give recommendations since he cannot compare the prospects from which the actual person has to choose with *R*. And he cannot say that the prospects are equally good since their expected values are equal. That is, he is not indifferent between the prospects, since that would presuppose a principle P: that you should be indifferent between prospects with equal expected values.

It might be objected that I may already have some risk-attitude towards these prospects, and it will be taken into account as an input to the determination of my fully informed and ideally rational preferences. But when we want to assess our actual preferences, we want to assess our preferences over prospects as well. What I am asking my ideal advisor to do in this case is precisely to tell me whether my preference based on my risk-attitude would be one that I would embrace in ideal conditions, and, if not, what sort of risk-attitude I should have when forming preferences over these prospects. Consequently, if P is not part of *R*, then the ideal advisor model is underdetermined: when the actual person has to choose from risky prospects, the theory does not specify what the person would prefer were she fully informed and ideally rational.

In order to avoid this problem, it is natural to assume that P is part of *R*. Thus, in the remainder of this section, I test the hypothesis that P is part of *R* for different versions of P. I argue that if it is, then ideal advisors may form preferences such that the welfare judgements which are based on them do not seem to be correct. I show this by arguing that if P is part of *R*, then actual persons might reject, for good reasons, the recommendations based on the preferences of their ideal advisors.

I will assume, for now, that if P is part of *R*, then it can be any of three simple principles. (I will discuss the possibility of more refined principles in the next section.) P might tell rational agents to be risk-averse towards well-being. Or it might tell rational agents to be risk-neutral towards well-being. Finally, it could tell rational agents to be risk-seeking towards well-being. However, I only mention this last possibility to discard it at the outset. I suspect that it would be quite extraordinary for our ideal advisors to tell us to take risks comprehensively. It is hard to see how a principle to seek risk could be a principle of rationality. Consider again the choice I have between becoming a philosopher and pursuing a risky career as a concert pianist. Suppose now I have the talent of a genius for playing the piano. If I do not develop rheumatoid arthritis, I will not only become a great concert pianist, but I will be the greatest concert pianist of the time: a talent like me is born only once in a century. Unfortunately, I am even more likely, in this scenario, to develop the condition in my fingers. Suppose the probability of this is 0.999 now. There is, however, a very low – 0.001 – probability that I do not develop the condition, and my life will be exceptional: its value will be not 10, but 1,000. The expectations of becoming a philosopher and risking the career in music are again equal. It nonetheless seems, given the extremely low likelihood of pursuing the concert pianist career successfully, that my ideal advisor could not recommend to take that risk. But, in any case, I will give a general argument against *any* principle later.

Let me now consider the remaining two cases. Suppose, first, that principle P of *R* tells rational agents to be risk-averse towards well-being. In particular, it tells rational agents that when they are faced with a sure prospect and a lottery prospect of the same value, they should prefer the sure prospect – in short, rational agents play it safe.

I will, once again, argue through an example. In the example of the choice between becoming a philosopher or a concert pianist, the outcome of the choice of pursuing the latter was influenced by factors outside of my control – by the state that may result following a 'move' by Nature. But our choices are not influenced by states of nature only. They may also be influenced by the consequences of the choices other people make. When giving us advice, our ideal advisors must take into account these influences as well.

Look at Figure 10.2 now. In this situation, there are two individuals, *A* and *B*. I suppose *A* is female and *B* is male. The first number at the endpoints stands for the value of the outcome for *A*, and the second number stands for the value of the outcome for *B*. Thus, *A* has a choice at node *A*: she can either move down, in which case she receives 1 unit of well-being and *B* receives 0; or she can move across. If *A* moves across, there is a 0.5 probability that she will receive 0 and *B* will also receive 0, but there is also a 0.5 probability that *B* gets to make a choice: he can also move down or across. (What p and $(1-p)$ stand for will become clear later.) If *B* moves down, *A* receives 0 and *B* receives 3 units of well-being. If, on the other hand, he moves across, there is a 0.5 probability that they both receive 2, and it is equally likely that *A* receives 2 and *B* receives 4.

I will assume that initially both *A* and *B* take the recommendations of their respective ideal advisors as authoritative – that they recognize the preferences of their ideal advisors as *reason-giving* – and they mutually know that they do. Furthermore, their ideal advisors form their preferences according to the canons of *R*, and *R* contains P: a principle that tells rational agents to be risk-averse towards well-being. What will the recommendations of the ideal advisors be?

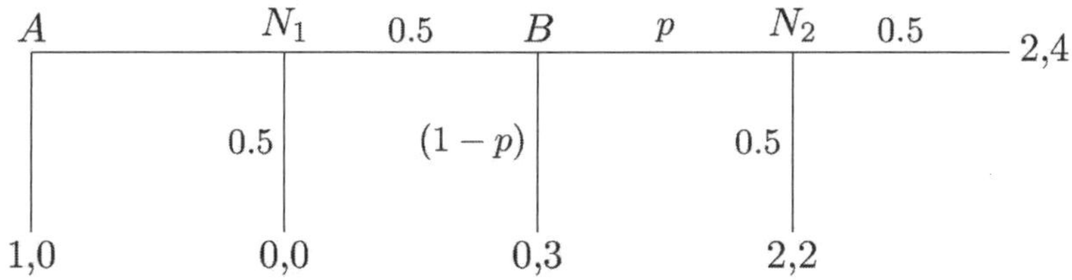

Figure 10.2 *A problem for actual persons*

Look at the situation from the perspective of *B* first. His ideal advisor reasons that if *B* moves down at his node, he will receive 3 for certain; if he moves across, he may receive either 2 or 4 with equal probabilities. The expectations of these two prospects are equal. But *B*'s ideal advisor follows P, which says that you should be risk-averse towards well-being. Hence, if *B* ever gets a chance to make a move, he should move down.

Consider *A* now, who will definitely have a chance to make a move. She can either move down or across. If she moves down, she will get 1 for sure. In order to find out whether she should move across, she will reason the following way:

> If I move across, Nature will either move down or across. If Nature moves down, I receive 0. If Nature moves across, *B* will make a move. He will either move down or across. If he moves down, I again receive 0. If he moves across, Nature will move again, but that move is irrelevant, since no matter what happens, I receive 2. So what I can expect if I move across partly depends on *B*. Suppose *B* moves across with probability p, and he moves down with probability $(1 - p)$. My expectation if I move across therefore is:
>
> $$0.5 \times 0 + 0.5((1 - p) \times 0 + p(0.5 \times 2 + 0.5 \times 2)) = p.$$
>
> So whether I should move across depends on what *B* is likely to do, whether he is willing to move across. But I know that he will take the preference of his ideal advisor as the reason for his move. And I also know that his ideal advisor forms his preference according to a principle of risk-aversion towards well-being, that is, he will prefer him to move down, should he get a chance to move. Hence I know that he would move down, that is, I know that $p = 0$. So I should move down myself.

This assumes, of course, that the preferences of the ideal advisors, as well as the reasons for those preferences, are known by the actual persons. This assumption enables us to check whether *A* and *B* can endorse the preferences of their ideal counterparts. The argument I make is that they have reasons not to. They have reasons to reject the recommendations of their ideal advisors.

To return to *B*. He realizes that if they both act in accordance with the preferences of their ideal advisors, he will never have a chance to move. But getting a chance to move by *A*'s moving across would be at least as good for him as not getting a chance to move by *A*'s moving down. That is, if only he got a chance to move – even if he *actually* could not move because Nature moved down at N_1 – he would not be worse off, and possibly he could end up being much better off. In short, he would not be worse off if *A* moved across, irrespective of what happens afterwards. And *B* starts to think now, and comes up with an idea.

Suppose *A* and *B* can communicate, and do it without costs. Then *B* can make the following offer to *A*: 'I promise to move across if I get a chance to make a move.' *B* has nothing to lose with promising this, since if *A* accepts the offer, he might end up better off, and if she rejects it, he ends up no worse off. The idea behind the offer is that by cooperating in ways not embraced by their ideal advisors, they might fare better than by strictly following their recommendations.

When *B* makes his offer, he promises that he will not act in accordance with the preference of his ideal advisor. In effect, he promises that at his move he will *not* be risk-averse towards well-being. In other words, he promises to reject the reasoning based on P. Instead of being risk-averse, he becomes risk-seeking, and he makes it the case that $p = 1$. We can think of *B*'s offer as choosing a *risk-disposition* towards well-being at the start of the choice problem: if he makes the offer, he promises to become risk-seeking, and if he declines to make the offer, he remains risk-averse. Similarly, we can think of *A*'s decision whether to accept the offer as choosing a risk-disposition which determines which way she moves at node *A*: on the one hand, if she accepts the offer, she becomes risk-seeking towards well-being and moves across; on the other hand, if she rejects the offer, she becomes risk-averse towards well-being and moves down.[11]

For the sake of the argument, assume that the agents are *transparent*, that is, their risk-dispositions are known with certainty. Of course, in many situations agents are not transparent, thus their risk-dispositions are not known with certainty. In such cases, whether *A* can accept the offer depends on how she evaluates the risk of accepting it, given her probability assessment of *B*'s risk-disposition – thus, whether she accepts the offer depends on the *degree* to which she is willing to become risk-seeking. However, at least in this case *B* has a reason to become transparent – as a way of assuring *A* that the promise of moving across at his node will be kept.

Assume also that *B*'s offer to commit himself to be a risk-seeker is *credible*: once he chooses his risk-disposition, he sticks with it, and he does move across at node *B*. Of course, prior commitments are not always credible. When the time for action comes, agents may find that they are better off breaking a prior promise. However, at least in this case, once *B* has chosen his risk-seeking disposition, he has no obvious reason to change it later. In other words, we may suppose that *B*'s risk-disposition is stable, in which case *A* can count on *B* to move across at node *B*. If risk-dispositions are less than perfectly stable, whether *A* can accept the offer depends on how she evaluates the risk of accepting it, given her probability assessment of *B*'s stability of risk-disposition – thus, whether she accepts the offer once again depends on the *degree* to which she is willing to become risk-seeking. Hence, *B* has a reason to develop a stable risk-disposition.

But should *A* accept the offer after all? If she moves down, she will get 1 for certain. If she moves across, she also expects 1, since now she knows that *B* will move across – that $p = 1$. Why would she reject the offer? One consideration is that her ideal advisor, who is ideally rational in the sense given by *R*, tells her to be risk-averse towards well-being, so she should still move down at node *A*, regardless of *B*'s promise. This consideration, however, is decisive only if she continues to believe that P is a principle of rationality or that it is relevant to deciding what she should do. But *B* now rejects P, and for sound reasons. With the offer, *A*'s situation has changed. Figure 10.3 illustrates how her original choice problem is simplified, given that the offer is made.[12]

B's offer requires that the actual persons cooperate by harmonizing their risk-dispositions towards well-being in ways not embraced by (and not open to) their ideal advisors. The offer works only if *B* gives up the recommendation based on the preferences of his ideal advisor by rejecting P, and *A* too gives up the recommendation based on the preferences of her ideal advisor, also rejecting P. The offer requires that they both become risk-seekers – that they both become irrational in light of *R*. If they do, *B* can end up better off: once *A* moves across and

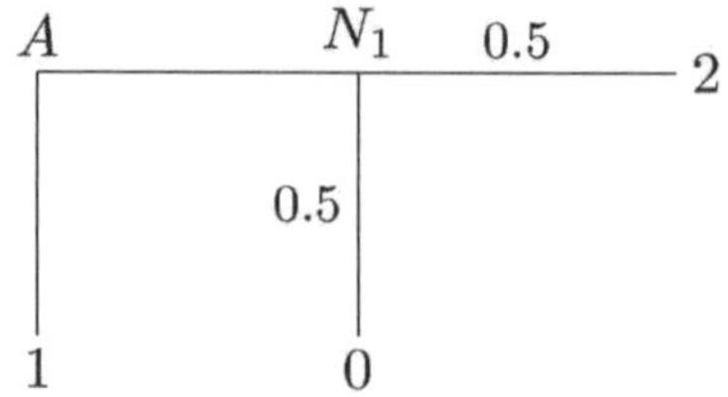

Figure 10.3 *The problem simplified*

if he gets lucky, he is guaranteed a pay-off of at least 2, and, with some further luck, 4. Moreover, *A* is no worse off, since the expectations of moving down and moving across are now equal, and she has no reason not to reject P and become a risk-seeker.

Their ideal advisors, in contrast, cannot cooperate in the same way. They cannot transform their situation in order to open up the possibility for realizing higher gains. Since ideal advisors, by definition, are 'in the grip' of their rationality, and their rationality, by hypothesis, prescribes risk-aversion towards well-being, their preferences cannot yield the recommendation to cooperate. *A* and *B* will realize this, since their ideal advisors are transparently risk-averse and their risk-dispositions are fixed.

B has a reason to reject the recommendation of his ideal advisor and make this known to *A*, because if he follows that recommendation, he forgoes benefits he might otherwise be able to obtain through cooperation. His ideal advisor, since he is ideally rational and this is known, cannot credibly commit himself to move across at node *B*. Thus, his offer would not be accepted. Actual persons therefore may be able to come to agreements which would be foreclosed to them if they were ideally rational.

A has no reason to accept the recommendation of her ideal advisor because she may fail to see why she should be risk-averse in a situation like the one depicted in Figure 10.3. She notices that there are many situations in which it is better not to follow the recommendation given by *R* (*B* is in such a situation), and she may start wondering why P should be considered a principle of rationality at all – or, if it is a principle of rationality, why a principle of rationality should determine what is likely to be better for her.

Notice that the argument is not that ideal advisors can *never* employ commitment or other mechanisms to come to advantageous agreements. Rather, the argument is that in virtue of their ideal rationality, certain mechanisms whose use can make people better off are foreclosed to them. Therefore, their preferences may fail to determine what is likely to make less than ideally rational persons better off.

Finally, let me ask what happens if principle P prescribes risk-neutrality towards well-being instead of risk-aversion. Actually, nothing changes in this case. *A* and *B* may similarly reject the recommendations of their ideal advisors. In order to see this, return to Figure 10.2. For *B*, the expectations of moving down and across at node *B* are equal, and if he adheres to the preferences of his ideal advisor, then he will, say, toss a fair coin to decide which move to make. That is, $p = 0.5$. Hence *A* will move down, because by doing so she expects 1. Once again, *B* will realize that this way he will never get to make a move, and he is thus eager to give up P and convince *A* to move across. He tells her that he will not follow the principle, attempting to make the expectations of *A* equal. If *A* listens to the recommendation of her ideal advisor, she will also toss a fair coin to decide whether to move down or across. But that is not good enough, for why jeopardize their cooperation by staying risk-neutral? She could make sure their cooperation gets a better chance to kick off if she also abandons P, and acts as a risk-seeker. She once again has reason to think that principle P does not determine what is likely to be better for her, given that there are situations when it is more beneficial to give it up – to become irrational in light of *R*. She may tell herself that sometimes it is better not to listen to what you would advise yourself to do were you ideally placed to give yourself advice.

Reasonable risks

In this section, I first consider the possibility that *R* contains some more refined principle of reasonable levels of risk-taking towards well-being. I argue that no such principle is possible, at least not within the context of rationality. I conclude by exploring some of the implications of my argument.

Of the three basic candidates for P, we found that one, risk-seeking, is implausible on its own right, and it is possible to construct situations in which the two other principles also become implausible – because actual persons may find incentives to abandon them. This means that if *R* contains any of these, actual persons may fail to take the preferences of their ideal advisors as reason-giving, since rejecting these principles can lead to outcomes which are better for them. At the same time, if *R* does not contain a principle that prescribes preference formation in risky situations, then ideal advisors cannot form preferences in these situations and the prospects remain incomparable. Either way, the ideal advisor model of welfare judgements fails to resolve which prospect is likely to be better. Hence we cannot base our prospective welfare judgements on the preferences people would form were they fully informed and ideally rational.

On the one hand, perhaps one can bite the bullet and argue that the ideal advisor model is incomplete for prospective welfare judgements. One may argue that there is a good reason for this: when we are faced with a risky situation, there is no answer to the question which prospect would be better, since a person's well-being is uncertain until the risk (or uncertainty) is resolved. Hence, the prospects are incomparable with respect to well-being.

This objection rests on an understanding of what we do when we try to make prospective welfare judgements that is different from mine. It assumes that these judgements try to determine how well lives *will* go, given that some action or policy is chosen. In contrast, I take it that prospective welfare judgements are about how well lives are *likely* to go, or can be expected to go, given that the action or policy is chosen. While it is certainly impossible to determine the answer to the former question until the risk is resolved, it should not be impossible to determine the answer to the latter question. In this respect, prospects do not seem to be incomparable. After all, when I am pondering whether I should try to be a reasonably good philosopher or an exceptionally good piano player (with a predisposition to develop rheumatoid arthritis), my complaint is not that I cannot compare these prospects – my complaint is that what risk-attitude I should have towards these prospects does not seem to be a matter resolvable by a principle of rationality. Comparing prospects is the most we are able to do, and we cannot avoid making these comparisons.

On the other hand, one could propose that principle P, in a fully developed theory of rational choice, will be much more complex. It will specify some particular *level* of risk-taking. So, for instance, it will tell me to try to become a concert pianist if the likelihood of developing rheumatoid arthritis is within tolerable limits, but choose the career in philosophy if its probability is too high. That is, the principle prescribes some rational level of risk-taking. What you should do, then, depends on the riskiness of the prospects you face.

But it is doubtful that you should have the same level of risk-taking in all situations, regardless of the context. Different attitudes towards risk seem warranted when you decide how to invest your savings for your old age and when you play a friendly poker game. So a complex principle must differentiate between different reasonable levels of risk-taking for different *objects* of preference. For example, the principle could say that you should be risk-averse when making a career choice, to ensure that your life does not turn out to be very bad. Hence I should choose to become a reasonably good, although not great, philosopher. But this complex principle could also tell me to be more risk-seeking when I am faced with the choice between staying at my current academic post or accepting a job offer from another country, where I may do my best work, but there is a fair chance that I will not be able to integrate into the academic community there, and my work will go poorly.

When we give advice in real life, we do distinguish between reasonable levels of risk-taking. We believe people should not jeopardize their health with smoking, and that they should save up money for their old age. But very often, we also advise people to take risks. We think it is a good thing to travel to other countries, to take reasonable financial risks, we admire people choosing risky professions. Hence, the proposal goes, a fully developed theory of rationality will incorporate a principle of reasonable levels of risk-taking for different objects of preference.

The problem with this proposal is twofold. First, given that there is no consensus on reasonable levels of risk-taking either in everyday situations or in philosophy, and it is controversial what these levels should be, it is hard to see where we could find the resources to formulate this complex principle. Even if disputes about what risk-attitudes are reasonable in different situations can be resolved, we end up on this proposal with a 'principle' which is merely an infinitely long conjunction associating reasonable risk-taking levels with descriptions of possible objects of preference and, perhaps, also contexts of choice. And this leads to the second problem, because it is hard to see how such a complex 'principle' could be considered a *principle*; and even if it was one, why it would be a principle of *rationality*.

Of course, one could argue that we need a more robust conception of rationality which incorporates principles of reasonable risks. But this just recreates the problem within this more robust theory of rationality. Moreover, on this proposal, prospective welfare judgements unavoidably involve substantive judgements – judgements about risks associated with the contents of preferences. If the complex principle was a principle of rationality, then the norms of rationality would appeal to objects of preference. In this case, when we evaluate the counterfactuals about a person's preference changes on the ideal advisor model in order to determine which prospect is better for the person, then at least sometimes we have to appeal to normative facts: what determines what can be expected to be better for the person is not the person's fully informed and ideally rational preferences, but, at least partly, normative facts about the objects of those preferences.

In my argument, I assumed a 'fully developed' theory of rational choice – a theory that we don't yet have, and perhaps we never will. This raises the question of how my argument relates to extant theories of rational choice, familiar from economics and game theory. Inevitably, all I can do here is to make some brief and cursory comments.

How do extant theories of rational choice deal with risk-attitudes? Typically, they take these attitudes as exogenous to the theory. That is, risk-attitudes are given either as empirical assumptions about people's reactions to risk in the context of particular goods (for instance, money), or they are incorporated into the utility functions which represent the decision-maker's preferences. Putting aside certain coherence assumptions on preferences, this means that risk-attitudes are not subject to norms of rationality. Hence, extant theories of rational choice typically cannot say anything about the reasonableness of people's risk-attitudes.

Perhaps this is not a serious problem for descriptive applications. But in normative contexts, and in particular in the context of making prospective welfare judgements, we are often interested in the reasonableness of risks – as in my example of a choice between becoming a philosopher or a concert pianist. In these cases, we cannot take preferences as given, and we cannot simply make assumptions about people's risk-attitudes. If we want to further develop some extant theory of rational choice for the purposes of the ideal advisor model, we need to appeal to normative facts about the objects of preferences.

If what I have argued in this chapter is correct, then prospective welfare judgements pose a special difficulty for the ideal advisor model.[13] Since such judgements involve the assessment of risks, the model is either deficient or needs to be augmented with appeals to substantive claims about the reasonableness of risks. Such claims, in turn, at least partly depend on the pursuits or goods which are the objects of the preferences. Moreover, the ideal advisor model cannot be an adequate model of how people ordinarily make prospective welfare judgements in their everyday lives. People reason about risks, and they reason about them in substantive terms; this sort of reasoning is not captured by the model.

In recent decades, we have learned a great deal about the heuristics people use when they form preferences in risky situations as well as the mistakes they are prone to make.[14] Most of these studies focus on how people judge probabilities. From a normative perspective, the ideal advisor model may help to avoid those mistakes when reasoning about risks. But it is not sufficient to base our judgements on the ideal advisor model: in order to make prospective welfare judgements, we also need to develop substantive criteria to distinguish between reasonable and unreasonable risks.[15]

References

Anderson, E. (1993) *Value in Ethics and Economics*, Harvard University Press, Cambridge, MA

Arneson, R. J. (1999) 'Human flourishing versus desire satisfaction', *Social Philosophy and Policy*, vol 16, pp113–142

Brandt, R. B. (1979) *A Theory of the Good and the Right*, Clarendon Press, Oxford

Brandt, R. B. (1992) 'Two concepts of utility', in R. B. Brandt (ed.) *Morality, Utilitarianism, and Rights*, Cambridge University Press, Cambridge

Brink, D. O. (1989) *Moral Realism and the Foundations of Ethics*, Cambridge University Press, Cambridge

Cowen, T. (1993) 'The scope and limits of preference sovereignty', *Economics and Philosophy*, vol 9, pp253–269

Darwall, S. (1983) *Impartial Reason*, Cornell University Press, Ithaca, NY

Darwall, S. (2002) *Welfare and Rational Care*, Princeton University Press, Princeton, NJ

Enoch, D. (2005) 'Why idealize?', *Ethics*, vol 115, pp759–787

Finnis, J. (1980) *Natural Law and Natural Rights*, Clarendon Press, Oxford

Gauthier, D. (1986) *Morals by Agreement*, Clarendon Press, Oxford

Griffin, J. (1986) *Well-Being: Its Meaning, Measurement, and Moral Importance*, Clarendon Press, Oxford

Hare, R. M. (1981) *Moral Thinking: Its Method, Levels, and Point*, Clarendon Press, Oxford

Harsanyi, J. C. (1982) 'Morality and the theory of rational behaviour', in A. Sen and B. Williams (eds) *Utilitarianism and Beyond*, Cambridge University Press, Cambridge

Kagan, S. (1992) 'The limits of well-being', *Social Philosophy and Policy*, vol 9, pp169–189

Kahneman, D., Slovic, P. and Tversky, A. (eds) (1982) *Judgment under Uncertainty: Heuristics and Biases*, Cambridge University Press, Cambridge

Loeb, D. (1995) 'Full-information theories of individual good', *Social Theory and Practice*, vol 21, pp1–30

McClennen, E. F. (1990) *Rationality and Dynamic Choice: Foundational Explorations*, Cambridge University Press, Cambridge

Parfit, D. (1984) *Reasons and Persons*, Oxford University Press, Oxford

Railton, P. (1986a) 'Facts and values', *Philosophical Topics*, vol 14, pp5–31

Railton, P. (1986b) 'Moral realism', *The Philosophical Review*, vol 95, pp163–207

Rawls, J. (1971) *A Theory of Justice*, Harvard University Press, Cambridge, MA

Raz, J. (1986) *The Morality of Freedom*, Clarendon Press, Oxford

Rosati, C. S. (1995) 'Persons, perspectives, and full information accounts of the good', *Ethics*, vol 105, pp296–325

Scanlon, T. M. (1993) 'Value, desire, and the quality of life', in M. C. Nussbaum and A. Sen (eds) *The Quality of Life*, Clarendon Press, Oxford

Sobel, D. (1994) 'Full information accounts of well-being', *Ethics*, vol 104, pp784–810

Sumner, L. W. (1996) *Welfare, Happiness, and Ethics*, Clarendon Press, Oxford

Notes

1 See, for example, Arneson (1999), Brandt (1979), Brink (1989, pp17–36), Darwall (2002), Finnis (1980, pp59–99), Griffin (1986), Kagan (1992), Parfit (1984, pp493–502), Railton (1986a), Raz (1986, pp288–320), Scanlon (1993) and Sumner (1996), among others.

2 Further questions can be raised about the *temporal unit* of welfare measurement. Suppose we want to establish how well off a person is, or how well off she is in comparison to other persons. Do we then assign a value to how well off she is for her whole life, for this very moment, or something in between? (See Brandt (1992) for a discussion of this and related problems.) These questions lead to controversial issues in metaphysics; for instance, whether persons persist through time or they are merely collections of persons at different time-slices. For a seminal discussion of such issues, see Parfit (1984).

3 For such accounts, see, for example, Brandt (1979), Darwall (1983, pp85–100), Hare (1981, pp101–106, 214–218), Harsanyi (1982), Railton (1986a) and Rawls (1971, pp407–424). For discussions, see Anderson (1993, pp129–140), Cowen (1993), Loeb (1995), Rosati (1995) and Sobel (1994).

4 For a discussion of the distinction between the two uses of idealization in value theory, see Enoch (2005).

5 Spelling out the model in terms of preference rather than, for instance, desire, allows us to make comparative welfare judgements, since preference is a comparative notion.

6 Note also that the ideal advisor's preferences range over the feasible options which are open to her non-ideal counterpart, even if that person is unaware of the availability of some of those options. This takes into account the possibilities that the person is unaware that some option is available to her or that she has not formed a preference over some of her options.

7 As a matter of fact, a similar restriction appears to be implicit in many informed desire theories of well-being. For instance, in Brandt's theory, the information ideal advisors have must be part of current scientific knowledge, available through inductive or deductive logic, or justified on the basis of available evidence (Brandt, 1979, pp111–113). In Railton's theory, even though ideal advisors have unlimited cognitive and imaginative powers, they have to base their preferences on factual and nomological information about the person's psychological and physical constitution, capacities, circumstances and history (Railton, 1986b, pp173–174). And in Harsanyi's view, a person's 'true' preferences are those that she would form if she reasoned with the greatest possible care about the relevant facts with a view to making a rational choice (Harsanyi, 1982, p55). None of these accounts of the ideal conditions include omniscience in the sense I am using the term.

8 The objections to the cognitive condition of full-information accounts of well-being and idealization in general tend to target component (b). For references, see notes 3 and 4.

9 We can think of these numbers as indices for valuable mental states, objects of intrinsic desires, items on the list of objective goods or whatever our theory of welfare proposes for having intrinsic value.

10 The expected values of the prospects do not have to be equal: principles for reasonable levels of risk-taking are relevant even if these values are unequal. I use the simplest case for purposes of illustration.

11 In order to model the offer, we can insert a node B_0 before node A in Figure 10.2, representing B's making the offer or declining to make the offer. The subsequent branches are the same on both branches leading from this node. The difference is in

the preferences that *B* forms over the prospects at node *B*, given the choice of his risk-disposition at the initial node.

12 Figure 10.3 shows only *A*'s perspective of the choice problem – assuming that *B* is transparent and his risk-disposition is stable – with the probabilities and payoffs relevant to deciding whether she should accept the offer (move across) or reject it (move down).

13 At least, they pose one sort of difficulty. I have left open the question whether other problems, familiar from the literature on strategic interactions, rational intentions and paradoxes of rationality, also raise difficulties for the ideal advisor model of welfare judgements (see, for example, Parfit (1984); Gauthier (1986); McClennen (1990)). The answer to this question at least partly depends on how we further specify component (b) when we give an account of the cognitive capacities of ideal advisors.

14 See, for example, the contributions to Kahneman et al (1982).

15 Earlier versions of this paper have benefited from discussions with Geoffrey Brennan, John Broome, Campbell Brown, János Kis, Michael Smith and an anonymous referee. I would also like to thank audiences at the Australian National University, the University of Adelaide, Central European University and the Conference on Ethical Aspects of Risk at the Delft University of Technology for useful comments.

Part IV

Involving the Public

Opening risk management to explicitly include ethical considerations also suggests including the moral views of the public. It has indeed been shown that laypeople already take into account broader and more complex ethical considerations than experts. Hence, the public can provide for important ethical expertise when it comes to assessing the moral acceptability of technological risks. The contribution by Paul Slovic, Melissa Finucane, Ellen Peters and Donald G. MacGregor discusses the strengths and weaknesses of the risk-emotions of the public, based on empirical psychological research. Sabine Roeser argues that emotions allow us to be practically rational, which means that the emotions of laypeople can be seen as a source of ethical wisdom about risk. Mark Coeckelbergh challenges the dismissive rhetoric implicit in the terminology in the sociological and psychological literature about the emotions and the imaginative capacities of laypeople concerning risks. Lotte Asveld shows that in the debate about mobile phone technology in the Netherlands, people who are worried about risks make claims that should be taken more seriously by policymakers and should lead to further research.

11 Risk as Feeling: Some Thoughts about Affect, Reason, Risk and Rationality[1]

Paul Slovic, Melissa Finucane, Ellen Peters and Donald G. MacGregor

Introduction

Risk in the modern world is confronted and dealt with in three fundamental ways. *Risk as feelings* refers to our fast, instinctive and intuitive reactions to danger. *Risk as analysis* brings logic, reason and scientific deliberation to bear on hazard management. When our ancient instincts and our modern scientific analyses clash, we become painfully aware of a third reality ... *risk as politics*. Members of the Society for Risk Analysis are certainly familiar with the scientific approach to risk and Slovic (1999) has elaborated the political aspect. In the present chapter we shall examine what recent research in psychology and cognitive neuroscience tells us about the third dimension, risk as feelings, an important vestige of our evolutionary journey.

That intuitive feelings are still the predominant method by which human beings evaluate risk is cleverly illustrated in a cartoon by Garry Trudeau (Figure 11.1). Trudeau's two characters decide whether to greet one another on a city street by employing a systematic analysis of the risks and risk-mitigating factors. We instantly recognize that no one in such a situation would ever be this analytical, even if their life was at stake. Most risk analysis is handled quickly and automatically by what we shall describe later as the 'experiential' mode of thinking.

Background and Theory: The Importance of Affect

Although the visceral emotion of fear certainly plays a role in risk as feelings, we shall focus here on a 'faint whisper of emotion' called *affect*. As used here, 'affect' means the specific quality of 'goodness' or 'badness': (1) experienced as a feeling state (with or without consciousness); and (2) demarcating a positive or negative quality of a stimulus. Affective responses occur rapidly and automatically – note

Copyright © 1994 by Garry Trudeau. Reprinted with permission.

Figure 11.1 *Street calculus*

how quickly you sense the feelings associated with the stimulus word 'treasure' or the word 'hate'. We argue that reliance on such feelings can be characterized as 'the affect heuristic'. In this chapter, we trace the development of the affect heuristic across a variety of research paths followed by ourselves and many others. We also discuss some of the important practical implications resulting from ways that this affect heuristic impacts on the way we perceive and evaluate risk and, more generally, the way it affects all human decision-making.

Two modes of thinking

Affect also plays a central role in what have come to be known as dual-process theories of thinking, knowing and information processing (Sloman, 1996; Chaiken and Trope, 1999; Kahneman and Frederick, 2002). As Epstein observed:

> There is no dearth of evidence in every day life that people apprehend reality in two fundamentally different ways, one variously labeled intuitive, automatic, natural, non-verbal, narrative, and experiential, and the other analytical, deliberative, verbal, and rational. (1994, p710)

Table 11.1 *Two modes of thinking: comparison of the experiential and analytic systems*

Experiential system	*Analytic system*
1. Holistic	1. Analytic
2. Affective: pleasure–pain oriented	2. Logical: reason oriented (what is sensible)
3. Associationistic connections	3. Logical connections
4. Behaviour mediated by 'vibes' from past experiences	4. Behaviour mediated by conscious appraisal of events
5. Encodes reality in concrete images, metaphors and narratives	5. Encodes reality in abstract symbols, words and numbers
6. More rapid processing: oriented towards immediate action	6. Slower processing: oriented towards delayed action
7. Self-evidently valid: 'experiencing is believing'	7. Requires justification via logic and evidence

Table 11.1, adapted from Epstein, further compares these modes of thought. One of the main characteristics of the experiential system is its affective basis. Although analysis is certainly important in some decision-making circumstances, reliance on affect and emotion is a quicker, easier and more efficient way to navigate in a complex, uncertain and sometimes dangerous world. Many theorists have given affect a direct and primary role in motivating behaviour (Mowrer, 1960; Tomkins, 1962, 1963; Zajonc, 1980; Clark and Fiske, 1982; Le Doux, 1996; Forgas, 2000; Barrett and Salovey, 2002). Epstein's view on this is as follows:

> The experiential system is assumed to be intimately associated with the experience of affect ... which refer[s] to subtle feelings of which people are often unaware. When a person responds to an emotionally significant event ... the experiential system automatically searches its memory banks for related events, including their emotional accompaniments ... If the activated feelings are pleasant, they motivate actions and thoughts anticipated to reproduce the feelings. If the feelings are unpleasant, they motivate actions and thoughts anticipated to avoid the feelings. (1994, p716)

Whereas Epstein labelled the right side of Table 11.1 the 'rational system', we have renamed it the 'analytic system', in recognition that there are strong elements of rationality in both systems.

It was the experiential system, after all, that enabled human beings to survive during their long period of evolution. Long before there were probability theory, risk assessment and decision analysis, there were intuition, instinct and gut feeling to tell us whether an animal was safe to approach or the water was safe to drink. As life became more complex and humans gained more control over their environment, analytic tools were invented to 'boost' the rationality of our experiential thinking. Subsequently, analytic thinking was placed on a pedestal and portrayed as the epitome of rationality. Affect and emotions were seen as interfering with reason.

The importance of affect is being recognized increasingly by decision researchers. A strong early proponent of the importance of affect in decision-making was Zajonc (1980), who argued that affective reactions to stimuli are often the very first reactions, occurring automatically and subsequently guiding information processing and judgement. If Zajonc is correct, then affective reactions may serve as orienting mechanisms, helping us navigate quickly and efficiently through a complex, uncertain and sometimes dangerous world. Important work on affect and decision-making has also been done by Isen (1993), Janis and Mann (1977), Johnson and Tversky (1983), Kahneman et al (1998), Kahneman and Snell (1990), Loewenstein (1996), Loewenstein et al (2001), Mellers (2000), Mellers et al (1997), Rottenstreich and Hsee (2001), Rozin et al (1993), Schwarz and Clore (1988), Slovic et al (2002), and Wilson et al (1993).

One of the most comprehensive and dramatic theoretical accounts of the role of affect and emotion in decision-making was presented by the neurologist Antonio Damasio (1994). In seeking to determine 'what in the brain allows humans to behave rationally', Damasio argued that thought is made largely from images, broadly construed to include perceptual and symbolic representations. A lifetime of learning leads these images to become 'marked' by positive and negative feelings linked directly or indirectly to somatic or bodily states. When a negative somatic marker is linked to an image of a future outcome, it sounds an alarm. When a positive marker is associated with the outcome image, it becomes a beacon of incentive. Damasio hypothesized that somatic markers increase the accuracy and efficiency of the decision process and their absence, observed in people with certain types of brain damage, degrades decision performance.

We now recognize that the experiential mode of thinking and the analytic mode of thinking are continually active, interacting in what we have characterized as 'the dance of affect and reason' (Finucane et al, 2003). While we may be able to 'do the right thing' without analysis (e.g. dodge a falling object), it is unlikely that we can employ analytic thinking rationally without guidance from affect somewhere along the line. Affect is essential to rational action. As Damasio observes:

> The strategies of human reason probably did not develop, in either evolution or any single individual, without the guiding force of the mechanisms of biological regulation, of which emotion and feeling are notable expressions. Moreover, even after

> reasoning strategies become established ... their effective deployment probably depends, to a considerable extent, on a continued ability to experience feelings. (1994, pxii)

THE AFFECT HEURISTIC

The feelings that become salient in a judgement or decision-making process depend on characteristics of the individual and the task as well as the interaction between them. Individuals differ in the way they react affectively, and in their tendency to rely upon experiential thinking (Gasper and Clore, 1998; Peters and Slovic, 2000). As will be shown in this chapter, tasks differ regarding the evaluability (relative affective salience) of information. These differences result in the affective qualities of a stimulus image being 'mapped' or interpreted in diverse ways. The salient qualities of real or imagined stimuli then evoke images (perceptual and symbolic interpretations) that may be made up of both affective and instrumental dimensions.

The mapping of affective information determines the contribution stimulus images make to an individual's 'affect pool'. All of the images in people's minds are tagged or marked to varying degrees with affect. The affect pool contains all the positive and negative markers associated (consciously or unconsciously) with the images. The intensity of the markers varies with the images.

People consult or 'sense' the affect pool in the process of making judgements. Just as imaginability, memorability and similarity serve as cues for probability judgements (e.g. the availability and representativeness heuristics; Kahneman et al, 1982), affect may serve as a cue for many important judgements (including probability judgements). Using an overall, readily available affective impression can be easier and more efficient than weighing the pros and cons of various reasons or retrieving relevant examples from memory, especially when the required judgement or decision is complex or mental resources are limited. This characterization of a mental short-cut has led us to label the use of affect a 'heuristic' (Finucane et al, 2000).

EMPIRICAL SUPPORT FOR THE AFFECT HEURISTIC

Support for the affect heuristic comes from a diverse set of empirical studies, only a few of which will be reviewed here.

Early research: dread and outrage in risk perception

Evidence of risk as feelings was present (though not fully appreciated) in early psychometric studies of risk perception (Fischhoff et al, 1978; Slovic, 1987). Those studies showed that feelings of dread were the major determiner of public perception and acceptance of risk for a wide range of hazards. Sandman, noting that dread was also associated with factors such as voluntariness, controllability, lethality and fairness, incorporated these qualities into his 'outrage model'

(Sandman, 1989). Reliance on outrage was, in Sandman's view, the major reason that public evaluations of risk differed from expert evaluations (based on analysis of hazard; e.g. mortality statistics).

Risk and benefit judgements

The earliest studies of risk perception also found that, whereas risk and benefit tend to be positively correlated in the world, they are negatively correlated in people's minds (and judgements; Fischhoff et al, 1978). The significance of this finding for the affect heuristic was not realized until a study by Alhakami and Slovic (1994) found that the inverse relationship between the perceived risk and perceived benefit of an activity (e.g. using pesticides) was linked to the strength of positive or negative affect associated with that activity as measured by rating the activity on bipolar scales such as good/bad, nice/awful, dread/not dread and so forth. This result implies that people base their judgements of an activity or a technology not only on what they *think* about it but also on how they *feel* about it. If their feelings towards an activity are favourable, they are moved towards judging the risks as low and the benefits as high; if their feelings towards it are unfavourable, they tend to judge the opposite – high risk and low benefit. Under this model, affect comes prior to, and directs, judgements of risk and benefit, much as Zajonc proposed. This process, which we have called 'the affect heuristic' (see Figure 11.2), suggests that, if a general affective view guides perceptions of risk and benefit, providing information about benefit should change perception of risk and vice versa (see Figure 11.3). For example, information stating that benefit is high for a technology such as nuclear power would lead to more positive overall affect that would, in turn, decrease perceived risk (Figure 11.3A).

Finucane et al (2000) conducted this experiment, providing four different kinds of information designed to manipulate affect by increasing or decreasing perceived benefit or by increasing or decreasing perceived risk for each of three technologies. The predictions were confirmed. Because by design there was no

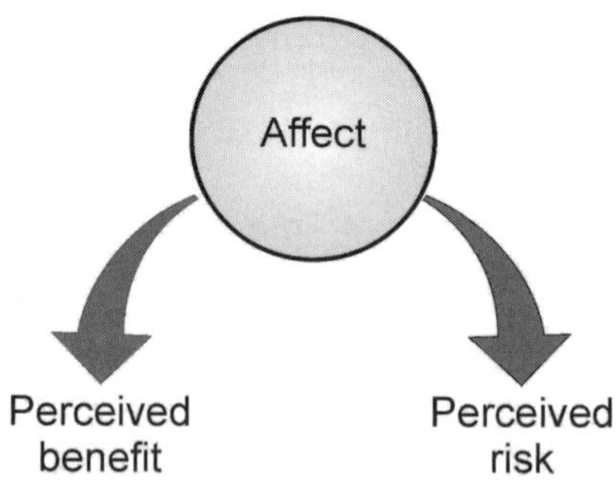

Source: Finucane et al (2000).

Figure 11.2. *A model of the affect heuristic explaining the risk/benefit confounding observed by Alhakami and Slovic (1994). Judgements of risk and benefit are assumed to be derived by reference to an overall affective evaluation of the stimulus item*

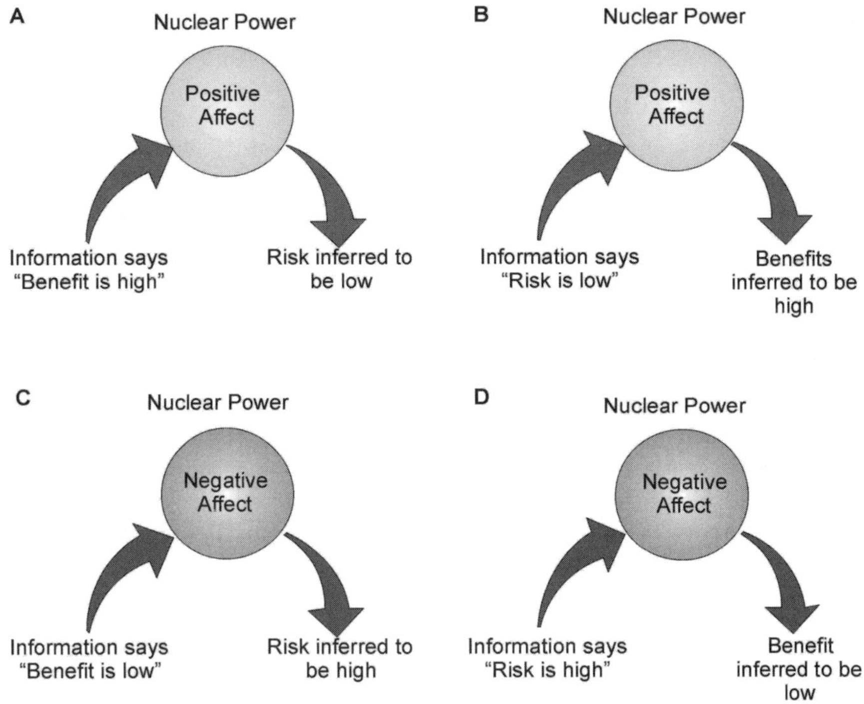

Source: Finucane et al (2000).

Figure 11.3. *Design for testing the inverse relation between risk and benefit*

apparent logical relationship between the information provided and the nonmanipulated variable, these data support the theory that risk and benefit judgements are influenced, at least in part, by the overall affective evaluation (which was influenced by the information provided). Further support for the affect heuristic came from a second experiment by Finucane et al, finding that the inverse relationship between perceived risks and benefits increased greatly under time pressure, when opportunity for analytic deliberation was reduced. These two experiments are important because they demonstrate that affect influences judgement directly and is not simply a response to a prior analytic evaluation.

Further support for the model in Figure 11.2 has come from two very different domains – toxicology and finance. Slovic et al (in preparation) surveyed members of the British Toxicological Society and found that these experts, too, produced the same inverse relation between their risk and benefit judgements. As expected, the strength of the inverse relation was found to be mediated by the toxicologists' affective reactions towards the hazard items being judged. In a second study, these same toxicologists were asked to make a 'quick intuitive rating' for each of 30 chemical items (e.g. benzene, aspirin, second-hand cigarette smoke, dioxin in food) on an affect scale (bad-good). Next, they were asked to judge the degree of risk associated with a very small exposure to the chemical, defined as an exposure that is less than 1/100 the exposure level that would begin to cause concern for a regulatory agency. Rationally, because exposure was so low, one might expect these risk judgements to be uniformly low and unvarying, resulting in little or no correlation with the ratings of affect. Instead, there was a strong correlation across chemicals between affect and judged risk of a very small exposure. When the affect rating was strongly negative, judged risk of a very small exposure was high; when affect was positive, judged risk was small. Almost every respondent (95 out of 97) showed this negative correlation (the median correlation was –50). Importantly, those toxicologists who produced strong inverse relations between risk and benefit judgements in the first study also were more likely to exhibit a high correspondence between their judgements of affect and risk in the second study. In other words, across two different tasks, reliable individual differences emerged in toxicologists' reliance on affective processes in judgements of chemical risks.

In the realm of finance, Ganzach (2001) found support for a model in which analysts base their judgements of risk and return for unfamiliar stocks upon a global attitude. If stocks were perceived as good, they were judged to have high return and low risk, whereas if they were perceived as bad, they were judged to be low in return and high in risk. However, for familiar stocks, perceived risk and return were positively correlated, rather than being driven by a global attitude.

Judgements of probability, relative frequency and risk

The affect heuristic has much in common with the model of 'risk as feelings' proposed by Loewenstein et al (2001) and with dual process theories put forth by Epstein (1994), Sloman (1996) and others. Recall that Epstein argues that individuals apprehend reality by two interactive, parallel processing systems. The *rational* system is a deliberative, analytical system that functions by way of established rules of logic and evidence (e.g. probability theory). The *experiential* system encodes reality in images, metaphors and narratives to which affective feelings have become attached.

To demonstrate the influence of the experiential system, Denes-Raj and Epstein (1994) showed that, when offered a chance to win $1 by drawing a red jelly bean from an urn, individuals often elected to draw from a bowl containing a greater absolute number, but a smaller proportion, of red beans (for example, 7 in 100) than from a bowl with fewer red beans but a better probability of winning (for example, 1 in 10). These individuals reported that, although they knew the probabilities were against them, they *felt* they had a better chance when there were more red beans.

We can characterize Epstein's subjects as following a mental strategy of 'imaging the numerator' (i.e. the number of red beans) and neglecting the denominator (the number of beans in the bowl). Consistent with the affect heuristic, images of winning beans convey positive affect that motivates choice.

Although the jelly bean experiment may seem frivolous, imaging the numerator brings affect to bear on judgements in ways that can be both non-intuitive and consequential. Slovic et al (2000) demonstrated this in a series of studies in which experienced forensic psychologists and psychiatrists were asked to judge the likelihood that a mental patient would commit an act of violence within six months of being discharged from the hospital. An important finding was that clinicians who were given another expert's assessment of a patient's risk of violence framed in terms of relative frequency (for example, 'of every 100 patients similar to Mr Jones, 10 are estimated to commit an act of violence to others') subsequently labelled Mr Jones as more dangerous than did clinicians who were shown a statistically 'equivalent' risk expressed as a probability (for example, 'patients similar to Mr Jones are estimated to have a 10% chance of committing an act of violence to others').

Not surprisingly, when clinicians were told that '20 out of every 100 patients similar to Mr Jones are estimated to commit an act of violence', 41 per cent would refuse to discharge the patient. But when another group of clinicians was given the risk as 'patients similar to Mr Jones are estimated to have a 20% chance of committing an act of violence', only 21 per cent would refuse to discharge the patient. Similar results have been found by Yamagishi (1997), whose judges rated a disease that kills 1286 people out of every 10,000 as more dangerous than one that kills 24.14 per cent of the population.

Follow-up studies showed that representations of risk in the form of individual probabilities of 10 per cent or 20 per cent led to relatively benign images of one person, unlikely to harm anyone, whereas the 'equivalent' frequentistic representations created frightening images of violent patients (example: 'Some guy going crazy and killing someone'). These affect-laden images likely induced greater perceptions of risk in response to the relative-frequency frames.

Although frequency formats produce affect-laden imagery, story and narrative formats appear to do even better in that regard. Hendrickx et al (1989) found that warnings were more effective when, rather than being presented in terms of relative frequencies of harm, they were presented in the form of vivid, affect-laden scenarios and anecdotes. Sanfey and Hastie (1998) found that compared with respondents given information in bar graphs or data tables, respondents given narrative information more accurately estimated the performance of a set of marathon runners. Furthermore, Pennington and Hastie (1993) found that jurors construct narrative-like summations of trial evidence to help them process their judgements of guilt or innocence.

Perhaps the biases in probability and frequency judgement that have been attributed to the availability heuristic (Tversky and Kahneman, 1973) may be due, at least in part, to affect. Availability may work not only through ease of recall or imaginability, but because remembered and imagined images come tagged with affect. For example, Lichtenstein et al (1978) invoked availability to explain why judged frequencies of highly publicized causes of death (for example, accidents, homicides, fires, tornadoes and cancer) were relatively overestimated and underpublicized causes (for example, diabetes, stroke, asthma, tuberculosis) were underestimated. The highly publicized causes appear to be more affectively charged, that is, more sensational, and this may account both for their prominence in the media and their relatively overestimated frequencies.

Proportion dominance

There appears to be one generic information format that is highly evaluable (e.g. highly affective), leading it to carry great weight in many judgement tasks. This is a representation characterizing an attribute as a proportion or percentage of something, or as a probability.

Proportion or probability dominance was evident in an early study by Slovic and Lichtenstein (1968) that had people rate the attractiveness of various two-outcome gambles. Ratings of a gamble's attractiveness were determined much more strongly by the probabilities of winning and losing than by the monetary outcomes. This basic finding has been replicated many times (Goldstein and Einhorn, 1987; Ordóñez and Benson, 1997).

Slovic et al (2002) tested the limits of this probability dominance by asking one group of subjects to rate the attractiveness of a simple gamble (7/36, win $9) on a 0–20 scale and asking a second group to rate a similar gamble with a small loss (7/36, win $9; 29/36, lose 5¢) on the same scale. The data were anomalous from the perspective of economic theory, but expected from the perspective of the affect heuristic. The mean response to the first gamble was 9.4. When a loss of 5¢ was added, the mean attractiveness jumped to 14.9 and there was almost no overlap between the distribution of responses around this mean and the responses for the group judging the gamble that had no loss.

Slovic also performed a conjoint analysis where each subject rated one of 16 gambles formed by crossing four levels of probability (7/36, 14/36, 21/36, 28/36) with four levels of payoff ($3, $6, $9, $12 in one study and $30, $60, $90, $120 in another). He found that, although subjects wanted to weight probability and payoff relatively equally in judging attractiveness (and thought they had done so) the actual weighting was 5 to 16 times greater for probability than for payoff.

We hypothesize that these curious findings can be explained by reference to the notion of affective mapping. According to this view, a probability maps relatively precisely onto the attractiveness scale, because it has an upper and lower bound and people know where a given value falls within that range. In contrast, the mapping of a dollar outcome (e.g. $9) onto the scale is diffuse, reflecting a failure to know whether $9 is good or bad, attractive or unattractive. Thus, the impression formed by the gamble offering $9 to win with no losing payoff is dominated by the rather unattractive impression produced by the 7/36 probability of winning. However, adding a very small loss to the payoff dimension puts the $9 payoff in perspective and thus gives it meaning. The combination of a possible $9 gain and a 5¢ loss is a *very attractive* win/lose ratio, leading to a relatively precise mapping onto the upper part of the scale. Whereas the imprecise mapping of the $9 carries little weight in the averaging process, the more precise and now favourable impression of ($9: –5¢) carries more weight, thus leading to an increase in the overall favourability of the gamble.

Proportion dominance surfaces in a powerful way in a very different context, the life-saving interventions studied by Baron (1997), Fetherstonhaugh et al (1997), Friedrich et al (1999) and Jenni and Loewenstein (1997). These studies found that, unless the number of lives saved is explicitly comparable from one intervention to another, evaluation is dominated by the proportion of lives saved (relative to the population at risk), rather than the actual number of lives saved.

The results of our lifesaving study (Fetherstonhaugh et al, 1997) are important because they imply that a specified number of human lives may not carry precise affective meaning, similar to the conclusion we drew about stated payoffs (e.g. $9) in the gambling studies. The gamble studies suggested an analogous experiment with lifesaving. In the context of a decision pertaining to airport safety, my colleagues and I asked people to evaluate the attractiveness of purchasing new equipment for use in the event of a crash landing of an airliner. In one condition, subjects were told that this equipment affords a chance of saving 150 lives that would be in jeopardy in such an event. A second group of subjects were told that this equipment affords a chance of saving 98 per cent of the 150 lives that would be in jeopardy. We predicted that, because saving 150 lives is diffusely good, hence only weakly evaluable, whereas saving 98 per cent of something is clearly very good, support for purchasing this equipment would be much greater in the 98 per cent condition. We predicted that other high percentages would also lead to greater support, even though the number of lives saved was fewer. The results, reported in Slovic et al (2002), confirmed these predictions (see Figure 11.4).

Insensitivity to probability

Outcomes are not always affectively as vague as the quantities of money and lives that were dominated by proportion in the above experiments. When consequences carry sharp and strong affective meaning, as is the case with a lottery jackpot or a cancer, the opposite phenomenon occurs – variation in probability often carries too little weight. As Loewenstein et al (2001) observe, one's images and feelings towards winning the lottery are likely to be similar whether the probability of winning is one in 10 million or one in 10,000. They further note that responses to uncertain situations appear to have an all or none characteristic that is sensitive to the *possibility* rather than the *probability* of strong positive or negative consequences, causing very small probabilities to carry great weight. This, they argue, helps explain many paradoxical findings such as the simultaneous prevalence of gambling and the purchasing of insurance. It also explains why societal concerns about hazards such as nuclear power and exposure to extremely

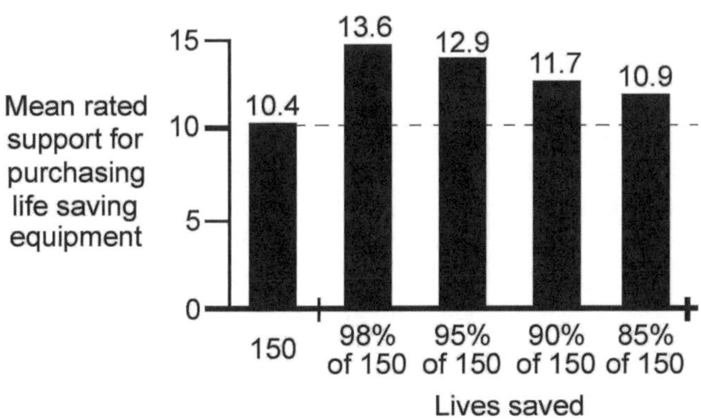

Source: Slovic et al, 2002.

Figure 11.4 *Saving a percentage of 150 lives received higher support than saving 150 lives*

small amounts of toxic chemicals fail to recede in response to information about the very small probabilities of the feared consequences from such hazards. Support for these arguments comes from Rottenstreich and Hsee (2001) who show that, if the potential outcome of a gamble is emotionally powerful, its attractiveness or unattractiveness is relatively insensitive to changes in probability as great as from 0.99 to 0.01.

Affect and insurance

Hsee and Kunreuther (2000) demonstrated that affect influences decisions about whether to purchase insurance. In one study, they found that people were willing to pay twice as much to insure a beloved antique clock (that no longer works and cannot be repaired) against loss in shipment to a new city than to insure a similar clock for which 'one does not have any special feeling'. In the event of loss, the insurance paid $100 in both cases. Similarly, Hsee and Menon (1999) found that students were more willing to buy a warranty on a newly purchased used car if it was a beautiful convertible than if it was an ordinary-looking station wagon, even if the expected repair expenses and cost of the warranty were held constant.

FAILURES OF THE EXPERIENTIAL SYSTEM

Throughout this chapter, we have portrayed the affect heuristic as the centrepiece of the experiential mode of thinking, the dominant mode of risk assessment and survival during the evolution of the human species. But, like other heuristics that provide efficient and generally adaptive responses but occasionally get us into trouble, reliance on affect can also mislead us. Indeed, if it was always optimal to follow our affective and experiential instincts, there would have been no need for the rational/analytic system of thinking to have evolved and become so prominent in human affairs.

There are two important ways that experiential thinking misguides us. One results from the deliberate manipulation of our affective reactions by those who wish to control our behaviours (advertising and marketing exemplify this manipulation). The other results from the natural limitations of the experiential system and the existence of stimuli in our environment that are simply not amenable to valid affective representation. The latter problem is discussed below.

Judgements and decisions can be faulty not only because their affective components are manipulable, but also because they are subject to inherent biases of the experiential system. For example, the affective system seems designed to sensitize us to small changes in our environment (e.g. the difference between 0 and 1 deaths) at the cost of making us less able to appreciate and respond appropriately to larger changes further away from zero (e.g. the difference between 500 deaths and 600 deaths). Fetherstonhaugh et al (1997) referred to this insensitivity as 'psychophysical numbing'. Albert Szent-Gyorgi put it another way: 'I am deeply moved if I see one man suffering and would risk my life for him. Then I talk impersonally about the possible pulverization of our big cities, with a hundred million dead. I am unable to multiply one man's suffering by a hundred million.'

Similar problems arise when the outcomes that we must evaluate are visceral in nature. Visceral factors include drive states such as hunger, thirst, sexual desire, emotions, pain and drug craving. They have direct, hedonic impacts that have a powerful effect on behaviour. Although they produce strong feelings in the present moment, these feelings are difficult if not impossible to recall or anticipate in a veridical manner, a factor that plays a key role in the phenomenon of addiction:

> Unlike currently experienced visceral factors, which have a disproportionate impact on behavior, delayed visceral factors tend to be ignored or severely underweighted in decision-making. Today's pain, hunger, anger, etc. are palpable, but the same sensations anticipated in the future receive little weight. (Loewenstein, 1999, p240)

THE DECISION TO SMOKE CIGARETTES

Cigarette smoking is a dangerous activity that takes place, one cigarette at a time, often over many years and hundreds of thousands of episodes. The questionable rationality of smoking decisions provides a dramatic example of the difficulty that experiential thinking faces in dealing with outcomes that change very slowly over time, are remote in time and are visceral in nature.

For many years, beginning smokers were portrayed as 'young economists', rationally weighing the risks of smoking against the benefits when deciding whether to initiate that activity (Viscusi, 1992), analogous to the 'street calculus' being spoofed in Figure 11.1. However, recent research paints a different picture. This new account (Slovic, 2001) shows young smokers acting experientially in the sense of giving little or no conscious thought to risks or to the amount of smoking they will be doing. Instead, they are driven by the affective impulses of the moment, enjoying smoking as something new and exciting, a way to have fun with their friends. Even after becoming 'regulars', the great majority of smokers expect to stop soon, regardless of how long they have been smoking, how many cigarettes they currently smoke per day or how many previous unsuccessful attempts they have experienced. Only a fraction actually quit, despite many attempts. The problem is nicotine addiction, a visceral condition that young smokers recognize by name as a consequence of smoking but do not understand experientially until they are caught in its grip.

The failure of the experiential system to protect many young people from the lure of smoking is nowhere more evident than in the responses to a survey question that asked smokers: 'If you had it to do all over again, would you start smoking?' More than 85 per cent of adult smokers and about 80 per cent of young smokers (ages 14–22) answered 'no' (Slovic, 2001). Moreover, the more individuals perceive themselves to be addicted, the more often they have tried to quit, the longer they have been smoking, and the more cigarettes they are currently smoking per day, the more likely they are to answer 'no' to this question.

The data indicate that most beginning smokers lack the experience to appreciate how their future selves will perceive the risks from smoking or how they will value the trade-off between health and the need to smoke. This is a strong repudiation of the model of informed rational choice. It fits well with the findings indicating that smokers give little conscious thought to risk when they begin to smoke. They appear to be lured into the behaviour by the prospects of fun and excitement. Most begin to think of risk only after starting to smoke and gaining what to them is new information about health risks.

These findings underscore the distinction that behavioural decision theorists now make between decision utility and experience utility (Kahneman and Snell, 1992; Kahneman, 1994; Loewenstein and Schkade, 1999). Utility predicted or expected at the time of decision often differs greatly from the quality and intensity of the hedonic experience that actually occurs.

MANAGING EMOTION, REASON AND RISK

Now that we are beginning to understand the complex interplay between emotion, affect and reason that is wired into the human brain and essential to rational behaviour, the challenge before us is to think creatively about what this means for managing risk. On the one hand, how do we apply reason to temper the strong emotions engendered by some risk events? On the other hand, how do we infuse needed 'doses of feeling' into circumstances where lack of experience may otherwise leave us too 'coldly rational'?

Can risk analysis benefit from experiential thinking?

The answer to this question is almost certainly yes. Even such prototypical analytic exercises as proving a mathematical theorem or selecting a move in chess benefit from experiential guidance. The mathematician senses whether the proof 'looks good' and the chess master gauges whether a contemplated move 'feels right', based upon stored knowledge of a large number of winning patterns (de Groot, 1978). Analysts attempting to build a model to solve a client's decision-making problem are instructed to rely upon the client's sense of unease about the results of the current model as a signal that further modelling may be needed (Phillips, 1984). A striking example of failure because an analysis was devoid of feeling was perpetrated by Philip Morris. The company commissioned an analysis of the costs to the Czech government of treating diseased smokers. Employing a very narrow conception of costs, the analysis concluded that smokers benefited the government by dying young. The analysis created so much hostility that Philip Morris was forced to issue an apology ('Philip Morris', 2001).

Elsewhere, we have argued that analysis needs to be sensitive to the 'softer' values underlying such qualities as dread, equity, controllability, etc. that underlie people's concerns about risk, as well as to degrees of ignorance or scientific uncertainty. A blueprint for doing this is sketched in the Academy report *Understanding Risk: Informing Decisions in a Democratic Society* (National Research Council, 1996). Invocation of the 'precautionary principle' (Wiener, 2002) represents yet another approach to overcoming the limitations of what some see as overly narrow technical risk assessments.

Someone once observed that 'Statistics are human beings with the tears dried off'. Our studies of psychophysical numbing demonstrate the potential for neglect of statistical fatalities, thus raising the question, 'How can we put the tears back on?' There are attempts to do this that may be instructive. Organizers of a rally designed to get Congress to do something about 38,000 deaths a year from handguns piled 38,000 pairs of shoes in a mound in front of the Capitol. After September 11, many newspapers published biographical sketches of the victims, a dozen or so each day until all had been featured. Writers and artists have long recognized the power of the written word to bring meaning to tragedy. *The Diary of Anne Frank* and Elie Weisel's *Night* certainly bring home the meaning of the Holocaust more powerfully than the statistic 'six million dead'.

How can an understanding of 'risk as feeling' help us cope with threats from terrorism?

Research by Rottenstreich and Hsee (2001) demonstrates that events associated with strong feelings can overwhelm us even though their likelihood is remote. Because *risk as feeling* tends to overweight frightening consequences, we need to invoke *risk as analysis* to give us perspective on the likelihood of such consequences. For example, when our feelings of fear move us to consider purchasing a handgun to protect against terrorists, our analytic selves should also heed the evidence showing that a gun fired in the home is 22 times more likely to harm oneself or a friend or family member than to harm an unknown, hostile intruder.

In some circumstances, *risk as feeling* may outperform *risk as analysis*. A case in point is a news story dated 27 March 2002 discussing the difficulty of screening 150,000 checked pieces of baggage at Los Angeles International Airport. The best analytic devices, utilizing x-rays, computers and other modern tools, are slow and inaccurate. The solution – rely upon the noses of trained dogs.

Some species of trouble – such as terrorism – greatly strain the capacity of quantitative risk analysis. Our models of the hazard generating process are too crude to permit precise and accurate predictions of where, when and how the next attacks might unfold. What is the role of risk analysis when the stakes are high, the uncertainties are enormous and time is precious? Is there a human equivalent of the dog's nose that can be put to good use in such circumstances, relying on instinctual processing of affective cues, using brain mechanisms honed through evolution, to enhance survival? What research is needed to train and test experiential risk analysis skills?

Conclusion

It is sobering to contemplate how elusive meaning is, due to its dependence upon affect. Thus the forms of meaning that we take for granted, and upon which we justify immense effort and expense towards gathering and disseminating 'meaningful' information, may be illusory. We cannot assume that an intelligent person can understand the meaning of and properly act upon even the simplest of numbers such as amounts of money or numbers of lives at risk, not to mention more esoteric measures or statistics pertaining to risk, unless these numbers are infused with affect.

Contemplating the workings of the affect heuristic helps us appreciate Damasio's contention that rationality is not only a product of the analytical mind, but of the experiential mind as well. The perception and integration of affective feelings, within the experiential system, appears to be the kind of high-level maximization process postulated by economic theories since the days of Jeremy Bentham. These feelings form the neural and psychological substrate of utility. In this sense, the affect heuristic enables us to be rational actors in many important situations. But not in all situations. It works beautifully when our experience enables us to anticipate accurately how we will like the consequences of our decisions. It fails miserably when the consequences turn out to be much different in character than we anticipated.

The scientific study of affective rationality is in its infancy. It is exciting to contemplate what might be accomplished by future research designed to help humans understand the affect heuristic and employ it beneficially in risk analysis and other worthy endeavours.

REFERENCES

Alhakami, A. S. and Slovic, P. (1994) 'A psychological study of the inverse relationship between perceived risk and perceived benefit', *Risk Analysis,* vol 14, pp1085–1096

Baron, J. (1997) 'Confusion of relative and absolute risk in valuation', *Journal of Risk and Uncertainty,* vol 14, pp301–309

Barrett, L. F. and Salovey, P. (eds) (2002) *The Wisdom in Feeling,* Guilford, New York

Chaiken, S. and Trope, Y. (1999) *Dual-Process Theories in Social Psychology,* Guilford, New York

Clark, M. S. and Fiske, S. T. (eds) (1982) *Affect and Cognition,* Erlbaum, Hillsdale, NJ

Damasio, A. R. (1994) *Descartes' Error: Emotion, Reason, and the Human Brain,* Avon, New York

de Groot, A. D. (1978) *Thought and Choice in Chess,* Monton, New York

Denes-Raj, V. and Epstein, S. (1994) 'Conflict between intuitive and rational processing: when people behave against their better judgment', *Journal of Personality and Social Psychology,* vol 66, pp819–829

Epstein, S. (1994) 'Integration of the cognitive and the psychodynamic unconscious', *American Psychologist,* vol 49, pp709–724

Fetherstonhaugh, D., Slovic, P., Johnson, S. M. and Friedrich, J. (1997) 'Insensitivity to the value of human life: a study of psychophysical numbing', *Journal of Risk and Uncertainty,* vol 14, no 3, pp282–300

Finucane, M. L., Alhakami, A., Slovic, P. and Johnson, S. M. (2000) 'The affect heuristic in judgments of risks and benefits', *Journal of Behavioral Decision Making,* vol 13, pp1–17

Finucane, M. L., Peters, E. and Slovic, P. (2003) 'Judgment and decision making: the dance of affect and reason', in S. L. Schneider and J. Shanteau (eds), *Emerging Perspectives on Judgment and Decision Research,* Cambridge University Press, Cambridge

Fischhoff, B., Slovic, P., Lichtenstein, S., Read, S. and Combs, B. (1978) 'How safe is safe enough? A psychometric study of attitudes toward technological risks and benefits', *Policy Sciences,* vol 9, pp127–152

Forgas, J. P. (ed.) (2000) *Feeling and Thinking: The Role of Affect in Social Cognition,* Cambridge University Press, Cambridge

Friedrich, J., Barnes, P., Chapin, K., Dawson, I., Garst, V. and Kerr, D. (1999) 'Psychophysical numbing: when lives are valued less as the lives at risk increase', *Journal of Consumer Psychology,* vol 8, pp277–299

Ganzach, Y. (2001) 'Judging risk and return of financial assets', *Organizational Behavior and Human Decision Processes,* vol 83, pp353–370

Gasper, K. and Clore, G. L. (1998) 'The persistent use of negative affect by anxious individuals to estimate risk', *Journal of Personality and Social Psychology,* vol 74, no 5, pp1350–1363

Goldstein, W. M. and Einhorn, H. J. (1987) 'Expression theory and the preference reversal phenomena', *Psychological Review,* vol 94, pp236–254

Hendrickx, L., Vlek, C. and Oppewal, H. (1989) 'Relative importance of scenario information and frequency information in the judgment of risk', *Acta Psychologica,* vol 72, pp41–63

Hsee, C. K. and Menon, S. (1999) *Affection Effect in Consumer Choices,* unpublished study, University of Chicago

Hsee, C. K. and Kunreuther, H. (2000) 'The affection effect in insurance decisions', *Journal of Risk and Uncertainty,* vol 20, pp141–159

Isen, A. M. (1993) 'Positive affect and decision making', in M. Lewis and J. M. Haviland (eds) *Handbook of Emotions,* The Guilford Press, New York

Janis, I. L. and Mann, L. (1977) *Decision Making,* The Free Press, New York

Jenni, K. E. and Loewenstein, G. (1997) 'Explaining the "identifiable victim effect"', *Journal of Risk and Uncertainty,* vol 14, no 3, pp235–258

Johnson, E. J. and Tversky, A. (1983) 'Affect, generalization, and the perception of risk', *Journal of Personality and Social Psychology,* vol 45, pp20–31

Kahneman, D. (1994) 'New challenges to the rationality assumption', *Journal of Institutional and Theoretical Economics,* vol 150, pp18–36

Kahneman, D. and Snell, J. (1990) 'Predicting utility', in R. M. Hogarth (ed.) *Insights in Decision Making*, University of Chicago Press, Chicago

Kahneman, D. and Snell, J. (1992) 'Predicting a changing taste', *Journal of Behavioral Decision Making,* vol 5, pp187–200

Kahneman, D. and Frederick, S. (2002) 'Representativeness revisited: Attribute substitution in intuitive judgment', in T. Gilovich, D. Griffin and D. Kahneman (eds) *Heuristics and Biases: The Psychology of Intuitive Judgment*, Cambridge University Press, New York

Kahneman, D., Slovic, P. and Tversky, A. (eds) (1982) *Judgment under Uncertainty: Heuristics and Biases,* Cambridge University Press, New York

Kahneman, D., Schkade, D. and Sunstein, C. R. (1998) 'Shared outrage and erratic awards: the psychology of punitive damages', *Journal of Risk and Uncertainty,* vol 16, pp49–86

Le Doux, J. (1996) *The Emotional Brain*, Simon and Schuster, New York

Lichtenstein, S., Slovic, P., Fischhoff, B., Layman, M. and Combs, B. (1978) 'Judged frequency of lethal events', *Journal of Experimental Psychology: Human Learning and Memory,* vol 4, pp551–578

Loewenstein, G. F. (1996) 'Out of control: visceral influences on behavior', *Organizational Behavior and Human Decision Processes,* vol 65, pp272–292

Loewenstein, G. F. (1999) 'A visceral account of addiction', in J. Elster and O-J. Skog (eds) *Getting Hooked: Rationality and Addiction*, Cambridge University Press, London

Loewenstein, G. F. and Schkade, D. (1999) 'Wouldn't it be nice? Predicting future feelings', in E. Diener, N. Schwartz and D. Kahneman (eds) *Well-Being: The Foundations of Hedonic Psychology*, Russell Sage Foundation, New York

Loewenstein, G. F., Weber, E. U., Hsee, C. K. and Welch, E. S. (2001) 'Risk as feelings', *Psychological Bulletin,* vol 127, no 2, pp267–286

Mellers, B. A. (2000) 'Choice and the relative pleasure of consequences', *Psychological Bulletin,* vol 126, no 6, pp910–924

Mellers, B. A., Schwartz, A., Ho, K. and Ritov, I. (1997) 'Decision affect theory: emotional reactions to the outcomes of risky options', *Psychological Science,* vol 8, pp423–429

Mowrer, O. H. (1960) *Learning Theory and Behavior,* John Wiley and Sons, New York

National Research Council. Committee on Risk Characterization (1996) *Understanding Risk: Informing Decisions in a Democratic Society,* National Academy Press, Washington, DC

Ordóñez, L. and Benson, L. III (1997) 'Decisions under time pressure: how time constraint affects risky decision making', *Organizational Behavior and Human Decision Processes,* vol 71, no 2, pp121–140

Pennington, N. and Hastie, R. (1993) 'A theory of explanation-based decision making', in G. Klein, J. Orasano, R. Calderwood and C. E. Zsambok (eds) *Decision Making in Action: Models and Methods,* Ablex, Norwood, NJ

Peters, E. and Slovic, P. (2000) 'The springs of action: affective and analytical information processing in choice', *Personality and Social Psychology Bulletin,* vol 26, pp1465–1475

'Philip Morris issues apology for Czech study on smoking', *The New York Times,* 27 July 2001, pC12

Phillips, L. D. (1984) 'A theory of requisite decision models', *Acta Psychologica,* vol 56, pp29–48

Rottenstreich, Y. and Hsee, C. K. (2001) 'Money, kisses and electric shocks: on the affective psychology of probability weighting', *Psychological Science,* vol 12, no 3, pp185–190

Rozin, P., Haidt, J. and McCauley, C. R. (1993) 'Disgust', in M. Lewis and J. M. Haviland (eds) *Handbook of Emotions,* Guilford, New York

Sandman, P. (1989) 'Hazard versus outrage in the public perception of risk', in V. T. Covello, D. B. McCallum and M. T. Pavlova (eds) *Effective Risk Communication: The Role and Responsibility of Government and Nongovernment Organizations*, Plenum Press, New York

Sanfey, A. and Hastie, R. (1998) 'Does evidence presentation format affect judgment? An experimental evaluation of displays of data for judgments', *Psychological Science*, vol 9, no 2, pp99–103

Schwarz, N. and Clore, G. L. (1988) 'How do I feel about it? Informative functions of affective states', in K. Fiedler and J. Forgas (eds) *Affect, Cognition, and Social Behavior*, Hogrefe International, Toronto

Sloman, S. A. (1996) 'The empirical case for two systems of reasoning', *Psychological Bulletin,* vol 119, no 1, pp3–22

Slovic, P. (1987) 'Perception of risk', *Science,* vol 236, pp280–285

Slovic, P. (1999) 'Trust, emotion, sex, politics, and science: surveying the risk-assessment battlefield', *Risk Analysis,* vol 19, no 4, pp689–701

Slovic, P. (2001) 'Cigarette smokers: rational actors or rational fools?', in P. Slovic (ed.) *Smoking: Risk, Perception, and Policy,* Sage, Thousand Oaks, CA

Slovic, P. and Lichtenstein, S. (1968) 'Relative importance of probabilities and payoffs in risk taking', *Journal of Experimental Psychology Monograph,* vol 78 (3, Pt 2), pp1–18

Slovic, P., Monahan, J. and MacGregor, D. M. (2000) 'Violence risk assessment and risk communication: the effects of using actual cases, providing instructions, and employing probability vs. frequency formats', *Law and Human Behavior,* vol 24, no 3, pp271–296

Slovic, P., Finucane, M. L., Peters, E. and MacGregor, D. G. (2002) 'The affect heuristic', in T. Gilovich, D. Griffin and D. Kahneman (eds) *Heuristics and Biases: The Psychology of Intuitive Judgment*, New York, Cambridge University Press

Slovic, P., MacGregor, D. G., Malmfors, T. and Purchase, I. F. H. (in preparation), *Influence of Affective Processes on Toxicologists' Judgments of Risk*, Decision Research, Eugene, OR

Tomkins, S. S. (1962) *Affect, Imagery, and Consciousness: Vol. 1. The Positive Affects*, Springer, New York

Tomkins, S. S. (1963) *Affect, Imagery, and Consciousness: Vol. 2. The Negative Affects*, Springer, New York

Tversky, A. and Kahneman, D. (1973) 'Availability: a heuristic for judging frequency and probability', *Cognitive Psychology*, vol 5, pp207–232

Viscusi, W. K. (1992) *Smoking: Making the Risky Decision*, Oxford University Press, New York

Wiener, J. B. (2002) 'Precaution in a multirisk world', in D. J. Paustenbach (ed.) *Human and Ecological Risk Assessment: Theory and Practice*, John Wiley and Sons, New York

Wilson, T. D., Lisle, D. J., Schooler, J. W., Hodges, S. D., Klaaren, K. J. and LaFleur, S. J. (1993) 'Introspecting about reasons can reduce post-choice satisfaction', *Personality and Social Psychology Bulletin*, vol 19, no 3, pp331–339

Yamagishi, K. (1997) 'When a 12.86% mortality is more dangerous than 24.14%: implications for risk communication', *Applied Cognitive Psychology*, vol 11, pp495–506

Zajonc, R. B. (1980) 'Feeling and thinking: preferences need no inferences', *American Psychologist*, vol 35, pp151–175

NOTE

1 Originally published as Slovic, P., Finucane, M. L., Peters, E. and MacGregor, D. G. (2004) 'Risk as analysis and risk as feelings: some thoughts about affect, reason, risk, and rationality', *Risk Analysis*, vol 24, no 2, pp1–12. With kind permission by the authors and Wiley-Blackwell.

12 The Relation between Cognition and Affect in Moral Judgements about Risks

Sabine Roeser

Introduction

It seems to be a platitude that emotions and feelings are irrational and need to be corrected by reason. We also see this reflected in studies about risk perception:

> Because *risk as feeling* tends to overweight frightening consequences, we need to invoke *risk as analysis* to give us perspective on the likelihood of such consequences. (Slovic et al, 2004, p320; italics in original)

In the literature on decision-making under uncertainty, affective responses are generally seen as biases but also as heuristics (cf the heuristics and biases literature, for example, Gilovich et al, 2002). In contrast, rational judgements are considered to be justified and reasonable. In accordance with this distinction there is Dual Process Theory, which states that there are two fundamentally different systems by which we process information and form judgements. The first system is taken to be spontaneous, intuitive and emotional, the second system is supposed to be slow, reflective and rational. This chapter questions this dichotomy, specifically by focusing on moral emotions such as sympathy and empathy, but also on fear. It will be argued that these emotions cross the boundaries between the two systems. They have features that are central to system 1 and features that are central to system 2. These emotions can provide epistemic justification for moral judgements about risks. Rather than being biases that threat objectivity and rationality in thinking about acceptable risks, emotions are crucial to come to a correct understanding of the moral acceptability of a hazard.

Emotions about risks

Paul Slovic has done pioneering work on the risk perception of laypeople. The risk judgements of laypeople differ substantially from those of experts. However,

Slovic has shown that this is not so much due to a *wrong* understanding of risk on the side of laypeople, but rather to a *different* understanding. Whereas experts define risks as a product of probabilities and undesired outcomes to which they apply cost-benefit analysis, laypeople include additional considerations in their judgements about risks, such as whether risks and benefits are fairly distributed, whether a risk is voluntarily taken, whether there are available alternatives and whether a risk might be catastrophic. According to Slovic, these are legitimate concerns (Slovic, 2000; for a philosophical justification of this claim, cf Roeser, 2007).

More recently, Slovic has also studied the role that emotion or affect plays in the risk perception of laypeople. According to Slovic, laypeople rely on an 'affect heuristic': their affective responses to a large degree determine their judgements about risks. However, I think that in this part of his work, Slovic threatens to undermine the emancipatory claims that underlie his more general work on risk perception. Whereas in his general work, the risk perception of laypeople is seen as the source of legitimate concerns, in his work on the affect heuristic Slovic seems to see the views of laypeople as biased and in need of correction by scientific evidence. I think that this is due to the theoretical framework that Slovic applies to his empirical findings. This framework is Dual Process Theory. In this chapter I will argue that this framework is not convincing, at least if applied to emotions. Starting out from a different theoretical framework, Slovic's empirical data can be interpreted in a different light which leads to claims that are much more consistent with Slovic's general work on the risk perception of laypeople. I will argue that affect or emotion is an invaluable source of wisdom, at least in so far as it comes to judgements about the *moral acceptability* of risks. Let me first discuss what Slovic says about the affect heuristic.

Slovic et al (2004) review various studies that point to the important role that affective mechanisms play in decision-making processes. An important author in this respect is Robert Zajonc who has emphasized the 'primacy of affect': non-cognitive, affective responses steer our behaviour and judgements (Zajonc, 1980, 1984a, 1984b). Affect serves as it were as a mental shortcut, specifically when it comes to value judgements. Slovic et al (2004) coin this the 'affect heuristic'. Empirical studies have shown that feelings (such as dread) are the major determinant for laypeople's judgements about risks (Fischhoff et al, 1978; Slovic, 1987; Sandman, 1989). Risk and benefit are negatively correlated in laypeople's judgements (Slovic et al, 2002, p410; Slovic et al, 2004, p315). Alhakami and Slovic (1994) point out that this is related to the strength of positive or negative affect associated with a hazard.

> This result implies that people base their judgments of an activity or a technology not only on what they *think* about it but also on how they *feel* about it. If their feelings towards an activity are favorable, they are moved toward judging the risks as low and the benefits as high; if their feelings toward it are unfavorable, they tend to judge the opposite – high risk and low benefit. Under this model, affect comes prior to, and directs, judgments of risk and benefit, much as Zajonc proposed. (Slovic et al, 2004, p315; italics in original)

Slovic claims that in the cases that he has examined, affect comes before judgement, and he also claims that often in those cases affect tends to mislead us, at least concerning judgements about the magnitude of a risk (Sunstein, 2005, p87 and Loewenstein et al, 2001 make similar claims). Slovic makes this point in various articles, but one formulation is especially interesting:

> That the inverse relationship [between risk and benefit, SR] is generated in people's minds is suggested by the fact that risks and benefits generally tend to be positively (if at all) correlated in the world. Activities that bring great benefits may be high or low in risk, but activities that are low in benefit are unlikely to be high in risk (if they were, they would be proscribed). (Slovic et al 2002, p410)[1]

This is a very peculiar passage. The last remark in parenthesis is question-begging: there is no guarantee that past or current risk legislation is adequate. That current risk legislation might *not* be adequate is exactly one of the possible outcomes of research about public risk perception and acceptable risk. More fundamentally, it is surprising that in this passage, Slovic seems to presuppose that there should be something like risk in the real world, independent of anybody's perception or conception of risk. The question is how this 'real risk' could be determined. In conversation, Paul Slovic has pointed out to me that this claim about the 'real' relationship between risks and benefits is based on a commonsensical hypothesis. However, this is inconsistent with Slovic's usual emphasis on the idea that there is no such thing as 'real risk', 'out there', independently of anybody's definition of what counts as a risk. All forms of risk assessment involve normative presuppositions and contestable assumptions (cf Slovic, 1999).

Furthermore, there is an ambiguity in the notion of 'risk': it can refer to the magnitude of a risk but also to the moral acceptability of a risk. It is not clear whether subjects in Slovic's studies were supposed to rate the former or the latter. Based on the information provided in Slovic's articles on these studies, it seems that subjects were not given definitions as to what is meant by risk or benefit. Hence, it is not surprising that subjects have various connotations invoked with these notions and have views of risk that diverge from those of experts. Based on Slovic's previous work, we know that this is frequently the case. Hence, it would be straightforward if Slovic would be more specific in the instructions for his research subjects as to which notion of risk he is interested in, in order to eliminate unnecessary ambiguities.

A problem might be how to distinguish between the magnitude of a risk and its acceptability. The conclusions of Slovic's earlier studies were that whereas scientists are supposedly mainly interested in the magnitude of a risk, they also make normative assumptions. It can be useful to distinguish conceptually between the magnitude of a risk and acceptable risk, but Slovic's work illuminates that it can be difficult to make such a distinction concerning concrete examples. A given measure of a magnitude of a risk implies normative assumptions as to what is a morally important aspect of risk. However, a possible setup of a study might be to provide subjects with information about annual fatalities related to a certain hazardous activity and then to ask them to judge how acceptable they find these hazardous activities. This latter question could also be further split up into 'personally acceptable' and 'socially/morally acceptable'. I will come back to this latter ambiguity at the end of this chapter.

In any case, it is far from clear that affective states are prone to biases. Admittedly, affect is an unreliable source if it comes to determining the magnitude of a risk. Scientific methods are much better equipped to measure quantitatively the occurrence of particular unwanted effects. But affect might be indispensable if it comes to determining acceptable risk, including what counts as an unwanted effect. This is a hypothesis which is an alternative to Slovic's acocunt of the affect heuristic, and it is this hypothesis which I will examine in this chapter. This hypothesis is based on the following two claims: (1) moral emotions are affective and cognitive at the same time; and (2) in their assessment of hazards, laypeople make an overall judgement as to the (moral) acceptability of a hazard rather than (often wrongly) weighing the magnitude of risks and benefits. Note that the latter claim is something Slovic generally emphasizes himself in his work (cf Slovic, 2000), that is why I will not develop this claim any further in this chapter but take it as a given. I will focus on the first claim.

I first want to study in more detail the theoretical underpinning of the position that Slovic defends, which is Dual Process Theory. I will argue that Dual Process Theory is a too simplistic view of categorizing ways in which we apprehend reality. Emotions, and especially moral emotions such as sympathy, but also instances of fear, do not fit into this account. On a different understanding of the affective responses of laypeople we can draw different conclusions as to the legitimacy of their concerns and as to how to treat affective responses to risks. This interpretation is much more in line with Slovic's usual emphasis on the wisdom that is entailed in laypeople's judgements about risks.

Dual process theory

Seymour Epstein claims that:

> There is no dearth of evidence in every day life that people apprehend reality in two fundamentally different ways, one variously labeled intuitive, automatic, natural, non-verbal, narrative, and experiential, and the other analytical, deliberative, verbal and rational. (Epstein, 1994, p710)

Several psychologists have defended the idea that human mental capacities with which we apprehend reality can be divided into two systems: 'system 1' and 'system 2'. This is generally called 'Dual Process Theory'. These are various labels psychologists use to distinguish between the two systems: Epstein (1994, p711) calls the one system experiential or emotional and the other rational. Slovic et al (2004) adopt this distinction and say that the experiential system is affect oriented and the analytic system reason oriented. Sloman (2002, p383) distinguishes between an associative system and a rule-based system. Sloman does not mention affective states of any sort (cf Sloman, 1996, p7, table 1), unless intuition is taken to be a specific form of feeling or emotion, which is at least a controversial use of terminology for many philosophers who also acknowledge the existence of rational intuition, for example concerning the insight of logical or mathematical axioms.

The labels for these two systems differ, but defenders of this view argue that there seems to be sufficient overlap between all these various models to justify some consensus that there are indeed two systems of mental processing (e.g. Epstein, 1994, p714). Let us call this general approach Dual Process Theory (DPT), although the specific versions of it are not in agreement about all the details. I will first discuss the specific ideas of some authors who are cited by Slovic. I will conclude this section with some general remarks why I am sceptical about DPT, specifically on how to locate emotions in such an approach. My critique will be twofold: (1) System 2 is not normatively more correct than system 1; rather, this depends on the domain of knowledge. System 1 is more adequate for some domains, system 2 is more adequate for other domains of knowledge. (2) DPT is too simplistic in subdividing all ways of apprehending reality in two opposed systems. There are ways of apprehending reality that transcend the boundaries of DPT; they fit into neither or both systems.

Specific versions of DPT

In this section I will discuss a couple of articles by defenders of DPT which are invoked by Slovic in his work on the affect heuristic. I will assess whether the claims made by the defenders of DPT are compatible with views on the nature of ethical reflection as endorsed by major moral philosophers. My answer will be that they are not. Ethical reflection comprises features of system 1 and of system 2. I will then focus more specifically on the role of emotions in ethical reflection, and I will argue that DPT in general is inadequate in categorizing moral emotions.

Sloman

Steven A. Sloman distinguishes between an associative and a rule-based system. He emphasizes that this is not the same as the distinction between induction and deduction. The latter distinction refers to different argument types, whereas he is interested in different psychological systems. According to him, the psychological distinction cross-cuts through the distinction in argument types (Sloman, 1996, pp17, 18). Still, the way Sloman characterizes what in his view are two different psychological systems invites the analogy with the inductive-deductive distinction: 'The associative system encodes and processes statistical regularities of its environment, frequencies and correlations amongst the various features of the world' (Sloman, 2002, pp380, 381). He also refers to William James who calls this empirical thinking (Sloman, 2002, p380). Hence, it seems as if the associative system at least has central features in common with induction. It is difficult to understand what Sloman means by the rule-based system because he only mentions some features of it without providing us with a definition. In any case, he says that '[r]ule-based systems are productive in that they can encode an unbounded number of propositions … A second principle is that rules are systematic in the sense that their ability to encode certain facts implies an ability to encode others' (Sloman, 2002, p381). Here are some features which distinguish the two systems that Sloman has identified: 'The associative system is generally useful for achieving one's goals; the rule-based system is more adept at ensuring that one's conclusions are sanctioned by a normative theory' (Sloman, 2002, p382), and '[r]ules provide a firmer basis for justification than do impressions' (Sloman, 1996, p15).

Hence, Sloman thinks that the second system, by being rule-based, is a better basis for justification than the first system. However, I think that in the case of empirical knowledge, the second system is inappropriate. In order to capture the empirical aspects of the world we need sense perception (in our daily life) and empirical research methods (in scientific research). In that respect it is remarkable that Sloman opposes perception versus knowledge:

> The Müller-Lyer illusion suggests that perception and knowledge derive from distinct systems. Perception provides one answer (the horizontal lines are of unequal size), although knowledge (or a ruler) provides quite a different one – they are equal. The *knowledge* that the two lines are of equal size does little to affect the *perception* that they are not. The conclusion that two independent systems are at work depends critically on the fact that the perception and the knowledge are maintained simultaneously. (Sloman, 2002, pp384, 385; italics in original)

The opposition that Sloman makes between knowledge and perception is very problematic and would probably not even be affirmed by the most fervent rationalist philosopher. Surely we can also have perceptual knowledge. Epistemologists would not contrast perception with knowledge as Sloman does. That seems to be a category mistake. Knowledge is a success term that can be ascribed to various sources of belief, amongst which are perceptual beliefs, provided that they are true, and justified or warranted.[2] Instead I would say that in the case of the Müller-Lyer illusion we have a false, direct perceptual belief versus a correct, mediated belief that is based on a ruler. But even concerning the correct belief, we still need perception to read the measurements on the ruler. In any case, the purely rule-based system is inadequate for certain forms of knowledge. According to some moral philosophers, this is also the case with moral knowledge (e.g. ethical particularism; see Dancy, 1993, 2004). I will discuss this in more detail in the next subsection.

Stanovich and West

This is what Keith E. Stanovich and Richard F. West say about DPT:

> System 1 is characterized as automatic, heuristic-based, and relatively undemanding of computational capacity. System 2 conjoins the various characteristics associated with controlled processing. System 2 encompasses the processes of analytic intelligence that have traditionally been studied by information processing theorists trying to uncover the computational components underlying intelligence.
> (Stanovich and West, 2002, p436)

It is noteworthy that Stanovich and West characterize system 1 as 'relatively undemanding of computational capacity', whereas system 2 is supposed to encompass the 'computational components underlying intelligence'. Intelligence is here mainly associated with computational processing. However, human intelligence possesses alternative resources such as narrative and emotional capacities (this has, for example, been argued for by phenomenologists such as Scheler

(1948) and Plessner (1961, 1975) and more recently by Dreyfus (1992)). These capacities cannot be captured in the computational terms of system 2, but since they are reflective and deliberative, they also do not fit into the more instinctive system 1.

Yet Stanovich and West seem to see 'the tendency toward a narrative mode of thought' (2002, p439) as a part of system 1 and as an obstacle to normative rationality, that is, system 2. They think that system 1 is evolutionarily primary and 'that it permeates virtually all our thinking' (Stanovich and West, 2002, p439). Characteristic for this system is amongst other things a high emphasis on context, whereas normative rationality, system 2, aims to abstract from context: 'If the properties of this system are not to be the dominant factors in our thinking, then they must be overridden by System 2 processes so that the particulars of a given problem are abstracted into canonical representations that are stripped of context' (Stanovich and West, 2002, p439). This might all be correct concerning areas where formal reasoning is the most appropriate mode of thinking, but I think that there are domains of knowledge where formal reasoning is not going to be sufficient. This holds concerning our knowledge of the material world, for which we need sense perception. In addition, it also holds concerning another important area, namely ethical knowledge, which is the focus of this article. For ethical knowledge, we need ethical reflection. Knowledge of the material world and of ethics cannot be achieved by formal reasoning only. In both domains of knowledge, contextualization is not necessarily a vice. It might even be unavoidable, as has been argued by moral contextualists or particularists (cf McDowell, 1998; Dancy, 1993, 2004).

There are some moral philosophers who insist that in ethical reflection we should abstract from the particular context, such as most famously Immanuel Kant. But present-day Kantians also wish to include contextual features in ethical reflection (e.g. Audi, 2003). Ethical intuitionists have argued for a long time that proper ethical decisions are to be made on a case-by-case basis, taking into account the features of specific contexts (for example, Prichard, 1912; Ewing, 1929; Broad, 1951; Ross, 1967, 1968; Dancy, 1993, 2004). The main argument behind it is that ethical reality is so complex that we cannot simply apply general rules. Instead, we have to look at the specific aspects of concrete situations. For example, sometimes it is best to be honest to somebody even if we might hurt that person. In other cases, it is better to be diplomatic about the truth in order to not hurt somebody (cf Dancy's work for various examples).

It is remarkable that Stanovich and West mention as one of the problems what they call 'evolutionary rationality' (system 1), as opposed to 'normative rationality' (system 2): 'the tendency to see *design* and patterns in situations that are either undesigned, unpatterned, or random' (Stanovich and West, 2002, p438). In the area of logic, this might indeed be a problem for what the authors call evolutionary rationality (system 1), but in the area of ethics, this is rather a problem for philosophers who defend a rationalist position (with rationality understood as part of system 2). Rationalists in ethics think that all ethical decisions can be justified by general principles, known by reason. Contextualists deny this. Whereas logic, by its very nature, operates in general, de-contextualized terms, our moral life is the messy, contextual world we live in. We would lose touch with our subject matter if in ethics we would try to reason in purely general terms. A contextualist in ethics would say that the moral world is unpatterned, and that this is exactly the reason why ethical reflection should take contextual features into account. An approach which does not do so will assume patterns that are not really there. Hence in ethics, this is a problem for system 2 rather than a problem for system 1, *pace* Stanovich and West.

Logic is not an ultimate normative standard of rationality in all domains of thinking. Logic might be necessary but it is definitely not sufficient for ethical reflection. However, this seems to be implied by Stanovich and West's claim that system 2 is generally normatively superior to system 1, with system 2 being more or less equated with formal, computational reasoning. The general deductive rules of logic apply in cases that are relevantly similar, but in determining what relevant similarities are, logic is completely inadequate. Logic is an empty system telling us which deductive inferences are valid given certain premises, but logic cannot tell us anything about the truth values of the premises themselves. To determine those, other modes of thinking are required. For example, concerning empirical premises, perception and other forms of empirical insight are needed in order to determine the truth values of such premises. And concerning ethical premises, we need ethical reflection.

Ethical intuitionists emphasize that we cannot avoid what Prichard calls 'an act of moral thinking' (Prichard, 1912). Moral thinking cannot be replaced by other modes of thinking. In any case, probably no moral philosopher thinks that a purely computational approach will be able to give us ethical insights. Kant's rationalist approach in philosophy distinguishes between 'pure reason' and 'practical reason', where the latter cannot be replaced by, for example, logic. Practical reason or 'moral thinking' requires that one *endorses* a moral point of view, something that computers are not able to do, and no system of formal logic can supply. In addition, there are philosophers who think that emotions are essential to our moral thinking, a view which I will defend in more detail further on.

To conclude, Stanovich and West wrongly think that narrativity and contextualization are normatively inferior to system 2 processing. Furthermore, the fact that narrativity, emotions and contextualization cannot be reduced to instinctive responses makes it doubtful whether these capacities can be located in system 1. On the other hand, these capacities do not fit into the computational paradigm of system 2. They seem to belong into both systems or neither of them.

Epstein

Seymour Epstein has developed an account called cognitive-experiential self-theory (CEST) according to which there are two 'interactive modes of information processing, rational and experiential' (Epstein, 1994, p710). Features of the experiential system (system 1) are the following:

1 holistic
2 affective
3 associative
4 behaviour mediated by past experiences
5 encodes reality in images, metaphors and narratives

6 more rapid processing
7 slower to change (changes with repetitive or intense experience)
8 stereotypical thinking
9 context-specific
10 'experienced passively and preconsciously: we are seized by our emotions'
11 self-evidently valid.

System 2 is characterized by the following features:

1 analytic
2 reason oriented
3 logical
4 behaviour mediated by conscious appraisal of events
5 encodes reality in abstract symbols, words and numbers
6 slower processing
7 changes more rapidly (with speed of thought)
8 more highly differentiated
9 cross-context processing
10 'experienced actively and consciously: we are in control of our thoughts'
11 requires justification via logic and evidence.

(Epstein 1994, p711)

At first sight, there seems to be a lot of plausibility in these oppositions. However, there are severe problems with them. For example, it seems that words (item 5, system 2) are needed for narrativity (item 5, system 1). Furthermore, reliabalists in epistemology maintain that even in logic and sense perception, justification comes to an end (Alston, 1989, 1993). Foundationalists say that all our thinking involves intuitions, i.e. non-inferential or self-evident beliefs (cf Ewing, 1941; Reid, 1969a).[3] This makes the opposition between items 11 on these lists debatable. In addition, many philosophers hold that the axioms of logic (item 3, system 2) are self-evident (item 11, system 1). Intuitionists would say that moral intuitions are self-evident (item 11, system 1), but they are not necessarily rapid, and for most intuitionists they are not emotional or affective. Far from always being preconscious and passive states (as suggested by item 10, system 1), many human emotions are conscious (item 4, system 2), rational and based on reasons (item 2, system 2). I will discuss this in more detail below. Hence, many important ways with which human beings apprehend reality transcend the boundaries of DPT as characterized by Epstein. Hence, although there is some plausibility in the oppositions that Epstein suggests, they are far too simplistic as to be able to capture many important ways with which we apprehend reality.

Slovic

Slovic and colleagues (Finucane et al, 2000) did experiments in which subjects had to rate different hazards on a seven-point scale for risks and benefits (from not at all risky/beneficial through very risky/beneficial). Some subjects were in a 'time pressure condition', that is, they were given limited time (5.2 seconds) to make their ratings, whereas other subjects were given more time to reflect. The subjects in the time pressure condition came up with significantly different ratings than the other subjects. Slovic and his colleagues presuppose that the subjects in the time pressure condition were using system 1, affect, and the others system 2, analytic thinking.

Slovic et al (2004) define affect as follows:

> As used here, 'affect' means the specific quality or 'goodness' or 'badness' (1) experienced as a feeling state (with or without consciousness) and (2) demarcating a positive or negative quality of a stimulus. Affective responses occur rapidly and automatically. (Slovic et al, 2004, p312)

Apparently, affect has three properties: (1) being a feeling state; (2) being evaluative; and (3) being rapid. There are some ambiguities here. Even if there are states that combine all these three properties, it does not follow that a state that has one of these properties also has all the others. Yet this seems to be the underlying assumption: in many articles on the affect heuristic, Slovic uses the words emotion, affect and value interchangeably.[4] However, rationalist philosophers would not equate evaluative states with affective states. Furthermore, from Zajonc's view it does not follow that every time pressure decision is based on affect. This assumption only holds if affect is the only mental activity that proceeds under time pressure. In other words, from the purported fact that affect always arises in a time pressure condition (affect implies time pressure), it does not as yet follow logically that all mental states that arise in a time pressure condition are forms of affect (not: time pressure implies affect). This would only hold if there would be a logical equivalence relation between affect situations and time pressure situations. Slovic does not provide any argument or evidence to this effect.

However, even if that assumption would be true, nothing follows as to which modes of thinking were used by the subjects who were not in the time pressure condition. Was it reason or emotion, or both? We would only know if system 1 could be equated with emotions and system 2 with reason, and if system 1 and system 2 could be unambiguously distinguished through time pressure. This might be the underlying assumption of DPT, but as I will argue in what follows, emotions can also have features of system 2, for example, being slow and rational.

Slovic has told me in conversation that he would distinguish between affect (system 1) and emotions (system 2, or both). With affect he means pro-con evaluations that we make all the time, often unnoticed. With emotions he means strong passionate feeling states that we are rarely in. Note that this is at odds with Epstein who does more or less identify emotions with system 1. But furthermore, I do not think we have captured the whole range of affective and cognitive responses to reality in this way. For example, moral emotions are evaluative judgements (similar to how Slovic understands affect), yet they do not always have to be intensely felt, and they can be slow, justified, rational and based on reasons. It is conceivable that subjects who were not in the time pressure condition used emotions understood in a broader way. I will expand on these issues in the remainder of this chapter.

General critique of DPT

It might be clear by now that I am not convinced by the framework of DPT. I do not think that system 2 is normatively superior to system 1. Note that Sloman nuances the claims of DPT by saying the following:

> The point ... is not that both systems are applied to every problem a person confronts, not that each system has an exclusive problem domain; rather, the forms have overlapping domains that differ depending on the individual reasoner's knowledge, skill, and experience. (Sloman, 2002, p382)

Sloman here seems to leave open the possibility that depending on the problem domain and/or a person's skills, system 1 can at least be as appropriate as system 2. But even on such a 'liberal' reading, Sloman still takes the existence of the two systems for granted. He just allows some leeway as to their application. However, in the previous subsection I have argued that our ways to apprehend reality are much more complex than what is claimed by DPT. Hence, I do not agree with what Epstein says in the quote at the beginning of this section ('There is no dearth of evidence'). As we saw, the various theorists do not agree on the labels for the two processes, which might be an indication that the conceptual distinctions are at least ambiguous. The question is also whether all these distinctions map. But more fundamentally, I do not think that we can distinguish all the diverse ways through which we apprehend reality into just two basic systems.

Most importantly for the purpose of this chapter is the question of where we should place emotions. Should there be one place for all affective states? On the one hand, emotions seem to fit into system 1 because they are affective states, but emotions can also be rational (system 2). They can be spontaneous responses but they can also be reflective, deliberative states. For example, moral emotions are not necessarily and not paradigmatically biases. In addition, many affective states are not quick but slow, especially moods, sentiments, dispositional emotions and character traits. Moral emotions such as sympathy, empathy and compassion can be rapid, but they can also be slow and require or at least allow scrutiny and reflection.

Emotions, and specifically moral emotions such as sympathy, seem to have a hybrid character on the model proposed by DPT. However, it is unclear what conclusions we should draw about their reliability and trustworthiness. Are they rather 'heuristics-but-biases' like system 1 operations, or are they reflective, justified concerns like system 2 operations? First of all, in the previous subsection, I already argued that it is far from clear that system 2 is normatively superior to system 1. But in addition, moral emotions cast into doubt the neat distinction between mental states that defenders of DPT propose. The distinction between these two systems reflects the traditional view of emotions and reason as categorically distinct states. Many modern theories of emotions challenge such a dichotomy in which reason is rational, objective and wise, and emotions are irrational, subjective and misleading (for example, de Sousa, 1987; Solomon, 1993; Little, 1995; Nussbaum, 2001). Of course emotions can lead us astray, but our purely rational system is even less competent in moral judgement and motivation (Damasio, 1994; Roskies, 2003).

In the following section I will give a positive account of emotions which will illustrate in more detail how emotions transcend the boundaries of DPT.

AN ALTERNATIVE VIEW OF EMOTIONS

We saw that proponents of DPT have a too simplistic understanding of our mental capacities with which we apprehend reality, and that this holds specifically regarding (moral) emotions. In this section I will discuss alternative views of emotions which allow for emotions to be reflective and permeated by rationality, or to be a form of rationality. Although my main focus is on moral emotions, I will sometimes also discuss other kinds of emotions. In the last section, I will apply these ideas to moral emotions about risks.

On the view underlying DPT, affect is not connected to judgement (cf Hume, 1975) or it precedes judgement (Zajonc, 1980, 1984a, 1984b). However, on this view, it is not clear where our affective states come from. They could be aroused by irrelevant conditions, which means that there is no reason to expect that the judgements resulting from such affective states are veridical. This might hold for some affective states, but surely not for all. Many of our moral emotions seem to be appropriate responses to situations in which they arise. One might conclude from this that judgement precedes feeling (e.g. Reid, 1969b). But then the feelings would be a mere add-on to our judgement that would not serve any purpose, except for maybe moral motivation. However, there are empirical and philosophical accounts that suggest that affective states also play an indispensable epistemological role in our practical and moral lives (see, for example, de Sousa, 1987; Frijda, 1987; Solomon, 1993; Damasio, 1994; Nussbaum, 2001; Roberts, 2003; for a review of recent philosophical theories of emotions, see de Sousa, 2003).

An alternative view of emotions runs as follows. Emotions are unitary states that consist of affective and cognitive aspects (e.g. Zagzebski, 2003; in addition, they have motivational and expressive elements, e.g. Scherer, 1984). There are also non-cognitive or precognitive feeling states, the ones that Zajonc emphasizes, but that does not mean that there cannot also be cognitive emotions (Zajonc actually did not deny that possibility, to the contrary; Zajonc, 1984a). Emotions are intentional states that incorporate beliefs. Many philosophers of emotions have argued that we cannot make sense of emotions such as fear, joy, love, etc. without reference to beliefs and intentional objects. This is also the case with explicitly other regarding emotions, such as sympathy, empathy and compassion. Moral emotions are focused on moral aspects of situations, often situations somebody else is in. These emotions let us see salient features of situations that purely rational states would easily overlook. An account of emotions as unities of cognitive and affective states has the advantage above the alternatives discussed before that in normal human beings, moral emotions are normative, veridical, appropriate, and not as a mere coincidence but because emotions are states that can track evaluative features of the world. This fits with our idea of virtuous moral agents who act from appropriate motives and who discern moral values through moral emotions (cf Aristotle, 1996; McDowell, 1998).

Robert C. Roberts (2003) has proposed an account of emotions as 'concern-based construals'. With this he means that emotions combine the following features: in emotions we are (1) concerned about something which we (2) construe in a certain way. With 'construing', Roberts means that we see a snake *as* dangerous, we see our partner *as* loveable, etc. With 'concern', he means that we care about the object of the construal. By talking about construals instead of cognitions, as for example Martha Nussbaum (2001) does, Roberts allows for the possibility that our emotions can be at odds with our considered judgements. I might be afraid of flying although I know that it is one of the safest means of transportation. Here we see an analogy with the Müller-Lyer illusion. Hence, Roberts' account *can* do justice to the intuitions underlying DPT. However, on Roberts' account, emotions are far from being *paradigmatically* prone to biases. To the contrary; Roberts thinks that in the normal case, emotions are supported by judgement (Roberts, 2003, p106).[5] The fact that his theory allows for irrational emotions does not mean that these are typical phenomena. In a similar vein, the Müller-Lyer illusion does not show that sense perception is always or generally misleading. Emotions can provide us with veridical, justified construals, that is, with evaluative judgements that can sustain deliberation and rational scrutinization, and they paradigmatically do so in virtuous moral agents.

Roberts gives a list of aspects that emotions paradigmatically, but not always have, which can serve to illustrate that emotions do not fit in either of the systems that DPT proposes. This is a summary of Roberts' list (2003, pp60–64):

1 Emotions are paradigmatically felt.
2 They are often accompanied by physiological changes (the feeling of which is not identical with, but typically an aspect of, the feeling of an emotion).
3 Emotions paradigmatically have objects.
4 The objects of emotions are typically situations that can be told about by a story.
5 An emotion type is determined by defining leading concepts (e.g. anger: about a culpable offence; fear: about a threat, etc.).
6 In paradigm cases, the subject believes the propositional content of his/her emotion.
7 Emotions typically have some nonpropositional content.
8 Many emotions are motivational.
9 Emotions can be controllable but also uncontrollable.
10 Emotions come in degrees of intensity.
11 Expression of emotion can intensify and prolong an emotion but it can also cause it to subside.
12 Emotions are praise- and blameworthy.

The following features of emotions let them seem to be part of system 1: features 1, 2, 7, 8, 9 (uncontrollable); whereas other features seem to be more related to system 2: features 3, 4, 5, 6, 9 (controllable) and 12. Some features do not seem to correspond clearly with either system: features 10 and 11. In any case, I think that Roberts' list of paradigmatic features of emotions gives reason to doubt the possibility to classify emotions in either system, and it is at least far from clear that emotions belong in system 1.

To sum up, Roberts' account of emotions as concern-based construals can do justice to some of the plausible intuitions underlying DPT, by allowing that emotions can be at odds with our considered judgements, while still showing that paradigmatically, emotions are rational. On this account, moral emotions transcend the boundaries that are set by DPT. This alternative account can shed a different light on affective responses to risks.

Reflective moral emotions about risks

By departing from DPT and embracing a richer conception of emotions, we can come to alternative interpretations of Slovic's data and reach different conclusions as to the role of the affect heuristic and emotions about risk in general. These conclusions are much more in line with Slovic's usual views about the legitimacy of the risk perception of laypeople. In the following, I will focus on two kinds of emotions: first, on fear or dread, since this is the emotion that Slovic and his colleagues focus on in their work on the affect heuristic; second, I will discuss explicitly other regarding moral emotions such as sympathy, empathy and compassion. They do not figure explicitly in most of Slovic's studies (except for his recent work on psychophysical numbing and genocide), but they can shed important light on the study of moral emotions about risk.

Fear and related emotions

Let us see how Roberts' account of emotions as concern-based construals can help us to a different understanding of the affect heuristic, by looking at what Roberts has to say about fear. Note that Slovic does not so much speak about fear but about dread, which is an important factor in the affect heuristic. According to Roberts, the notions 'fear' and 'dread' originally had a similar meaning but do nowadays have different connotations (cf Roberts, 2003, p199, n21). Roberts interprets dread as an emotion about an unavoidable situation. Unavoidability does not seem to be a necessary ingredient to dread in Slovic et al's studies. Hence, I will focus on Roberts' analysis of fear as I think that this comes closest to what Slovic means by 'dread'.

Roberts proposes the following defining proposition for fear:

> *X presents an aversive possibility of a significant degree of probability; may X or its aversive consequences be avoided.* (Roberts, 2003, p195; italics in original)

This proposition curiously is more or less identical to the standard account of risk as probability times unwanted effect ('aversive possibility'), although it goes further than that by referring to a 'significant degree of probability' and by stating that X or its consequences should be avoided. Fear is a concern-based construal. We try to avoid the object of our fear, we feel an aversion of the object (concern), and we construe it as something worth avoiding. Fear transcends the boundaries of system 1 and 2. It can be invoked spontaneously and it can operate very rapidly like a gut reaction (system 1-like), but it also incorporates justifiable factual and evaluative beliefs (system 2-like). Roberts (in criticizing David Hume) emphasizes that fear is paradigmatically based on reasons:

> If someone fears a slippery sidewalk, it makes perfectly good sense to specify his reason(s) for fearing it: He needs to traverse it, his shoes do not have good traction on ice, he is unskilled at remaining upright on slippery surfaces – in short, the conditions are such that the slippery sidewalk may well occasion an injurious fall. Apart from some such reasons, it may be as hard to see why a slippery sidewalk would be an object of fear as it is to see why, apart from reasons, a self would be an object of pride. (Roberts, 2003, p194)

Note that Roberts not only cites reasons for a specific fear, he also claims that without such reasons, we could not see how something could be an object of fear. If this holds for fear of slippery sidewalks, surely this holds even more for fear of nuclear power plants, pesticides, explosives and chemical plants, to mention just a few of the hazardous activities that subjects had to rate in Slovic et al's studies on the affect heuristic (see, for example, Finucane et al, 2000, p7, exhibit 3). We are able to cite justifiable reasons why people would fear such activities, such as the destruction of our environment and the possible deaths of human beings (cf Roeser, 2006). This involves factual beliefs about the possible consequences and evaluative beliefs about the desirability of these consequences.

This is what Harvey Green says about fear:

> Imaginative fears, for example, are secondary to ordinary fears involving beliefs about dangers, not just in being less common, but in a more basic sense. Our emotional sensitivity to imaginative representations of danger is explained by our sensitivity to beliefs about danger, for it is in those cases that our emotional representations have the adaptive value which accounts for their evolutionary origin. (Green, 1992, p38)

Here Green makes some interesting remarks: (1) fear is based on beliefs about dangers; (2) it is evolutionary adaptive; (3) irrational fears such as in imaginative representations are anomalous and derived from these as it were rational states of fear. Fear has adaptive value; it can guide us away from destructive situations. A being without fear would probably not survive for a very long time.

To sum up, fear can be a justified, reasonable concern (system 2ish) rather than merely a blind impulse (which would be the case if it would be a pure system 1 state).

Other regarding moral emotions: sympathy, empathy and compassion

There is an ambiguity in the kinds of surveys that research subjects in Slovic's study have to fill in. Often, subjects have to rate how far they find the current level of risk of a specific hazard acceptable or not. However, this is ambiguous between whether a subject finds a risk acceptable for herself or acceptable for society. She might fear or dread to be herself the victim of the manifestation of a hazard, but she could also be concerned about the well-being of other people.

The latter kind of concerns are involved in explicitly other regarding emotions such as sympathy, empathy and compassion.

Many emotions are spontaneous responses to what is nearby, but sympathetic emotions are exactly the kinds of emotions that can lead us to extend our 'circle of concern', as Nussbaum (2001) phrases it. If we think about the suffering that other people might undergo by being the victims of a disaster, we cannot help but feel touched and shocked about this. This realization involves emotions. These are emotions that are reflective, justifiable and based on reasons (unlike system 1), and they are even inevitable in our moral assessment of risks. Through these emotions we see how morally unacceptable a certain hazard might be (cf Roeser, 2006). Purely rational reflection would not be able to provide us with the imaginary power that we need to envisage future scenarios and to take part in other people's perspectives and to evaluate their destinies. Hence, such moral emotions neither fit neatly into system 1 nor into system 2.

Re-assessing the affect-heuristic

I have argued that fear and sympathy are not typically system 1 states, and yet they can be expected to play an important role in people's affective responses to risks. Going back to Slovic's studies about the affect heuristic, this could mean several things. The subjects in the non-time pressure condition were not necessarily in an unemotional state. They might have experienced reflective, reason-based, justifiable emotions such as fear, sympathy, empathy and compassion, rather than having made purely rational judgements, so they also were not in pure system 2 states as defined by DPT. But even in so far as the emotional responses of subjects were spontaneous, this does not necessarily mean that they were irrational. We have seen that typical system 1 features can be more adequate for certain domains of knowledge than system 2 features. However, it is not clear whether the more complex emotions that philosophers are interested in can be elicited in a time pressure condition lasting 5.2 seconds. What is definitely clear is that the time pressure condition could not filter out all the responses that are affective states of some sort. We know that the subjects in the different situations came up with different ratings, but it is far from clear that the responses of the subjects in the non-time pressure condition were not emotional. It might very well be that the non-time pressure subjects used reflective, rational moral emotions that led them to more well-considered judgements than the other subjects. Different experiments would be needed to figure out which mental activities were involved in the non-time pressure-condition; for example, MRI-scanning of brain activities or self-assessment surveys. But furthermore, nothing is said yet about the normative status of the various responses to risk. To simply invoke DPT is question begging, because DPT fails on two levels: it wrongly suggests that system 2 is normatively superior to system 1; and it wrongly places emotions in system 1.

Conclusion

Paul Slovic's work on the affect heuristic is based on DPT, a theoretical framework that can be cast into doubt by various philosophical approaches. Rather than providing us with fully satisfying theoretical conclusions, Slovic's work invites possible alternative interpretations which are not yet considered in the literature on risk perception and acceptable risk, where DPT seems to be an unquestioned paradigm. This is probably due to the fact that most authors in that field have an empirical training in sociology or psychology. (Neuro)psychologists commonly are interested in very different emotions, and from a very different perspective, than philosophers. The emotions studied by many psychologists are the instinctive responses that we share with animals. Instead, philosophers are interested in different kinds of emotions, some of which we might share with animals, but many of which we don't because they involve mental capacities that only human beings have. These are emotions that involve a high degree of reflectivity and narrativity, such as emotional responses to fictional characters or to people or events who or which are far away (cf Roberts, 2003, especially pp49–52). Based on such a different view of emotions, the empirical results of Slovic's studies on the 'affect heuristic' can be interpreted in a different light: emotions are a source of moral wisdom in thinking about risks. This interpretation is much more in line with Slovic's general work in which he stresses that public risk perception is based on legitimate concerns.

From a philosophical point of view, the field of risk and emotions is severely underdeveloped. A different theoretical framework with a different view of emotions challenges the standard view of emotions about risks as heuristics but biases. Rather, emotions might be an inevitable route to coming to a proper understanding of the moral acceptability of risks. This would not only significantly change the academic literature on risk perception and decision-making under uncertainty, it would also have direct implications for risk policy from which emotions are generally banned.[6] At most, emotions are officially acknowledged as an unfortunate fact of life that we have to accept ('the emotional, hence irrational public'; this is, for example, the approach of Loewenstein et al (2001)). An alternative approach to emotions about risks would invite people's emotions explicitly into the arena of debates about acceptable risks, as an invaluable source of ethical wisdom.[7]

References

Alhakami, A. S. and Slovic, P. (1994) 'A psychological study of the inverse relationship between perceived risk and perceived benefit', *Risk Analysis*, vol 14, pp1085–1096

Alston, W. P. (1989) *Epistemic Justification. Essays in the Theory of Knowledge*, Cornell University Press, Ithaca and London

Alston, W. P. (1993) *The Reliability of Sense Perception*, Cornell University Press, Ithaca and London

Aristotle (1996) *The Nichomachean Ethics*, trans. with notes by Harris Rackham, intr. by Stephen Watt, Wordsworth, Ware

Audi, R. (2003) *The Good in the Right. A Theory of Intuition and Intrinsic Value*, Princeton University Press, Princeton

Broad, C. D. (1951 [1930]) *Five Types of Ethical Theory*, Routledge & Kegan Paul Ltd., London
Damasio, A. (1994) *Descartes' Error*, Putnam, New York
Dancy, J. (1993) *Moral Reasons*, Blackwell, Oxford
Dancy, J. (2004) *Ethics Without Principles*, Oxford University Press, Oxford
de Sousa, R. (1987) *The Rationality of Emotions*, MIT-Press, Cambridge MA
de Sousa, R. (2003) 'Emotion', *The Stanford Encyclopedia of Philosophy*, Edward N. Zalta (ed), http://plato.stanford.edu/archives/spr2003/entries/emotion/
Dreyfus, H. (1992) *What Computers Still Can't Do. A Critique of Artificial Reason*, MIT-Press, Cambridge MA
Epstein, S. (1994) 'Integration of the cognitive and the psychodynamic unconscious', *American Psychologist*, vol 49, no 8, pp709–724
Ewing, A. C. (1929) *The Morality of Punishment*, Kegan Paul, London
Ewing, A. C. (1941) 'Reason and intuition', *Proceedings of the British Academy*, vol 27, pp67–107
Finucane, M., Alhakami, A., Slovic, P. and Johnson, S. M. (2000) 'The affect heuristic in judgments of risks and benefits', in *Journal of Behavioral Decision Making*, vol 13, pp1–17
Fischhoff, B., Slovic, P., Lichtenstein, S., Read, S. and Combs, B. (1978) 'How safe is safe enough? A psychometric study of attitudes towards technological risks and benefits', *Policy Science*, vol 9, pp127–152
Frijda, N. (1987) *The Emotions*, Cambridge University Press, Cambridge
Gilovich, T., Griffin, D. and Kahnemann, D. (eds) (2002) *Intuitive Judgment: Heuristics and Biases*, Cambridge University Press, Cambridge
Green, O. H. (1992) *The Emotions*, Kluwer Academic Publishers, Dordrecht
Hume, D. (1975) *A Treatise of Human Nature*, ed. by L. A. Selby-Bigge, 2nd edn revised by P. H. Nidditch, Clarendon Press, Oxford
Little, M. O. (1995) 'Seeing and caring: the role of affect in feminist moral epistemology', *Hypatia*, vol 10, pp117–137
Loewenstein, G. F., Weber, E. U., Hsee, C. K. and Welch, N. (2001) 'Risk as feelings', *Psychological Bulletin*, vol 127, pp267–286
McDowell, J. (1998) *Mind, Value and Reality*, Harvard University Press, Cambridge MA
Nussbaum, M. (2001) *Upheavals of Thought*, Cambridge University Press, Cambridge
Plessner, H. (1961) *Lachen und Weinen*, Francke, Bern
Plessner, H. (1975) *Die Stufen des Organischen und der Mensch*, Walter de Gruyter, Berlin
Prichard, H. A. (1912) 'Does moral philosophy rest on a mistake?', *Mind*, vol 21, pp21–37
Reid, T. (1969a [1785]) *Essays on the Intellectual Powers of Man*, introduction by Baruch Brody, The M.I.T. Press, Cambridge, Massachusetts, and London, England
Reid, T. (1969b [1788]) *Essays on the Active Powers of the Human Mind,* introduction by Baruch Brody, The M.I.T. Press, Cambridge, Massachusetts, and London, England
Roberts, R. C. (2003) *Emotions. An Essay in Aid of Moral Psychology*, Cambridge University Press, Cambridge
Roeser, S. (2006) 'The role of emotions in judging the moral acceptability of risks', *Safety Science*, vol 44, pp689–700
Roeser, S. (2007) 'Ethical intuitions about risks', *Safety Science Monitor*, vol 11, pp1–30
Roskies, A. (2003) 'Are ethical judgments intrinsically motivational? Lessons from "acquired sociopathy"', *Philosophical Psychology*, vol 16, pp51–66
Ross, W. D. (1967 [1930]) *The Right and the Good*, Clarendon Press, Oxford
Ross, W. D. (1968 [1939]) *Foundations of Ethics. The Gifford Lectures*, Clarendon Press, Oxford

Sandman, P. M. (1989) 'Hazard versus outrage in the public perception of risk', in V. T. Covello, D. B. McCallum and M. T. Pavlova (eds) *Effective Risk Communication: The Role and Responsibility of Government and Nongovernment Organizations*, Plenum Press, New York, NY

Scheler, M. (1948) *Wesen und Formen der Sympathie*, Schulte-Bulenke, Frankfurt/Main

Scherer, K. R. (1984) 'On the nature and function of emotion: A component process approach', in K. R. Scherer and P. Ekman (eds) *Approaches to Emotion*, Lawrence Erlbaum Associates, Hillsdale, London

Sloman, S. A. (1996) 'The empirical case for two systems of reasoning', *Psychological Bulletin*, vol 119, pp3–22

Sloman, S. A. (2002) 'Two systems of reasoning', in T. Gilovich, D. Griffin and D. Kahnemann (eds) *Intuitive Judgment: Heuristics and Biases*, Cambridge University Press, Cambridge, pp379–396

Slovic, P. (1987) 'Perception of risk', *Science*, vol 236, pp280–285

Slovic, P. (1999) 'Trust, emotion, sex, politics, and science: surveying the risk-assessment battlefield', *Risk Analysis*, vol 19, pp689–701

Slovic, P. (2000) *The Perception of Risk*, Earthscan, London

Slovic, P., Finucane, M., Peters, E. and MacGregor, D. G. (2002) 'The affect heuristic', in T. Gilovich, D. Griffin and D. Kahnemann (eds) *Intuitive Judgment: Heuristics and Biases*, Cambridge University Press, Cambridge, pp397–420

Slovic, P., Finucane, M., Peters, E. and MacGregor, D. G. (2004) 'Risk as analysis and risk as feelings: some thoughts about affect, reason, risk, and rationality', *Risk Analysis*, vol 24, pp311–322 (reprinted in this volume)

Solomon, R. (1993) *The Passions: Emotions and the Meaning of Life*, Hackett, Indianapolis

Stanovich, K. E. and West, R. F. (2002), 'Individual differences in reasoning: Implications for the rationality debate?', in T. Gilovich, D. Griffin and D. Kahnemann (eds) *Intuitive Judgment: Heuristics and Biases*, Cambridge University Press, Cambridge, pp421–440

Sunstein, C. R. (2005) *Laws of Fear*, Cambridge University Press, Cambridge

Zagzebski, L. (2003) 'Emotion and Moral Judgment', *Philosophy and Phenomenology Research*, vol 66, pp104–124

Zajonc, R. B. (1980) 'Feeling and thinking: preferences need no inferences', *American Psychologist*, vol 35, pp151–175

Zajonc, R. B. (1984a) 'The interaction of affect and cognition', in K. R. Scherer and P. Ekman (eds) *Approaches to Emotion*, Lawrence Erlbaum Associates, Hillsdale, London, pp239–257

Zajonc, R. B. (1984b) 'On primacy of affect', in K. R. Scherer and P. Ekman (eds) *Approaches to Emotion*, Lawrence Erlbaum Associates, Hillsdale, London, pp259–270

Notes

1 In more or less the same formulation, this passage can be found in various other articles by Slovic on the affect heuristic, e.g. Slovic et al (2004, p315).

2 I do not wish to enter here into the epistemological debate on criteria of knowledge, whether knowledge is justified true belief, justified warranted belief or what have you. But it is generally agreed upon by epistemologists that knowledge can be applied to perceptual beliefs that are at least true (plus possibly other criteria).

3 Note that the notions 'intuition' and 'self-evident' do not entail infallibility (see, for example, Ewing, 1941; Audi, 2003).

4 See, for example, Finucane et al (2000, p2) and Slovic et al (2002, p398), which both contain the following passage: 'According to Zajonc, all perceptions contain some affect. We do not just see "A House": We see a *handsome* house, an *ugly* house, or a *pretentious* house' (Zajonc, 1980, p154). Also see Finucane et al (2000, p2, note 1): 'Affect may be viewed as a feeling state that people experience, such as happiness or sadness. It may also be viewed as a quality (e.g. goodness or badness) associated with a stimulus. These two conceptions tend to be related. This paper will be concerned with both of these aspects of affect.' Note that this is a more careful formulation: here it is said that evaluation and feeling tend to be related, whereas in the quote about Zajonc they are equated.

5 See also Green (1992, pp36, 37) for an alternative approach of what he calls 'anomalous emotions': he says that they lack cognitive commitment and the rational properties of belief.

6 The banning of emotions from risk policy might be inherently impossible since many risk judgements that are not taken to be emotional are in fact emotional, on the broader view of emotions defended in this chapter.

7 Earlier versions of this chapter have been presented at the conference 'Ethical Aspects of Risk', Delft University of Technology, 14–16 June 2006, at the departmental colloquium of the Philosophy Department of Delft University of Technology, at the departmental colloquium of the Philosophy Department of Twente University and at the Bioethics Work in Progress Series at Georgetown University. Thanks to the comments by the audiences at those meetings, especially to Steve Clarke, Niklas Möller, Jeroen de Ridder and Paul Slovic.

13 Risk and Public Imagination: Mediated Risk Perception as Imaginative Moral Judgement

Mark Coeckelbergh

Introduction

Public discussions about technological risk tend to be polarized between experts and the public. Consider the controversy about the risks of genetically modified food in Europe. Many people support a ban on such food by claiming that there are serious health and environmental risks, whereas many experts argue that such risks are small or at least manageable. Experts typically accuse the public of biases and 'emotional' responses, to which they oppose their own views based on 'scientific evidence'. A similar polarization can be observed in worldwide discussions about the risks of nuclear energy, another highly contested technology. Opponents refer to disasters such as Chernobyl and Hiroshima; experts try to counter this public 'imagination' with results from 'scientific research' on the risks of radiation and nuclear waste disposal. Experts argue, therefore, that the public should be informed about and educated on the 'real' risks attached to these technologies. This expert position received support from psychological and social research. For instance, Paul Slovic and others have studied emotional factors that play a role in risk perception (e.g. Slovic, 2000; Slovic et al, 2004). Their intention is to defend the legitimacy of the public's position: emotions do and should count. Their work, however, appears to undermine this claim. Lay people are said to *perceive* risks, using their feelings and imagination, whereas experts *analyse* and *assess* it. In this way, opposition to genetically modified foods or nuclear energy can be dismissed as distorted perception, as the outcome of an 'affect heuristic' (Slovic et al, 2004), as a typical instance of social amplification of risk (e.g. Smith and McCloskey, 1998, p46) and stigmatization (e.g. Flynn et al, 2001). Risk communication, then, is a one-way process based on a paternalistic attitude: experts claim to know what the public should think about the risk related to technology.

Assuming that it is good for a society to move towards more consensus on issues related to technological risk,[1] this polarization and paternalism is

undesirable. But can it be avoided, and how? In this chapter, I criticize the expert position and the related psychological and social studies, and propose an alternative approach to avoid polarization between expert and public positions by focusing on the moral role of imagination. In particular, I argue that the public views should be taken seriously as moral judgements that crucially depend on the use of imagination. First I show that in spite of good intentions and while there is much to learn from recent literature on the psychological and social aspects of public risk perception, its conceptual framework implies an unfair evaluation of the role of public imagination concerning risk. I argue that more work needs to be done to close the gap between feeling and analysis, and between imagination and reason. Then I look for an alternative approach. Inspired by contemporary philosophical accounts of moral imagination, I explore what it means to understand public imagination of risk as an imaginative moral judgement. I conclude that more philosophical reflection and empirical research is needed to further work out the role of imagination in risk judgements by public and experts. I end with a call for a new distribution of moral and epistemological power and responsibility, and for new mediators and interfaces between different perspectives on risk.

RISK CONCEPTS, PERSPECTIVES AND IMAGES

Concepts

The social and psychological literature on risk uses concepts such as 'risk perception', 'risk assessment', 'risk management', 'risk as feelings', 'stigma' and 'the social amplification of risk'. By making explicit the normative assumptions related to these concepts, I will argue that this literature enforces the expert view of the role of the public, and therefore the polarization between the two positions. Furthermore, I will pay special attention to how this literature approaches the role of imagination with regard to technological risk. This double focus will allow me to suggest an alternative approach in the next sections of this chapter, which aims to avoid polarization and paternalism.

Risk perception and risk assessment

In the literature on risk a distinction is made between risk assessment, done by experts, and risk perception, done by the public. Experts estimate the chances of a specific event occurring and the potential consequences (Kunreuther, 2002, p656), whereas risk perception is 'concerned with the psychological and emotional factors' (Kunreuther, 2002, p657) related to risk. Paul Slovic and others have studied such factors. The normative conclusion many have drawn from such studies is that we should not ignore the perception of risk of the public, and that we should include psychological and emotional factors as part of risk assessment processes. For example, in his introduction to *The Perception of Risk*, Slovic suggests that we should respect laypeople's perception of risk (Slovic, 2000, pxxxii) and explicitly defends an approach to risk 'that focuses on introducing more public participation into both risk assessment and risk decision-making' (ibid, pxxxvi). However, this view is contradicted by the normative implications of the concepts Slovic and others use in their studies. In spite of their good intentions, they still hold on to the dichotomy risk perception (public) versus risk assessment (expert), which assumes that expert judgement concerns 'real' risk, and that therefore part of risk management consists of informing and educating the public about that 'real' risk. If we really want to take seriously risk perception as risk judgement, this distinction between risk assessment and risk perception is far too sharp. I propose to view both 'risk assessment' and 'risk perception' as moral risk judgements, in which factors such as emotion and imagination play a role, and this holds both for the public and for experts. I will further develop this view below.

Note that an additional and more radical conclusion would be to drop the distinction altogether and think of other concepts. Whether or not we should opt for this solution depends on how much work the conceptual pair can still do in increasing our understanding of risk. I shall not discuss this question further here. But whatever option is chosen, we must be beware of the normative shadow attached to these concepts.

Risk management and communication

Risk management that involves the public is often still seen as a one-way process: experts are to communicate information to the public. It's the technology, stupid! Studies have shown that people do not think in terms of probabilities. Under the so-called *availability heuristic*, people 'estimate the likelihood of an event by the ease with which they can imagine or recall past instances of the event' (Kunreuther, 2002, p658). Furthermore, they do not only imagine past and future events, affect and emotions also play an important role (Slovic et al, 2004 – see further below). Although these types of 'biases' hold for *all* people, that is, not only for laypeople but also experts, it is the *public* judgement that is accused of bias. Although Slovic and others do not wish to support the view that the public has to be educated to judge risk by adopting the scientific perspective, this conclusion is sometimes suggested by their terminology and some of their claims. Emotions and imagination are taken into account, but sometimes it looks as if they are factors that stand in the way and that should not really be taken seriously. The research results are ambiguous in this respect: emotions are shown to be involved in both expert and laypeople's judgement, but in applications to the risk discussion it often appears that only laypeople are charged with bias. More effort is needed to exclude this interpretation of the risk perception studies.

The view that risk communication should be a one-way process is enforced by the risk perception versus risk assessment distinction discussed above. Risk perception denotes emotional bias, it is not a proper risk judgement; risk judgement can only be risk assessment. Again, by using the word 'perception', experts (and politicians, journalists, ...) take the views of the public into account – they're not ignored but registered with the help of an army of social scientists and marketing people – but they do not take those views seriously as proper judgement. Therefore, even in the case of two-way communication as part of risk management, the polarization between expert and public positions in the discussion remains. If, however, we look at public perception as a moral judgement, we can allow for various approaches to risk. This avoids extremely paternalistic approaches to risk management, avoids unnecessary polarization between expert and public views and improves our understanding of the moral dimension of risk. I will argue for this claim below, when I apply the term 'perspectives' to this discussion and when I explore the imaginative and moral aspects of public risk perception.

Risk as feelings

In 'Risk as analysis and risk as feelings' (Slovic et al, 2004), Slovic and others distinguish between two ways to comprehend risk. The analytic system relies on calculus and is usually called risk assessment, whereas the experiential system is intuitive: it relies on images and associations, which are linked by experience to emotion and affect (Slovic et al, 2004, pp311–313). Reality is encoded in 'concrete images, metaphors, and narratives' (ibid, p313). However, the authors argue that to understand 'risks as feelings' (ibid, p311) need not entail the view that affective responses are irrational. Rather, they claim that both systems depend on each other: rational decision-making requires integration of both modes of thought. Although they admit that the interplay between emotion and reason is complex, they put forward the following claim about their relation when they consider the implications for risk management:

> Because *risk as feeling* tends to overweight frightening consequences, we need to invoke *risk as analysis* to give us perspective on the likelihood of such consequences. (Slovic et al, 2004, p320)

Although Slovic and others do seem to value risk as feeling, they suggest that it needs to be corrected by reason. The authors use the language of error and failure:

> It [the affect heuristic] works beautifully when our experience enables us to anticipate accurately how we will like the consequences of our decisions. It fails miserably when the consequences turn out to be much different in character than we anticipated. (Slovic et al, 2004, p321)

In other words, it is suggested that emotion is an inaccurate measure, which therefore needs to be corrected by science, and science is an approach to reality that provides measures worthy of that name. Although Slovic stresses that both ways of reasoning depend upon each other – he subscribes to Damasio's view that 'emotional processes interact with reason-based analysis in all normal thinking' and that they are essential to rationality (Slovic, 2000, pxxxii) – the passage about failure may suggest that whereas the 'affect' of the public can be inaccurate and can 'fail miserably', expert judgement cannot fail. Slovic and others have not done enough to exclude this interpretation and to show in their own research that the gap between feeling and analysis can be closed.

Stigma

The use of the stigma concept in a technology context faces the same limitation. The idea of the stigma concept here is that a mark is placed on a technology associated with a negative emotion. For example, in a recent study Peters and others observe that 'nuclear objects appear to carry strong associations with our society's early experiences with radiation and nuclear war' (Peters et al, 2004, p1351). So we end up with 'a class of risk objects that are generally regarded as disgraceful and unacceptable' (p1353). First, this falsely suggests that people are completely unreasonable if they rely on historical experiences such as Hiroshima for their view on nuclear technology. Emotions and reason are connected in normal thinking (see Slovic's reference to Damasio above), whereas the discussion of risk perception in terms of 'stigma' suggests that to rely on emotions is by definition unreasonable. If emotions play a role in a view on nuclear technology, this does not itself render it unreasonable. Moreover, an historical experience such as Hiroshima may well play a role in the perception of nuclear technology of both opponents and defenders, but their moral *judgement* of its technological risk obviously differs. By approaching risk with the stigma concept, there is no room for moral risk judgement on the part of the public. Peters and others point to evidence that people learn by experience that they should not like certain things. I do not question this, but to stop at such observations and interpreting them in terms of stigma does no justice to other factors that play or can play a role in the moral judgement of the public, and neglects the plurality of images and emotions that can be attached to one technology. The stigma model has only room for one kind of emotions, that is, negative ones. But there are many more, and there can be multiple images that can compete and conflict. Again we get only a very partial view of the complex process of moral risk judgement. Furthermore, to talk about a public that 'stigmatizes' is again to say that experts always know better. The assumption is that the public stigmatizes, experts judge.

The social amplification of risk

Another example of a one-sided view on moral risk judgement is the concept of 'social amplification of risk' (e.g. Smith and McCloskey, 1998, p46), which suggests that there are the scientific facts (the risk) which then get distorted by public perception. The concept assumes a distinction between 'real risk' (experts) versus 'amplified risk' (public). I do not want to deny the reality of so-called 'moral panics' (p42); think of the BSE crisis: panic has been observed in that and other crises. I also endorse the view defended by Smith and McCloskey that this is a complex multi-actor process that includes the behaviour of media, regulators, politicians, action groups, etc. It would be interesting to think about the distribution of moral responsibility going on in such processes. But the concept of risk amplification does little justice to the value and moral significance of the public imagination and judgement. For example, if the public is so much worried about small probability – large consequences types of technological risk – this is not just an 'amplification' or exaggeration, but a moral judgement saying that large consequences matter a lot to us regardless of the probability. Whether or not this moral judgement is adequate is a hard moral question, but the point is that it is not something for experts (alone) to decide. Experts are not necessarily moral experts – provided that 'moral expertise' is a concept that makes sense at all. In the next section, therefore, I propose an alternative approach to discussions about technological risk.

Perspectives

I have shown that in spite of the good intentions of Slovic and others to take seriously the views of the public, good intentions for which there is plenty of evidence, a study of the assumptions related to the conceptual framework used reveals a deep-rooted mistrust of public risk 'perception'. Rather than talking about public risk 'perception' that needs to be corrected by the science of risk assessment, I propose that it is best to view various ways of looking at risk – by experts, public and media – as different perspectives on risk that all have moral significance and deserve to be taken seriously as informants and elements in risk judgements, including that of the public. If polarization between expert and public views is to be avoided, experts should do their homework as well. Moral imagination can help to expand their perspective. While no-one should be blamed for starting off with a certain perspective, developed under the influence of one's education and environment, it is everyone's moral duty and responsibility to use one's imagination to transcend it, to look beyond, here: to consider the perspective of the public. This is a duty since it is an acceptable way that allows the discussion to move on beyond polarization. Another way would be to simply impose the expert perspective on the public, but this is unacceptable in a social and political system that claims to adhere to democratic principles. Even if a model of direct citizen's participation is rejected, it can be reasonably expected from a democracy seriously to take into account views of the public. This is possible only if a real understanding of the views of the public is achieved, an understanding which is enabled by the use of imagination.

Transcending one's own perspective is both harder and easier than it may seem. It is difficult since our social-cultural environment, for example our profession, exerts a lot of influence on us and shapes our way of thinking. But it is not very hard either to take on another perspective, since professional experts have other roles as well, for example parent, friend, lover, consumer or driver, and they can connect to the feelings, imagination and values of these other roles if needed. The perspective of the public, with its imagination and feeling, is not alien; experts just tend to block it out while they are playing their role. Usually that's fine and functional; sometimes it's dysfunctional and morally unacceptable. Imagination has the critical function to 'disengage us from the perspective with which we are dealing with a situation so that we will be able to consider new possibilities', beyond those prescribed by one's context or one's role (Werhane, 1998). To conclude, if we want to take seriously public 'perception' as judgement, we need to acknowledge that there are various ways and perspectives of looking at risk and judging its acceptability, perspectives that all have moral significance, and that therefore all should be taken into consideration. To make the gap between experts and public less wide, then, we need to make sure that all risk stakeholders, including experts, acknowledge the role of imagination, emotions, etc. in their risk judgements, acknowledge other perspectives than their own, and use their imagination to enter into the perspectives of others and consider new ways of dealing with risk. Going beyond one's own perspective may be difficult, given the influence of the context of professional education and socialization, but this importance of context also points to the possibility of change: we can change education and training processes in such a way that imagination and emotion are not excluded.

Note that considering various perspectives on risk does not release any risk stakeholder of their moral responsibility; rather the question of responsibility is one of distribution: various risk stakeholders have their responsibility within their area of praxis. Citizens and experts are not the ones who are involved in risk discussions and have a stake in it; the mass media are risk stakeholders and participants in the discussion as well. What is their role in risk judgement, and what kind of perspective do they take on risk? In 'The media and genetically modified foods', Frewer et al, (2002) argue that the media often trigger public fears. This suggests again that fear or other emotions are out of place. The concept used is 'social amplification of risk'. But the moral question we want to ask is whether or not the fear of the public is justified. This requires that we assume that the emotions and imagination of the public reflect a genuine and serious risk judgement. The authors, however, use the term 'risk perception', which apparently increased during high levels of media reporting, whereas the perception of benefits decreased (Frewer et al, 2002, p708). I propose to understand what is going on here as a moral judgement process in which risk and benefits are weighted, a process in which the media play a key role, since they influence the way we imagine a technology and the risks and benefits associated with it. Risk studies, however, often hold a particular normative view about the role of the media. Just as the public is often seen as irrational or ignorant, the media are accused of a limited understanding of science (Smith, 2005, p1474) and of distorted representation of the risk (p1476). In their book *Risk, Media and Stigma* (2001), Flynn, Slovic and Kunreuther also (rightly) criticize the media: they are selective and focus on the dramatic, the rare and the 'story value' of the event, since they want to catch the imagination of the people. But to speak of distorted representation assumes that there is an 'objective' risk somewhere out there that can be correctly or incorrectly represented. Is that the case? Or is the process of imagination itself both a construction and judgement of risk? The latter view allows for a study of the judgement of various actors, which does not exclude questions of responsibility and blame, but rather asks these questions for all actors involved, including experts.

Slovic could respond to this criticism by making a distinction between real 'hazards' and construed 'risk', and given his view that the public should be involved in risk decision-making he would agree that such a construction should involve many views on risk. But this response also assumes a strong distinction between an 'objective' realm that includes hazards and a 'subjective' sphere of construction. I have shown that by speaking of distorted representation the view of Slovic and others does too little to take seriously risk judgement by non-expert stakeholders, including the media.

Given the important role of the media, it is good to be critical. It is true that journalists tell stories that are not very complicated and lack some level of abstraction (Smith, 2005). But simplification, concreteness and narrative are not necessarily morally undesirable. Surely experts should give critical feedback (Smith, 2005), but the model in which the public is always wrong and the expert is always right is inadequate. We know by now that hard facts do not exist, that there is a social-cultural side to science and technology. Science is one perspective on the world, which both enables and constrains what is thinkable (see also the notion of 'framing' in STS and risk studies literature). The moral implication for risk judgement, however, need not be the relativistic 'everyone his truth'. Rather, the lesson to learn is that if we want to avoid polarization between experts and public, if we want to bring closer the various distinct moral judgements of technological risks, perhaps even aim at a consensus, the burden of going imaginatively beyond one's perspective should not be put on the shoulders of the public alone. For risk experts in academia and elsewhere, this includes seeing the limitations of concepts such as risk perception and social amplification of risk, and reviewing the accusation of limited understanding and distorted representation. The perspective of the expert is also limited. We should find a way of talking about public and media that takes seriously all views of risk judgements while acknowledging and criticising the limitations to each particular perspective, including one's own.

Images

So far, I have only speculated about a role of imagination in risk judgement. But what does the literature on the psychological and social aspects of risk perception tell us about imagination? Although the literature has mainly focused on the emotional aspects of risk perception rather than imaginative aspects, there has been some attention for the role of imagery, in particular in connection with the role of emotions and the role of images in creating stigma (Slovic, 2000; Flynn et al, 2001). Let me take a closer look at how images figure in the literature on risk perception.

Focus on emotions and some attention for imagination. One route to say something more about the role of imagination is to compare it and link it with the role of emotions. In *The Perception of Risk*, Paul Slovic and others argue that risk perception is not simply analytical information processing but is dependent upon 'intuitive and experiential thinking, guided by emotional and affective processes' (Slovic, 2000, pxxxi). This does not mean that risk perception is derived from emotion only. Rather than seeing emotion as opposed to reason, Slovic refers to Damasio's work to make the point that 'research shows that affective and emotional processes interact with reason-based analysis in all normal thinking' (pxxxii), and there's no reason to think that this is different in the case of risk perception. In *Risk, Media and Stigma*, he also refers to Damasio's argument that human thought is made largely from images (Damasio, 1994; Flynn et al, 2001, p332). In *The Perception of Risk*, Slovic concludes that 'the public is not irrational' and that both scientists and publics are influenced by emotion and affect. Although (to my knowledge) little work has been done on showing how exactly reason and emotion work together in risk perception, this is an important result of this kind of study. It is attractive to apply these claims about the role of emotions to imagination as well. If imagination is a part of the intuitive and experiential thought processes Slovic refers to, it plays a role in how experts and publics view risk. But what does that mean? Imagination has many meanings and usages (I will return to this point below). In the risk literature the most frequently used term is 'image' or 'imagery'. For example, studies show that 'perceived risk is influenced (and sometimes biased) by the imaginability and memorability of the hazard' (Slovic, 2000, p119), or experts are accused of a lack of imagination (Slovic, 2000, p43). Let me take a critical look at what the literature says about the role of images in risk perception.

Focus on images but not in visual form. Slovic and others have conducted a series of studies about the perception of risk related to nuclear waste (e.g. Slovic et al, 1991a). The context of these studies was a political and public controversy about a plan to dispose high-level nuclear waste in Yucca Mountain, Nevada. Respondents were asked to indicate the first thoughts and images that come to mind when they think of an underground nuclear waste repository. People came up with images and these were categorized by the researchers. The results show that positive imagery was rare (only 1 per cent of the images). There were almost no associations related to possible benefits. In other words, a clear case of what is called 'stigma' in the literature. But I'm interested in the imaginative aspect in these studies. Rather than image categories such as 'dangerous/toxic' or 'destruction' as provided by Slovic and others, I am interested in the visual images themselves, in the non-verbal representations of nuclear waste. A glimpse of this can be seen in Slovic's discussion of why nuclear waste is stigmatized. He mentions the fact that people tend to associate nuclear activities with the bombings of Hiroshima and Nagasaki, nuclear accidents (e.g. before and after Chernobyl) and media stories of contamination (Slovic et al, 1991, p281). If he would elaborate this point by focusing on the images of Hiroshima and Nagasaki, of Chernobyl, etc., we could gain more insight in how the public views on nuclear waste emerge. An important source of such images is the media. This brings me to my next point.

Focus on stigma but no visual images. Research presented in the collection In *Risk, Media and Stigma* (Flynn et al, 2001) confirms the important role of images and media in stigmatization. Above I questioned the use of the term 'stigma': I argued that to talk of 'stigma' implies the moral statement that 'we' researchers or experts know what is acceptable risk and what is not, whereas the public can only have a distorted risk judgement. Furthermore, using the concept of stigma is also a moral judgement on the particular case. To talk about 'stigma' refers to misconception, misrepresentation of risk (Walker, 2001, p354), and is therefore a judgement by researchers that the public is wrong in the case at hand. But let us look at an account of how stigma is constructed to say more about the role of images. Again, research on nuclear stigma is instructive here. Slovic and others asked respondents to indicate the first thoughts or images that come to mind when they think of an underground nuclear-waste repository. The thoughts and images were then categorized and listed. The 'negative consequences' category included terms such as 'death', 'horror', 'desert', 'big business', etc. Positive imagery was rare: the general category labelled 'positive' included only 1 per cent of the images (Slovic et al, 1991). I infer that images are reasons for stigmatization, and the media play an important role in communicating these images to the public. It seems that the media often show only one part of the Janus face of technology: risks rather than benefits. However, in this account no concrete images are presented. The definition of image used is very broad, and seems to refer to verbal elements only. The same holds for other articles on nuclear images in the *Risk, Media and Stigma* collection. Therefore, I propose to look at the images themselves. Compare images of genetically modified foods published on the internet. Images of GM foods by Greenpeace convey a very different message from those of Monsanto, a well-known producer of GM foods. For example, Greenpeace shows their campaigners in white coats entering fields where GM crops are grown, suggesting danger of contamination, whereas Monsanto shows a happy farmer in his fields, supporting their claim that GM foods are a great help to farmers and to the survival of their business.[2] This comparison does not only show that images are not neutral with regard to risk judgement (a point to which I will return below), it also indicates that images play a significant role in relation to those judgements. Hence, risk research would benefit considerably by paying attention to visual images and by studying their precise role in discussions about technological risk.

Focus on stigma but attention for photographs: words and images. My proposal to look at the images as images is motivated by the recognition that visuality is part of our epistemological make-up. Let us look at an interesting description of the process of stigmatization in the literature. In 'From vision to catastrophe' (Ferreira et al, 2001), Ferreira and others explain the way from image to stigma. They argue that knowledge is not primarily organized in a language way but in a non-language way, for example in images. The power of images is that they can become independent of the facts, events or contexts in which they were formed. In this way, symbols, stigma and stereotypes are produced. The authors explain that 'a certain photograph will not "stand for" a certain risk event but becomes in itself the embodiment of the risk event. As a symbol, the photograph becomes autonomous of the context in which it was first formed' (Ferreira et al, 2001, p298), and it becomes 'portable' between events (ibid, p299). The media play a crucial role in this process. For example, a picture of a technological disaster is taken in the context of that particular event, but later on it embodies any similar disaster. Paying attention to such processes allows us to develop a better understanding of public risk judgements, and hence improve the discussion about risk. Note that the outcome of this need not be another devaluation of the public risk judgement by experts. The observation that photographs are taken out of their original context does not necessarily render the judgement of the public 'distorted'. For example, when realizing that images of Hiroshima or Chernobyl are used today to oppose nuclear energy production, experts may point out the differences between the risks involved in both cases, but they are also invited to consider seriously the arguments of the public based upon the similarities. In this way, the discussion benefits from explicitly considering the images, how experts and public use them, and the contexts in which they are used.

Constraints. Talking about imagination may suggest to some readers free day-dreaming or similar mental activities that seem to have no connection with the real world. But this is an inadequate understanding of imagination. Consider images again. Images (interpreted as stigma or otherwise) draw on existing ideas of how the world is constructed. Imagination does not stand alone. First, since research shows that risk perception depends on social, political and cultural factors such as worldviews (e.g. Jenkins-Smith, 2001), it is plausible that imagination is also connected with such factors. For example, if our worldview assumes a strong distinction between nature and culture, or between humanity and technology, this has implications for how we think of technology. Second, if imagination relies on memory and experience, it has individual and social-cultural aspects. For example, most of us do not have personal experience with Hiroshima, fortunately, but such experiences have become part of collective history and culture. Public imagination, then, is also embedded in cultural frameworks, including 'worldviews' and ways of giving meaning to our lives. I will elaborate this argument below when I discuss the limits and constraints of public imagination.

To conclude, in the literature there are at least three ways imagination receives attention: (1) in studies with a focus on emotions; (2) in studies that focus on images but treat these images in a verbal and categorizing way without attention for visual images; and (3) exceptionally in studies that focus on images as images, such as Ferreira's study of how photographs come to embody risk. The latter approach is promising, especially if we do not only look at the role of images but also at the way they are embedded in worldviews, ways we give meaning to our lives and other constraints related to the context of risk judgement.

Note that we do not need to view words and images as competitors; it is perfectly sensible to hold that both play, and must play, a role in public imaginative risk judgement.

So far I have talked about 'imagination' and 'images' that play a role in public risk 'judgement' as a 'moral' judgement. In the next sections I sketch a more systematic picture of what I mean by this. I go beyond the social-psychological literature on risk perception and seek inspiration in philosophical reflections on moral imagination. In this way, I want to support the main claim of my chapter, that we should take seriously the public imagination of risk as imaginative moral judgement.

PUBLIC MORAL IMAGINATION

Roles and levels of moral imagination

What do I mean by 'imaginative moral judgement'? Cognitive science and neuroscience show that non-language elements such as imagination and emotions play a much larger role in our thinking than is suggested by most philosophical approaches, including most accounts of moral reasoning. Inspired by such scientific work and by the pragmatist or Aristotelian philosophical tradition, some philosophers have argued that moral reasoning is for an important part if not fundamentally imaginative. They propose the concept of 'moral imagination'. What is meant by this term, what does imagination mean here and what does it do for moral judgement concerning technological risk?

Roles

Imagination can mean various things, and we can conceive of its role in moral judgement in various ways. For example, based on research in cognitive science and linguistics, Mark Johnson has argued for a key role of metaphors in our moral reasoning (Johnson, 1993) and Steven Fesmire has used Dewey's work to argue for the importance of moral imagination (Fesmire, 2003). Imagination helps us to explore the consequences of our actions and allows us to place ourselves in the shoes of the other. Martha Nussbaum has argued that reading literature aids our moral development (e.g. Nussbaum, 1990, 1995, 1997, 2001).

If we consider risk judgement as a moral judgement, we can apply these ideas to how we judge risk. Risk is usually defined in terms of probability and consequences. If we consider technological risk, it seems plausible that part of what we do when we judge risk is to imagine the consequences of a technological disaster. We can explore various scenarios, including worst-case scenarios. We can imagine ourselves being a victim of a disaster: we can not only imagine the event, but also that it happens to ourselves. In risk literature we find evidence that people often fail to imagine that it can happen to themselves, it always happens to others.[3] And we can place ourselves in the shoes of potential victims of the disaster and explore the consequences for them. We can read narratives of past disasters and learn from them. Furthermore, we can think of the role of metaphors and images related to risk (see below). Let me further develop some of these rather general suggestions in more detail below.

Levels

If we discuss imaginative risk judgement we must ask who *is* judging with imagination and who *should* be judging with imagination. We can distinguish at least three levels of imagination and judgement: individual, professional and public. I do not regard these levels as mutually exclusive, but I believe this categorization may clarify my use of the term 'public' in relation to imagination. By *individual*, I mean individual laypersons whose judgement is not expressed in the public sphere or not aggregated on a collective level. By *professional*, I mean experts whose task it is to judge risk. The term *public* is far more ambiguous. It can refer to the aggregation of individual risk judgements, for example in an opinion poll, or it can refer to any individual or collective judgement expressed in the public sphere. But even with these definitions the term 'public' remains vague, and potentially misleading. For example, the term 'public' suggests homogeneity, whereas there is no such thing as a single public risk judgement. An alternative could be to talk about the way *citizens* judge, and should judge, risk and its acceptability. This approach suggests ideas about active citizenship and involvement of citizens in decisions about technology. Judging risk, then, is a task for experts *and* citizens. I will return to this point below, but since the term 'public' is used in risk literature I used the term so far in this chapter and propose to continue to use the term 'public' for the time being while keeping in mind these reservations.

Note that policy-makers, politicians, pressure groups, etc. do not appear here as a separate category. Perhaps they fit all three categories: as individuals they may have their own judgement, but in their role as politicians, lobbyists, etc. they are 'public professionals' with regard to risk, since they are informed by expert judgement as well as by public judgement, and act and express their judgement in the public sphere.

Science, technology and public imagination

So far I have said what I mean by the notions imagination and public; let me now further elaborate the term public imagination and its relation to risk judgement. Let me start with a common, trivial claim: 'Science and technology catch the public imagination.' For example, people are amazed by TV documentaries on the workings of the human body, or are outraged when they watch the images of a technology disaster. These examples allow me to qualify and further discuss the claim about public imagination.

Selective imagination. First, public imagination is selective. *Some* scientific stories and *some* technologies and events catch public attention. For instance, there is far more attention for genetic engineering than for mechanical engineering, and ICT technology is far more in the spotlight of public attention than washing machine technology. In addition, slow long-term improvement of technology receives less public attention than what is defined as sudden breakthroughs or shown as spectacular catastrophes. This selectivity limits the area public risk judgements engage with.

Moral imagination. Second, images and stories are not neutral but are connected with how the risk associated with science and technology is morally valued. Public imagination is not morally neutral. I have argued above that *images* are not neutral with regard to risk judgement. They are also not morally neutral; for example, the contamination image from Greenpeace is part of an argument that it is morally wrong to produce and consume GM foods. Similarly, the argument about the benefits to the farmer by Monsanto, supported by the image, is a moral argument: it is not only permitted to produce GM foods; production is a duty derived from the duty to help farmers to survive. Now consider the role of *metaphor* in how the public views science and technology. Scientific research may be presented as an exciting exploration narrative, where risk has the connotation of adventure and thrill. In this metaphorical frame, gaining scientific knowledge is analogous to the discovery and indeed colonization of new, unknown territories – a metaphorical frame that fits unsurprisingly well with the historical geopolitical context in which modern science expanded. In such a world, risk is excitement, and it is part of the game. To pick up on the latter metaphor: the heartbeats of the hunter who is getting closer to its prey are comparable to those of the scientist who feels that she is on to something; they are the symptoms of risk as excitement. A positive value is attached to risk. A very different imaginative valuing goes on when technological risk is presented in the story and imagery of a catastrophic event. In the public imagination, the risks associated with nuclear technology may take on the shape of the nightmare stories and images of Hiroshima or Chernobyl. The imagination transforms nuclear power plants into ticking bombs, waiting only for a small error to explode in the face of humanity. In the frame of such apocalyptic narratives, technological risk takes on the shape and face of death and destruction. Risk becomes fear. The pleasant experience of watching a science thriller is replaced by a history of horror documented by images that leave very little to discover. Obviously, the moral value attached to this technology is negative, which gives the risk judgement a strong moral significance.

Mediated imagination. Third, the selective imagination and moral (e)valuation and judgement of science and technology by the public does not usually take place as a result of a direct confrontation with science and technology, but is mediated. Images and stories of science and technology and the risks associated with them reach most of us via the mass media (TV, radio, internet). Ethically speaking, this raises questions about the responsibility of the media for how the public imagines risk and, therefore, how society deals with risk.

We can conclude that public imagination, and therefore public risk judgement, is selective, morally engaged and mediated.

Public imagination: limits and constraints

Limits. Although the examples above suggest that public imagination plays an important role in risk judgements, there are limits to public imagination and what it can do for risk judgement.

First, imagination as a capacity has limits of its own. The public cannot imagine all possible scenarios and events, and neither can experts or politicians. In terms of moral responsibility, this implies that although no one is responsible for the limits of one's imagination (for example, it may be that some accidents were 'unimaginable' by both experts and public), one *is* responsible for (not) *using* one's imagination. Therefore, it is not enough to demand that professionals, experts and scientists should take into account public imagination, or that expert and non-expert citizens should engage in inter-subjective dialogue and imaginative reasoning, being aware of, and making explicit, each other's images of (this or that particular) technology. The morally significant issue remains how imagination is used. My normative claim now is that risk stakeholders should use their imagination at least in such a way that polarization of the debate is avoided; that is, in a way that enables serious consideration of, and engagement with, each other's positions. This is a formal requirement only, it stands apart from potential substantive claims about how we should judge technological risk. It is derived from my starting position in the beginning of this chapter: the aim is to avoid polarization, and above I argued that this is a reasonable aim in a democratic society. It is also a minimum requirement: in whatever other way risk stakeholders use their imagination, and whatever other arguments can be made in relation to their use of imagination and their judgement of risk, this is a necessary condition to avoid polarization.

Second, imagination is only one element in the process of risk judgements. It would be mistaken to see imagination as taking over the mind, suppressing rationality, emotion and other elements such as principles that play a role in reasoning and moral reasoning. Such an image of mental hijacking misrepresents what goes on. Rather, I propose to view moral reasoning in terms of a complex interplay between various elements and capacities. I will return to this point below.

Constraints. To some people imagination may suggest to be some kind of free play, and therefore to be epistemologically unreliable and unsuitable to use in moral judgement. However, the relation between imagination and knowledge is more complex than this 'imagination as free play' view assumes. Imagination is not the same as fantasy. It is not to be compared with building 'castles in the air', a metaphor which suggests that imagination does not have a base in reality. Rather, imagination is based on existing knowledge, experience, memory, etc. I have argued this in the first part of this chapter: images are embedded in political, social and cultural frameworks. This is also the case with metaphors. To pick up an example from the second part of this chapter: if we imagine science as a discovery adventure, we may base our imagination on our memory of images that were presented to us in the media. Furthermore, if an expert imagines various scenarios related to a technological system, her imagination will be based on her knowledge of, and experience with, the system at hand. In this way, imagination can help us to fill a knowledge gap in case of uncertainty about a risk. Thus, this is another sense in which imagination is limited, but in an enabling way: these are constraints on imagination that give it a higher epistemological status than 'mere' fantasy and allow it to play its role in moral judgements, including moral judgements of the acceptability of risk.

CONCLUSION

Mediated public risk perception as imaginative moral judgement. I started with the observation that public discussions about technological risk tend to be polarized between experts and public. The former accuse the latter of a biased, emotional and stigmatizing view. I have shown that this polarization is enforced by psychological and social research on public risk perception. While there is much to learn from such literature, its conceptual framework has unfair normative implications which enforce polarization and paternalism. I argued that the public views should be taken seriously as moral judgements that crucially depend on the use of imagination. Inspired by contemporary philosophical accounts of moral imagination, I explored what this means. I conclude that risk stakeholders should use their imagination in a way that enables serious consideration of, and engagement with, each other's position in the debate. This is a way to avoid polarization and unwarranted paternalism, which I assume to be a minimum requirement for discussions about technological risk in a democratic society. More philosophical reflection and empirical research is needed to further elaborate the role of imagination in public and expert risk judgements. If in both judgements imagination plays an important role, we need further philosophical reflection as well as more empirical research on how this imaginative process works, and a more careful use of the concepts used to guide such research. Studies of the role of imagination should pay special attention to the limitations of imagination and the role of other elements in moral judgement, and to the constraints that enable our use of imagination. For example, we could study which and how images of technology are communicated to us by the media, how they are embedded in our worldviews and our cultural environment, and what the implication is for public risk judgements. How do these images facilitate and constraint our perspective on technology? And how can we transcend our perspective? The same questions can and should be asked for experts. Let's compare images used by public and scientists, and study how both risk stakeholders can transcend their own perspective and understand that of others.

Public and citizens. In this chapter I have used the term 'public'. But if the 'public' perspective is indeed as important as any other, we may want to consider replacing the term 'public' by 'citizens', which may be a better expression of the moral significance of the role each of us has and should have in judging the risks we face in a technological world and culture. What is needed in practice, it seems, is an explicit and public discussion about and (re)negotiation of a new distribution of moral and epistemological power and responsibility. What is the share citizens should have in the resources for, and praxis of, risk judgement? What do they know and what should they know, and – correspondingly – what is and should be their responsibility and that of other risk stakeholders? This requires an openness for mutual criticism and a public space where different perspectives on risk can meet. If our aim is not merely more information (e.g. informing the parties of each other's images, views) but also to bring different perspectives closer to one another, we must think about ways all risk stakeholders, citizens and experts should be stimulated to use their imagination to transcend their own perspective. We should not underestimate the difficulties of such a process, given the constraining influence of education and training (e.g. the professional training of experts) on the way we view the world. Philosophers and risk researchers could develop and offer tools for reflection on visual images as well as on words and numbers. Generally, an ambitious transformation of risk culture as suggested here also requires thinking about creating (new) mediators and interfaces between perspectives. This involves a philosophical discussion about the problem regarding the status of the view of the mediator and its normative significance and force. Who or what is suitable as a mediator, as 'inter-face'? In this chapter I have argued for considering different perspectives on risk. But philosophers also argue from a perspective. Or do they manage to take a kind of meta-perspective? What does this mean? Generally, is the view of the mediator itself 'a view from nowhere', or 'just' a perspective? Should it also be open to questioning, reflection, discussion? On what basis can someone or something claim its role as mediator? How to cope with the danger of manipulation? Finally, there is no good reason to view the current media landscape and organization of the public sphere as the most suitable tools and spaces to understand, mediate, communicate and manage technological risk. Efforts to connect the study of the ethical aspects of risk with discussions in political theory and media studies should be encouraged.

Risk and meaning. I have argued that imagination is not free standing, instead it is anchored in cultural and other frameworks. Culture includes morality or ethics in a descriptive sense. Public imagination is intrinsically linked with how and what we value. Our imaginative perspectives on risk are deeply embedded in our worldviews and the way we give meaning to our lives. Once we realize this, we can take a reflective stance. To think about how we judge the moral acceptability of risks, then, involves reflection on how we view the world, on the world we create with our actions, and on the ideals we hold. And that should not be a task for experts alone.[4]

References

Damasio, A. (1994) *Descartes' Error: Emotion, Reason, and the Human Brain,* Putnam, New York

Ferreira, C., Boholm, Å. and Löfstedt, R. (2001) 'From vision to catastrophe: a risk event in search of images', in J. Flynn, P. Slovic and H. Kunreuther (eds) *Risk, Media and Stigma: Understanding Public Challenges to Modern Science and Technology*, Earthscan, London

Fesmire, S. (2003) *John Dewey and Moral Imagination*, Indiana University Press, Bloomington/Indianapolis

Flynn, J., Slovic, P. and Kunreuther, H. (eds) (2001) *Risk, Media and Stigma: Understanding Public Challenges to Modern Science and Technology*, Earthscan, London

Frewer, L. J., Miles, S. and March, R. (2002) 'The media and genetically modified foods: evidence in support of social amplification of risk', *Risk Analysis*, vol 22, issue 4, pp701–711

Jenkins-Smith, H. C. (2001) 'Modeling stigma: an empirical analysis of nuclear waste images of Nevada modeling stigma', in J. Flynn, P. Slovic and H. Kunreuther (eds) *Risk, Media and Stigma: Understanding Public Challenges to Modern Science and Technology*, Earthscan, London

Johnson, M. (1993) *Moral Imagination: Implications of Cognitive Science for Ethics*, The University of Chicago Press, Chicago/London

Kunreuther, H. (2002) 'Risk analysis and risk management in an uncertain world', *Risk Analysis*, vol 22, no 4, pp655–664

Mouffe, C. (2000) *The Democratic Paradox*, Verso, London

Nussbaum, M. C. (1990) *Love's Knowledge: Essays on Philosophy and Literature,* Oxford University Press, New York

Nussbaum, M. C. (1995) *Poetic Justice: The Literary Imagination and Public Life*, Beacon Press, Boston, MA

Nussbaum, M. C. (1997) *Cultivating Humanity: A Classical Defense of Reform in Liberal Education*, Harvard University Press, Cambridge, MA

Nussbaum, M. C. (2001) *Upheavals of Thought: The Intelligence of Emotions*, Cambridge University Press, New York

Peters, E., Burraston, B. and Mertz, C. K. (2004) 'An emotion-based model of risk perception and stigma susceptibility: cognitive appraisals of emotion, affective reactivity, worldviews, and risk perceptions in the generation of technological stigma', *Risk Analysis*, vol 24, no 5, pp1349–1367

Smith, D. and McCloskey, J. (1998) 'Risk communication and the social amplification of public sector risk', *Public Money & Management*, vol 18, no 4, pp42–43

Smith, J. (2005) 'Dangerous news: media decision making about climate change risk', *Risk Analysis*, vol 25, no 6, pp1476–1477

Slovic, P. (2000) *The Perception of Risk,* Earthscan, London

Slovic, P., Flynn, J. and Layman, M. (1991) 'Perceived risk, trust, and the politics of nuclear waste', *Science*, vol 254, pp1603–1607. Reprinted in Slovic (2000)

Slovic, P., Layman, M., Kraus, N., Flynn, J., Chalmers, J. and Gesell, G. (1991) 'Perceived risk, stigma, and potential economic impacts of a high-level nuclear waste repository in Nevada', *Risk Analysis*, vol 11, pp683–696. Reprinted in Flynn et al

Slovic, P., Finucane, M. L., Peters, E. and MacGregor, D. G. (2004) 'Risk as analysis and risk as feelings: some thoughts about affect, reason, risk, and rationality', *Risk Analysis*, vol 24, no 2, pp311-322 (reprinted in this volume)

Walker, V. (2001) 'Defining and identifying "stigma"', in J. Flynn, P. Slovic and H.

Kunreuther (eds) *Risk, Media and Stigma: Understanding Public Challenges to Modern Science and Technology*, Earthscan, London

Werhane, P. H. (1998) 'Moral imagination and the search for ethical decision-making in management', *Business Ethics Quarterly*, special issue no 1, pp75–98

NOTES

1 This assumption is not shared by all theorists and is therefore not trivial. Some have argued for an 'agonistic' view, which questions consensus as the primary aim of democratic political processes. For example, Mouffe has proposed agonistic democratic politics, putting more emphasis on space for strife and disagreement than on consensus (e.g. Mouffe, 2000).

2 Compare the image on: www.greenpeace.org.uk/gn/what-we-are-doing with that on: www.monsanto.com/monsanto/layout/products/seeds_genomics/cornfarmer.asp.

3 Kunreuther gives the example of wearing seat-belts: people who refuse(d) to do that do not deny that accidents happen, but believe that 'I won't have an accident' (Kunreuther, 2002, p659).

4 I would like to thank the organizers of the 'Ethical Aspects of Risk' conference for what has turned out to be a very stimulating and fruitful event, and I am grateful to those who commented on my presentation, for example Johan Melse (Netherlands Environmental Assessment Agency). I would also like to thank Lotte Asveld and Sabine Roeser for their useful editorial comments.

14 Trust and Criteria for Proof of Risk: The Case of Mobile Phone Technology in the Netherlands

Lotte Asveld

Introduction

Participation of the public in debates on the acceptability of risk has been recognized in both academic literature and public institutions as an important contribution to the resolution of such debates (Slovic, 1999; Wynne, 2002; Bijker, 2004). This importance has been recognized for both ethical (Shrader-Frechette, 1991, 2002; Sclove, 1995; Van Asselt et al, 2001) and for instrumental reasons (Kluver et al, 2000; Van Asselt et al, 2001). However, the most appropriate methodology for such participation remains a contentious issue, the answer to which may depend on the specific characteristics of the issue at hand (Poortinga and Pidgeon, 2004).

This chapter offers an analysis of a specific case in the Netherlands: the controversy over the alleged risks attached to mobile digital communication, also known as Global System for Mobile communication (GSM), second generation mobile phone technology and Universal Mobile Telecommunication System (UMTS), third generation mobile phone technology. The controversy exists mainly between authorities and operators on the one hand and lay-audiences on the other hand, although the disagreement extends to the scientific community as well.

It is argued that a specific means of participation is required to stimulate a resolution that can be considered adequate for both ethical and instrumental reasons. The assumption of this analysis is that the lack of trust by the opponents in the authorities and the operators of mobile digital communication is the main obstacle to a satisfactory resolution. This lack of trust is difficult to solve simply by taking precautionary measures or producing additional research as it centres on the issue of criteria for proof of risk. An open and transparent process of establishing these criteria for proof of risks will help foster trust.

In what follows, first a short account of the debate is given, followed by an overview of the reasons for the lack of trust, after which the possibilities for restoring trust are discussed.

The data for this chapter were collected partly via interviews with different actors and partly via literature-studies (including internet-resources).

THE DEBATE

Since the erection of the GSM network in 1993, digital mobile communication has become an integral part of modern society. Since then it has sparked some controversies. In the Netherlands, concerned individuals protested against the placement of antennas and took to the streets in a national demonstration,[1] several cities restricted the amount and positions of antennas within their city borders (Van Dijk, 2005), and questions were asked in the Dutch parliament with regard to the alleged risks attached to mobile phone technology.

Aside from concerns about the effect of this technology on the social fabric of society, many have voiced worries about the effects on human health. The opponents fear that the Ultra High Frequency Electro Magnetic Radiation (UHF EMR) emanating from the antennas as well as from the telephones themselves interferes with basic biological processes. However, regulatory authorities in general state that scientific research so far has shown no indication of any adverse effects and therefore protective measures are unnecessary.

The advent of UMTS as a successor of the familiar GSM has fuelled the debate once again since this new technology might bring about new adverse health effects. The main question in this chapter is: how can the debate about this technology be resolved?

The parties involved

This section contains an overview of the parties involved and their general point of view. The division between proponents and opponents is very rough, as the different positions are more nuanced, especially for the proponents camp, than is reflected in this crude division. However, these are the actors that oppose each other and as such it can be an informative division, and that is why it is included here.

Proponents

Government: the Dutch government auctioned the UMTS (3rd Generation) frequencies and is ultimately responsible for the establishment of the safety norms. Balancing out the different interests and sentiments that are relevant in this case, the government takes the position that there are no reasons to take precautionary measures, as the available scientific knowledge at this point does not provide convincing evidence about risks. The government does recognize a duty to take concerns of citizens seriously, however valid the reasons for these concerns may be.[2] The government is willing to invest a limited amount of money in research.

Health Council (HC): This is the main advisory body to the Dutch government. The HC determines the safety norms in practice. The point of view of the Health Council largely coincides with that of the government with regard to the need for precautionary measures, although the Health Council advised to invest more in research than the government actually does.[3]

Operators: These are the companies that operate mobile phone technology. These companies are usually willing to invest in research concerning possible risks attached to mobile phone technology. They do have a strong interest in a smooth enrolment of the third generation mobile phone technology. They do not see reasons to take any precautionary measures as the evidence for risks is minimal.[4]

Opponents

The camp of the opponents consists of a wide variety of concerned individuals, both laypeople and experts,[5] and more or less organized groups. This chapter focuses on both an individual and a group.

Mr ing. Teule: he wrote several popular books (e.g. Teule, 2002) about the possible adverse health effects of mobile phone technology and the injustices, as he sees it, related to imposing these risks on the general population. He is a concerned, independent individual with a background in engineering.

Stop UMTS website: this website (www.stopumts.nl) was founded by Mr E. Goes and is maintained by several people. This website reports about developments concerning the enrolment of third generation mobile phone technology. It contains links to scientific sources that are providing evidence or indications of the adverse health effects of mobile phone technology. The reliability of these sources is difficult to establish and probably varying.

TRUST

If the government, the operators and the Health Council were trusted in their ability to adequately manage risk, the debate would not be as fierce as is currently the case. The opponents claim that there are sufficient reasons to suppose a causal relationship between the reported adverse health effects and mobile phone technology exists.

According to Baier, 'trusting is rational in the absence of any reason to suspect in the trusted strong and operative motives which conflict with the demands of trustworthiness as the truster sees them' (1986, p254). Likewise, Hardwig states that it is reasonable for laypeople to trust experts except if there are reasons to suspect a conflict of interest or a yielding to social pressure from peers, or any other influence that distorts the production of reliable knowledge (1985, p342).

The main reason for the lack of trust between the parties is a disagreement over (1) what the relevant scientific material consists of, and (2) what the relevant scientific material pertains to, or put differently what actions are justified on basis of the available scientific material. This disagreement leads the opponents to suppose that the regulatory authorities are guided by unjustified scientific views at the best, and unwarranted conflict of interests at worst. Vice versa, the regulatory authorities and the operators suspect that the opponents do not really understand what electromagnetic radiation is and additionally that they do not comprehend what good science is all about.

It is in the interest of the government, the operators and the HC to maintain a trusting relationship with citizens and costumers. Without this trust, their functioning would become increasingly problematic: for the government, because it requires a mandate from the people to legitimately govern the people; for the HC, because it needs to function as a neutral arbitrator; and for the operators, because they need costumers to trust their products in order to survive as a company.

Moreover, ethically seen, institutions such as the government and the Health Council, but also industry, ought to be reasonably trustworthy. It is their duty to adequately manage risks. In this case, however, it appears that the opponents have some good reasons for distrust.

The disagreement over scientific material

The major issue in the debate on health effects concerns the alleged effects of electromagnetic radiation under the conditions of the mobile digital communication network. Electro Magnetic (EM) radiation at the extreme high end of the spectrum, that is, with high frequencies, is known for its property of breaking down molecular bonds. This kind of radiation is known as ionizing radiation. It emanates for instance from radioactive material. Other kinds of radiation are thought to be relatively harmless.

Heating tissue is considered the main health effect arising from Ultra High Frequency Electromagnetic Radiation. These EM fields include those that are usually produced by man-made utensils including mobile phones and antennas. Mobile phones are the most probable source for tissue heating. Characteristics of mobile phones should legally[6] fall within a specific technical scope which ensures the SAR value (Specific Absorption Rate) does not exceed the norm of 2 w/kg. Most mobile phones have a SAR between 0.3 w/kg and 1.6 w/kg.[7] Adverse health effects due to mobile phones within this range are expected to be minimal. These expectations fall within the scope of established, mainstream science.

The International Commission on Non-Ionising Radiation Protection (ICNIRP) has established norms which indicate at which strengths electromagnetic radiation emanating from antennas can still be considered safe (ICNIRP, 1998). These norms are based on the available scientific literature. The exposure levels advised by the ICNIRP are 41 V/m for 900 MHz, 58 V/m for 1800 MHz and 61 V/m for 2050 MHz. In the Netherlands the limits are set at 49.13 V/m for 900 MHz, 80.92 V/m for 1800 MHz and 87 V/m for 2050 MHz (UMTS).

Opponents of GSM and UMTS antennas state that these norms are misguided. They contend that worrisome effects besides heating occur as well. Radiation emanating from mobile phones and antennas is said to cause various adverse physical effects ranging from headaches, panic attacks and sleeplessness to cancer. These symptoms are thought to be effects of the interaction of the human body, which is an electromagnetic organism, and radiation from antennas and the like. Other artefacts producing electromagnetic radiation are in this view suspect as sources of physically damaging emission as well.

The Dutch Health Council, however, considers the likelihood of such effects occurring due to electromagnetic radiation at the frequencies used for mobile communication to be highly unlikely. This opinion is based, the HC states, on the available scientific evidence. The occurrence of additional effects in relation with Ultra High Frequency electromagnetic fields is not scientifically proven, or not sufficiently shown to be plausible. Reliable scientific sources for the HC include peer-reviewed publications in established journals which report research that adheres to the values of good science such as reproducibility and compatibility with other scientifically established knowledge.[8]

Nonetheless, several people report adverse health effects such as dizziness, sleeplessness, headaches and depression due to living next to mobile phone antennas. Moreover, there are several scientific reports, some of them published in peer-reviewed journals, and most of them apparently in accordance with standards for good scientific research, that seem to indicate that adverse health effects do indeed occur due to exposure to UHF EMR.[9] Additionally, some scientists working in standard research institutes or with standard scientific training warn against the possible adverse health effects of mobile phone technology and the distorting influence of commercial interests on the outcome of scientific studies.[10]

The availability of information that contradicts the position of the Health Council, which appears to stem from the same scientific community the HC draws from itself, creates distrust amongst the opponents of mobile phone technology towards regulatory authorities. The opponents feel that for some reason, some scientific material is unduly excluded from scrutiny by the HC.

Authorities claim, however, that a substantial amount of research has been done which might have been able to scientifically describe the various complaints that have been put forward, but that nothing emerged from that. The slight amount of scientific sources that seems to contain evidence to the contrary is either marginal and lacking in quality, or misinterpreted (by the opponents). Therefore, a causal relationship between UHF EMR emanating from mobile phone technology is highly unlikely. As E. Van Rongen, secretary of the standing committee on Radiation Protection of the Health Council, says:

> There are numerous people who have complaints they ascribe for instance to living in the vicinity of GSM-antennas, or to the use of mobile phones.
>
> The question is whether those complaints are indeed invoked through exhibition to those electromagnetic fields or whether other causes are conceivable. It is certain that there is a strong psycho-somatic component. … The point is that those complaints those people have could be caused by many different things.[11]

Opponents agree that it is hard to establish beyond doubt that there is a causal relationship between the radiation and reported adverse health effects; however, they do think that, in addition to excluding certain scientific material, the HC is taking an unwarranted position with regard to the uncertainties that still surround the effects of mobile phone technology on the human body. As Mr Teule states:

> And concerning all those other effects about which people complain, except heating of tissue, the Health Council says: sorry, we do not understand this, we don't know how this works, biologically seen, and therefore we can't establish a norm. This is a bit peculiar as an argument.[12]

Here the disagreement over criteria for proof of risk manifests itself. First, both parties differ over what counts as a reliable scientific source. The unclarity in assessing this reliability does not help this difference. Some scientific articles that seem to live up to at least some of the criteria of the HC are not taken seriously or not seriously enough according to the opponents.

Second, given the difficulty in properly assessing the risks involved, the parties differ in their estimation of the existence of a causal relationship between UHF EMR and adverse health effects. The HC sets higher standards for considering the likelihood of risks substantial enough to take measures than do the opponents. The HC requires more indications than are currently available from good scientific sources, whereas for the opponents, each indication is enough to stir their worries once more. This divergence in assessment of adequate criteria for proof of risk leads the opponents to suppose that the HC, the government and the operators are not to be trusted with giving the interests of the general population due concern.

Suspicion of unwarranted motives

The claim made here is not that the proponents, who also happen to be the authorities, are indeed influenced by unwarranted interests, or succumb to peer pressure, but that from the perspective of the opponents there are reasons to suspect that they are. The financial interests of the government and industry (the Dutch government is a large shareholder of a big telecom operator and has auctioned the third generation mobile phone frequencies for considerable amounts of money) and the close links between the Health Council and the government, combined with lack of clarity about the criteria used for assessing scientific knowledge, do provide reasons to doubt the motives of the authorities and the operators (cf Baier, 1986).

The motives the authorities and the operators have may be nothing more extraordinary than an interest in smooth technology development and a healthy economical system. However, there could be situations in which such motives conflict with concerns over public health, the opponents fear.

The opponents state that the view of the proponents may be distorted by their interest in the smooth enrolment of mobile phone technology. This distortion may lead them to be very selective in their assessment of scientific sources. According to the opponents, there is scientifically sound material available, and has been for years, that supports their view on the risks. This material also lives up to criteria for sound science as they are set by the Health Council, the opponents claim. So, the complaint goes, even if science is available that undermines the established conventional view on effects of UHF EMR, the relevant institutions do not acknowledge this.

To support their complaints about the bias of the authorities and the operators, the opponents draw parallels with the case of asbestos where scientific evidence for adverse health effects was weak and later even deliberately suppressed. In drawing this parallel they feel supported by large insurance companies who do not want to risk covering liabilities for technologies that may turn out to have damaging effects.[13]

Moreover, their bias in favour of technology development makes the authorities and the operators reluctant to extensively search for possible risks, the opponents think. This reluctance is reflected, according to the opponents, in the sober set-up of most of the relevant research. The opponents say that the criteria for proper research into the existence of risks attached to mobile phone technology were never met. Therefore, the evidence about the risks is inconclusive. On the *Stop UMTS* site, criteria for acceptable research are spelled out. Such requirements include among others: focus on long-term effects; a control group which has been exempt from radiation for a considerable period of time; and a focus on the effects on subtle biological mechanisms.

Until now, a lot of the research into the effects of antennas did not live up to these criteria. Many studies about the effects of antennas focus on short-term effects. One study which focused on the long-term health effects in the neighbourhood of antennas found an increased risk for cancer, but this study was dismissed by German authorities as failing in methodology (Federal Office of Radiation Protection, Germany, 2005). Long-term effects have been studied for mobile phones: the results vary. One study has found detrimental effects to the eyeball, some have found evidence of an increased chance of brain cancer, but this could not be confirmed by other studies (Health Council, 2003). Although the results from long-term effects provide little indication that harm does indeed occur due to UHF EMR, there are good reasons to pursue this line of research, as the HC also acknowledges (Health Council, 2003). The recommendation of the HC for more long-term studies has not been picked up by the government at this point.

Considering the demand for a control group: it is very hard to find such a control group, because the amount of electro-magnetic radiation in our environment has increased substantially over the past few decades, subjecting most people in society to this radiation. The opponents state that a proper control group should have been isolated from this radiation for some period of time to function adequately as a control group. Related to this point is that research on subtle biological mechanisms takes both a 'clean' control group as well as a long-term study which so far has not been conducted in a manner that satisfies the criteria of the Health Council for good research. Considering the scientific material produced in this area so far, it appears to me that there is little proof for the existence of risk. However, the possibility cannot be excluded that other types of research will produce evidence of harm.

Scientific conservatism

The objection of the opponents about a supposed technology bias among the proponents of UMTS technology may possibly be relevant in assessing the motives of the government and the operators. The Health Council however does not have any direct economical or societal objectives. Its views appear to be in accordance with the criteria for good research as they are proposed by the opponents.

But the opponents have a second objection to the adequacy of the policies of the HC and the government and the operators, which boils down to an accusation of unwarranted scientific conservatism. This accusation implies that the Health Council and with it many established scientists do not dare to look outside the confines of mainstream knowledge. Nothing is found that sustains the complaints of people claiming to suffer from adverse health effects, because scientists are looking in the wrong direction. This leads them both to pursue the wrong questions and to interpret the findings in the wrong vein. Scientists are thus, according to the opponents, unwilling to look beyond the conventional boundaries of their disciplines, and as such they may be understood as succumbing to peer pressure (cf Hardwig, 1985).

Mr Teule states for instance that given the complexities surrounding the interaction of electromagnetic radiation and biological processes, determining the likelihood of effects depends to a large extent on the kind of models used to describe the working of the human body. Teule thinks that most of the models employed by conventional science are flawed because they are too mechanistic and do not sufficiently take into account the delicate electromagnetic structures and balances that make up the human body. Many scientists do therefore not sufficiently recognize the risks involved in mobile digital communication. Indications that other models may be more apt at describing the workings of the human body are largely ignored, he states (Teule, 2003).

The moral conflict underlying this accusation of conservatism is related to an avoidance of type 1 errors as opposed to avoiding type 2 errors. Type 1 errors refer to acceptance of a false positive; type 2 errors refer to avoidance of a false negative. Avoiding type 1 errors is part of conducting good science. Before something is added to the existing body of scientific knowledge, it has to be well established. We want to be careful not to be too hasty in accepting something as true, hence the conservatism that is common among scientists and that is reflected in the attitude of the Health Council.

However, when it comes to risk-assessment, there are convincing ethical reasons to focus on the avoidance of type 2 errors (Cranor, 1990; Wandall, 2004). When dealing with risks, the less desirable outcome is not taking something to be true which isn't, but to disregard a potential danger. The opponents of mobile phone technology, although they do not themselves formulate it as such, put their finger on the clash between sound science and morally desirable risk assessment. In their perspective, all indications and explanations for the existence of risks ought to be taken seriously, not just those that provide conclusive evidence.

RESTORING TRUST

There are several strategies that have been proposed and indeed undertaken in the course of this debate to resolve the dispute. So far none of them appears to have sorted any tangible results. One option is to do additional research, a second option is to resort to precautionary measures and a third option is participation.

Additional research

As said before, trust is a main problem in this debate. Part of this lack of trust is a suspicion of a distorted assessment of the risks due to a technology bias of the authorities and the operators.

In order to show that it is taking the possibility of risks attached to UHF EMR seriously, the Dutch government is willing to invest in research, as a representative of the Dutch Department of Housing, Spatial Planning and the Environment, Directorate Chemicals says.[14]

Plans exist to start up a research fund shared between the government and industry. The research would have to be conducted by independent researchers so there would be no suspicion of an unwarranted conflict of interests. As such, government-funded research might foster trust with the opponents. They might feel that some of their main concerns at least are addressed if the government (and industry) shows it is willing to invest in research. This might indicate to the opponents that the motives of the proponents are trustworthy.

However, one may doubt whether additional research will be sufficient in restoring trust. The main fissure in this debate centres on what are criteria for proof of risk. The government and industry may feel they have provided sufficient evidence for the relative safety of GSM and UMTS technology; this evidence will not satisfy the opposition as long as the dispute about the criteria for proof of risk remains. Additional research just by itself will not help to resolve the debate (cf Wynne, 1980).

Precautionary measures

Precautionary measures may in some cases help to foster trust (Gee and Stirling, 2003) as it shows that the government holds public health paramount. According to the demands of the opponents, precautionary measures would in this case amount to a lowering of the safety norms, which would probably imply that the existing network would have to undergo radical changes, such as the installation of different or more antennas.

However, if the scientific evidence for precautionary measures is flimsy this strategy may have the opposite effect (Wiedemann and Schutz, 2005). This is the position of the Dutch authorities and the operators in this case. The Dutch authorities state that as long as there is no reliable scientific indication of physical harm associated with the use of mobile telephones or living close to antennas, precautionary measures such as lowering the exposure limits are unnecessary and would not help to foster trust. It might be perceived as a move motivated by pressure from the opponents, rather than by considered scientific evidence.

A representative of the Dutch Department of Housing, Spatial Planning and the Environment, Directorate Chemicals says:

> It turns out in practice, that field strengths are 20 times as low as the ICNIRP numbers. We could adjust the norms. One could wonder however, whether that does indeed foster trust. One needs a basis for such decisions. The norms we have now are based on scientific information. We have got a story to back up the norm, so to say. But one can also, as has happened in Italy or in Greece, take a different norm, but one has to motivate that … One has to have an explanation. Just saying something will not foster trust.[15]

A representative of a large Dutch operator of UMTS technology likewise doesn't see any need for precautionary measures. First, a lack of reasonable scientific indications of physical harm makes it very hard to take precautionary measures:

> If that would be proved, that that thing would be unsafe, then we would have a very big problem. Then we should instantly modify or adapt the whole network. But at least we would know what to do. Now we don't know at all what we could do. Is diminishing the field strength something? The reason? Is that it that causes people's complaints? Nobody has got that proof.[16]

The representative of a large operator states that his company would be willing to alter the antennas as long as it is based on solid evidence so that it makes sense to make alterations. There are other considerations relevant as well while thinking about the antennas, as he points out. If antennas were to be placed higher, they would have a negative aesthetic effect. If the strength of the signal were diminished, the reception for individual telephones would deteriorate.

According to the opponents of this technology, the uncertainty should not be a reason not to take precaution, the costs of which, as they see it, are small. The authorities and the operators, however, feel there is a substantive lack of certainty about adverse effects on health. Moreover, the costs would be large (diminished coverage, halt of technological development). Both these considerations lead them to dismiss precautionary measures, at least those that are proposed by the opponents.

Introducing precautionary measures at this stage will not provide a resolution to the debate as it is not acceptable to the proponents and would, as they point out, possibly unduly harm other societal interests and would even deteriorate the trust relationship with the general population if the reasons for taking them are flimsy.

In light of the evidence the government and the operators rely on at this point, the reasons for taking precautionary measures might indeed be flimsy. The possibility remains, however, that if other criteria for proof are applied the evidence for the existence of risks becomes more solid. Should this be the case, the reasons for taking precautionary measures become less flimsy. The government and the operators could then alter their stance on the desirability of precautionary measures without necessarily losing trust from the rest of the population, as their change of position is induced by a new assessment of the scientific evidence or of new scientific evidence itself.

Of course, it may be questioned, if it emerged from applying new criteria for proof of risks that risks do indeed exist, whether the government was doing a good job before. However, new risks will emerge always and the government will probably gain more trustworthiness by acknowledging mistakes in the past than to continue on a path that has proven to be false. These reflections do not assume that the risks do indeed exist, but that the possibility remains that new scientific evidence will emerge or that existing evidence assessed differently may lead to new policies.

Participation

A third strategy for increasing trust is to let people participate in the risk assessment that determines the acceptability of a given technology (Slovic, 1999, 2003), in this case mobile phone technology.

Trust requires a belief from one party that the other party will sufficiently accommodate their interests, either through a perception that the trusted party has a good will towards the trusting party (Baier, 1986) or that the system of checks and balances is sufficiently in place to prevent abuse of power (O'Neill, 2002).

Participation by laypeople in decisions on risk provides an indication to laypeople that both these conditions are met. Participation gives people an opportunity at least to articulate their concerns and to know that they are heard by the authorities. Participation can additionally function as an element of a system of checks and balances.[17]

Participation is furthermore ethically important since it can function as a form of consent (Van Asselt et al, 2001). The imposition of risks on individuals without their consent is ethically unacceptable since this is an infringement on their personal autonomy. Consent should be regarded in a broad manner in the context of technological risks as traditional forms of individual consent are often impractical in the matters that concern larger groups of people. Consent can be given through different forms of participation, such as citizens' juries and public debates. As a matter of fact, consent procedures already exist. However, they apparently are not sufficient to foster (warranted) trust. What are their shortcomings?

The consent procedures as they currently take place in the Netherlands involve a written notification of the planned installation of an antenna, some information on possible health effects, as well as a request to return a form on which one's preference regarding the placement of the antenna can be revealed.

The consent procedures as they are now reflect a typical downstream inclusion of laypeople (Wynne, 2002; Bijker, 2004). At the end of the line, people can assent or dissent to a development which is already fulfilled. At this stage a technology has already gained a certain momentum that may make it look like an inevitable fact of life which leaves the individual little options for influence or even the incentive to try and influence that technology, whereas such options should possibly be available and indeed are theoretically available. The consent procedures as they are designed cannot be considered adequate because they shy away from the more fundamental issues. It can furthermore be questioned whether the assent that is given through these procedures can be considered actual consent. The premises on which participation is shaped are in this case not shared by the different parties involved. It is as such not true participation.

These premises include for instance the way the question is framed. Individuals can consent or assent to the placement of a UMTS antenna on their roof. They cannot give their opinion on the safety norms. They cannot demand additional research. The premises include that the safety norms and the research as it is conducted at present are beyond discussion.

For the government, to convince the opponents that it does indeed properly protect the interests of its citizens, the true concerns of those citizens need to be addressed. If the government is willing to alter the premises or at least put them up for discussion, it may be able to regain the trust of all citizens in its capacities to adequately handle new technologies and the alleged attached risks.

In doing this, the government needs not compromise the interests of those citizens that fully embrace mobile phone technology. Participation on the basis of different premises from those that the government applies now may eventually support a smooth development of this technology as it can resolve the disputes that spur resistance at the present time.

Recommendations for participation

In this debate, the criteria for proof of risk are the main problem. They are dominant in determining the acceptability of UMTS and GSM technology. Participation of laypeople in the establishment of criteria for proof of risk is desirable as a means of actual participation.

On the *Stop UMTS* site some requirements have been put forward concerning the set-up of new research that are viewed as paramount by opponents of UMTS and GSM technology. Setting up a research which specifically takes into account the above-mentioned requirements seems an appealing option to restore trust and do justice to the concerns of the opponents. Such research obviously needs to take into account the criteria set by the Health Council for sound science. An agreement should be reached beforehand about how the results will be interpreted. As such it is an instance of participatory risk assessment that may help to bring the different parties together.

If concerned individuals can contribute to what the requirements for good research are, they will be more compelled to accept the outcome as it suits their requirements for sound scientific evidence. It would show them that the Health Council does not unduly exclude certain questions from the onset and is willing to consider alternative hypotheses.

The inclusion of opponents in the process of risk assessment may also diminish their worries about the motives of the proponents: the suspicion that government and industry do not really care about the problems of individuals. This suspicion is brought about by the perception that the proponents are being sloppy with the criteria for proof so as to be able to adjust them to their own particular interests. If they are willing to adjust the criteria for proof to the interests of the opponents, they are exempt of the above-mentioned suspicion. Moreover, it would give the authorities a ground on which to base decisions with regard to precautionary measures.

Both the government and industry may feel they are succumbing to the irrational (in their eyes) fears of a small group of frantic people, but if that is so, there is nothing they have to fear from such research. The money to be spent on such research is negligible compared with the potential loss of profit if the breach of trust continues to exist.

Discussion

The issue of the acceptability of the technology cannot be isolated from the disputes about the identification and estimation of risks. These aspects of risk assessment can be conceived as criteria for proof of risk. Once the dispute over these criteria is solved, it will be easier to arrive at an agreement about the policies that should be employed with regard to this technology. Such disputes may be addressed through participatory strategies.

It may not always be clear in which cases participation by lay-audiences in risk assessment is desirable. In some instances, increased participation may lead to a decrease in trust as the authority of the expert is undermined (O'Neill, 2002). Participation may expose the fallibility of experts to the public, which harms trust (Giddens, 1990).

The government may feel that accommodating the views of the opponents may lead to a loss of trust in the eyes of other groups in society. If the criteria for proof of risk are adjusted, then the old criteria for proof of risk may be questioned and likewise the accompanying policies. Moreover, having a minority dictate the spending of communal money is not a warranted policy option. The government needs to take into account plural interests in society. It cannot let its agenda be dominated by particular concerns.

In many cases these considerations are valid. However in this case there are several reasons why the criteria for proof of risk of the opponents ought to be accommodated, for both ethical and instrumental reasons.

First, the experts and authorities involved had already lost their reliability in the eyes of the opponents. There is little fear of breaking trust down even further as it is already extremely low. If the government does not act on the demands of the opponents, the resistance to this technology may spread even further. The trust of other parties need not be eroded if the government listens to the demands of the opponents. Listening and taking the demands seriously does not equal immediate action in the form of precautionary measures. It is also in the interests of other groups in society that the government invests in additional research according to additional criteria.

Second, the demands of the opponents are not that radical that they are incompatible with the views of the government and the operators. The old criteria for proof of risk can be maintained. The criteria for proof of risk as proposed by the opponents are mainly additions.

Third, where they are not, but touch on a fundamental disagreement about what is good risk-assessment (i.e. the choice between avoiding type 1 or type 2 errors), they appear to be desirable. Research about such risks is not just for the benefit of a small, limited group of people. There is much reason in the demands of the opponents. Research conducted as they envision it may be to the benefit of the whole of society.

Conclusion

The debate on the acceptability of the risks associated with UMTS technology in the Netherlands revolves around the issues of the reliability of scientific evidence and the legitimacy of the resulting safety norms. The government-initiated participation procedures fail to foster trust because they do not offer true options for participation. The opponents do appear to have a reasonable claim about the necessity of additional research. This makes the lack of options for influence of the decision procedure even more problematic as the government appears to exclude reasonable perspectives on the alleged risks from the decision procedures, thereby harming the interest of society at large.

REFERENCES

Baier, A. (1986) 'Trust and anti-trust', *Ethics,* vol 96, pp231–260

Bijker, W. E. (2004) 'Sustainable policy? A public debate about nature conservation in the Netherlands', *History and Technology*, vol 20, no 4, pp371–391

Cranor, C. F. (1990) 'Some moral issues in risk assessment', *Ethics,* vol 101, pp123–143

Gee, D. and Stirling, A. (2003) 'Late lessons from early warnings: improving science and governance under uncertainty and ignorance', in J. Tickner (ed.) *Precaution, Environmental Science and Preventive Public Policy*, Island Press, Washington, DC

Giddens, A. (1990) *The Consequences of Modernity*, Stanford University Press, Stanford

Hardell, L., Carlberg, M. and Mild, K. H. (2006) 'Case-control study of the association between the use of cellular and cordless telephones and malignant brain tumors diagnosed during 2000–2003', *Environmental Research*, vol 100, pp232–241

Hardwig, J. (1985) 'Epistemic dependence', *The Journal of Philosophy*, vol 82, no 7, pp335–349

Health Council of the Netherlands (2002) 'Mobile telephones; an evaluation of health effects', *Publication no 2002/01E*, Health Council of the Netherlands, The Hague

Health Council of the Netherlands (2003) 'Health effects of exposure to radiofrequency electromagnetic fields: recommendations for research', *Publication no 2003/03*, Health Council of the Netherlands, The Hague

ICNIRP (1998) 'Guidelines for limiting exposure to time-varying electric, magnetic, and electromagnetic fields (up to 300 GHz)', *Health Physics*, vol 74, no 4, pp494–522

Igumed (2002) *Freiburger Appell*, Bad Säckingen, 9 October 2002

Klüver, L. et al (2000) 'Europta: European Participatory Technology Assessment', The Danish Board of Technology, Copenhagen

Neitzke, H.-P. (2001) 'ECOLOG-study by order of the German T-Mobile refers to health risks' (press-release)

O'Neill, O. (2002) *Autonomy and Trust in Bioethics*, Cambridge University Press, Cambridge

Pacini, S. et al (2002) 'Exposure to global system for mobile communication (GSM) cellular phone radiofrequency alters gene expression, proliferation, and morphology of human skin fibroblasts', *Oncology Research*, vol 13, no 1, pp19–24

Poortinga, W. and Pidgeon, N. F. (2004) 'Trust, the assymetry principle, and the role of prior beliefs', *Risk Analysis,* vol 24, no 6, pp1475–1486

Sclove, R. E. (1995) *Democracy and Technology*, The Guilford Press, New York

Shrader-Frechette, K. (1991) *Risk and Rationality: Philosophical Foundations for Populist Reforms*, University of California Press, Berkeley

Slovic, P. (1999) 'Trust, emotion, sex, politics and science: surveying the risk-assessment battlefield', *Risk Analysis*, vol 19, no 4, pp689–701

Slovic, P. (2003) 'Going beyond the red book: Sociopolitics of risk', *Human and Ecological Risk Assessment*, vol 9, no 5, pp1–10

Teule, G. (2002) *GSM-straling en de grondwettelijke onaantastbaarheid van het lichaam,* Sigma, Tilburg

Teule, G. (2003) *GSM, straling en de grondwettelijke onaantastbaarheid van ons lichaam,* Sigma, Tilburg

Van Asselt, M., Mellors, J., Rijkens-Klomp, N., Greeuw, S. C. H., Molendijk, K. G. P., Beers, P. J. and Notten, P. (2001) 'Building blocks for participation in integrated assessment: a review of participatory methods', *ICIS working paper I01-E003 I*, ICIS, Maastricht

Van Dijk, B. (2005) 'Spanning loopt op bij uitrol van umts', *Financieel Dagblad*, 16 April

Wandall, B. (2004) 'Values in science and risk assessment', *Toxicology Letters*, vol 152, pp265–272

Wiedemann, P. M. and Schutz, H. (2005) 'The precautionary principle and risk perception: experimental studies in the EMF area', *Environmental Health Perspectives*, vol 113, no 4, pp402–405

Wynne, B. (1980) 'Technology, risk and participation: on the social treatment of uncertainty', in J. Conrad (ed.) *Society, Technology and Risk Assessment*, Academic Press, London

Wynne, B. (2002), 'Risk and environment as legitimatory discourses of technology: Reflexivity inside out?', *Current Sociology*, vol 50, pp459–477

Zwamborn, A. P. M., Vossen, S. H. J., van Leersum, B. J. A., Ouwens, M. A. and Makel, W. N. (2003) 'Effects of global communication system radio-frequency fields on well being and cognitive functions of human subjects with and without subjective complaints', *TNO Reports* (FEL03C148), pp1–89

Notes

1 On 16 April 2005, a national demonstration was organized in Amsterdam.
2 A government official explained this in an interview, 8 April 2005.
3 Information obtained from an interview with Dr van Rongen, 11 November 2004.
4 Information obtained from an interview with a representative of a large operator of UMTS technology.
5 Among the opponents are people with a higher education in related technological fields and with positions at universities in relevant fields.
6 EU-directive 1999/519/EG.
7 www.nrg-nl.com/public/straling_mobi_nl/straling_mobi.html, accessed 2 March 2005.
8 As stated by Dr van Rongen, 11 November 2004, and Health Council (2002).
9 See among others Hardell et al (2006), www.verum-foundation.de/www2004/html/pdf/euprojekte01/REFLEX_ProgressSummary_231104.pdf (accessed 23 August 2005), Neitzke (2001), Pacini et al (2002), Zwamborn et al (2003).
10 See amongst others www.powerwatch.org.uk/news/20041222_reflex.asp (accessed 23 August 2005), Igumed (2001).
11 Interview, 11 November 2004.
12 Interview, 17 November 2004.
13 Financieel Dagblad, 16 April 2005.
14 Interview, 8 April 2005.
15 Interview, 8 April 2005.
16 Interview, 9 December 2005.
17 If participation were to be the only check on the decision procedures of policy-makers and experts, it might be counterproductive as it would render laypeople the ultimate authority which would significantly diminish the authority of experts and policy-makers. The input of laypeople can however add valuable insight to the information on which the official decision-makers base themselves.

Part V

Instruments for Democratization

Once it has been established that the public should be granted a stronger voice in risk management, this calls for instruments by which risk management should be made more democratic. Gero Kellerman discusses the value but also the limits of national ethics councils. Anke van Gorp and Armin Grunwald discuss so-called regulative frameworks that constrain the work of engineers, which especially in the case of fundamentally new forms of design should be supplemented by the moral responsibilities of the engineers themselves.

15 Risk Management through National Ethics Councils?

Gero Kellermann

Introduction

The national ethics councils are interdisciplinarily or transdisciplinarily composed commissions for political counselling on the exposure to risks in biomedical fields. They make concrete several issues discussed by philosophy. Ethics councils try to use ethical analysis for solving political and social problems. Therefore, when studying the functioning of national ethics councils, the philosophical problem of the possibility of ethical expertise must be considered. One further problem, that will not be considered here, is to subsume the councils under the popular but still poorly defined terms of inter-, trans- and multidisciplinarity. This chapter concentrates on the analysis of the outcome of the work of ethics councils. By considering typical forms of their statements I want to investigate the problem of the possibility of ethical expertise. Is there such a thing as ethical expertise, can the work of the council be described by the term 'ethical expertise', is this kind of expertise desirable for the estimation of risks? First I want to give a short overview of the origins, typical tasks and composition of national ethics councils. This descriptive part of the chapter also presents an analysis of typical forms of the design of their outcomes of deliberations. The main focus in the normative part of the chapter is on the philosophical question whether there actually is such a thing as ethical expertise, and whether ethics as an academic discipline can be translated into documents of political counselling. In this context the question arises whether the recommendations of committees like the national ethics councils can be regarded as ethical expertise, and whether they are adequate instruments to evaluate the risks of technologies. Special emphasis is placed on the fact that ethics councils provide a specific kind of ethical knowledge by incorporating knowledge from different spheres, that is, from different scientific disciplines as well as practical experience. It will be analysed whether this can also be applied to other modern technological developments that raise ethical questions, in particular concerning the new information and communication technologies.

The dynamic progress of science, in particular of the life sciences, and the expansion of their applications has brought out new institutions. The national ethics councils are examples of such new institutions. They are dealing with the handling of possible risks caused by the involved scientific disciplines. There are approximately 30 of these councils operating at national level all over the world. Examples are the French 'National Consultative Bioethics Committee' (founded in 1983), the American 'President's Council on Bioethics' (2001) and the 'National Ethics Council of Germany' (2001). The establishment of national ethics councils shows the growing awareness of ethical implications of science and technology. These ethical implications are caused by an increasing awareness of risks and the collision of different moral values. By establishing ethics councils, it seems that ethics has found a new institutional basis for a kind of counselling that crosses academic borders. These institutions estimate possible consequences of scientific or technical innovations, but do so in a particular manner. This new way of counselling consists of an explicit extensive consideration of ethical values and the social consequences of scientific progress for the individual and for society (cf Fuchs, 2005; Endres and Kellermann, 2007). In doing so, ethics councils try to bring together different scientific disciplines and professions, which constitutes the core of their special handling of risks. The handling of scientific risks is not left to the scientific system itself anymore, since its forms of self-control only have a limited capability to consider moral consequences of research. Similarly politics is faced with complex questions and it cannot be expected that political decision-makers have the personal competence to solve all the bioethical problems (Kuhlmann, 2002, p26). At the same time the counselling of conventional expert boards is regarded as insufficient. Also the public often is not able to come to soundly based judgements because the people are faced with complicated scientific matters, the detailed understanding of which requires a large temporal as well as intellectual investment.

This development is connected with the progress in the life sciences. In particular this field of knowledge has enforced the setting-up of national ethics councils. The main reason for this is the fact that even the basics of the life sciences can affect moral beliefs in a fundamental way (Bayertz, 1991, p287). Besides, biotechnology refers to 'basic bodily processes, that our timely existence and our identity depend on' (Kemp, 2000, p40). It is obvious that the public reacts extremely sensitively if questions of stem-cell research, pre-implantation diagnostics or genetic manipulation come into play. The same applies for classical matters of medical ethics, such as euthanasia and abortion. In contrast, other fields of modern science do not lead to a comparable public ethical discussion. Particularly innovations in communication and computer science have far-reaching consequences for daily life, for example the huge possibilities of data transfer via mobile phones or PCs, and give rise to questions of data protection, justice, etc. But in this domain there is not such a high level of demand for political solutions or ethics as there is in the life sciences (although the UN has recently initiated an international debate by organizing the 'World Summit on the Information Society' that was held in 2003 in Geneva and in 2005 in Tunis).

One topic where the ethical problematic situation shows itself very clearly is the question of normative limits of research. There are several parties coming to different conclusions (cf Nida-Rümelin, 2002). In accordance with a strict approach, which underlines the autonomy of science, science should be kept free from any limits that are implemented from the outside. Instead science should confine itself to mechanisms of self-limitation. This approach underlines the basic law of freedom of research. But in view of the scientific developments, above all in the life sciences, there are many doubts whether science itself can consider the consequences of its results in a sufficient way. Therefore, science should accept limits that are set up outside the science system (cf Nida-Rümelin, 2002, p325 ff). But it is still difficult to fix these limits. In the meantime it has become generally accepted that norms concerning rapid technological development cannot be implemented without time-lag (cf Sommermann, 2003, p77). In this context it must be clarified who should be responsible for drafting these limits. At this point, above all, politics acting through law and decrees must be taken into account, but also society acting through social values. National ethics councils constitute a new interface between science, politics and society for solving the normative problems of modern life sciences.

STRUCTURE OF THE COUNCILS

Origins

In many countries national ethics councils have been constituted since the 1980s in connection with the accelerated process of biomedical research. Their institutional precursors are the ethics committees that have been set up since the 1970s at many faculties of medicine, medical associations and hospitals. While these latter committees are initially focused on individual cases, national ethics councils reflect on more fundamental issues. Their main task is to generate orientation guidelines at the interface of science, politics and society. Typical results are expert reports or recommendations. They often deal with drafts of legislative bodies; they rarely develop drafts on their own. In a survey,[1] some councils stated that the political bodies followed up to 75 per cent of their proposals, for others their rate of acceptance of their recommendations was at least 50 per cent. This shows that these councils often have an influential political role.

Nearly all councils were constituted through government initiatives, partly in connection with the parliament. Exceptions are the Danish Ethics Council which was initiated solely by parliament, and the British Nuffield Council on Bioethics which was constituted within a private foundation. Further agents promoting the set-up of national ethics councils are, for example, nationwide acting academies of sciences or councils for research and professional organizations. When politicians initiate or ask for such councils this means for them an extraordinary approach because they do not take recourse to conventional counselling, for example by ad-hoc committees or parliamentary commissions. Ethics councils do not fit into earlier schemes of political counselling, and therefore must be considered as institutions sui generis for a special kind of reflection on the moral implications of science. Politicians have set their hope on these councils because they are seen to be more capable to respond quickly to new scientific developments than, for example, parliamentary commissions, because the councils are standing committees and have the opportunity to choose their issues themselves (Endres and Kellermann, 2007).

Tasks

The comparison of the statutes of the ethics councils shows distinct tasks that appear in nearly all cases. The main task is regularly described as ethical counselling and evaluation of new developments in biology, medicine or the life sciences. Partly it is presupposed that issues of natural sciences with legal or social implications should be considered. The broadest thematic range can be found in Norway where, according to the so called 'Norwegian Model', there is one council for ethics of medical research, one for ethics of science and technology, and a third one for ethics of research in the humanities and social sciences. The political counselling of national ethics committees is aimed at different institutions. In the USA and Austria the councils primarily advise the government. The German Ethics Council and the Swiss National Advisory Commission on Biomedical Ethics can make recommendations on request both by the government and by parliament. The Danish Council and the Human Genetics Commission first of all advise the ministers of health. In Australia and the Netherlands the councils primarily concentrate on decisions of administrative bodies, for example the national health councils (Endres and Kellermann, 2007; cf Fuchs, 2005).

However, political counselling is not the only task of ethics councils. It is regularly underlined in the statutes that the councils shall address, integrate and inform the public. Often it is a statutory duty to stimulate public debate in ethical questions of life sciences. For instance, the German Ethics Council, according to its statutes, organizes conferences on ethical questions. Public education is also an explicit task of the President's Council in the USA. In contrast to conventional expert boards (including ethical committees at hospitals, churches or pressure groups) one can speak of 'socially oriented' ethics councils (Taupitz, 2003, p818). There are further tasks of the councils, such as cooperation with other ethics councils and committees or initiatives for international regulation. But the main purpose remains the same: the transformation of scientific knowledge into the political and societal dimension under consideration of its moral relevance (Endres and Kellermann, 2007).

Composition

The councils try to fulfil their role by a mixed composition. They normally consist of between 10 and 25 members, who are supposed to represent particular knowledge that is relevant for the tasks of the councils. Typically, they consist of representatives of several sciences, above all medical doctors, lawyers, philosophers, theologians and social scientists (interdisciplinary aspect). Apart from that, they integrate knowledge from outside the science system, such as representatives of trade unions, churches and politics (transdisciplinary aspect). Normally, it is not easy to assign the members of the councils to certain scientific disciplines or other spheres: politicians are often declared as laypersons, and many members have a double qualification, for example in medicine and ethics. Although the councils are called 'ethics councils' there are only few or even no philosophers represented. In some cases there are more, mainly moral philosophers, but their maximum rate of participation normally does not exceed 25 per cent. Nearly all councils also call in external experts (see above-mentioned survey in Endres and Kellermann, 2007).

STATEMENTS OF ETHICS COUNCILS ON HUMAN CLONING

Normally, as a form of their political advice, the councils present expert opinions or recommendations that sometimes answer single questions, but they mainly serve as guidelines for political decisions. Approximately one-third of the councils evaluate bills, only a quarter see it as a task to develop drafts itself. Due to the number of national ethics councils there is a huge amount of experts' recommendations, statements, reports, popular scientific publications and conference articles. Concerning the main task, political counselling, the most important results of the councils are the statements and recommendations for legislative bodies, even if in the Anglo-American countries big parts of their activities refer to single questions and projects. An international comparison shows that it is not constitutive for the councils to reach a consensus. Depending on their preferences the councils have developed procedures to present different opinions or a common position (for more details, see Endres and Kellermann, 2007).

In the preceding discussion the concrete way in which ethics councils make their decisions has played only a minor role. In order to illustrate how they come to their recommendations, I have chosen two examples that I think are paradigmatic. The case study refers to the expert opinions of the German National Ethics Council and the American President's Council on the question of cloning, strictly speaking their recommendations on cloning-to-produce-children and cloning for biomedical research. These councils have presented quite extensive statements that clarify the way of counselling of the ethics councils.

German National Ethics Council

The German National Ethics Council was established in 2001 and has up to 25 members appointed by the federal chancellor. In the future, according to a current bill, one half of the council will be appointed by the Federal Government, the second half by the parliament (Nationaler Ethikrat-Infobrief, 2006). The members represent the scientific, medical, theological, philosophical, social, legal and economic spheres (cf Nationaler Ethikrat Homepage). In comparison with other councils, the German ethics council has tried to integrate as many social actors as possible. Both of the main churches in Germany (Catholic and Protestant) are represented, as well as trade unions and patient groups for certain diseases and for disabled people.

In 2004, the German Ethics Council submitted its expert opinion on 'Cloning' (Nationaler Ethikrat, 2004). In this case it had decided to produce this report not because of a government's query but due to disagreements among several countries and scientists (p9 ff), above all in the field of cloning for biomedical research. The statement consists of three parts. In the first part (p12 ff) the report presents relevant definitions and scientific fundamentals. What is cloning, which techniques do exist, what is the success rate of cloning of mammals, what is the state of the art concerning cloning? In regard to cloning for biomedical research, different techniques are presented, divergent opinions of scientists and open questions. The second part (p26 ff) goes into the details of the legal framework. Relevant legal documents at national, European and international level are pointed out (above all the European Council Convention on Human Rights and Biomedicine and UNESCO's Universal Declaration on the Human Genome). Finally, the legal part of the report analyses the legal situation in other countries.

On the basis of the descriptive part, the normative part of the report presents one statement concerning cloning-to-produce-children, and three statements dealing with cloning for biomedical research. Each of these statements is argued for in detail, and mainly ethical and constitutional aspects are taken into account. Concerning cloning-to-produce-children (p37 ff) the council votes unanimously for a ban, independent of the technical state of the art. There are 11 arguments founding this decision that express different preferences in the argumentation of the council members. The statement of the council on cloning for biomedical research is more differentiated and consists of three different positions. The first position (p49 ff) is in favour of the perpetuation of the ban, irrespective of the technical possibilities. That position is grounded in an argumentation that considers constitutional laws like respect for human dignity and the right to live, and ethical consideration, above all the concept of 'a preventive ethic of responsibility' (p57). The second position (p60 ff) is in favour of a limited admission of cloning for biomedical purposes. It states that it cannot be assumed that there is a person or a subject of human dignity at the early stage of the embryo. To argue for this position the members of this group point out that in the ethical and constitutional debate the theories of human dignity afford no justification for regarding early embryonic life (i.e. at the stage prior to nidation and individuation) as a subject of the guarantee of human dignity. This position emphasizes the freedom of research. A permission of relevant research could help to reduce diseases and to avoid harm, and that is a constitutional duty of the government. The admission of biomedical cloning should be limited by strong regulation and control of research (cf p73 ff).The third position (p80 ff) proclaims a ban on cloning for biomedical research for the time being. But this position underlines that there might be ethically unproblematic possibilities in the future (in this context they cite the studies of Hwang Woo Suk that were accepted at this time but later had been uncovered as fraudulent). The members of this group point out, among other things, that the therapeutic prospects are still uncertain, and according experiments are still inefficient (p80 f). Therefore research should be supported and encouraged that could gain stem cells without embryos. After consideration of all three positions, the council passes the unanimous recommendation not to permit cloning for biomedical research at the current time (p103).

President's Council on Bioethics

The American ethics council also passed a statement on this issue. The President's Council on Bioethics was founded in 2001 and consists of 18 members who are appointed by the president. The members are lawyers, natural scientists, medical doctors, philosophers, theologians and social scientists. The council presented a 300-page statement on cloning in 2002 (President's Council, 2002).

The composition of the statement is similar to the German example: at first relevant definitions and scientific fundamentals are presented, followed by the normative assessment and policy recommendations. But unlike the German council, it tries to show all conceivable arguments pro and contra to cloning. For example, the council presents the argument that 'human cloning would allow couples with fertility-problems to have biologically related children' (p79) or to replicate a dead child. After that the council presents the contra-arguments (p87 ff) that are more or less the same as in the German case and passes the unanimous recommendation to prohibit cloning-to-produce-children. In regard of biomedical cloning there are two positions based on the pro/contra-pattern. The council discusses for example duties with respect to the embryo and to society. The majority is in favour of a four-year moratorium, the minority is eager to see the research proceed, and recommends permitting cloning for biomedical research to go forward, but under strict federal regulation. One difference to the German case is that also a broad range of policy options is considered. This part entails reflections on 'science and society', comparative law and, above all, various legislative options (p173 ff).

These are of course not the only ethics councils devoting their attention to this issue. The Danish Council of Ethics for example produced a statement of a similar pattern in 2001 (Danish Council of Ethics, 2001), but not as extensive as the two examples. The purpose was not to enter the ethical discussion regarding cloning, but to make clear the basic method of the ethics councils of producing expert statements on ethical problems. The statements normally consist of a descriptive and a normative part. The descriptive part comprises scientific and medical definitions and disambiguations, and sometimes the legal situation entailing comparative law. Concerning the normative part, the councils assess ethical problems of technologies and show certain values and goods that could be affected and discuss possible consequences for society. The length of each part can differ. The presentation of policy options for example can be short and distinct, sometimes several possible options are explained in more detail. There is also the possibility to pass more than one opinion. These opinions are sometimes presented one after another, each with an extensive reasoning, or there can be something like a collection of all pro/contra-arguments in advance, before passing distinct opinions. And there is a third established way of presenting an output which I have not considered here, namely to produce a consensus. The aim of all three kinds of presentation is to pass a recommendation that is normally addressed to political decision-makers.

Expertise of ethics councils

Is this kind of interdisciplinary counselling really valuable in evaluating and handling the risks of biomedical research? The national ethics councils ground their legitimacy in being expert boards. But their expertise differs from conventional expertise: on the one hand because of their mixed, that is, interdisciplinary and transdisciplinary composition, on the other hand because they are dealing with moral issues. There is one basic problem, namely whether there is something like ethical or moral expertise and whether such expertise would be desirable.

The nature of expertise

Ordinarily, expertise means the possession of special knowledge or capability of a person or a board. These knowledge and skills gain authority, because they are in some way exclusive, which means that only a few people possess them, and it is not easy to obtain them (Caplan, 1992, p29 f). Normally, the result is a statement that entails a judgement on the quality of something, for example a wine, or that recommends acting in a certain way, for example councils of economic experts do that. There is no doubt that expertise is possible on the value of a diamond or the best economic decisions, but what about evaluating moral problems? The first objection is that there is no exclusive knowledge on morals, because everybody has some moral competence.

Nevertheless, ethics is more and more demanded as expertise. This can be seen not only in context with the national ethics councils. Ethical experts are consulted by legislative bodies, sometimes they are even asked to give advice in lawsuits (cf Caplan, 1992, p19 f; Nussbaum, 2002, p502 ff) and they inform public health authorities, medical associations and international boards (cf Birnbacher, 1999, p267). After all there seems to exist a higher qualified moral evaluation and an exclusive knowledge that can be achieved by special training. Analogically lots of persons are able to assess the quality of a wine, but their judgements are regarded less than the opinion of a famous wine journalist. There have been many efforts to establish applied ethics as an expertise for practical questions. That can be seen by the existence of scholarly centres, research institutes and specialized journals (cf Engelhardt, 2002, p62). It seems that there is a debatable idea 'that there are methods of evaluative thought that can be applied to particular practical issues so as to produce specific answers' (Noble, 1982, p7).

In order to show why ethical expertise is possible their advocates normally refer to the role of the professional ethicist. As we have seen before, philosophers are regularly represented in the ethics councils but only at a low percentage. But, with some complements, the relevant arguments (as well as the objections against ethical counselling) are transferable to the councils as a whole.

Basic concept of ethical expertise

The discussion about ethical expertise in a pluralistic society was enforced by a short article of Peter Singer at the beginning of the 1970s (Singer, 1972). He tried, against all scepticism of other moral philosophers, to promote the adequacy of ethical expertise. As an advocate of the existence of such expertise he argued that, because there are no or only a few generally binding rules in a pluralistic society, everyone has to find out on his own what to do if there is a moral problem. Therefore he needs information, and he should try to gain all the background information about the problem. After that he might assess the problem and bring it together with the moral views he has. This procedure is not easy. But for this, the moral philosopher would be the appropriate expert, because he is familiar with moral concepts and with moral arguments, has enough time to gather information, and may reasonably reach a more soundly based conclusion (p116 f). Like experts of other domains the moral philosopher would have a higher-than-average competence. Due to his education he or she would have more knowledge about moral concepts and the logic of a moral argument. The result would be a higher degree of clarity that could contribute to error-free arguments (p117). Thus, Singer underlines the technical qualities of the philosopher that can be used for solving practical issues.

Martha Nussbaum (2002) also pleads for philosophical expertise, among other reasons because the expert philosopher can contribute to the public democratic culture by the survey of all necessary considerations, asking about interentailments and their consequences, and appreciation of different views (Nussbaum, 2002, p510 f). She points out further aspects, for example the Socratic 'gadfly-function' that could help philosophical laypersons to clear up the unordered beliefs (p508). She also underlines that such an expertise could help to avoid 'self-serving rationalization', which means that people often just try to legitimate their own interests by ethical deliberation (p511). Furthermore, according to Nussbaum, the philosopher could help to bring about a moral progress, but only if the ethics expert would consider the views of other experts and 'ordinary people'. That is a task that laypersons rarely perform. It should be a part of ethical expertise to systematize the views of non-philosophers and to bring in the knowledge of specialized ethical debate (p509).

Limits of the basic concept of ethical expertise

Some proponents of ethical expertise underline its potential but suggest some modifications. These supporters of ethical expertise often explicitly assume a certain methodology of the ethicist. Some note that an ethical expert should confine himself to assist other people with finding the morally relevant aspects and weighing them up in a comprehensible way (Birnbacher, 1999, p271). According to Friele, the ethicist, like other experts, could refer to a foundation of knowledge such as technical literature, moral conventions, principles and dilemmas, the check of arguments by philosophical analysis, but she points out that in ethics commissions, the ethicist should argue solely negatively. That means that an ethicist should try to avoid contradictions, inconsistencies and incoherences (Friele, 2003, p314 f).

Kymlicka (1993) regards the technical role of a philosopher as too narrow. Instead, he is in favour of a certain catalogue that could represent a common basis for decisions of ethics expert boards. This catalogue entails certain principles, among others autonomy, responsibility, respect of life and equality (p11 f).

He points out that the members of expert ethics boards should not be obliged to be experts in ethical theory but rather they should be able to apply these basic values 'in a serious and sensitive way' (p26). Similarly, Caplan (1992), who has been a member of several ethics boards, points out that expertise in ethics would presuppose that the expert has a broad range of knowledge and experience on the norms and values of the relevant life sphere, such as hospitals, courts or political boards. Otherwise, ethical expertise would be an 'engineering model' grounding on axioms, laws or principles that can be applied to various content, whereas ethical expertise implies content-specific 'analogical reasoning' (p35 ff). Therefore, knowing moral traditions and theories is not enough for moral expertise. The ability to identify and recognize moral problems is not limited to persons with training in ethics (p38).

Martha Nussbaum refuses a kind of ethical expertise that deals with what John Rawls calls 'constitutional essentials' and 'matters of basic justice'. Regarding constitutional questions, ethics experts would be positioned in authority over fellow citizens and that would threaten political democracy (Nussbaum, 2002, pp507, 516 f). In view of different notions of good life in a pluralistic society, Nussbaum points out that it would be against democratic virtues to upgrade oneself on the moral ladder. When performing in public as an ethical expert, one should lay out the arguments carefully and in sufficient detail, and make clear that the judgements might be shared among many different comprehensive conceptions. In addition, one should always avoid a kind of hierarchy that would hurt 'the equality of respect democratic citizens owe one another in a context of debate about fundamental ethical and political questions' (p518).

Objections against ethical expertise

There are several objections against the idea of ethical expertise that also emerge in the discussion on national ethics councils. The first objection against such expertise is that everyone has ethical knowledge. That is because everybody can take some time to produce coherent ethical reflection. The evaluation of actions as good or bad can already be found in many daily life situations. Moral evaluation is an integral part of education and people normally have their own moral preferences. Besides, a religious person will probably not change her opinion on adultery or abolition when there is an 'expertise' that contradicts his view. The question of good or bad life belongs to the private liberties and it would be an undue influence to patronize people by ethical authorities. An ethical expert would just be someone who unwarrantedly puts himself in the foreground. In addition, to be an expert in ethics would be against the philosopher's duty to be modest if questions of legislation are involved. The philosopher should confine himself regarding such questions in order not to appear too pretentious, for example not to appear as a philosopher-king who wants to act as a guardian for the public (for a more detailed view on these arguments, see Singer, 1972; Caplan, 1992; Birnbacher, 1999; Nussbaum, 2002).

One further objection is that politics and philosophy have different goals. For politics moral questions play a role, particularly regarding the consequences of political decisions, but questions of power are more relevant. In contrast, philosophy's intention is to reach the truth. There cannot be an omnipotent philosopher who is also able to switch between these goals. Instead, philosophers as counsellors would always just help politicians to convince the public of their decisions. But this aim would contradict the scientific virtues, above all the scholarly virtue of the unconstrained search for the truth, and therefore the philosopher should abstain from that (Brock, 1987).

The special theoretical background of philosophy leads to another objection against the concept of ethical expertise. It states that there is no theory that guarantees a binding orientation. There is no 'objective moral theory' and thus there is not any expertise. Unlike the sciences that have a broad empirical basis, like economics or engineering science, ethics deals with values, and there is not even a commonly accepted ground of knowledge (cf McConnell, 1984; Friele, 2003, p312).

So ethical expertise remains a controversial matter, and the national ethics councils are still confronted with analogous objections. Nevertheless, I think that the concepts of the proponents of ethical expertise lead to a plausible understanding of ethical expertise. However, there must be a special notion of being an expert in ethics. Taking the unique personal composition of the ethics councils into account, one can face the arguments against ethical expertise. I think that national ethics councils are, under certain conditions, a convenient instrument for information and counselling in the field of normative risks. Their output should, however, not be regarded to be more than a kind of soft expertise. I shall now elaborate this in more detail.

Expertise sui generis

In general the expertise of the national ethics councils can be regarded as an expertise sui generis. The special quality of the councils is their mixed composition that allows them to achieve a broad overview of all various problems that need to be discussed in a public setting, and in addition allows them to reach more clarity, for example by excluding inconsistent argumentation. The extraordinary character of these councils which cannot be found in other kinds of expertise is connected with a certain understanding of ethics that is the basis for their work. In this case ethics is not solely academic ethics but a special connection of humanities and social sciences such as law, philosophy, theology and sociology, which work hand in hand with biology, genetics and medicine, and, further, with knowledge from outside the science system, in a broad sense, with society. Although the councils pass yes/no recommendations, the emphasis is placed on the heuristic procedure for risk management. The examples of the American and the German ethics councils show that a large part of their work consists of the analysis of the basic terms, the legal conditions and the ethical problems. The recommendations are based on a broad range of arguments that are presented systematically. The emphasis in the councils' reports strongly lies on the presentation of the work that was done to reach a recommendation, and not so much on the recommendation itself. This manner is appropriate for several reasons. The councils can for example make use of the advantages which the proponents of ethical expertise point out. This is above all the capability and knowledge of scientists, ethicists and experts from other academic disciplines, as well as experts working outside the scientific system. Over and above they integrate the experience of different life spheres. Finally, they have enough time to gather information and evaluate the ethical issues of life sciences and medicine.

One objection against the use of ethics councils was that everyone has ethical knowledge. This notwithstanding, the ethics councils fulfil expert functions because they unite diverse professional competences, have enough time resources and are able to focus on ethical problems systematically. Both recommendations of ethics councils discussed above show that relevant arguments are unfolded systematically and consider the contemporary discussion. In the recommendation of the German Council, for example, the proponents of a limited permission of biomedical cloning consider different current arguments of the contemporary bioethical discussion. For example, they deal with the validity of arguments of the bioethical debate that are in favour of an extension to the earliest embryonic stage of the guarantee of human dignity and the right to life (cf Nationaler Ethikrat, 2004, pp66 ff). The argument from identity for example emphasizes that the embryo in vitro or in vivo and the human being born later are the same living organism. In contrast, the council members assume the existence of a temporal boundary, namely the formation of the primitive streak about 14 days after fertilization. At the earlier stage, that constitutes the relevant stage in research cloning, a multiple birth is still possible and therefore life is not yet individuated and the backward projection of personal identity fails (p67). Even if one does not share this point of view the discussion regards important opinions and arguments that cannot be presupposed as 'everyday knowledge'. Besides, by presenting divergent opinions, the councils attempt not to patronize but to clarify the normative situation, and to contribute to the public debate. Also they can provide support to make the 'everyday knowledge' more well founded. With regard to the problem of cloning-to-produce-children any member of the public might find his or her intuitive position among one of the presented arguments. Some members of both councils point out that cloning-to-produce-children offends the dignity, respect and self-determination of the human being; some emphasize that it would lead to instrumentalization of human beings and positive eugenics, others that it would contradict self-determination of women and our understanding of generation and family, and that it would lead to experimentation on human subjects.

Another objection was that politics and philosophy have different goals. In this context one has to consider that also other sciences that fulfil expert functions have their specific goals that do not always correspond to political goals. Admittedly the ethicist uses a different scientific basis than the engineer, but that does not exclude him from political counselling which asks for his exclusive abilities. I think that the typical composition of the statements of the councils and the language in which they are written, that is, a language that is intended to address a broad public, show their potential to clarify the normative problems. As it can be seen in the statement of the American council, a broad range of policy options is presented. The council presents seven options, for example professional self-regulation with no legislative action, a ban on cloning-to-produce-children with or without regulation of the use of cloned embryos for biomedical research, governmental regulation by a new federal agency, etc. (President's Council, 2007, p173 ff). By presenting these options ethics councils do not want to fulfil a 'political goal' but want to provide a scientifically founded organizational background where political aims can be realized. So, the aims of the experts and politicians do not have to be identical. Besides, in contrast to the presumptions of this objection one main task of the national ethics councils is not to perform political power but rather to advise politicians and inform the public of the ethical problems involved, so that there is a broader basis in the political decision-making process. Therefore, in the statutes of the councils it is often pointed out emphatically that they shall facilitate a greater understanding of these issues, and shall provide a national forum for according discussion.

The objection that expertise on ethics is not based on an 'objective theory' does not take into account that other sciences dealing with 'hard facts' do not provide binding orientation in all cases. For example, it is typical that expertises grounding on a strong empirical basis do not usually come to converging results concerning one and the same question. As the scientific system is highly differentiated and provides many ways of gaining knowledge, the assumption of a clear objectivity would be unrealistic. In contrast, since they deal with morals, it is preferable that there is pluralism of expert opinions that prevents the councils from becoming dogmatic. In order to advance the pluralism in the bioethical discussion, the councils also facilitate international collaboration which is often presupposed by their statutes (e.g. in the case of the American and German councils), and they cooperate with one another. In doing this, the different ways of coming to conclusions and presenting arguments also become apparent.

The special character of the expertise of the councils has even more aspects. The history of the ethics councils from their beginnings in the 1980s up to now shows that interdisciplinarity and transdisciplinarity are not a temporary fashion, but have established themselves because they are perceived as leading to an understanding that make the handling of risks easier. Their mixed composition, their way of working and the acceptance of their results prove the growing importance of approaches that cross academic and disciplinary borders. That is the reason I think that they should not consist solely of professional ethicists. For example, constitutional law is authoritative for political basic decisions and has to be represented by legal experts, just as the relevant technical and medical background must be apparent in the councils.

But there are further questions of legitimacy, particularly because the main purpose of the councils is political counselling concerning ethical questions. Therefore, the councils have to obey conditions that are irrelevant for other forms of expertise. The ethics councils must keep in mind that they only play a modest role in the political process. The legislator has the last word and therefore nobody should suppose that the councils anticipate parliamentary decisions. The influence of the councils must remain limited in order to avoid a de facto loss of power of the parliament. Even if, in reality, it is mainly their conclusions and recommendations that are discussed by the public, their main contribution lies in the systematically presented arguments rather than in their conclusions. Making their recommendations into binding decisions would lead to the image of a closed council of wise women and men that is not democratically legitimized and that is anachronistic in a pluralistic society. As it is, their statements are only one among many that feature in the political process even if they have the status as expert recommendations. Needless to say, there must not be any impression of partiality.

Hence, there should not be an ethics council for every morally relevant issue. With regard to biomedicine there are many open questions, for example which goods and values are concerned, which arguments are coherent or not, and how to politically deal with different ethical points of view. Similar problems arise in the field of information and communication technology. In this domain one can also find a dynamic development and the need to gather knowledge for normative orientation. Ethics councils could possibly contribute expertise for public education and political counselling, for example concerning privacy, data protection, intellectual property rights, access to knowledge in the world-wide web and so on. An appropriate council could consist of representatives of computer science, media, philosophy, etc. But in these cases there is no clash of deeply held moral views pertaining to life, the integrity of the human body, human dignity, religion, etc., issues that play important roles in the field of the applications of the life sciences. It is true that a national council for information technology could incite public discussions and deliver important arguments, but I think that building up further specialized nationwide operating ethics institutions would be overdone. The establishment of such institutions could divert the relevant discussion from parliament to commissions that do not usually operate publicly, which in turn could lead to a development that dilutes the frontiers between democratic processes of decision-making and expert advice. However, that does not mean that there should not be *any* ethical expertise at all concerning new developments in science and technology. The *design* of the statements of the ethics councils, as presented in the two cases dealing with human cloning, could be used as an example of how further studies dealing with the ethical evaluation of new technologies could be composed. The concept of the existing councils should not be extended to further institutions but to more interdisciplinary and transdisciplinary assessments. These assessments could deliver important heuristic contributions for dealing with new risks.[2]

References

Bayertz, K. (1991) 'Wissenschaft als moralisches Problem: Die ethische Besonderheit der Biowissenschaften', in H. Lenk (ed.) *Wissenschaft und Ethik*, Reclam, Stuttgart

Birnbacher, D. (1999) 'Für was ist der "Ethik-Experte" Experte', in K. P. Rippe (ed.) *Angewandte Ethik in der pluralistischen Gesellschaft*, Universitätsverlag, Freiburg (Switzerland)

Brock, D. W. (1987) 'Truth or consequences: the role of philosophers in policy-making', *Ethics*, vol 97, no 4, pp786–791

Caplan, A. L. (1992) 'Moral experts and moral expertise: does either exist?', in A. L. Caplan (ed.) *If I Were a Rich Man, Could I Buy a Pancreas?*, Indiana University Press, Bloomington

Danish Council of Ethics (2001) *Cloning: Statement from the Danish Council of Ethics*

Endres, K. and Kellermann, G. (2007) 'Nationale Ehikkommissionen: Funktionen und Wirkungsweisen', in P. Weingart, M. Carrier and W. Krohn (eds) *Nachrichten aus der Wissensgesellschaft – Analysen zur Veränderungen der Wissenschaft*, Velbrück Wissenschaft, Weilerswist

Engelhardt, T. H. Jr (2002) 'The ordination of bioethicists as secular moral experts', *Social Philosophy and Policy*, vol 19, pp59–82

Friele, M. B. (2003) 'Do committees ru(i)n the bio-political culture? On the democratic legitimacy of bioethics committees', *Bioethics*, vol 17, no 4, pp301–318

Fuchs, M. (2005) *Nationale Ethikräte: Hintergründe, Funktionen und Arbeitsweisen im Vergleich*, Nationaler Ethikrat, Berlin

Kemp, P. (2000) 'Ethik, Wissenschaft und Gesellschaft', in D. Mieth (ed.) *Ethik und Wissenschaft in Europa: Die gesellschaftliche, rechtliche und philosophische Debatte*, Alber, Freiburg/München

Kuhlmann, A. (2002) 'Kommissionsethik: Zur neuen Institutionalisierung der Moral', *Merkur*, vol 56, pp26–37

Kymlicka, W. (1993) 'Moral philosophy and public policy: the case of NRTs', *Bioethics*, vol 7, no 1, pp1–26

McConnell, T. C. (1984) 'Objectivity and moral expertise', *Canadian Journal of Philosophy*, vol 14, no 2, pp193–216

Nationaler Ethikrat (2004), *Cloning for Reproductive Purposes and Cloning for the Purposes of Biomedical Research: Opinion*, Nationaler Ethikrat, Berlin

Nationaler Ethikrat Homepage (August 2006), www.ethikrat.org

Nationaler Ethikrat (2006), *Nationaler Ethikrat-Infobrief*, no 11, Geschäftsstelle des Nationalen Ethikrates, Berlin

Nida-Rümelin, J. (2002) 'Wissenschaftsethik', in J. Nida-Rümelin (ed.) *Ethische Essays*, Suhrkamp, Frankfurt a.M.

Noble, C. N. (1982) 'Ethics and experts', *Hastings Center Report*, vol 12, no 3, pp7–9

Nussbaum, M. C. (2002) 'Moral expertise? Constitutional narratives and philosophical argument', *Metaphilosophy*, vol 33, no 5, pp502–520

President's Council on Bioethics (2002) *Human Cloning and Human Dignity: An Ethical Inquiry*, President's Council on Bioethics, Washington, DC

Singer, P. (1972) 'Are there moral experts?', *Analysis*, vol 32, pp115–117

Sommermann, K. P. (2003) 'Ethisierung des öffentlichen Diskurses und Verstaatlichung der Ethik', *Archiv für Rechts- und Sozialphilosophie*, vol 89, pp75–86

Taupitz, J. (2003) 'Ethikkommissionen in der Politik: Bleibt die Ethik auf der Strecke?', *Juristenzeitung*, vol 58, no 17, pp815–821

Notes

1 This survey was carried out by the Center for Philosophy and Ethics of Science of the Leibniz University of Hannover, under the direction of Dr Kirsten Endres, in 2003; the results are in part published in Endres and Kellermann (2007).

2 I would like to thank Thomas Reydon for helpful comments on an earlier draft of this paper.

16 Ethical Responsibilities of Engineers in Design Processes: Risks, Regulative Frameworks and Societal Division of Labour

Anke van Gorp and Armin Grunwald

Introduction

Engineers and their societal environment

Engineers are professionals with respect to designing technology and other technology related fields of action, such as production, marketing, maintenance. Talking about the responsibility of engineers must, on the one hand, take its point of departure at their specific professional competence, their obligations and their opportunities to exert influence. On the other hand, however, engineers are living and working in a specific societal environment. They are professionals but not only professionals. They are also citizens acting as members of society in many different roles.

According to our observation, the point mentioned first – the professionalism of engineers – has been widely taken into account in existing work on their responsibilities (e.g. Schaub et al, 1983; Ladd, 1991). The other point, however – the role of the societal environment of engineers for defining their responsibilities – has been investigated to a much lesser extent. In the notion of responsibility as a 'notion of attribution' (Grunwald, 1999), the surrounding societal context is of crucial importance for questions of responsibility. In addition, recent observations of an increasingly 'thinned' responsibility due to increased division of labour, specialization of work and more complex processes of design and production of technology in the globalized world make clear that the societal environment of engineers also has to be taken into account for empirical reasons.

In our chapter, we will focus on what the normative idea of a deliberative democracy (Barber, 1984; Habermas, 1988) would imply for the responsibilities of engineers, looking especially at their relation to regulative frameworks. Deliberative democracy can be characterized by a focus on solving problems in social and political life *by argumentation* as far as possible. The idea is, generally speaking, that the positions and values of all persons involved or affected are represented in the problem-solving procedure. The problem-solving itself shall then be performed by the exchange of arguments following the model of discursive ethics (Habermas, 1988). It is essential to ensure principles of fairness regarding access to information and the possibility to intervene in the dialogue. The majority rule dominating the classical understanding of democracy is seen only as the second-best approach. The recourse to problem-solving by argumentation and to participation of people involved and those affected – which relates deliberative democracy to ideas of a 'civil society' – indicates that deliberative democracy is a 'strong' model of democracy (Barber, 1984). Participatory approaches of Technology Assessment (Joss and Belucci, 2002) can be regarded as specific operationalizations of such philosophical ideas.

Our question in this context will be what follows from these very general ideas for the more concrete operating field of engineers and their responsibilities.

Value-neutrality or value-ladenness of technology?

The debate on the relation between ethics and engineering in the last decades showed two extreme positions: the traditional postulate of the value-neutrality of technology, denying completely the relevance of ethics to engineering, on the one hand, and the position that every step in engineering should be subject to ethical reasoning, on the other.

One author who argues that engineers are not, and should not be, involved in the formulation of design requirements, criteria or goals is Florman (1983). According to Florman, the formulation of requirements and goals is ethically relevant, but this should not be done by engineers. Managers, politicians, customers, etc. should formulate the requirements. In this line of thinking, the

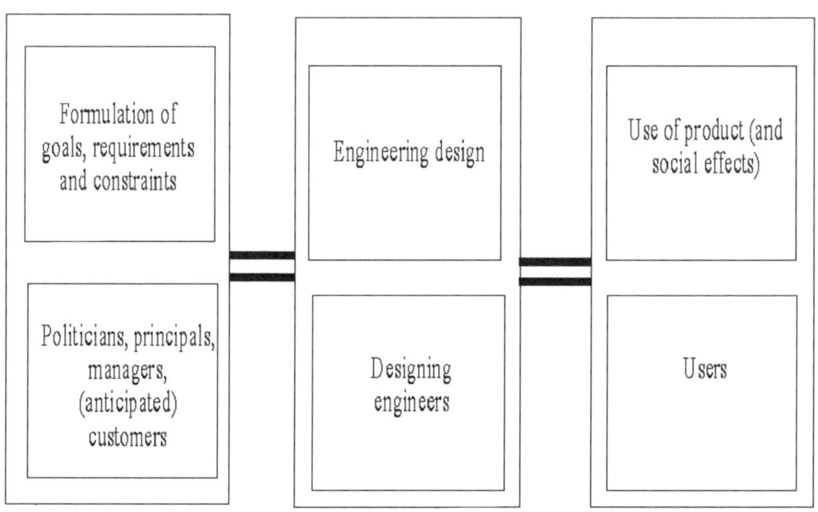

After Van Gorp and Van de Poel (2001).

Figure 16.1 *Division of labour with respect to engineering design, if design problems are well-structured problems in which the requirements fully determine the solution*

task of engineers is to discover the technologically best solution, given certain requirements. This task is seen as ethically neutral. In this model, the sole responsibility of engineers is to carry out a task, formulated by others, in a competent way (Florman, 1983).

Design problems are, however, usually not problems where a clear set of requirements is available that completely determines the solution. Design problems are more or less ill-structured problems (Simon, 1973; Cross, 1989). There may be no or more than one solution to a specific design problem. These solutions score differently on the design criteria and have, amongst other things, different consequences for users and the environment. During design processes, engineers have to choose between solutions, for example between a safer or a cheaper solution. Hence it is not tenable that engineers have to find the technologically best solution to a given design problem and that this is a value-neutral activity.

The acknowledgement of the value-ladenness of engineering, especially of engineering design, however, implies a tendency to burden engineers with very high – and perhaps unrealistic and unfulfillable – expectations in moral respect. Some optimists in the field believe that if each engineer were to grasp all the consequences of his own actions, to responsibly assess them and to act accordingly, any negative and unintended consequences of technology could be largely or completely avoided (Sachsse, 1972; VDI, 1992). This assumption leads to the demand that engineers should always engage in ethical reflection parallel to their engineering work. This position has been shown to be unrealistic for several reasons (Grunwald, 2000). Therefore, new and more precise models than the extreme positions mentioned are needed concerning the moral responsibility of engineers. In this chapter, we are going to develop a position *in between* the extreme positions.

Societal division of responsibilities

Our basic observation is that engineering – and especially *engineering design* as our main field of interest – takes place in a normatively structured environment: there are rules of professional action, codes of conduct, laws and other prescriptions. We will denote the set of such normative elements of the environment within which engineers act as *regulative frameworks*. Our assumption is that these frameworks are an expression of a *societal division* of responsibilities and accountabilities.

In modern society, division of labour is not only realized in factories and enterprises, but also to a high degree in societal affairs. Economy, law, customers, the media, politics, science and further parts of society are building complex interconnected networks of regulation, decision-making, behaviour and communication. Technology development as a social process (Bijker and Law, 1994) is, to a large part, driven by market forces, but also has to take into account external boundary conditions like law or public acceptance issues or knowledge input from science. Division of labour in technology development, therefore, also comprises the division of responsibilities and accountabilities among the actors involved at the different levels. The question of the responsibility for technological advance, for technical products and systems, and for the impacts of their use, therefore, dissolves into subquestions to the various actors involved in the field.

Against this background, complaints regarding the division of reponsibilities and accountabilities are frequently expressed, for example the fear that the distribution among various actors would lead to a 'thinning' of responsibility and, as a final consequence, to its vanishing. According to our diagnosis, however, we have to take division of labour and its impact on the distribution of responsibilities seriously as a given part of modern reality. The challenge is then to establish and implement models of distributed responsibilities. Our work shall contribute to this line of thought.

A major challenge to any theory of the moral responsibility of engineers in design processes is, therefore, to cope with this complexity of modern society in an adequate way. Oversimplified images of the role of the engineer have to be avoided. They would only lead to oversimplified attributions of responsibilities, without any concrete resonance in practice (Grunwald, 2000). The call for engineers as 'moral heroes' (Alpern, 1982) – as well as Florman's position mentioned above – is such an oversimplified picture, supposing a role of engineers which – if at all – they might have played in the nineteenth century's technology development. There is still neither a societal nor a scientific or philosophical consensus on what the responsibilities of engineers consist of and how they should be defined.

The model

Our basic model is as follows: engineering design does not take place autonomously, far away from society; rather it is embedded within specific normative environments. We will conceptualize these normative environments as *regulative frameworks* governing the specific situation. If it is possible to design procedures and processes of formulating regulative frameworks in a way that all relevant actors give their informed consent to the regulative frameworks, then the regulative frameworks provide engineers with what is morally and legally allowed, desired or justified in the respective context. The strong postulate for an informed consent of all relevant actors in the respective field has its justification in the normative model of a deliberative democracy (see the first section of this chapter), which itself draws upon counterfactual ideals of a discursive, argument-based way of dealing with human affairs in general (Habermas, 1988). This model is counterfactual in the sense that it cannot yet be assumed to be part of reality, but it can and should be taken as a normative idea to provide orientation for societal practice to move into this direction.

The central questions then are: first, is there an informed consent or are there ways to ensure informed consent for regulative frameworks? Second, what is the overlap between the informed consent given with respect to the regulative framework and the set of moral questions in the respective design processes? Third, what are the implications of the availability or lack of a consented-to regulative framework on the responsibilities of engineers during design processes?

Moral responsibilities of engineers differ depending on the case. In the case of complete overlap between the moral questions addressed in the engineering design process and the moral questions addressed in the consented-to regulative framework, there will be no obligation for engineers to start ethical reflection during their daily work (Grunwald, 2000). This situation might be called a *standard situation* from a moral point of view (Grunwald, 2003).

This model represents the above-mentioned idea of societal division of responsibilities. Engineers are not responsible for the regulative frameworks established by societal mechanisms like law making, but they have to follow those regulations. In this way, the degree of freedom of engineers is restricted while simultaneously their burden of responsibility is lowered. As long as engineers follow the regulative frameworks, and insofar as these frameworks cover the normative questions to be considered, they are acting prima facie in a legally and morally 'safe' environment. Often, however, the engineering design leads to questions, indifferences, moral challenges or even conflicts which are not covered by the scope of the informed consent in place. The informed consent might be insufficient, deficient or in need of being developed further. In these cases, ethical reflection, including other actors, groups and parties than engineers alone, is required to find a morally sound and socially robust solution.

Overview

In order to use well-defined terms in our work it is necessary to introduce our basic distinctions and notions in some more detail; this will be done in the next section. This concerns the distinction between normal and radical design and the clarification of what we understand by the notion of regulative frameworks. To obtain empirical data, four case studies in the field of engineering design have been conducted: two case studies of radical design and two of normal design. The evaluation of these case studies with respect to our topic leads to two major ethical challenges. First, the question is whether regulative frameworks are adequate and what criteria an adequate regulative framework should meet in standard design . Second, it has to be asked what design processes can be considered standard design processes. Therefore, standard situations have to be defined more precisely. In the last section we will arrive at attributing moral responsibilities to engineers concerning the judgement of the applicability of the regulative frameworks, concerning the application itself and concerning the 'maintenance' of those frameworks.

ANALYTICAL DISTINCTIONS: ENGINEERING DESIGN AND ETHICS

We will use a common-sense notion of 'ethics', in order to avoid having to go into terminological debates. Essential for our use of this term is the involvement of the moral dimension of decision-making in engineering design (criteria, goals, values, moral questions, etc.). All decisions concerning risks have a moral dimension and are therefore considered ethical issues.

Normal and radical design

Vincenti has introduced the notion of design type to characterize design processes. Design types range from normal to radical. Vincenti uses the terms 'operational principle' and 'normal configuration' to indicate what normal design as opposed to radical design is (Vincenti, 1990). 'Operational principle' is a term introduced by Polanyi (1962). It refers to how a device works. The normal configuration is described by Vincenti as 'the general shape and arrangement that are commonly agreed to best embody the operational principle' (Vincenti, 1990, p209). In normal design, both operational principle and normal configuration are kept the same as in previous designs. In radical design, the operational principle and/or normal configuration are unknown or it is decided that the conventional operational principle and normal configuration will not be used in the design.

Vincenti's description of radical design focuses on the structure and material aspects of the design. These aspects will only become apparent during the design process. For our purpose, it is useful to introduce a somewhat broader definition of radical design. We will allow for a design to be radical with regard to its *function* or *design criteria*. An explicit choice can be made at the beginning of the design process to change the usual idea of a good product of a certain product type. This means setting different criteria or changing the relative importance of criteria. For example, in the design of a car, speed is often accorded some importance, but it is usually not the most important criterion. The usual idea of a good car is a safe, reliable and perhaps fast car. If the aim of a design process is to design a car that can break the sound barrier, this is a radical design process. Radical designing in this functional way may require reconsideration of the operational principle and the normal configuration. Reconsidering may, but does not have to, lead to changes in the operational principle or normal configuration. Thus, a radical design process with regard to the function may lead to a radical design of the physical structure, but this is not necessarily so. It is also probable that a new operational principle leads to new criteria.

Regulative frameworks

A regulative framework comprises the normative aspects of the environment in which human action – like engineering – takes place. It is constituted by the sum of all codified norms of action, principles or other kinds of customs guiding the concrete actions in technological development. In particular, regulative frameworks include laws and other regulations, codes of conduct, liability prescriptions, standardizations, etc. They comprise *procedural* as well as *substantial* normative elements. Examples for substantial elements are the duties to follow specific regulations like environmental or safety standards implemented by law. Procedural elements are, for example, the series of steps that engineers have to follow in order to get an approval for a fabrication plant or a new type of car.

To be more specific: in the European Union a regulative framework for a certain product consists of all relevant regulations, national and international legislation, technical codes and standards, and rules for controlling and certifying products.[1] A regulative framework is socially sanctioned, for example by a national or the European Parliament or by organizations that approve technical codes. Besides the technical codes and legislation, interpretation of legislation and technical codes by the controlling and certifying organizations is part of the regulative framework. Engineering societies can also formulate a code of ethics.

In the European Union, the main goal of standardization is to ensure a free market and to remove technical barriers to trade within the EU (European Committee, 1999). Only products or product types complying with the general requirements written down in EU directives obtain a CE mark and are allowed on the EU market. The EU directives usually refer to codes for the operationalization of the general requirements. Therefore, for most products a regulative framework can be expected, with one or more EU directives, corresponding national legislation, and national and EU codes and standards. A lot of standards and codes address product and process safety.

Regulative frameworks are highly context dependent. At the working place usually other frameworks are more valid than at home or in automobile traffic – obviously with overlaps between them. The context dependency corresponds to a dependency on roles played by people. For the same person different frameworks are valid if he or she is acting as a professional, as a car driver or as a parent. There are also different degrees of specificity involved. Some very general elements – like human rights or elements of state constitutions – will be valid over a large variety of frameworks, while others – like professional codes of conduct – will be applicable only in those specific environments.

CASE STUDIES

In the empirical case studies,[2] observations were made of design meetings, the engineers were interviewed, design documents were read and background information was gathered. In the following sections, we will give short descriptions of the ethical issues encountered by the engineers and of how the engineers dealt with them. In the case studies, we focused on ethical issues related to safety and sustainability.[3]

Bridge

The preliminary construction design phase of an arched bridge over the Amsterdam-Rijncanal in Amsterdam was studied. This was a normal design because the operational principle and normal configuration of arched bridges have been known for a long time and were used in this bridge. During this preliminary construction design phase, the engineers encountered ethical questions about the operationalization of safety and sustainability of the bridge. Safety of the bridge referred to different aspects: safety during use, safety during construction and hindrance of ships passing under the bridge.[4] The engineers expected to encounter ethical issues concerning the attribution and division of responsibilities in later design phases.

Most of the decisions concerning safety during use were taken using a regulative framework. This regulative framework was based on the Dutch Building

Decree. The Building Decree is detailed and contains prescriptions, for example on strength calculations, insulation for buildings, and static and dynamic loading of the bridge. The Building Decree, like many other regulations, refers to codes and standards, for example the Dutch codes for concrete and steel bridges (NEN 6723:1995 and NEN 6788:1995 respectively). The regulative framework guided most of the decisions concerning safety and sustainability of the construction. Not all safety and sustainability decisions were, however, covered by the regulative framework. An example of a safety issue that was not covered was misuse. People can climb onto the arches of the bridge, especially because the arches are not very steep. There were no rules concerning misuse in the regulative framework. Even in this (rather straightforward) design process, Florman's position mentioned at the beginning is not tenable.

Piping and equipment

The design process of pipes and pressure vessels was normal design; the operational principle and normal configuration were known and used. Pipes for transporting fluids and gases have been designed for some decades. Similar to the bridge case, the ethical issues were related to the operationalization of safety, the making of trade-offs involving safety, and the division and attribution of responsibilities.

In the case studies, the engineers used a regulative framework in the design process to make decisions concerning safety. The regulative framework for pipes and pressure vessels was based on the European Pressure Equipment Directive (PED) (European directive 97/23/EC).[5] The PED makes reference to codes. The PED, but especially the codes and standards, prescribed many of the choices regarding safety during the design process; for example, detailed equations were provided for strength calculations, required material qualities and safety provisions. Some choices regarding safety were not specified in the regulative framework and had to be made by the engineers and/or customer. For example, the engineers in the studied design process mentioned that accident and load scenarios were not defined in European codes and legislation. Under the PED, engineering companies are obliged to conduct a risk analysis of their design, but which accident and load scenarios should be used is not specified. According to the engineers, they usually discussed the issue with their customer or asked advice from a certification organization. This means that also in this case of normal design Florman's idea of value-neutrality in engineering does not hold.

DutchEVO

The DutchEVO project was the conceptual design of a very light, sustainable car. The weight of the car was set at a maximum of 400kg. The design requirement to produce a sustainable car with an empty mass of about a third of that of regular cars is what made the design radical.

The ethical issues encountered by the engineers were related to the operationalization of safety and sustainability and the trade-off between safety and sustainability. There was an extensive regulative framework for cars. This framework included rules for a variety of issues ranging from rules for tail-lights to rules for crash tests. It was not possible to design a really light car and still aim at very good results on the EuroNCAP crash tests.[6] After analysis of these crash tests, the design team decided that these crash tests would only lead to heavy unsustainable cars that make people feel protected in their car and overestimate their performance as a driver. The design team decided to make a car that would make people feel a bit vulnerable so they would drive carefully, while the car would protect people during crashes but probably score not very high on the crash tests.[7] The design team rejected the EuroNCAP crash tests and with that, part of the regulative framework. The regulative framework for cars included some regulations on sustainability, but the engineers wanted to make a more sustainable car and therefore could not rely on the regulative framework with regard to sustainability. Decisions about ethical issues were based on internal design team norms. These norms developed during the design process. These internal design team norms were based on the education of the engineers in the design team, their previous design experience and their personal experience.

Trailer

The other radical design case was the preliminary design and feasibility study of a light composite trailer with a new loading/unloading system. This was a radical design: the normal configuration and operational principle were changed. A new loading/unloading system was included and composite material was used. The engineers encountered ethical issues related to the operationalization of safety and the division and attribution of responsibilities.

There was a regulative framework incorporating rules on maximum loads on the axles, maximum heights, pneumatic springs, turning circles, guards to prevent cyclists from coming under the wheels of a truck and rules for certification. The engineers did not use the complete regulative framework, they only referred to maximum weights and heights. The reason the engineers disregarded the rest of the regulative framework is that they did not consider it relevant for their design task. The engineers construed their design task as making a structurally reliable trailer in composite material, that is, a trailer that will not fail during foreseeable use. The use of composite material meant that parts of the regulative framework that were tailored for trailers made of metals were not applicable. In the engineers' operationalization of safety, traffic safety was disregarded (cf Van der Burg and Van Gorp, 2005). The engineers attributed the responsibility for safe traffic to the government who should make traffic safety regulations, to the driver who should drive carefully, and to the customer who should have included traffic safety as a separate requirement if he wanted a trailer that was particularly safe in traffic.

The engineers made decisions about safety based on internal design team norms. In this case, these norms were based on the education of the engineers at the engineering company and the design experience of the engineers and the engineering company. The engineering company had a lot of experience in lightweight design and the use of and design in fibre reinforced plastic composites. This experience had led to norms about what a good design was. There was no experience with traffic safety and therefore there were no internal norms about including traffic safety in trailer design. Personal experience did not play a large role in this design process.

REGULATIVE FRAMEWORKS IN ENGINEERING DESIGN – SCOPE AND BOUNDARIES

Adequacy of regulative frameworks

The criteria a regulative framework should meet in order to be adequate can be procedural, concerning how the parts of the regulative framework are formulated, as well as substantive, concerning criteria on the framework itself. We will start with some remarks on the procedural and substantial criteria for adequate regulative frameworks. We will show what kind of ethical and even meta-ethical questions will play a role in formulating criteria for adequacy of regulative frameworks.

Procedural criteria of adequacy

The investigation of procedural criteria of adequate regulative frameworks needs a clear and transparent normative point of departure. We will rely, in this respect, on the theory of deliberative democracy. This normative approach claims that the regulation of public affairs should, to the largest extent possible, be organized by deliberative procedures in which citizens have the chance to bring their arguments and values into these processes and to participate in public opinion formation and argumentation.

Coming back to the challenge of identifying procedural criteria of adequate regulative frameworks governing standard design situations, this means that we have to look for the possibilities of citizens, persons and groups affected or concerned to contribute to shaping the regulative frameworks, for example, for specific product lines. The most important procedural criteria are therefore related to who is and who should be involved in the process of defining the elements of the regulative frameworks and how informed consent of affected actors should be interpreted. At this moment, only some specific groups are included in the formulation of large parts of the regulative frameworks. EU regulation is formulated by European committees and approved by the European Parliament. Therefore, all actors concerned are in a way represented in the process of formulating European directives. The European directives are, however, usually quite vague and refer to codes and standards for further operationalization. A European directive might require that a product is safe, but what safe means for the product at hand and how it should be measured is specified in codes and standards but not in the directives. The processes of codes and standards, however, are not in the same way democratically legitimated like the parliamentary processes of passing directives. They are formulated by groups of people that represent industry, some independent standardization organization, or a consumer organization. Codes of conduct and codes of ethics are usually defined by professional organizations, which means that only professionals are included in this process. Not all actors concerned have the resources to contribute to standardization or normalization processes; this requires considerable knowledge and money. As can be seen from this very short overview, only specific groups are represented in the formulation of large parts of the regulative framework, for example norms, standards and codes of conducts, and there is no informed consent procedure that includes all actors concerned.

If a kind of passive acceptance of the regulative framework would be enough to deduce an informed consent from affected actors, then the formulation of the regulative frameworks by specific groups would not be a problem. As long as affected actors do not protest against the regulative frameworks, they could be expected to consent to the regulative framework. However, there are two problems with this kind of reasoning. First, there might be other reasons than consent to a regulative framework to explain a lack of protests or discussion; people might not be familiar with the regulative framework or they might not realize the consequences of a regulative framework for them. Second, there are reasons to doubt that mere acceptance is a justifiable operationalization of informed consent (Grunwald, 2005). There might be regulative frameworks that are accepted by the actors concerned but which are not justifiable from an ethical point of view. One could imagine a situation in which poor people accept poor working conditions because doing this dangerous work in unhealthy conditions is their only opportunity to support their families. The fact that someone consents to a regulative framework is not sufficient; the context in which consent was given also has to be taken into account.

Because of these problems, the way in which regulative frameworks are formulated at present is not the way to obtain adequate regulative frameworks regarding the ideal of a deliberative democracy. A kind of informed consent procedure for regulative frameworks has still to be defined, taking into account the normative requirements of deliberative democracy but also the current societal situation including the necessity for a division of labour and responsibilities. Such an analysis, however, would go far beyond the scope of this chapter (see, for a further elaboration, Shrader-Frechette, 2002). Inspiration and ideas can also be gained from literature on participatory processes for technology development.[8]

Substantial criteria of adequacy

The normative point of departure to identify substantial criteria for adequacy of regular frameworks is the functional requirement that the regulative framework should guide the decision-making on ethical issues in the design process. This means that some vague statements about safety or mere appeals to the responsibility of engineers – as they sometimes are part of codes of ethics – are not enough. Important issues are, in the safety example, what safety means in a case at hand, how to measure safety, what is safe enough, and what trade-offs with safety are acceptable. Some detailed prescriptive rules can empower engineers with regard to their customers; some minimum requirements need to be met in order for the product to be certified in terms of safety. This means that if customers pressure the engineers to make designs cheaper, there is a lower legal limit for example with regard to safety. Some clear and detailed prescriptive criteria are required to make the overall concepts like safety or sustainability operable in concrete cases.

However, for two reasons we do not want to plead for *very* detailed prescriptive regulative frameworks. First, it is impractical, if not impossible, to prescribe every little detail in a regulative framework. The more detailed and prescriptive a regulative framework is, the fewer situations it will cover. This problem, amongst others, has led some philosophers to claim that it is impossible and undesirable to formulate universal principles in ethics. According to these philosophers, context- and situation-specific features should play a role in moral deliberation (see, for example, Dancy, 2004). Thus, formulating a regulative framework that is completely clear and unambiguous is impractical and perhaps even impossible or undesirable. Second, a balance needs to be found between clear frameworks and providing some freedom for engineers to make decisions. Very detailed prescriptive regulative frameworks might lead to engineers just living by the book instead of relying on their engineering judgement and experience (Pater and Van Gils, 2003). Some moral and professional autonomy is necessary for engineers to behave morally and professionally (see, for example, Ladd, 1991). This need not be irreconcilable with informed consent. One can consent to a regulative framework that still allows some room for engineering judgement but within certain boundaries.

Another point is the coverage of relevant ethical issues by the regulative framework. In the bridge case, misuse of the bridge was not covered. Ethical issues that are not covered by the regulative framework can easily be disregarded or not recognized during the design process. It is, however, too strict to require that regulative frameworks are complete and address all ethical issues, even those remotely connected to designs.[9] For example, requiring that the poverty of underdeveloped countries is addressed in all parts of the design of a coffee maker might be too strict, although one could require that the users of the coffee maker can use ecological fair-trade coffee.[10]

Following these arguments, the substantial criteria for adequate regulative frameworks will have to include a way of balancing the freedom of engineers in design processes with the empowerment and guidance of detailed prescriptive rules. An idea might be to include some detailed *minimum* requirements, but allow engineers to deviate from these requirements if they can provide good arguments why this is better or even necessary. In the details of the regulative framework, some inconsistencies or even contradictions might occur, leading to problems of orientation (Grunwald, 2000), for example between detailed technical codes. Some technical codes can be part of different regulative frameworks; for example, there are codes that regulate materials properties and testing, and a lot of regulative frameworks include these codes. As codes are referred to in very different contexts and codes are combined with very different codes, there are usually some contradictions on details between different codes of a regulative framework. Moreover, a regulative framework may point to alternative codes, for example the PED refers to EU codes, but some of these EU codes have not yet been formulated and, at the moment, all national codes of the European countries can be used instead of the not yet formulated EU codes. Allowing engineers to deviate from the minimum requirements is a way to handle inevitable inconsistencies. The regulative framework should include a certification organization to check whether designs actually meet the minimum requirements and to judge whether the reasons for deviating provided by the engineers hold water. A way of making normal designs is then to follow the minimum requirements and have the design certified. In case of special requirements, for example of the customer, it would be possible to deviate from the minimum requirements. Deviation requires some effort to argue why the deviation is necessary, but this probably only means that the engineers need to write down the arguments they probably already had when they started thinking about deviating.

This idea might seem very minimalist and even conservative because it could mean that every design is made with reference to the lower limits, which could hamper innovation. However, this does not need to be a problem, because regulative frameworks are and should be dynamic. Technological development enables the use of new processes and materials and regulative frameworks are regularly updated with regard to technological development and new information. Moreover, we are discussing normal design here; engineers can always choose to make a radical design and then the regulative framework is usually inapplicable (see the next section).

To conclude these preliminary ideas about the substantial criteria for an adequate regulative framework, the regulative framework should:

- be clear: it should define very clear minimum requirements for all relevant ethical issues;
- be pragmatically complete: it should address all ethically relevant issues directly related to the design of the product at hand;
- allow for deviation: if good argumentation is provided why the deviation leads to a better design;
- be updated and reformulated regularly ('maintenance' of the framework); and
- include a certifying organization: it should check whether the minimum requirements are met and whether the argumentation for deviations is acceptable.

In the two normal design processes, the bridge case and the piping and equipment case, the regulative frameworks did not meet all requirements. A first remark is that regulative frameworks as they exist at the moment do not meet the procedural requirements we discussed in the previous section. The most important problem with regard to the regulative framework governing the piping and equipment design is that it is not accepted by all actors concerned. For example, people living near a chemical installation that uses hydrocyanic acid usually consider this installation not to be safe enough even though this installation meets all requirements of the regulative framework (Van Corven, 2002). In the bridge case, the regulative framework concerning safety during use does not address all ethically relevant issues because it does not address misuse.

Boundaries of standard situations in engineering design

If a regulative framework is available and applicable, it is a standard situation. Therefore, normal design processes are usually standard situations. Regulative frameworks are applicable in normal designs (cf the case studies 'bridge' and 'piping equipment'). A regulative framework can be expected for most products, but there is no guarantee that every normal design process is covered by a regulative framework. Examples of normal designs made without a regulative framework can be found in history. Pressure vessels for steam engines existed and a normal configuration and working principle were established long before a regulative framework was formulated. Moreover, the regulative frameworks might not meet the above described criteria and therefore might be inadequate.

In radical design, the existing regulative frameworks might not be applicable, for example because another operational principle is used. We distinguish three ways in which (parts of) the regulative frameworks are not applicable:

1 In some radical designs, the working principle is not changed but the normal configuration is changed, for example if another material is used. Designing something from a different material usually changes the normal configuration because the properties of the new material are different (cf the trailer case).
2 In a radical design where the working principle and the normal configuration have been changed or are new, elements of the existing regulative frameworks may lead to contradictions. Some of the goals of the regulative frameworks might still be relevant. For example, one goal of a regulative framework is to produce a safe product, but elements of the framework that should lead to safe designs can come into conflict with the goals of the radical design project.
3 Radical designs can also be radical at a functional level. An explicit choice can be made at the beginning of a design process to change the usual idea of a good product of this type or to introduce a new product type. This means setting different criteria for a product or changing the relative importance of the criteria. It is possible that the regulative framework or parts of it pertaining to such a product are explicitly rejected (cf the DutchEVO case) or that there is no relevant regulative framework for the new product. If it is decided to make a functional radical design then, it is not clear from the start of the project what parts of the normal configuration or working principle will be used and what parts will not be used, there may be no normal configuration and working principle to be used for the design.

From the foregoing it can be concluded that a regulative framework may be available in radical design, but this will be rejected or will not be (completely) applicable. Only in the first instance of radical design can engineers use parts of the current regulative framework. This means that, in general, radical design processes are not standard situations and are not covered by regulative frameworks. Normal design processes are usually covered by regulative frameworks and are therefore standard situations, provided that the regulative framework is adequate.

Conclusions – Roles and Responsibilities of Engineers

What does the above imply for the responsibilities of engineers? Engineers should start every design process by judging whether the design process is standard design. If it is standard design, then there is an applicable regulative framework that engineers should use, provided that the regulative framework is adequate. This means that engineers need to understand the importance of the design type to judge whether a regulative framework is applicable. In normal design, a regulative framework is usually applicable, for most radical designs it is not. The divide between radical and normal design is not clear cut, design can be more or less normal or radical. In cases where the design is not completely normal but still not very radical, engineers should not use the relevant regulative framework without carefully investigating which elements of the framework are applicable and which elements are not. Petroski states that many design failures are due to an extrapolation of engineering knowledge outside the experience at that moment (Petroski, 1994). This means that even if a design seems more or less normal design, a small change in normal configuration might render some parts of the regulative framework inapplicable. Engineers should therefore always be prudent in relying on the rules and guidelines of the regulative frameworks.

Engineers are also responsible for supporting and 'maintaining' the regulative framework. The framework needs to be adapted to new information and technologies. Sometimes engineers will experience problems with the application of parts of the regulative framework; they should report these difficulties to the organization that has formulated this part. The most pressing issue at the moment is that the existing regulative frameworks are not adequate. A considerable number of frameworks do not meet the substantive criteria and most regulative frameworks do not meet the procedural criteria. Only some specific groups are involved in formulating large parts of the regulative frameworks. Part of the responsibility of engineers is to help in changing this, for example by raising awareness of the importance of regulative frameworks, by motivating people and groups to engage in the respective processes, and by providing knowledge to groups that want to participate in standardization or codification processes.

References

Alpern, K. D. (1987) 'Ingenieure als moralische Helden', in H. Lenk and G. Ropohl (eds) *Technik und Ethik*, Reclam, Stuttgart, pp177–193

Barber, B. R. (1984) *Strong Democracy. Participatory Politics for a New Age*, University of California Press, Berkeley, CA

Bijker, W. E. and Law, J. (eds) (1994) *Shaping Technology/Building Society*, Cambridge, MA

Cross, N. (1989) *Engineering Design Methods*, Wiley, Chichester

Dancy, J. (2004) *Ethics without Principles*, Oxford University Press, Oxford

Decker, M. and Ladikas, M. (eds) (2004) *Bridges between Science, Society and Policy. Technology Assessment – Methods and Impacts*, Springer, Berlin

European Committee (1999) *Guide to the Implementation of Directives Based on New Approach and Global Approach*, European Committee, Brussels

European directives accessed at http://europa.eu.int/eur-lex/en/:

89/391/EC Health and Safety at Work

92/57/EC Health and Safety at Construction Sites

97/23/EC Pressure Equipment Directive

Florman, S. C. (1983) 'Moral blueprints', in J. H. Schaub, K. Pavlovic and M. D. Morris (eds) *Engineering Professionalism and Ethics*, Wiley, New York

Grunwald, A. (1999) 'Verantwortungsbegriff und Verantwortungsethik', in A. Grunwald (ed.) *Rationale Technikfolgenbeurteilung. Konzeption und methodische Grundlagen*, Springer, Heidelberg

Grunwald, A. (2000) 'Against over-estimating the role of ethics in technology', *Science and Engineering Ethics*, vol 6, pp181–196

Grunwald, A. (2003) 'Methodical reconstruction of ethical advises', in G. Bechmann and I. Hronszky (eds) *Expertise and Its Interfaces*, Edition Sigma, Berlin

Grunwald, A. (2005) 'Zur Rolle von Akzeptanz und Akzeptabilität von Technik in der Bewältigung von Technikkonflikten', *Technikfolgenabschätzung – Theorie und Praxis*, vol 14, no 3, pp54–60

Habermas, J. (1988), *Theorie des kommunikativen Handelns*, Suhrkamp, Frankfurt am Main

Joss, S. and Belucci, S. (eds) (2002) *Participatory Technology Assessment – European Perspectives*, Westminster University Press

Kleinman, D. L. (2000) 'Democratizations of science and technology', in D. L. Kleinman (ed.) *Science, Technology and Democracy*, State University of New York Press, New York

Klüver, L., Nentwich, M. et al (2000), *Europta, European Participatory Technology Assessment; Participatory methods in technology assessment and technology decision-making*, Copenhagen, The Danish Board of Technology

Ladd, J. (1991) 'The quest for a code of professional ethics: an intellectual and moral confusion', in D. G. Johnson (ed.) *Ethical Issues in Engineering*, Prentice Hall, Englewood Cliffs

NEN (1995a) *Regulations for Concrete Bridges (VBB 1995): Structural Requirements and Calculation Methods* 6723:1995, Nederlands Normalisatie-instituut, Delft

NEN (1995b) *The Design of Steel Bridges, Basic Requirements and Simple Rules* 6788:1995, Nederlands Normalisatie-instituut, Delft

Pater, A. and Van Gils, A. (2003) 'Stimulating ethical decision-making in a business context. Effects of ethical and professional codes', *European Management Journal*, vol 21, no 6, pp762–772

Petroski, H. (1994) *Design Paradigms; Case histories of error and judgement in engineering*, Cambridge University Press, Cambridge

Polanyi, M. (1962) *Personal Knowledge*, The University of Chicago Press, Chicago

Sachsse, H. (1972) *Die Verantwortung des Ingenieurs*, VDI-Verlag, Düsseldorf

Schaub, J. H., Pavlovic, K. and Morris, M. D. (eds) (1983) *Engineering Professionalism and Ethics*, Wiley, New York

Shrader-Frechette, K. (2002) *Environmental Justice. Creating Equality, Reclaiming Democracy*, Oxford University Press, New York

Simon, H. A. (1973) 'The structure of ill-structured problems', *Artificial Intelligence*, vol 4, pp181–201

Van Corven, T. (2002) 'Chemieconcern DSM tornt aan veiligheidsgrens', *Trouw*, 17 June

Van der Burg, S. and Van Gorp, A. (2005) 'Understanding moral responsibility in the design of trailers', *Science and Engineering Ethics*, vol 11, no 2, pp235–256

Van Gorp, A. (2005) 'Ethical issues in engineering design: safety and sustainability', *Simon Stevin Series in the Philosophy of Technology*, Delft and Eindhoven

Van Gorp, A. and Van de Poel, I. (2001) 'Ethical considerations in engineering design processes', *IEEE Technology and Society Magazine*, vol 20, no 3, pp15–22

VDI – Verein Deutscher Ingenieure (1992) *Ingenieur-Verantwortung und Technikethik*, VDI, Düsseldorf

Vincenti, W. G. (1990) *What Engineers Know and How They Know It*, The Johns Hopkins University Press, Baltimore and London

NOTES

1 The cases that are described in section 3 are design processes in the European Union; therefore, the regulative frameworks that we will refer to are regulative frameworks that are typical for the EU.

2 Case studies were performed by Anke van Gorp; for elaborate case descriptions, see Van Gorp (2005).

3 For an argumentation that safety and sustainability are ethical issues, see Van der Burg and Van Gorp (2005) and Van Gorp (2005).

4 We will not focus on the hindrance of ships on the canal and the working conditions during construction; an elaboration of this can be found in Van Gorp (2005).

5 Other regulations relevant to the design of (petro)chemical installations are those encompassing environmental regulations and regulations regarding noise and smell, but we will not consider those.

6 EuroNCAP is a cooperative of different European consumer and governmental organizations designing crash tests and testing all cars on the EU market.

7 Not including various kinds of active and passive safety systems like airbags will automatically lead to very meagre results in the EuroNCAP crash test, because airbags are required in these tests. The main goal of the design process was to start a discussion about car safety and sustainability within the car industry and society.

8 For some case studies on participatory methods in Europe and problems with these methods, see Klüver et al (2000) and Decker and Ladikas (2004), and for a more general discussion on democratization of technology, see Kleinman (2000).

9 This argument was the reason to weaken hard requirements for such frameworks by adding attributes like 'pragmatic', 'sufficient' or 'local' in preceding analytical work (Grunwald, 2000).

10 The Senseo coffee maker, designed and developed by Philips and Douwe Egberts, required the use of (Douwe Egberts) coffee pads, thus excluding the use of biological fair-trade coffee in the first years or so. At the moment, a few years after the introduction of the Senseo coffee maker, all major brands produce the required coffee pads including ecological fair-trade coffee pads.

Part VI

Conclusion

In the concluding chapter to this volume, Michael Baram discusses how official systems of risk regulation and self-regulation have to supplement each other in order to do justice to moral considerations.

17 Governing Technological Risks

Michael Baram

Perspectives

Technological advance is highly valued as a powerful enabler of social and economic progress, major business ventures, and national power and prestige. Since the industrial revolution two centuries ago, it has been encouraged by public policies and private interests.

But technological advance often threatens health, safety and the environment. The 'dark satanic mills' of the industrial revolution belched clouds of pollutants, contaminated streams, injured workers, exploited child labour and natural resources, and degraded the lives of many (Jennings, 1985), conditions which persist today in developing nations struggling to benefit from the globalization of commerce.

The technological enterprises which followed in chemical, energy, transport, manufacturing, mining and other industrial sectors have threatened a broader range of harms, from the physical and chemical to the biological and psychological. Over time, democratic societies have sought to govern these technological activities by subjecting them to an ongoing process of social control which strives to prevent types and levels of harm which are unacceptable (Baram, 1973). This is a continuous process comprised of many actors and deliberations and operates at two levels.

At the macro-level, the social control process illuminates the intrinsically hazardous features of a technology and indicates uses of the technology for which the hazards will be manageable. At the micro-level, the process is applied to particular uses of the technology, estimates the extent to which the hazards threaten or actually cause harm to persons, property, environment and other societal interests, and then strives to reduce these particularized threats or risks to levels which are acceptable.

Another perspective on governance of technology disregards the hazards that technologies present and prescribes how to manage the risks that arise when a hazard-bearing technology is applied in specific contexts. According to the International Risk Governance Council:

> Governance refers to the actions, processes, traditions and institutions by which authority is exercised and decisions are taken and implemented. Risk governance applies the principles of good governance to the identification, assessment, management and communication of risks. It incorporates such criteria as accountability, participation and transparency within the procedures and structures by which risk related decisions are made and implemented … The challenge of better risk governance lies here: to enable societies to benefit from change while minimizing the negative consequences of the associated risks. (IRGC, 2008)

This is a prescription for governance which essentially calls for society to accept technology and channel all interests and concerns into a collabourative process for exploitation when benefits exceed risks.

To return to the broader descriptive vision of how technology is actually governed, the social control process addresses hazards and risks, but is not centrally managed, nor is it systematic or efficient. But it enables all sectors of a democratic society to work independently at shaping a technology to fit their interests and satisfy their concerns. This is a dynamic process because interests and concerns and concepts of acceptable risk undergo continual change.

For example, change may arise because experience with a technology produces a stream of new knowledge and perceptions about its hazards and their manageability which may intensify or diminish concerns. Changes in economic circumstances, which cause job insecurity or more affluence and consumer demand, may influence risk tolerance. The technology itself may subtly change societal beliefs and attitudes, as seems to be the case with research into genetic contributions to health and behaviour. And other concerns about societal well-being may grow and cause many of the actors in the social control process to reconsider their earlier judgements about hazards and risks, as exemplified by global competition in commerce, terrorist activities, climate change and corporate wrongdoing.

In recent years, health-related applications of biotechnology have presented new types of risks, ranging from loss of privacy and the re-emergence of discriminatory and even eugenic impulses to the creation and release of new life forms, and the clinical testing of new therapies on thousands of human subjects under extreme conditions of scientific uncertainty. And in its agricultural applications, biotechnology is being used to create genetically modified crops and foods, raising concerns about consequences for health and the environment. New versions of older industrial technologies are also being put to use in more threatening ways, as in the case of the oil and gas industry's move into vulnerable arctic regions for exploration and production. And the rapidly advancing, newest technologies, such as synthetic biology and nanotechnology, make social control highly speculative and tentative because of their scientific uncertainties.

Thus, as technologies proliferate and accelerate, it is increasingly important to develop a more complete understanding, conceptual and pragmatic, of the capacity of our existing social control process for assuring that the technologies do not cause unacceptable harm. This seems to be the main reason for growing concern about the governance of technological risks.

THE SOCIAL CONTROL PROCESS

In the democratic nations of North America and the European Union, social control of technology is a dynamic process in which many actors engage in evaluating facts and uncertainties and make decisions or take positions that favour or restrain the advance of a particular technological enterprise (Rasmussen and Svedung, 2000). These are taken into account by the corporate and governmental proponents of the technology in determining whether or how to proceed. Corporate proponents weigh these developments against their business interests and goals, whereas governmental proponents weigh these developments against much broader political and societal objectives.

The most visible actors include law-making legislators, rule-making and rule-enforcing regulators, courts which hear claims of harm and other disputes and decide about liability and other remedies, industrial associations and professional societies which enact voluntary standards, labour unions and established interest groups which take positions and make petitions or demands. Less visible but also important are consumers who express preferences in the marketplace, and shareholders, investment analysts and insurers whose views and decisions are taken into consideration by company boards and top management.

The proponents or prime movers of the technology, usually a corporation or industrial grouping of companies, are required to comply with those outcomes of the social control process that are legally enforceable, such as a law, regulation or a court decision regarding actual or threatened harm to workers, consumers, the environment or property interests.

Some of the decisions and views that are not legally enforceable are likely to be voluntarily followed by corporate proponents if they have high relevance to potential legally enforceable decisions. For example, when mandatory standards for an industrial activity have not been enacted by a regulatory agency, many companies will adhere to industrial standards or best practice determinations because these are likely to be significant when company performance is being evaluated in a future proceeding before an agency or court.

Other decisions or expressions of opinion may also be persuasive because of their relevance to the business interests and obligations of the proponent companies. Such is the case with judgements by financial analysts, and decisions by insurers about coverage of the potential losses that may be incurred by a company's use of a particular technology. Favourable decisions from these parties may be interpreted as signals that the company's technological activity is sufficiently safe.

Finally, views expressed by the public, often motivated by beliefs, values, perceptions and personal interests rather than scientific or technical analysis, are taken into account by companies because they may influence legislators, regulators and investors, and obviously serve as indicators of the level of public acceptance of the company's technological venture.

Corporate proponents do not passively await these outcomes. Instead, they work at gaining favourable decisions and opinions from many of the actors involved in the social control process, often by emphasizing the economic and social value of their venture, the loss of jobs and other distress that would follow from a less than fully favourable decision, and the threats posed by foreign competitors working under allegedly more favourable conditions. Proponents also sponsor scientific and technical studies, participate on key advisory committees, help political supporters gain office, mobilize other firms and industrial organizations, and indulge in public relations for additional support.

Arrayed against such corporate campaigns are a resolute group of sceptics and opponents that usually lack sufficient financial and technical resources and organizational skills, and depend on gaining media coverage and arousing public opposition in order to prevail.

A technological enterprise is therefore steered by its corporate proponents to follow a course they have charted after considering the many decisions and judgements made by the actors in the social control process about hazards, risks and their financial implications. As changes occur among these actors, corporate proponents will adjust the course they had been following. For example, a major accident is usually a course-changing event because it arouses public outrage and causes regulatory intervention and sanctions, liability lawsuits, business losses and shareholder distress (US House. Rep., 2008).

Changes are now occurring in several components of the social control process which relate to the roles of regulators and corporate proponents in dealing with hazardous technology. The following discussion focuses on the regulatory component and its transition from a 'command and control' form to one in which regulatory functions are delegated to corporate proponents, and briefly illustrates this development and searches for its implications in two technological sectors.

Moving from regulation to self-regulation

Regulation by government agencies has been the most notable component of the social control process. For most of the twentieth century, regulation involved agency development and enforcement of detailed standards and rules which prescribe the equipment, operational procedures, training programmes and other aspects of an industrial activity for companies to follow.

This 'command and control' approach usually relies on cost-benefit analysis to justify each new requirement and to support an ALARA process ('as low as reasonably achievable') for improving operational safety. It is also intended to assure that other standards for worker safety and health and environmental protection are met. The most complete version of this approach can be seen in the regulatory programmes governing the operation of nuclear power plants in Western nations and Japan. (Note: regulation of product safety is not included in this discussion.)

But this approach in technological sectors other than nuclear has waned for several reasons. It is difficult to apply to all the details of company activities which determine process safety, particularly as companies outside the nuclear power field reorganize and outsource tasks to contractors. It inevitably leads to an accumulation of regulatory requirements which are extremely burdensome to coordinate, decipher and use in practice. As a result, managers, workers and contractors frequently substitute simpler, deviant practices for the complex regulatory dictates, despite the risk of enforcement and sanctions. It also prevents companies from using their expertise to devise more cost-effective methods of operation which would yield equivalent or greater safety, and thereby stifles innovation (Hale and Baram, 1998).

Because of these and other problems, and growing objection to the 'command and control' approach by industry, economists, and by political forces such as the Reagan-initiated deregulation movement in the USA, softer or less prescriptive regulatory approaches have been introduced over the last 25 years (Kirwan et al, 2002). These include rules requiring companies to disclose more fully risk information to workers and the public for the purpose of exposing safety issues and thereby stimulating various means of addressing them, and the creation of economic incentives to persuade companies to voluntarily improve their performance. In addition, 'performance-based' regulations have been developed, which enable companies to use their own methods for managing their technological activities safely, provided they do not breach performance parameters. These approaches reduce the prescriptive role of regulators, and disappoint those who mistrust industry.

In parallel, new approaches for improving corporate compliance with the accumulation of diverse regulatory requirements for environmental and occupational safety have been developed (Coglianese and Nash, 2001). In the USA, the main approach attempts to improve compliance by having companies adopt better corporate management systems, and relies on corporate fear of criminal prosecution to accomplish this. Thus, American agencies have developed enforcement policies which threaten criminal prosecution of companies which disregard compliance or which repeatedly fail at compliance because of their inferior management systems. Reinforcing these policies are 'Sentencing Guidelines' developed for the courts to use in applying penalties and other sanctions to successfully prosecute companies. The guidelines enable judges to significantly increase the penalties for such companies if they have maintained inferior management systems and failed to cooperate with government investigators (Baram, 2002).

The most recent regulatory reforms taking place in the USA and EU nations are producing regulatory programmes often described as 'co-regulation' or 'enforced self-regulation' (Bamberger, 2006). These further reduce the prescriptive role of the regulator and delegate to companies the responsibility to self-regulate their own activities consistent with established practices of their industrial sector. The governmental authorization for self-regulation usually requires that the company follow standard industrial practices or industrial voluntary standards in carrying out its operations, and also comply with any governmentally established parameters, including previously enacted agency standards for protecting worker health and safety and the environment. When industrial standards or practices are not available as guidance for addressing a safety-related matter, the company may be authorized to use some form of risk-benefit or cost-benefit analysis to decide 'how safe is safe enough', and then conduct its activities accordingly.

Most versions of this approach require regulator oversight of the corporate effort, and authorize regulator intervention, enforcement and sanctions when companies fail to fulfil their responsibilities. Hence, it is accurate to refer to this approach as 'enforceable self-regulation'. Some versions further require more transparent interactions between regulators and companies, and call for participation by labour, non-governmental organizations, or other interested and recognized parties. In its most advanced version, self-regulation is translated into a contractual relationship between government and company, and the terms of the contract may include additional obligations for the company to carry out certain non-safety-related actions of social importance that have been specified by the government.

Self-regulation has taken hold in the EU where it is publicly and officially encouraged and many versions are now in effect (Hey et al, 2006). In the USA, the concept of self-regulation has been critically viewed by many observers as an inappropriate delegation of governmental responsibilities to private interests, and has not received official public support.

Nevertheless, self regulation has emerged in the USA, as evidenced by the relaxed regulatory outlook and practices of several agencies which rely to a considerable extent on companies to self-regulate and self-certify the quality of their performance. At this time, there is only one officially acknowledged programme of enforceable self-regulation, the Voluntary Protection Program for workplace health and safety sponsored by the federal Occupational Safety and Health Administration (OSHA, 2004; Baram, 2007). This programme has received favourable reviews and could become a model for other agencies to follow.

Thus, the regulatory component of the social control process in many developed nations is changing, and its capacity for sufficiently controlling technological threats is highly uncertain. Many are worried and critical of this increasing transference of responsibility to companies, and believe that self-regulation will prove to be no regulation because it will have weak forcing effect on companies to do anything more than 'business as usual'. Many other concerns have been expressed and some will be discussed subsequently.

CHANGING REGULATION IN TWO TECHNOLOGICAL DOMAINS

To illustrate the breadth and importance of the regulatory component, and the implications of the trend towards self-regulation, two cases are briefly presented: exploitation of offshore oil and gas resources, and applications of biotechnology to agriculture and food.

Offshore oil and gas technology

Regulation in many forms is applied to the technological enterprise of exploiting offshore oil and gas resources, such as resources in the US portion of the seabed of the Gulf of Mexico and the Norwegian share of the seabed of the North Sea. The USA and Norway, by separate legislative actions, have authorized the leasing of portions of their seabeds to qualified companies, and are now moving towards extending their leasing programmes into Arctic seabed regions of the Beaufort, Chukchai and Barents Seas which they have claimed as national territory.

The lead companies (producers) that have secured leases from the US and Norwegian programmes have similar responsibilities under each national regime. They must develop comprehensive operational plans and detailed technological designs for government approval, enter into contractual arrangements to lease drilling rigs and construct pipelines and other infrastructure, hire contractors, show financial capacity and provide evidence of managerial capability to comply with rules and standards that have been enacted for protection of workers and the environment, and special protections and lease stipulations designated by government for shipping and fishing activities, and other important interests (Petroleum Safety Authority, 2004; Minerals Management Service, 2008).

The Norwegian programme authorizes producers to self-regulate their functional responsibilities by doing risk assessments and following industrial standards and best practices. It also calls for producers to continuously reduce risks posed by their activities when 'costs are not significantly disproportionate to the risk reduction achieved' (Petroleum Safety Authority, 2004, section 9). The American programme does not announce a self-regulatory approach. Instead, it references numerous standards and rules for environmental and worker protection that must be complied with, as well as environmental assessment procedures. But producer self-regulation is implicit in the programme because few standards applicable to functional activities are indicated. In addition, the legal authorization for the programme provides that all new production operations are to use the best available and safest technologies economically feasible, 'except where the Secretary determines the incremental benefits are clearly insufficient to justify the incremental costs of using such technologies' (US Code, 2000).

Once licensed to operate, the companies working under the American and Norwegian regimes are expected to comply with these requirements and implement these authorizations on an ongoing basis. Regulators are authorized to inspect, to investigate harmful incidents and to bring about government intervention and impose sanctions when appropriate. Certain equipment and facilities needed by the producers, such as mobile drilling rigs, pipelines and harbour installations, which may be owned or operated by contractors, are also subject to government evaluation and certification.

In the Norwegian programme, the government has sought to eliminate some of the technological hazards and is now creating special performance parameters for producer activities, such as zero oil spills, zero discharge of toxic chemicals and zero discharge of drilling muds and other wastes. This forces producers to design operations and equipment which will be inherently safe in these respects. As producers move into highly vulnerable Arctic regions, such hazard-eliminating measures will be needed because the ecological context is more fragile, poses more dangerous operating conditions such as extreme weather, and a polluting incident would cause public outrage and have major political consequences.

In both the US and Norwegian programmes, self-regulation by the producer companies, consistent with standard industrial practices, plays an important role. For example, the Norwegian programme, administered by the Petroleum Safety Authority, provides that the basic principle for fulfilling health, safety and environmental responsibilities is consistent with recognized norms in the form of industrial standards (Petroleum Safety Authority, 2008). The counterpart US law, the Outer Continental Shelf Lands Act, does not, possibly to avoid stimulating public concern and litigation, but the regulatory agency which implements the law, the Minerals Management Service, operates in a de facto self-regulatory mode by letting producers determine the details of their operational functions and accepting their use of industrial practices and voluntary standards.

Both programmes raise many issues with regard to their reliance on producer self-regulation, albeit enforceable, to govern the technology so that it does not cause unacceptable harm (Lindoe, 2008). For example, do regulators responsible for oversight have the real time access to information about activities of the producers and their many contractors that is necessary for timely oversight and possible intervention, and do they have the expertise and resources needed to evaluate performance of functional activities by the producer and a host of contractors? When producers consult regulators on carrying out a safety-related function and the outcome is a harmful incident, who is held accountable? Do regulators have the courage to intervene and halt an inappropriate activity or inferior performance when doing so will obstruct or suspend the vast offshore enterprise and cause substantial business losses? Given that offshore production activities have caused spills, deaths and other harms, including major disasters such as the explosion and fire on the Piper Alpha production platform, will increased reliance on industrial customary practices and voluntary standards improve safety performance? These are some of the working level issues raised by the introduction of enforceable self-regulatory programmes (Baram, 2008).

Biotechnological agriculture

Another significant technological enterprise subject to the social control process involves applications of biotechnological expertise to create genetically modified (GM) crops and foods for human and farm animal consumption. As an ardent promoter of this enterprise, the US government has established a highly permissive regulatory framework intended to facilitate the entry of new GM crops and foods into domestic and international commerce. Funding for basic and applied research is provided by Congress and a small cluster of very large multinational companies.

Three agencies have been assigned to regulate activities and products. Their responsibilities encompass safety evaluations of GM seed and crops to ensure they will not be harmful to other agricultural activities or the environment, the siting and conduct of field testing and the decommissioning of test sites, methods of managing commercial growing of GM crops to minimize cross-pollination and other routes of genetic transference to other plants and also to minimize the evolution of more resistant pest species, methods of ensuring the separation of GM from non-GM crops throughout storage and distribution systems, and ensuring by scientific studies and cost-benefit analysis that GM food products do not pose 'unreasonable risk' (Environmental Law Institute, 2002).

This GM enterprise clearly poses many scientific uncertainties and management challenges which cause concern about its implications for health, the environment, the stability of traditional agrarian cultures and the many circumstances which enable its 'contamination' of conventional crops and thereby impact on a consumer's ability to choose conventional foods. Nevertheless, driven by rising global demand for food at affordable prices and corporate profit potential, GM agriculture now extends beyond the USA and flourishes in many other nations such as Argentina, Australia, Canada, Brazil, India and China, and is obviously transforming global agriculture and food systems (International Service, 2008).

American regulators, following directives issued by the President's Office of Science and Technology Policy, have practised a relaxed form of regulation by relying on company-sponsored scientific studies and self-certifications of compliance with testing and growing requisites and food safety criteria. In addition, the agencies have enacted several policies which have the effect of exempting virtually all new GM crops and foods from agency field testing requisites and agency food safety evaluation, have denied consumer petitions for labelling GM food, and continue to withhold the company studies they rely on from public scrutiny on grounds that they contain proprietary information (Mandel, 2004; Bratspies, 2007).

In direct contrast, regulators in the European Union (EU), strongly supported by public concerns and precautionary policy, have created a labyrinth of regulatory and economic obstacles, scientific studies, review processes, and imposed requirements for labelling and the tracing and verification of foods claimed to be GM-free (European Commission, 2008). Since many American crop growers and food producers rely on exports to EU nations, the stringent EU regulations are included in their business calculus and therefore have influence within the USA.

Although the US regulatory framework has been criticized for its reliance on, and deference to, company proponents for resolving uncertainties and managing risks, and industry has low credibility with the general public, no incidents of harm to human health and no unmanageable harm to local environments have occurred in the USA and other countries thus far. Adverse incidents have been limited to several instances of low-level 'contamination' of conventional crops and foods caused by cross-pollination, and by mishaps in harvesting and distribution of GM crops which caused their mixing with conventional crops. These few incidents, such as the Starlink corn episode, caused cancellation of many orders for conventional crops from US sources that had been placed by European and American customers (Early, 2005).

The consequent business losses suffered by the growers led to lawsuits, court decisions and out-of-court settlements which have cost GM seed companies hundreds of millions of dollars. Regulators are now working to prevent low-level contamination, thus far an economic risk. Another work in progress is their effort to prevent more significant contamination incidents, likely to have adverse consequences for human health, which could arise because certain GM crops are now being grown to produce vaccines and other medicinal products more efficiently than the fermentation methods traditionally used by the pharmaceutical industry. The prospect that human food will be inadvertently contaminated by medicinal versions of GM crops has created conflict between the pharmaceutical and food product industries. Preventing such incidents will require more stringent regulation and more responsible corporate practices.

This case indicates that the creep towards corporate self-regulation with regulatory oversight has advanced into food, environmental and agricultural agencies in the USA, but remains officially unacknowledged because of public mistrust. It also indicates that the robust common law system of the USA is serving as a supplement to safety regulation by raising the prospect of numerous lawsuits and ruinous liability if personal injury and other serious harms arise from the growing and consumption of GM crops and foods, a prospect which may be deterring the corporate proponents of GM agriculture from looser practices.

Finally, to be fair-minded, it just might be that the regulators, although relaxed and deferential to industry, have nevertheless had the requisite expertise and played oversight roles sufficiently to allow the industry to essentially self-regulate and grow without causing unacceptable harm. Clearly, this case is not comforting to those who prefer a systematic, predictable and probative form of regulation with progressive features of transparency, public participation and respect for public perceptions.

Conclusion

This description of the complex process by which democratic and capitalistic societies govern technological risks has not provided any prescriptions for improving the process or more efficiently gaining preferred outcomes. Its main message is quite neutral ... technology is steered by its corporate and governmental proponents along a course they have charted after considering the many decisions and judgements about hazards and risks made by participants in the social control process. And as changes occur in the process, the course is adjusted.

But at least two other messages are implicit in the description.

One is the reminder that risk arises from doing a hazardous activity in a specific context, and that disregarding reduction of the hazard beforehand creates the burden for society of bearing at least some measure of the risk that could have been eliminated by previously reducing the hazard. Thus, it is a moral obligation to reduce hazard in order to lessen the societal risk burden. This sense of moral obligation is lacking in most technocratic approaches to risk governance.

The second message is that governmental and industrial standards and rules, substantive and procedural, are important but do not conclusively answer the eternal societal question of 'how safe is safe enough'. Although compliance is an essential social responsibility, it should not distract organizations and individuals from also developing their own moral views and ethical principles of what is fair and right, and robustly applying these principles when dealing with the eternal question.

References

Bamberger, K. (2006) 'Regulation as delegation: private firms, decisionmaking, and accountability in the administrative state', *Duke Law Journal*, vol 56, no 2, pp377–468

Baram, M. (1973) 'Technology assessment and social control', *Science*, vol 180, no 4085, pp465–473

Baram, M. (2002) 'Improving corporate management of risks to health, safety and the environment', in B. Wilpert and B. Fahlbruch (eds) *System Safety*, Pergamon, Amsterdam
Baram, M. (2007) 'Alternatives to prescriptive regulation of workplace health and safety', *Safety Science Monitor*, vol 11, no 2
Baram, M. (2008) Robust Regulation seminar, Stavanger, Norway, 22 May
Bratspies, R. (2007) 'Some thoughts on the American approach to regulating genetically modified organisms', *Kansas Journal of Law and Policy*, vol XVI, no 3, pp101–131
Coglianese, C. and Nash, J. (eds) (2001) *Regulating from the Inside: Can Environmental Management Systems Achieve Policy Goals?*, Resources for the Future, Washington, DC
Early, J. (2005) 'Potential grower liability for biotech crops in a zero-tolerance world', *Agricultural Management Committee Newsletter*, American Bar Association, vol 9, no 1, pp 8–13
Environmental Law Institute (2002) *Biotechnology Deskbook*, Environmental Law Institute, Washington, DC
European Commission (2008) *Food Safety: Biotechnology*, http://ec.europa.eu/food/food/biotechnology
Hale, A. and Baram, M. (eds) (1998) *Safety Management: The Challenge of Change*, Pergamon, London
Hey, C., Jacob, K. and Volkery, A. (2006) 'Better regulation by new governance hybrids?', Report 02-2006, Freie Universität Berlin
International Service for the Acquisition of Agri-Biotech Applications, http://www.isaaa.org/kc/cropbiotechupdate
IRGC: Risk Governance Framework, International Risk Governance Council (2008) http://www.irgc.org/
Jennings, H. (1985) *Pandaemonium*, Macmillan, New York
Kirwan, B., Hale, A. and Hopkins, A. (eds) (2002) *Changing Regulation*, Pergamon, Amsterdam
Lindoe, P. (2008) Robust Regulation seminar, Stavanger, Norway, 22 May
Mandel, G. (2004) 'Gaps, inexperience, inconsistencies and overlaps: crisis in the regulation of genetically modified plants and animals', *William and Mary Law Review*, vol 45, no 4, pp2172–2173
Minerals Management Service (2008), *Gulf of Mexico Region: Overview of OCS Regulations*, http://www.gomr.mms.gov/homepg/regulate/regs/laws/postsale.html (accessed 22 September 2008).
OSHA (2004) *Fact Sheet: Voluntary Protection Programs,* Occupational Safety and Health Administration, Washington, DC
Petroleum Safety Authority (2004) *Framework Regulations*, Petroleum Safety Authority, Norway
Petroleum Safety Authority (2008) *The Continental Shelf*, www.ptil.no/regulations/the-continental-shelf (accessed 11 February 2008).
Rasmussen, J. and Svedung, I. (2000) *Proactive Risk Management in a Dynamic Society*, Swedish Rescue Services Agency, Karlstad
US Code (2000), Title 43, part 1346, section 21, The Outer Continental Shelf Lands Act
US House of Representatives (2008), Committee on Education and Labor, BP-Texas City Disaster, http://edlabor.house.gov/micro/workersafety_bptexascity.shtml (accessed 22 September 2008)

Index